Impurity and Sin in Ancient Judaism

Impurity and Sin
in Ancient Judaism

Jonathan Klawans

OXFORD
UNIVERSITY PRESS

2000

OXFORD
UNIVERSITY PRESS

Oxford   New York
Athens   Auckland   Bangkok   Bogotá   Buenos Aires   Calcutta
Cape Town   Chennai   Dar es Salaam   Delhi   Florence   Hong Kong   Istanbul
Karachi   Kuala Lumpur   Madrid   Melbourne   Mexico City   Mumbai
Nairobi   Paris   São Paulo   Shanghai   Singapore   Taipei   Tokyo   Toronto   Warsaw
and associated companies in
Berlin   Ibadan

Copyright © 2000 by Jonathan Klawans

Published by Oxford University Press, Inc
198 Madison Avenue, New York, New York 10016

Oxford is a registered trademark of Oxford University Press

Library of Congress Cataloging-in-Publication Data
Klawans, Jonathan
    Impurity and sin in ancient Judaism / Jonathan Klawans
    p   cm
    Includes bibliographical references and index.
    ISBN 0-19-513290-4 **ISBN 0-19-517765-7 (pbk.)**
    1 Purity, Ritual — Biblical teaching   2 Purity,
Ritual — Judaism — History of doctrines   3   Sin — Biblical teaching
4. Sin (Judaism) — History of doctrines   5. Bible O T — Theology
6 Rabbinical literature — History and criticism   I Title
    BS1199 P95 K55 2000
    296 3'2 — dc21   99-34714

Printed as an Oxford University Press paperback, 2004

9 8 7 6 5 4 3 2 1
Printed in the United States of America
on acid-free paper

Preface

The goal of this book is to gain a better understanding of the relationship between impurity and sin in ancient Judaism. In the course of this study, we will examine passages from the Hebrew Bible, the New Testament, the Dead Sea Scrolls, rabbinic literature, and other ancient Jewish texts. In so doing, we will see how various groups of ancient Jews disagreed in subtle and not-so-subtle ways regarding impurity, sin, and their interrelationship. The nature of these disputes is complex, and for this reason their full dimensions will be revealed gradually. The reason for the disputes, however, is actually rather simple, and can be stated here. The Hebrew Bible, the foundation of all ancient Jewish literature, presents ambiguities to interpreters, both modern and ancient. One ambiguity is in evidence in full force with regard to the relationship between impurity and sin. We begin by looking at two passages. Standing alone, each passage is clear enough, but once they are juxtaposed, questions arise.

> (19) When a woman has a discharge, her discharge being blood from her body, she shall remain in her defilement seven days; whoever touches her shall be impure until evening. (20) Anything that she lies on during her defilement shall be impure; and anything that she sits on shall be impure. (21) Anyone who touches her bedding shall wash his clothes, bathe in water, and remain impure until evening; (22) and anyone who touches any object on which she has sat shall wash his clothes, bathe in water, and remain impure until evening. (23) Be it the bedding or be it the object on which she has sat, on touching it he shall be impure until evening. (24) And if a man lies with her, her defilement is communicated to him, he shall be impure seven days, and any bedding on which he lies shall become impure. (Lev. 15.19–24)[1]

> (24) Do not defile yourselves in any of those ways, for it is by such that the nations that I am casting out before you defiled themselves. (25) Thus the land became defiled; and I called it to account for its iniquity, and the land spewed out its inhabitants. (26) But you must keep My laws and My rules, and you must not do any of those abhorrent things, neither the citizen nor the stranger who resides among you; (27) for all those abhorrent things were done by the people who were in the land be-

fore you, and the land became defiled (28) So let not the land spew you out for defiling it, as it spewed out the nation that came before you. (29) All who do any of
those abhorrent things — such persons shall be cut off from their people. (30) You
shall keep My charge not to engage in any of the abhorrent practices that were carried on before you, and you shall not defile yourselves through them: I the Lord am
your God. (Lev. 18:24–30)

The first passage can be understood readily enough. Menstrual blood was considered by ancient Israelites to be a source of "uncleanness" or "impurity." (Most
Bible translations prefer the term "uncleanness," but I will consistently use the more
accurate term preferred by scholars, "impurity.") If someone touched a menstruant,
he or she became ritually impure. And whoever became impure had to keep away
from all holy things (Lev. 15:31). In order to become ritually pure once more, such a
person would have to bathe and perhaps even launder his or her clothes. What is
more, if a couple had sexual relations while a woman was in such a state, the man
contracted from her a longer-lasting form of ritual impurity (Lev. 15:24). According
to subsequent passages, Leviticus 18:19 and 20:18, that couple has also committed a
capital crime. There is much more to say on this passage — what is ritual impurity,
and why did ancient Israelites believe in it? But nonetheless, even without defining
our terms we know what we are dealing with here: ancient beliefs — taboos if you
will — regarding substances that exude from the body.

The second passage quoted has posed greater difficulty. This passage comes at
the end of a long list of various incestuous, adulterous, and otherwise "abhorrent"
sexual sins which the Israelites are not to commit. The passage uses some language
similar to that in the passage from Leviticus 15. The terms "impure" and "defile" in
both passages stem from the same Hebrew root: *tameh* (טמא). Yet some of the terminology is *not* shared. The second passage speaks forcefully of "abominations"
(תועבות). Menstruation is certainly viewed in the first passage with a great deal of concern, but it is not referred to as an "abomination." Moreover, in the first passage the
impurity is conveyed by a substance that exudes from the body (in this case, menstrual blood) to a person (the menstruant), and from that person to another by means
of close physical contact. This impurity, however, is not all that severe: in most cases
a bath and the passing of the day are sufficient to remove the defilement. But in the
second passage the impurity that is contracted by the performance of sin is conveyed
to the land; the passage says nothing about sinners conveying impurity to another
person by means of close physical contact. Also unlike the first kind of impurity, the
impurity discussed in the second passage is not short-term. Nor can this impurity be
simply washed away. The impurity discussed in Leviticus 18 — in contrast to that discussed in Leviticus 15 — is brought about by abominations, is apparently permanent,
and brings about dire consequences.

With the assumption that we know what Leviticus 15 means, we have three options in
trying to understand Leviticus 18. The first is the option taken here: both passages discuss defilement, but the defilements are not of the same sort. This is the option espoused by many biblical scholars, and it is the one I will follow in this book. A second
option is to telescope the two passages and assume that they both speak about disparate
aspects of the same kind of defilement. Following this logic, a menstruant would in-

deed defile the land (as Leviticus 18 says of the sinner), and someone who commits a sexual sin would indeed defile the bed and clothes they touch (as Leviticus 15 says of the menstruant). This option can hardly be correct, because a great deal of evidence from within the purity laws of Leviticus argues against it, as we will see in chapter 1.

The remaining option is to understand Leviticus 18 as a metaphor. Generally the assumption of this argument is that Leviticus 15 must be taken literally: What is discussed in Leviticus 15 is the real impurity, and what is discussed in Leviticus 18 is a figurative one. This is an attractive approach, for it allows for a more abstract conception of sin (as favored in western thought), as opposed to the more physical, concrete conception of sin that results if Leviticus 18 is taken literally. Attractive or not, this approach is problematic. The more we learn about impurity — as manifested in both Leviticus 15 and Leviticus 18 — the more we realize that the "metaphor–literal" dichotomy is insufficient to account for the differences between Leviticus 15 and 18. We will return to this point later in this book.

A fundamental tenet of this book (and arguments for this tenet will be presented in chapter 1) is that Leviticus 18, and other passages like it, can and ought to be taken as literally — and as seriously — as passages like Leviticus 15. Both must be discussed as defilements, for the texts themselves use this language. But that fact does not mean that the differences between them (which are substantial) can be overlooked. To the contrary, a full understanding of impurity in the Hebrew Bible and ancient Judaism requires that we remain aware of both the similarities and the differences between these two types of defilements. The defilement discussed in passages like Leviticus 15 will be referred to here as "ritual impurity," and the defilement discussed in passages like Leviticus 18 will be referred to as "moral impurity."

But this is just the beginning. The purpose of this book is not so much to make the point that the Hebrew Bible knows of two types of defilements, but to demonstrate the impact that this point has on the study of ancient Judaism.

Before going any further, one issue of nomenclature must be addressed. References to "ancient Jews" and "ancient Judaism" in this work, following scholarly convention, apply to people who lived and texts that were composed during and after the second temple period (from the late sixth century BCE to the second century CE). The terms "Israelite" and "biblical" apply to the people who lived and the texts that were composed before the building of the second temple, sometime toward the end of the sixth century BCE. Breaking the past into historical periods is an inexact science, to say the least. Yet the convention adopted here is both common and useful. It is widely recognized that second temple period Judaism is quite distinct from first temple period Israelite religion, resulting in the widespread convention of distinguishing between "Israel" and "ancient Judaism." Also, the study of the Hebrew Bible on the one hand and ancient Judaism on the other are often considered to be two distinct fields. Yet the dividing line between the two fields is frequently drawn too deeply, and our topic is a case in point. In part, this work will serve to confirm a point that Jacob Milgrom has made in his authoritative commentary on Leviticus: the better one understands the Hebrew Bible, the better one can understand the literature of ancient Judaism.[2]

The argument of this book is that the distinction drawn between ritual and moral impurity in the Hebrew Bible — and in particular a correct understanding of the nature of moral impurity — allows for a better understanding of ancient Jewish literature broadly speaking. Scholars of ancient Judaism have been very interested in *ritual* impurity but not so interested in *moral* impurity. This fact has had two unfortunate results. First, passages that in fact discuss *moral* impurity have been misinterpreted in light of the more prevalent notion of *ritual* impurity. For instance, certain passages in the ancient Jewish book of Jubilees are commonly cited as evidence that ancient Jews considered Gentiles to be ritually impure. However, the passages in question in fact discuss *moral* impurity and not ritual impurity. A number of passages of ancient Jewish literature have been similarly misconstrued, as we will see, especially in chapter 2. Such misunderstandings are particularly conspicuous in contemporary scholarship on the New Testament. For this reason, this book expands the scope of previous analyses and takes into account evidence concerning John the Baptist, Jesus, and Paul.

In addition to the misunderstanding of various texts, a second unfortunate result of moral impurity's not receiving due attention is that an extremely important aspect of the dynamic of ancient Jewish sectarianism has been overlooked. Not only do a number of ancient Jewish texts discuss *moral* impurity, but some actually reveal that ancient Jews held different attitudes about the nature of moral defilement. This should not be surprising, since we know that ancient Jews disagreed on how ritual impurity was understood (rabbinic literature is full of such disagreements). Surprising or not, the fact that ancient Jews disagreed about the defiling force of sin has barely been recognized.

The purpose of this book is to counter these trends. It will argue that the notion of the defiling force of sin is articulated in a number of ancient Jewish texts. And it will argue that issues of moral impurity play an important role in the greater dynamic of ancient Jewish sectarianism. The writings and sayings of the Dead Sea sectarians, the early rabbinic sages, the Pharisees, and even Jesus will all make a good deal more sense when we give due attention to the notion of moral defilement.

The structure of this work strikes a balance between chronology and phenomenology. The overall structure is a chronological one: the book begins with the Hebrew Bible, and then it analyzes the interpretation of the Bible in the literature of ancient Judaism. But the primary concern is phenomenological: the goal is not so much to trace the history of ancient Jewish conceptions of impurity as to analyze the different approaches to these conceptions. Thus when phenomenological clarity stands to gain, the chronological structure will be abandoned. Therefore the treatment of Philo (whose thinking on impurity and sin is dealt with in some detail in the introduction to part II) precedes the treatment of the Dead Sea Scrolls, and the treatment of rabbinic literature precedes that of the New Testament. I believe that the logical flow of the claims made in these chapters will justify breaking with chronology.

The starting point is the observation that the Hebrew Bible addresses two distinct types of defilement, the first caused by natural and largely unavoidable bodily functions ("ritual impurity"), and the second brought about by certain sins ("moral impurity"). The bulk of the first chapter will categorize in simple terms these two distinct conceptions of biblical impurity.

The next step is to trace the early history of attitudes toward both types of defilement in ancient (postbiblical) Judaism. The importance of the notion of ritual impurity to ancient Judaism is well known; what remains virtually unnoticed is the fact — to be proven in chapter 2 — that the notion of *moral* impurity is also articulated in Jewish literature of the second temple period. As will be seen, in order to understand properly the approach to impurity taken in any ancient Jewish text, one must pay attention not only to ritual impurity but to moral impurity as well. ✳

With the understanding that there were two distinct conceptions of defilement at work in the literature of ancient Judaism, we turn to the main question: What did ancient Jews believe with regard to the nature of the relationship between ritual and moral impurity? In the Hebrew Bible the two conceptions are juxtaposed, and no explanation of their interrelationship is given. The same is true of the postbiblical literature surveyed in chapter 2. But later in the second temple period, ancient Jews addressed the question of the relationship between ritual and moral impurity. This book will take a look at the various answers to this question, as offered by Philo (introduction to part II), the Dead Sea sectarians (chapter 3), the early rabbinic sages (chapters 4 and 5), and important New Testament figures including Jesus and Paul (chapter 6). We will find, in the end, that the question of the relationship between impurity and sin was answered differently by various groups of Jews. That fact, in turn, will demonstrate further the importance of this topic. But to say any more would be jumping too far ahead.

Acknowledgments

This project was conceived during my graduate studies in the Department of Religion at Columbia University. While in New York, I also studied at the Jewish Theological Seminary, Union Theological Seminary, and New York University. I owe a great debt to my teachers at all of these institutions. But I am particularly indebted to my dissertation supervisors, Professors David Weiss Halivni, Alan F. Segal, and Holland L. Hendrix. I am very grateful for all the advice and support I have received from all three of my advisors, from the time when I was an undergraduate at Columbia and JTS, and throughout the writing of this book.

The bulk of my graduate work was funded by Columbia University. Yet the research and writing of my dissertation were financed generously by Har Zion Temple in Penn Valley, Pennsylvania, where I served for two years as Scholar-in-Residence. During those same two years, the Religious Studies Department at the University of Pennsylvania generously extended to me the status of a visiting student. I am grateful to both Har Zion and Penn for welcoming me into their communities.

The thorough revision of this work took place at Boston University. I have been profoundly influenced by the experience of teaching at BU, and a great number of my colleagues have affected my thinking on religion generally, and on purity specifically. I particularly thank Professors John Clayton and Steven T. Katz, who have both offered a great deal of advice to one of their youngest and newest colleagues.

A number of peers and colleagues helped me write this book. Various chapters, at various stages, were read by Albert I. Baumgarten, David Damrosch, Mary Douglas, Paula Fredriksen, Christine E. Hayes, Kim Haines-Eitzen, Maxine Grossman, Ross Shepard Kraemer, Jeffrey L. Rubenstein, and Michael Stanislawski. Cynthia Read, Robert Milks, and the editorial and production staff at Oxford also improved this book immensely and saved me from a number of errors. In truth, this book would probably have been even better had I accepted more of the advice offered by these friends and colleagues. Of course, the responsibility for all remaining errors and shortcomings is mine alone.

Parts of this book have appeared in the following publications, and I thank the editors of these journals for permission to reprint this material: "Idolatry, Incest, and Impurity: Moral Defilement in Ancient Judaism," *Journal for the Study of Judaism* 29, no. 4 (1998): 391–415; "The Impurity of Immorality in Ancient Judaism," *Journal of Jewish Studies* 48, no. 1 (1997): 1–16; and "Notions of Gentile Impurity in Ancient Judaism," *Association for Jewish Studies Review* 20, no. 2 (1995): 285–312.

My family and friends also contributed to this work, whether by listening to me talk about parts of it, or by adamantly refusing to do so, and thus forcing me, as is so important sometimes, to just forget about it for a while. To my sisters, my step-father, and other family and friends, thank you. Special thanks, of course, goes to my mother, Paula Madansky, for her constant encouragement and support.

Two family members deserve special mention, for they played a very important role in the completion of this book: my maternal grandparents, Dr. Irving and Sarah Barkan. My grandfather—who holds a Ph.D. in classics from the University of Chicago—read each chapter as I completed it with great care. He checked countless references, found many typographical errors, and saved me from many misstatements. This book is vastly better as a result of his efforts. And all three of us—my grandfather, my grandmother, and I—discussed many aspects of this work and my progress on it during our traditional, weekly, Friday afternoon telephone conversations.

From the time I was a teenager, I would spend practically every Shabbat afternoon at my grandparents' house, studying traditional Jewish texts with my grandfather. But it was never all work—I would have something to eat while I was there too. For as long as I can remember, my grandparents' hospitality, humor, and love has inspired me. I follow in their footsteps in more ways than I can count, and this work—in love and gratitude—is dedicated to them.

Less than a year after I received my degree from Columbia, my father, Harold L. Klawans, MD, died suddenly. My father was a tremendous source of encouragement and support—both morally and materially—to me throughout my life, but particularly while I was writing my dissertation. He would have loved his son's becoming an author, and he would have ordered a whole box of books. Maybe two.

And now, just as this book is about to be published, my fiancée, Helaine D. Denenberg, and I are planning our wedding. Helaine's editorial expertise has helped me every step of the way along the process of turning a dissertation into this book. More important, Helaine's generosity and devotion have enriched my life in countless ways. I thank her for her kind understanding and unfailing support throughout this process.

The dissertation upon which this book is based was originally dedicated to my grandparents, and I feel that it is only fitting that this book retain that dedication, in recognition of their dedication to this work specifically, and my education generally. More recent events—both happy and tragic—will have to be remembered elsewhere. I hope that both Helaine and my father understand.

Contents

PART I

RITUAL AND MORAL IMPURITY
IN THE HEBREW BIBLE
AND ANCIENT JUDAISM

Introduction

It is no exaggeration to say that recent scholarship on ancient Jewish conceptions of impurity is vast.[1] In the wake of the publication of Mary Douglas's *Purity and Danger* (1966) and, subsequently, Jacob Neusner's *The Idea of Purity in Ancient Judaism* (1973), modern scholarship on biblical and ancient Jewish conceptions of impurity has become a virtual growth industry. There are well over one hundred articles and dozens of books devoted to different aspects of this topic, only a selection of which can be discussed here in any detail. Indeed—especially once one has glanced at the bibliography—one may be tempted to ask: Why another book on impurity in ancient Judaism? Yet despite the fact that so much has been written of late, many misunderstandings of the nature of impurity in ancient Judaism persist. A good many of these misunderstandings, moreover, relate precisely to the topic of this book: the relationship between impurity and sin. Too often, scholars assume that defilement and sin are identical or closely identified. When it comes to the Hebrew Bible and ancient Judaism, however, such assumptions prove to be simplistic and even misguided.

Nearly seventy years ago Adolph Büchler devoted two chapters to the topic of the defiling force of sin in his *Studies in Sin and Atonement*.[2] Surprisingly enough, these chapters constitute the first and last systematic treatment of the issue of the defiling force of sin in ancient Judaism. Yet even Büchler's work, which will be evaluated in more detail shortly, cannot be considered complete, or even adequate for today's needs.

In the seventy years since, significant progress had been made with regard to historical and comparative methodologies in the study of religion. Büchler wrote his work long before anthropologists like Mary Douglas provided a sounder basis for the study of biblical purity laws. Büchler also wrote decades before the discovery of the Dead Sea Scrolls. With the discovery (and now, publication) of the Qumran corpus, we have much more literature relating to the subject of purity in ancient Judaism.

Additional recent phenomena come together to make a reevaluation of the question of sin and defilement in ancient Judaism particularly timely. For one, the re-

3

newed interest in the historical Jesus has yielded a wealth of scholarship, a good deal of which attempts to come to grips with Jesus's attitude toward ritual impurity.[3] Second, the discussion of biblical impurity has been greatly enhanced by the masterful commentary on Leviticus now being completed by Jacob Milgrom.[4] Third and finally, we are fortunate that Mary Douglas has returned to the subject of biblical impurity law. She has recently devoted a number of studies to the subject, many of them reevaluating the influential conclusions of her earlier works.[5] Indeed, in these recent works Douglas has pulled the carpet out from under almost all scholarship on impurity in ancient Judaism. And it is her own carpet that she has pulled: Virtually all work on impurity in ancient Judaism builds in one way or another on her influential books, especially *Purity and Danger*, but in her more recent writings she has either refuted or modified many of the fundamental tenets of *Purity and Danger*. I will say something more about these exciting developments later in this introduction.

Even if the topic of impurity and sin were addressed head-on over the last seventy years, all that has happened of late would necessitate a reevaluation of the topic. All the more is such a reevaluation necessary since the question of the relationship between impurity and sin in ancient Judaism has not been adequately addressed since Büchler's *Studies* appeared in 1928.

Impurity and Sin in Contemporary Research on Ancient Judaism

Now that impurity has a prominent place on the map of modern scholarship, it would be desirable to present here a thorough review of approaches taken on the subject going back to the publication of *Purity and Danger* in 1966. But to do so would produce a book-length work of its own, and we would never get to the topic at hand. Furthermore, such a work would in some ways be superfluous, for a number of the many recent books on impurity in ancient Judaism contain helpful bibliographic surveys.[6]

The section that follows will discuss in some detail a few classic works on impurity in ancient Judaism, scholarship that has had, for better or worse, a significant impact on the scholarly discussion about the topic of this book.

We begin with two "classics" — works of scholarship from before the Second World War, which remain significant today. The first is Adolph Büchler's *Studies in Sin and Atonement* with its two chapters on the defiling force of sin. We turn then to Gedalyahu Alon's essay "The Bounds of the Laws of Levitical Cleanness." This essay, as we will see, does not address the question of the relationship between impurity and sin at all, and that is precisely why his article is discussed here. It has been extremely influential, and thus his reluctance to address issues relating to the defiling force of sin is responsible in part for the fact that this topic has not received due attention.

Next we will consider Douglas's *Purity and Danger*. Douglas's work provides the basis for practically all scholarship on conceptions of defilement in the field of religious studies. Thus although the work does not directly address the relationship between impurity and sin in ancient Judaism, it remains relevant to us, because it does present a number of general statements regarding ways in which notions of defilement and morality can interconnect. As we will see, a number of the scholars who do address the dynamic between impurity and sin in ancient Judaism are echoing or developing perspectives that can be traced back to Mary Douglas's work.

Then we will examine Neusner's *The Idea of Purity in Ancient Judaism*. Unlike Douglas's book and Alon's essay, Neusner's *The Idea* does address the question of the relationship between impurity and sin in ancient Judaism. But as we will see, it addresses the issue inadequately. Finally, we will briefly survey the scholarship in the field since the publication of Neusner's book.

The second section of this introduction identifies and reviews scholarship devoted to clarifying the relationship between impurity and sin in the Hebrew Bible. At that point we will begin to address the themes touched on in the preface: the observation that the Hebrew Bible articulates not one, but two conceptions of defilement.

Two Classic Perspectives: Adolph Büchler and Gedalyahu Alon

Adolph Büchler (1867–1939)[7] wrote his *Studies in Sin and Atonement in the Rabbinic Literature of the First Century* in 1927, at a time when Judaism generally did not receive fair treatment in the academic world. (The first volume of George Foot Moore's *Judaism* appeared that same year.) There is an undoubtedly apologetic tone to the work, but that fact does not diminish its significance.[8] Apologetic or not, Büchler's *Studies* constitute an important contribution to the study of biblical Israel and ancient Judaism,[9] yet his work has been virtually ignored.

There are, as far as we are concerned here, two great merits of Büchler's *Studies*. The first is the scope of his work, which extends from the Bible to the Talmud in order to make sense of Judaism in the first century, as the title of his work suggests. It has already been claimed that the understanding of ancient Judaism is often enhanced by a better understanding of the Hebrew Bible. Büchler's work is a case in point. The second merit of his work for our concerns is the fact that he takes very seriously the notion of the defiling force of sin, recognizing its distinctive features. In one sense, at least, these two merits boil down to the same thing: Büchler, the scholar of ancient Judaism, explicitly based his analysis of ancient Judaism on the achievements of biblical scholarship.

In the *Studies*, Büchler establishes a conceptual framework that allows him to categorize two distinct types of biblical defilement. He distinguishes between what he calls "levitical" defilement and "spiritual" or "religious" defilement. By levitical defilement he means the regulations of Leviticus 11–15 and Numbers 19, which I will refer to as "ritual impurity." These defilements, as we will see in chapter 1, are natural (and thus not sinful), and they convey to people a generally impermanent contagion. Büchler's category of "religious" defilement refers to the impurity that comes about as the result of certain sinful acts and affects the land of Israel:

> The land of Israel being the property of God, idols, bloodshed, incest and adultery, and the Canaanite enormities defile it, not levitically, but religiously [10]

In other words, while ritual impurity is natural and not sinful, primarily affecting persons, grave sin produces a serious defilement that affects the land of Israel itself. Following Büchler's lead, this book will set up a similar conceptual framework and will attempt to cover the same scope, from the Hebrew Bible to rabbinic literature.

In drawing this distinction between "levitical" and "religious" impurities, Büchler was preceded, as he himself recognized, by the biblical scholarship of David Z. Hoffmann.[11] Hoffmann's contribution will be discussed in greater detail in the second section of this introduction, but I will note here that even Hoffmann was not the first to build this distinction. Indeed Hoffmann's work is informed both conceptually and terminologically by talmudic and medieval rabbinic literature. But more important, Hoffmann and the medieval Jewish exegetes were preceded by Philo and the early rabbinic sages (the tannaim), who very clearly distinguished between ritual, bodily impurities on the one hand, and the defilement that results from sin on the other.

As we will see later, a number of biblicists have of late returned to this kind of conceptual framework, recognizing that sin is the source of its own distinct kind of defilement. Scholars of ancient Judaism, however, have not grasped the utility of this important observation, and this book seeks to argue, as did Büchler in his own day, that it is useful — even necessary — to make this distinction in order to understand properly much of the literature of ancient Judaism.

Büchler's work, despite its merits, is by no means free of problems. Thus current scholarly confusions regarding the issues of impurity and sin would not be alleviated if scholars were to just read *Studies in Sin and Atonement*. The greatest problem with Büchler's *Studies* is, of course, the fact that it is outdated, because of both advances in method and the discoveries at Qumran. Büchler's work is also incomplete, for he chose not to deal with the bulk of the New Testament evidence. Another important problem with Büchler's work is that a number of his conclusions were not correct. He argued that the doctrine of the defiling force of sin was held by most Jews, more or less continuously, throughout the time frame he covers.[12] Where Büchler saw unity and continuity, however, we will find disagreement and evolution.

As J. H. Hertz conceded in his otherwise complimentary preface to the *Studies*, Büchler's works are "not easy reading."[13] This judgment may come as no surprise to the reader who struggled to make sense of the brief quotation cited earlier. The difficulty of Büchler's prose may well be one of the reasons that his *Studies* failed to make the impact they should have. Related to this problem is the fact that Büchler never settled on fixed terminology for the phenomena he sought to describe. What will be referred to here as "moral" impurity was referred to by Büchler variously as "moral," "spiritual," and "religious" defilement.[14] And throughout his work Büchler shifts back and forth from "purity" to "cleanness" and from "purify" to "cleanse." These terminological shifts and imprecisions further complicate the issue and in no way help the reader to understand what Büchler was trying to say.

Thus in a way it is not so surprising that the two most influential treatments of impurity in ancient Judaism — Alon's "The Bounds of the Laws of Levitical Cleanness" and Neusner's *The Idea of Purity in Ancient Judaism* — both decline to deal adequately either with Büchler's work or the topics he addressed. And the same can be said for practically all of the literature written of late on impurity in ancient Judaism. Of the books cited in the first note to this chapter, only a few refer to

Büchler's *Studies,* and none discuss it — or, for that matter, the issue of sin — in any detail.

Gedalyahu Alon (1901–1950) published his essay "The Bounds of the Laws of Levitical Cleanness"[15] in 1937, only two years before Büchler's death in 1939. Alon put forth the now widely accepted thesis that *the* major impurity debate among ancient Jews concerned the geographical boundaries of the realm of purity. According to Alon, one position limited the sphere of purity to the temple and priesthood, while the other position "taught that the laws of uncleanness applied to all Israel."[16] According to this model, the Pharisees were "maximalists" who expanded the realm of purity beyond the confines of the temple, while the Sadducees were "minimalists" who restricted the realm of purity to the bounds of the temple. Alon's method as well as his interpretation of the evidence can be quite problematic.[17] Nonetheless, his view is often taken as axiomatic.[18] Even Milgrom speaks of "maximalist" and "minimalist" positions, though he sees the difference as developing from Scripture itself.[19] Yet, as we will see, when the notion of moral defilement is properly accounted for, the dichotomy between "maximalist" and "minimalist" (or "expansive" and "restrictive") positions is simply not sufficient to account for all the possibilities. Ancient Jewish attitudes toward the defiling force of sin cannot be analyzed in spatial terms alone.

It is striking that Alon's "The Bounds" does not address at all Büchler's thesis concerning the defiling force of sin. When Alon's work on impurity does touch on the question of sin, it does so in a way that is less than satisfying.[20] Moreover, the omission is even more striking when one considers that in another of his well-known studies of impurity he refutes an argument of Büchler's: that, indeed, is the entire thrust of Alon's "The Levitical Uncleanness of Gentiles."[21] In "The Bounds," however, he left unrefuted Büchler's key arguments concerning the defiling force of sin, and Alon's overall argument suffers as a result. As we will see, one cannot set out to discuss impurity in ancient Judaism without coming to terms with sin and its defiling force. Indeed, once one has taken into account the defiling force of sin as well as ritual impurity, one may be in a much better position to try to map out the dynamics of ancient Jewish sectarianism.

Impurity and Its Place: Mary Douglas's Purity and Danger

Douglas's work on impurity can be divided into two stages. The first stage, which will be dealt with in this section, is the comparative enterprise that began in 1966 with *Purity and Danger* and ran for about a decade, through the publication of *Natural Symbols* and a number of other essays, including "Self-Evidence" and "Deciphering a Meal."[22] The second stage of her work on impurity in ancient Israel began in the early 1990s with of a series of essays reevaluating her earlier interpretations of Leviticus. We will examine Douglas's newer work toward the end of this introduction.

It need hardly be said that Mary Douglas's work has proven tremendously influential in the fields of anthropology and religious studies. And her work is almost as wide-ranging as it is influential: the topic of pollution constitutes only one of her many interests in the field. Since fuller treatments of her work are readily available,[23] we can restrict ourselves to noting the impact she has had on the study of ancient Israelite purity law.

I know I am not alone in tracing my interest in defilement back to my first encounter with *Purity and Danger*. But in addition to inspiring lasting interest in the topic, *Purity and Danger* also laid the theoretical foundation for all subsequent work on ritual impurity in the Hebrew Bible. Indeed, virtually every academically oriented treatment of impurity in ancient Israel since 1966 has built on Douglas's work in some way. Of course, all this attention also means that some of her ideas have been refuted, or even in some instances shown to be in error.[24] Nonetheless a number of her basic claims have withstood the test of time.

One lasting achievement of *Purity and Danger* is the breaking of the conceptual barrier that lumped notions of defilement with the category of "primitive," thereby separating the category from supposedly "higher" religions. At one time it was rather common for anthropologists and scholars of religion alike to operate on the assumption that notions of defilement were something wholly different from our own schema of categorization. Virtually everyone concerned now recognizes that all sorts of peoples — "primitives" and "moderns" alike — have concepts of dirt and pollution that are structurally similar and that therefore can constructively be compared (even if significant differences remain).[25]

A second lasting achievement of *Purity and Danger* is Douglas's recognition of the systemic nature of any given culture's conceptions of defilement. For Douglas, "where there is dirt, there is system," and within such systems, dirt (and by analogy, pollution) can profitably be understood as "matter out of place."[26] Among the things that will be considered defiling are "anomalies" — things that violate categories. But there are no universal anomalies, just as there are no universal categories.[27] Defilement is, then, a *structure*, whose individual components are not to be analyzed as if they were freestanding. Thus we cannot understand, for example, the menstrual taboo simply by collecting examples of cultures that shun this substance and then comparing the results.[28] What must be studied, and then compared, are systems of defilement: the totalities of things that pollute, and the ways in which pollution can be conveyed.[29] Most who study ancient Israelite impurity these days would accept the soundness of Douglas's structural insight. Still, not all have been convinced of the usefulness of her definition of defilement as matter out of place.[30] Nevertheless, her insistence on seeing *systems* of defilement remains virtually unchallenged, and rightly so.

A third lasting achievement of *Purity and Danger* is the claim that once purity rules are understood systemically, the next step is to understand those systems symbolically. Why certain animals are shunned, why specific body fluids will be avoided — there is, according to Douglas, a symbolic system at work here. More specifically, in both *Purity and Danger* and *Natural Symbols*, Douglas champions the centrality of body symbolism to a proper understanding of systems of defilement. Because the body symbolizes the society, Douglas theorizes, there will be a correspondence between attitudes toward societal and bodily boundaries, with closed societies paying much more attention to the substances that exude from or enter the body.[31] Douglas also, and quite famously, sets forth a symbolic interpretation of the Israelite dietary laws. In this instance, however, the symbolism is to be found in the correspondence not between body and society, but between diet and the categories of creation. In other words, she interpreted Leviticus 11 in light of Genesis 1.[32] Of course, these interpretations are not universally recognized.[33] There are important theorists who continue to insist that the ancient Israelite impurity system is, at its root, arbitrary.[34] Nonetheless, most who deal with ancient Israelite impurity recognize the need to come to terms with the likelihood of a symbolic basis to the system.

Finally, *Purity and Danger* also illumines the social functions of these symbolic systems.[35] In particular, Douglas sheds light on the ways in which systems of defilement serve as means of influencing or controlling human behavior and interaction. Pollution beliefs function as powerful tools of social control. Such systems can be used to lower the social status of women or some other social class, and they can serve to control (disliked) social or sexual behavior.[36] Yet Douglas's discussion of the purposes of defilement is more complex than is generally assumed. The irony is, according to Douglas, that such systems are likely to flourish precisely when more effective (and more violent) forms of social control are desired but actually lacking. In Douglas's words:[37]

> When male dominance is accepted as a central principle of social organization and applied without inhibition and with full rights of physical coercion, beliefs in sex pollution are not likely to be highly developed. On the other hand, when the principle of male dominance is applied to the ordering of social life but is contradicted by other principles such as that of female independence, or the inherent right of women as the weaker sex to be more protected from violence than men, then sex pollution is likely to flourish.

According to Douglas, the relationship between systems of impurity that problematize women's bodies and behavior, on the one hand, and systems of patriarchy, on the other hand, is in reality more complex than what one might readily assume.

Douglas's approach to the relationship between impurity and sin is similarly sophisticated. On the one hand, Douglas categorically states that an impure person "is always in the wrong."[38] The truth of that statement can no longer be accepted, but what is important to point out here is that even in 1966 Douglas did not blindly identify impurity and sin. Here too, Douglas recognized that there is no one-to-one correspondence: impurity systems "only high-light a small aspect of morally disapproved behavior."[39]

As we will see later in this introduction, many of the studies of purity in ancient Judaism that are ostensibly built on Douglas's work operate on the assumptions that impurity systems are always indicative of oppressive or patriarchal societies, and that impurity and sin are to be similarly closely identified. These ideas are certainly traceable, in part, to *Purity and Danger*, but Douglas's take is usually much more nuanced than the arguments of those who base their work on hers.

There is much more to be said about *Purity and Danger*. We cannot even begin to cover the many and varied reactions to this work. During the decade that followed its appearance, Douglas responded to some critics by refining and revising her approach in a number of key ways. As was noted already, she soon came to rethink her assessment of anomalies in purity systems. And of course, the grid/group schema introduced in *Natural Symbols* allows for a much more sophisticated analysis of purity in ancient Israel.[40] Still, upon the publication of *Purity and Danger*, both Alon's and Büchler's work — already outdated after the discovery of Qumran — became virtually obsolete. What was needed was a new detailed analysis of biblical and ancient Jewish purity law, in historical perspective, and cognizant of Douglas's insights. The mantel was quickly picked up by Jacob Neusner.

Impurity and Its Metaphors: Jacob Neusner's The Idea of Purity

Neusner's *The Idea of Purity in Ancient Judaism* begins with a description of the system of impurity as it appears in the various strands of the Hebrew Bible. Neusner then proceeds chronologically, isolating and analyzing pertinent passages in various ancient Jewish texts from the second temple and rabbinic periods. He concludes his historical analysis with a thematic essay, which discusses a number of issues raised by Douglas in *Purity and Danger*. Neusner rightly recognizes various systemic, symbolic, and social aspects of the Israelite and Judaic systems of defilement. Where his book is problematic, however, is with regard to the defiling force of sin. Büchler's *Studies* are listed in Neusner's bibliography, and Büchler's work is noted as at least historically significant in Neusner's preface.[41] Still, it appears as if Büchler's work had little impact on Neusner. Indeed, upon discussing Büchler's work, Neusner explicitly notes his appreciation of the work of Alon over that of Büchler.[42]

Neusner introduces the concluding chapter of *The Idea of Purity* with the following assessment:

> Two important ideas about purity and impurity come down from ancient Israel: first, purity and impurity are cultic matters; second, they may serve as metaphors for moral and religious behavior, primarily in regard to matters of sex, idolatry, and unethical action.[43]

Neusner steps away from this dichotomy twice. When discussing the texts from Qumran, Neusner grants that the sectarians, "treat committing a sin not as a metaphor for becoming unclean, but as an actual source of defilement." Neusner even goes on to recognize that for the Qumran sectarians, "one cannot distinguish between cultic and moral impurity."[44] When discussing the rabbinic view that impurity can come about as a punishment for sin, Neusner suggests that the biblical metaphor of sin as defilement has been "shattered." In the Hebrew Bible, sins were *like* impurity, but for the rabbis, certain sins now *produce* impurity.[45] In almost all other cases, impurity as sin remains in the realm of metaphor.

On the face of it, Neusner's description of rabbinic and Qumranic views of impurity is accurate enough. I too will claim, albeit in a different way, that sin and defilement become closely connected at Qumran (chapter 3, "Identification of Ritual and Moral Impurity"). We will note too that the rabbis were willing to view impurity as a possible punishment for sin (chapter 4, "*Negaim*: 'Leprosy' and Sin in Tannaitic Sources"). But I will attempt to trace the history and development of such notions, and I will also do away with Neusner's dichotomy. Indeed, it is a fundamental tenet of this book that one cannot simply describe biblical uses of impurity language as either cultic or metaphorical. While purity and impurity *may* "serve as metaphors for moral and religious behavior" (as in certain prophetic passages), I will argue, following Büchler, that many biblical and postbiblical traditions believed sin to have its own distinct and *nonmetaphorical*[46] defiling force. Neusner's dichotomy cannot account for this phenomenon.

One need not look far and wide for a criticism of Neusner's dichotomy. To Neusner's credit, Mary Douglas was invited to submit a response to Neusner's lectures, and her critique was published as an appendix to his *The Idea of Purity in Ancient Judaism*. The main point of Douglas's comments, for our purposes, is her argument that all of the biblical discussions of impurity—those that Neusner applies to the cult and those that he sees as metaphorical—are part of a single symbolic system. In Douglas's words:[47]

> Since it is clear that the temple rules and sex rules and food rules are a single system of analogies, they do not converge on any one point but sustain the whole moral and physical universe simultaneously in their systematic interrelatedness

This perspective allows the anthropologist to criticize Neusner further for overlooking the coercive power of impurity laws:[48]

> However, the coercive effects of the rules [Neusner] describes are so obvious that I hardly need to do more than cite some of them. . . .
>   As to all the manifold rules which attribute impurity to women, in menses, or childbirth, if in doubt ask the Women's Liberation Movement about the intention to sustain male dominance. And to declare adultery and all improper sex impure, is not that a blow struck in defense of marriage and the family?

Douglas is correct here insofar as she rejects Neusner's dichotomy and insists on coming to terms with the fact that these texts consider certain sinful acts to be defiling. Douglas's critique falls short, however, in her reluctance to see the ways in which the defiling force of sin is different from the defiling force of bodily flows. As we will see, these types of defilement are different indeed.

Neusner's *The Idea of Impurity in Ancient Judaism* made a tremendous contribution to the study of ancient Jewish impurity law, and it remains the most wide-ranging survey of sources. But there is one major drawback of this work that is, in a way, only reinforced by Douglas's appendix: The reader is left without any clear idea of what to make of the defiling force of sin. Neither of the two possibilities presented—that the defiling force of sin is merely a metaphor (Neusner), or that it is part of a single symbolic system (Douglas)—gives the reader an adequate way of making sense of the biblical impurity system. Is the defiling force of sin merely a metaphor? Neusner incorrectly says yes, and Douglas correctly says no. But is the adulterer considered to be ritually defiling? Neusner correctly says no, and Douglas incorrectly implies that the answer should be yes. The reader of Neusner's *The Idea* is not made aware of the third possibility—which is spelled out clearly in Büchler's *Studies*—that certain sins defile in their own distinct way. Indeed, in part because of the popularity of Neusner's work, that third possibility has been virtually ignored in all scholarship on ancient Judaism since Neusner's *The Idea*.

*The Current Scene: Scholarship Since
Neusner's* The Idea

With regard to the defiling force of sin, one can discern two trends in current scholarship on impurity in ancient Judaism. The first trend is to follow in the footsteps of Neusner and Alon, either dismissing the issue or simply avoiding it altogether. The second trend is blindly to equate impurity and sin.

One of the more useful recent works on impurity in ancient Judaism is Hannah K. Harrington's *The Impurity Systems of Qumran and the Rabbis*. This work is particularly important for its emphasis on the scriptural basis of the rabbinic and Qumranic systems of impurity. Unfortunately, however, it does not come to grips with the question of sin and its defiling force. Surprisingly, Harrington does not count sin among the sources of impurity for the Qumran sectarians, despite the fact that scholars have long noted that for the sectarians sin and impurity were closely related.[49] The second appendix to her book, which compares the rabbinic and Qumranic systems, thus overlooks the significant differences between Qumran and early rabbinic (tannaitic) literature with regard to the defiling force of sin.

In his important study of Pharisaic purity rules, "Did the Pharisees Eat Ordinary Food in Purity?" E. P. Sanders provides a helpful summary and schematization of biblical ritual purity law, as a necessary first step in his review of Pharisaic purity practices.[50] In addition to recognizing the need to review and make sense of the biblical evidence in order to understand ancient Judaism, Sanders provides an analysis of ritual impurity that is sound and sensible and that will be referred to with some frequency below. Yet he dismisses out of hand the issue of moral impurity.[51] While Sanders accurately describes *ritual* impurity, his decision to discount the importance of *moral* impurity greatly diminishes the overall value of his work, for he cannot fully describe the dynamic of impurity in ancient Judaism without accounting for both systems.[52] Similar criticisms can be raised against other detailed studies on impurity in ancient Judaism.[53]

We turn now to a few works that make a different mistake: that of equating impurity and sin. A number of scholars have tried to incorporate Mary Douglas's insights into an improved understanding of various New Testament texts. There are many such treatments; among the most frequently cited are Jerome H. Neyrey's "The Idea of Purity in Mark's Gospel," Bruce J. Malina's "Clean and Unclean: Understanding Rules of Purity," and David Rhoads's "Social Criticism: Crossing Boundaries."[54] A full evaluation of these works must wait until an analysis has been presented here in some detail. I note here, however, that one can find in each of these works statements to the effect that sinners were considered to be impure and that, by extension, those who associated with sinners were violating norms of purity.[55] This erroneous view has gained widespread acceptance, and at least one popular construction of the historical Jesus—that of Marcus J. Borg—is based explicitly on this assumption.[56]

This rapid survey of recent literature is far from complete; I have mentioned here only the better known and more wide-ranging works. Other important studies devoted to specific texts or times will be discussed in their proper place in the following chapters. Still, the sample that has been surveyed here is, I believe, representative enough to justify the need for the present work: Scholars of ancient Judaism have not paid enough attention to the question of the defiling force of sin.

The Right Foundation: Systems of Defilement in the Hebrew Bible

While scholars of ancient Judaism have not paid enough attention to the relationship between impurity and sin, it is our good fortune that a number of biblical scholars have indeed given this issue the attention it deserves. The Hebrew Bible is, of course, the foundation upon which much of ancient Jewish literature is built. And since a number of biblical scholars have dealt with the defiling force of sin, their work will provide the foundation upon which this study can be constructed. We cannot, of course, trace here the history of the scholarly discussion of impurity in the Hebrew Bible.[57] Instead we will focus exclusively on those scholars who have contributed positively to the understanding of the fact that certain grave sins have their own distinct defiling force in the Hebrew Bible.

David Z. Hoffmann

To my knowledge, the first scholar in modern times to articulate clearly that the Pentateuch presents two systems of defilement was David Zvi Hoffmann (1843–1921). In his seminal commentary on Leviticus, Hoffmann distinguished between what he referred to as the defilement that stands in opposition to purity (which he called טומאת הגויות) and the defilement that stands in opposition to holiness (which he called טומאת הקדושות).[58] In drawing this distinction, Hoffmann drew on various traditional Jewish sources.[59] In Hoffmann's scheme, the first sort of defilement originates in human corpses, certain animal carcasses, bodily flows, and "leprosy" — the sources of impurity delineated in Leviticus 11–15 and Numbers 19, which we will refer to as "ritual" impurity.[60] These sources of defilement leave the affected person in a temporary state of defilement, a situation that can be ameliorated by ritual purification.[61] Hoffmann's other type of impurity (טומאת הקדושות) originates in sinful behavior, including eating forbidden foods, performing idolatrous acts, and violating sexual taboos.[62] This impurity is defined in opposition to holiness, not purity. More significantly, there are no ritual purifications for the amelioration of this type of defilement. It is the sacrificial rituals for the Day of Atonement (Lev. 16) that provide the means to rectify this defilement.[63] As Leviticus 18:24–25 suggests, this impurity results in the defilement of the land and the exile of its inhabitants.[64] And as Leviticus 11:43 and 19:31 suggest, this defilement affects the sinner's being as well. It is for this reason that this type of impurity can also be referred to as the defilement pertaining to the soul (טומאת הנפשות).[65]

Hoffmann can too easily be misunderstood on this point. Although he does emphasize the defiling effect that sins have upon the soul, he believes that this defilement affects the body of the sinner as well. Yet the body of the sinner is not affected in the same way as the body of one who is ritually defiled. In his comments on the sexual prohibitions delineated in Leviticus 18—where sexual sins are viewed as defiling—Hoffmann emphasizes that the impurity contracted here is not of the same sort as that which is the concern in Leviticus 15.[66] While Leviticus 15 is concerned with a temporary defilement, which can be removed by ablution, Leviticus 18 is concerned with a different defilement, one that affects both body and soul and that cannot be removed by ablution.[67] When commenting on Leviticus 19:31, where necromancy is viewed as a defilement, Hoffmann articulates more precisely what effect the defilement of sin has upon the sinner. It affects the sinner's body and soul, the result being that the sinner is rejected by God.[68] Hoffmann emphasizes that this defilement is not symbolic but concrete. Indeed, it is the other type of impurity (טומאת הגויית) that is symbolic.[69] This last aspect of Hoffmann's view will prove particularly helpful when we take up again the question of metaphor in chapter 1. It is unfortunate that Hoffmann's work has been virtually ignored, even by those few who have paid due attention to the defiling force of sin.

Jacob Milgrom

In an article that first appeared in 1976, Jacob Milgrom advanced the thesis that the so-called "sin-offering" (חטאת) does not, as is commonly believed, serve as a ritual of atonement.[70] The sacrifice serves, rather, as a ritual of purification, and the name of the sacrifice should therefore be translated as "purification-offering."[71] What is purified, in Milgrom's view, is not the sinner who brings the sacrifice, but the altar of God, which is subject to defilement by sin. That sin defiles the sanctuary is evidenced first of all by Leviticus 20:3, which states explicitly that Molech worship defiles the sanctuary. Milgrom bolsters his case by referring to other biblical traditions as well as parallels in ancient Near Eastern literature.[72] Yet Milgrom is careful to note that the impurity that results from sin is distinct from the "physical" impurities described elsewhere. These "physical" impurities—like Büchler's "levitical" impurities—leave the person ritually defiled, and these impurities are resolved with rites of purification. But grave sin defiles in a different way altogether, and the sinner needs not ritual purification, but forgiveness.[73] What is defiled by sin? Not the sinner, Milgrom suggests, but the sanctuary. Recalling Oscar Wilde's novel, Milgrom speaks of the priestly *Picture of Dorian Gray*: "Sin may not leave its mark on the face of the sinner," Milgrom asserts, "but it is certain to mark the face of the sanctuary; and unless it is quickly expunged, God's presence will depart."[74]

The process of the defilement of the sanctuary by sin occurs, according to Milgrom, on three levels simultaneously. On the first level, the inadvertent sins of individual Israelites defile the outer altar. The sacrificial ritual described in Leviticus 4:27–35 ameliorates this situation: the priest puts some of the blood of the sacrificed animal on the horns of the altar and pours the rest at its base (vv. 30, 34). The inadvertent sin of the high priest, or of the entire community, is more severe: it defiles the shrine. The sacrificial rituals described in Leviticus 4:3–21 ameliorate these situations. In these ceremonies, the sacrificial blood is placed on the veil of the shrine and on the inner altar and then poured about the outer altar as well. The most severe form of sin-defilement, according to Milgrom, is that produced by the "wanton, unrepented sin."[75] This defilement reaches even further than the defilements caused by inadvertent sins, penetrating into the Holy of Holies, where the ark of the Lord is kept. The sinners who produce this defilement are not permitted to bring *chattat* sacrifices (Num. 15:27–31). This defilement of the sanctuary is ameliorated by the rituals performed on the Day of Atonement, which include purgation of the inner altar and shrine.[76]

Milgrom's theories about the "purification-offering" have not been universally accepted.[77] Yet these debates, though interesting, are ancillary to our project. For our purposes, the following aspects of Milgrom's work are the most important, and neither of these propositions has been refuted. First, like Hoffmann and Büchler before him, Milgrom recognizes the distinctive nature of the defiling force of sin. Second, Milgrom develops a specific description of the process by which various types of sins defile a holy place — in this case the sanctuary of God. Building on Milgrom's analysis — and eagerly awaiting his forthcoming commentary on the second half of Leviticus — we will focus in this work on the fact that three sins in particular have the force to defile not only the sanctuary of God, but also the land of Israel: Bloodshed, idolatry, and sexual immorality are explicitly described in various traditions as defilements that have a deleterious effect on the land.[78] They produce a defilement that is therefore analogous to, but distinct from, the sin defilement that Milgrom has clearly described in his articles and commentaries.

Tikva Frymer-Kensky

Without a doubt the most successful recent attempt at systematizing the various types of purity is that undertaken by Tikva Frymer-Kensky, in the *festschrift* for David Noel Freedman.[79] The article is not well known, which is unfortunate because her analysis is astute and provocative.[80] Right from the start, Frymer-Kensky notes:[81]

> Some forms of pollution could be eradicated by rituals; the performance of these purifications and expiations was a major function of the priesthood. The pollution caused by the performance of certain deeds, however, could not be eradicated by rituals; Israel believed that the person intentionally committing these acts would suffer catastrophic retribution. Wrongful acts could cause the pollution of the nation and of the land of Israel, which could also not be cured by ritual

The distinction Frymer-Kensky builds here is essentially similar to that of both Büchler and Hoffmann: all three recognize that grave sin defiles in a way that is altogether different from the ways in which the ritual impurities defile. After reviewing and schematizing the major and minor forms of the ritual type of pollution, Frymer-Kensky makes some important general observations about this kind of impurity. For one, she is careful to describe the dynamic between ritual impurity and danger. Although it is contagious, this sort of defilement is not necessarily dangerous. Of course, there is a dangerous aspect to it, in that it is forbidden for what is ritually impure to come into contact with what is sacred. Thus the impure priest who comes into contact with the sancta is to suffer a most severe punishment: *karet* (כרת).[82] And all Israelites must take care to keep impurity away from the sacred (Lev. 15:31).[83] Still, the Israelite — priest, Levite, or layperson — was not in danger when affected by these pollutions, *provided the purity laws were obeyed*. Frymer-Kensky also carefully describes the dynamic between this type of defilement and sin. Ritual impurity is generally not sinful, it is often unavoidable, and at times it is even required (as in the case of burial).[84]

Frymer-Kensky then moves on to discuss the defiling force of sin. She correctly recognizes the idea — which she refers to as a "danger belief" — that sins place individuals and society in danger by polluting the land and the sanctuary, even though the sinner does not suffer any contagious defilement. She builds on the work of Milgrom in this respect, drawing on his analogy to the *Picture of Dorian Gray*. Taking Milgrom's work one step further, Frymer-Kensky focuses on the defilement of the land, identifying the three possible causes of land defilement: sexual sins, bloodshed, and idolatry.[85]

One could raise some questions about specific aspects of Frymer-Kensky's analysis,[86] but the fundamental disagreement to be raised here concerns terminology. The terminology I will suggest — "ritual" and "moral" impurity — is much more pliable than "contagious pollutions" and "danger-beliefs." There are no adjectives or adverbs that go hand-in-hand with Frymer-Kensky's terms, and thus they become cumbersome in any attempt to describe literature as reflecting one idea or another, or even sources of impurity that may defile in one way or another. The terms employed here are much more useful for this purpose.

But it is not only that the terminology suggested here is more useful, it is also more accurate. As Frymer-Kensky herself concedes, there is a degree of danger surrounding the ritual defilements, and that is reason enough to avoid using "danger-belief" to refer to only one type of impurity. But there is also a problem with the second half of the phrase, "danger-*belief*." At one point Frymer-Kensky states that ancient Israel had two sets of pollution beliefs, as described in her statement quoted above.[87] Yet she then goes on to use the term "belief" primarily with regard to the second, graver type of defilement. It is true, of course, that the defiling force of sin is an ancient Israelite belief. But the idea that lepers, for example, defile, in any way whatsoever, is also a *belief*. Similarly, that the carcasses of reptiles are defiling is also a belief. In fact, all of ancient Israel's conceptions of purity and impurity are beliefs, as Frymer-Kensky herself recognizes. The logical extension of this observation is to avoid using the term "belief" with regard to one type of defilement over another. As will be seen, even scholars who recognize the distinctive nature of the defiling force of sin often underestimate the importance of the issue (see discussion of metaphor in chapter 1). While Frymer-Kensky is not one of those scholars, her more frequent use of the term "belief" in reference to that type of impurity is unlikely to contribute to general awareness of the importance of the defiling force of sin.

David P. Wright

In two recent detailed studies, David P. Wright offers an alternative schematization of biblical purity law.[88] Building on the work of Büchler and Milgrom (Frymer-Kensky is not cited in either article), Wright also divides the purity laws into two major categories. Yet the distinction he draws is not as sharp as Büchler's (or Frymer-Kensky's), nor is it drawn along the same lines. In his *Anchor Bible Dictionary* article,

Wright sets up two major categories of defilements: those that are permitted, and those that are prohibited.[89] In his related article "The Spectrum," Wright rejects the term "permitted" and refers to that type of purity as "tolerated."[90]

The permitted, or tolerated, impurities include most, but not all, of the impurities that were included in the analogous categories set up by Hoffmann, Büchler, and Frymer-Kensky. That is, the permitted impurities are generally the laws laid out in Leviticus 11–15 and Numbers 19. There are some important exceptions, however. Wright would put almost all of the prohibitions related to these regulations in the second category, though food laws, for Wright, remain in the first.[91] Thus, for Wright, the restriction incumbent on priests and Nazirites to avoid corpse impurity (Lev. 21:1–4, 10–11; Num. 6:6–9) falls in the category of prohibited impurity, along with the three defilements we have discussed before: idolatry, murder, and sexual sins.[92] While there is something to be said for this categorization, I believe that the distinction drawn between ritual and moral defilements is simpler and will therefore prove more useful, especially for the description of ancient Judaism. The difference between the two systems of categorization is essentially this: While Wright's schema is based on the abstract categories of permission and prohibition, the categorization suggested in this work focuses on the ability of certain sins to defile the land and bring about exile. – Defile the land

One problem with Wright's schema is the fact that his terminology, like that of Frymer-Kensky, is cumbersome: Without both adverbial and adjectival forms, it is difficult to describe one substance as defiling in one way or another. But putting matters of grammar and syntax aside, the term "permitted" is instrinsically problematic, for as Wright himself recognizes, many of the defilements so described result not just from permitted activities, but also from activities that are obligatory, including procreation and burial.[93] In "The Spectrum," Wright recognizes this difficulty, and for that reason he suggests "tolerated" as a better referent than "permitted."[94] But we have the same problem with "tolerated." What is commanded is not merely "tolerated"; it is, rather, "right and proper," to use Sanders's phrase.[95] In the end, all that has been said argues against using the categories of permission and prohibition alone as the major conceptual basis when schematizing biblical impurity law.

To sum up, David Zvi Hoffmann's early twentieth-century commentary on Leviticus is important for its recognition of two types of defilement, its insistence that the defilement that results from sin is both concrete and serious, and its suggestion that this defilement is defined not in opposition to purity but in opposition to holiness. Jacob Milgrom's work is important to us for its development of an understanding of how sinfulness in general has the power to defile the sanctuary from afar. Although Milgrom's work to date does not go into the details that we are concerned with here (how grave sins defile the land), his description of how lesser sins defile the sanctuary proves to be an illustrative analogy. Finally, Frymer-Kensky and Wright have both provided detailed treatments of biblical purity that try to come to terms with the relationship between sin and defilement. While the terminology used in these works is cumbersome, both contribute to a better understanding of the topic at hand. All four of these works, in the final analysis, lead us in the right direction and provide the right foundation for further research on impurity and sin in ancient Judaism.

Re-placing Ritual Impurity: The Recent Work of Mary Douglas

In the early 1990s, Mary Douglas embarked on a project that involved rethinking many of the major tenets of *Purity and Danger*. Influenced by recent progress in biblical studies, especially by the work of Jacob Milgrom, and armed with a newly acquired facility with the Hebrew language, Douglas took on the daunting task of understanding better the books of Leviticus and Numbers. She published a number of studies in quick succession.[96] Douglas then worked these insights into two complete volumes, one treating Numbers and the most recent treating Leviticus.[97] As we will see, much of her new work differs markedly in a number of respects from her earlier work, and because of her influence, it is fitting to point out some of the changes. Moreover, it is especially appropriate to do so here because her new approach to ritual impurity is to a large degree commensurate with the approach taken in this book.[98]

What has changed? For one, Douglas's new work in the field is decidedly less comparative in nature than *Purity and Danger*. This is so not because she has abandoned the comparative enterprise, by any means, but rather she has come to believe that there is something distinctive about the Israelite purity system. The second notable change is her reevaluation of the function of ritual impurity in biblical Israel. She has now come to believe that the Israelite ritual impurity system does not serve to exclude or subordinate people belonging to inferior classes or castes. In the Israelite system, as we will see, all Israelites are subject to ritual impurity, and ritual purification is available to all Israelites. In her words:[99]

> In short, pollution ideas normally maintain the accepted moral and social codes and at the same time separate categories of the same population. . .
>
> In so far as the Levitical rules for purity apply universally they are useless for internal disciplining. They maintain absolutely no social demarcation. It is true that only the priest can make atonement, and that the priest's dedicated food must not be eaten by outsiders, but the book insists over and over again that the poor and the stranger are to be included in the requirements of the laws, no one is excluded from the benefits of purification.

With this observation — and the same sentiment is expressed throughout her new work[100] — Douglas has made virtually an about-face, and in so doing, she has pulled the carpet out from under those who, working with *Purity and Danger*, set themselves to the task of understanding ritual impurity in biblical Israel and ancient Judaism. Those who would understand ritual impurity in such a way as to draw an overly hierarchical picture of biblical priests or ancient Jewish Pharisees would do well to take seriously Mary Douglas's new work.

This new understanding of ritual impurity by no means exhausts the significance of Douglas's new work. Indeed, Douglas has greatly widened her scope in regard to biblical Israel. In her new work, impurity is just one of many themes, as it is just one of the many themes in the books of Leviticus and Numbers. Douglas has tried to tackle Leviticus and Numbers in their entirety; and in order to do so, she has drawn on the full resources of the Bible, interpreting defilement in light of doctrines of atonement, and food laws in light of notions of justice. Along the way, she has completely rethought her earlier understanding of the Israelite food laws,[101] and she has worked toward an important reevaluation of the achievements of Ezra.[102]

And yet this is still the same Mary Douglas. Despite its staggering scope, there is an overall unity to her work.[103] She remains a disciple of Durkheim, emphasizing the need to grapple with the social functions of ritual categories.[104] And even with regard to defilement, she is still interested in structures, and she still emphasizes the importance of body symbolism.[105] Moreover, she remains engaged in a critique of "anti-ritualistic" understandings of religious behavior.[106] In her words:[107]

> One serious look at Leviticus shows that there is no lineup of priest and prophet, and no conflict between internal versus external religion, or justice versus ritual. As I read it, Leviticus makes a truly brilliant synthesis of two equations. justice of people to people, and justice of people to God.

Her tenacity in sticking to this message is welcome, for the demon she would wish to exorcise remains among us.

Impurity and the Comparative Enterprise

It is not at all uncommon to find scholars speaking very generally of "purity systems," or "purity societies," as if all societies that had purity systems functioned in more or less the same way.[108] Those who articulate such views have been too seriously affected by a perfunctory reading of Mary Douglas's early work. But just as there are no universal taboos, there are no universal models of "purity societies." In this work no such generalizations about purity systems will be made. The more I learn about the different ways in which impurity was perceived in ancient Judaism, the more convinced I become of the complexity and subtlety of the topic as a whole.

To illustrate the peril of overgeneralization, let us quickly compare one aspect of the impurity systems of Islam and Zoroastrianism. The Zoroastrian system of impurity is clearly—and I can only hope, accurately—described in Jamsheed K. Choksy's *Purity and Pollution in Zoroastrianism: Triumph over Evil.*[109] I do not know of any book-length treatments of impurity in Islam, but a detailed description can be found in A. Kevin Reinhart's article, "Impurity/No Danger."[110] A difference between Zoroastrianism and Islam is manifest even in the titles of these works. In Zoroastrianism, impurity and evil are quite closely identified and thus defilement is a great source of danger. Moreover, there is a great moral need to maintain purity.[111] In Islam, in contrast, impurity is not particularly dangerous at all. It is conceived of as natural and unavoidable, and there are none of the overwhelming moral concerns indicative of Zoroastrianism.[112] We could offer other brief comparisons as well: in Hinduism, purity and class are closely related,[113] while that was not at all the case in, for example, ancient Greek religion.[114] And it stands to reason that impurity systems would differ markedly from one another. If indeed such systems serve in part to demarcate external religious and cultural boundaries, then there is an inherent necessity for any one system to function differently than the systems of any other cultures with which the first comes into contact. If the systems functioned too similarly—problematizing the same classes, substances, or phenomena—then they would interact interchangeably. In other words, if purity systems of distinct societies were not significantly different, no boundaries would be demarcated.[115] Impurity systems, in order to perform their function, ought to be rather distinct.

All this is to say nothing of differences that could be pointed out even *within* religious systems. Shiite and Sunni Muslims, for instance, disagree over the status of outsiders with regard to purity.[116] And this work is devoted to clarifying some disagreements about impurity among various groups of ancient Jews. To account for differences and evolution within a single religious tradition is a daunting task in itself. To offer broad comparisons between the various Judaic approaches and other systems of impurity in the Greco-Roman world is simply beyond the limitations of this work.[117] Certain points of comparison will be made along the way, but the effort is, admittedly, not a sustained one. It is hoped, however, that this work will find its way to scholars who have intimate knowledge of other religious traditions. It is by provoking reactions from such reachers that this work may in the end contribute to the comparative enterprise.

The task, again, is to understand disagreements and debates among ancient Jews concerning the relationship between impurity and sin. But to understand these ancient Jewish debates, we must first understand the dynamic between sin and impurity in the Hebrew Bible. That is the task of chapter 1.

1

Ritual and Moral Impurity
in the Hebrew Bible

[handwritten marginal note: Problem addressed → Grave sins have defiling force]

The introduction argued that many of the recent treatments of impurity in ancient Judaism do not fully take into consideration the fact that certain grave sins have their own distinct defiling force. Yet some biblical scholars, as we have seen, have indeed paid due attention to this phenomenon. Building especially on the work of Hoffmann, Milgrom, Frymer-Kensky and Wright, this chapter will schematize the two main conceptions of impurity in the Hebrew Bible (first two sections).

Once the schematization is spelled out clearly, some ancillary questions will be addressed in the next four sections. First, how do the food laws fit into this picture? Second, can moral impurity be understood as metaphorical? Third, what is the relationship between the two impurity systems? And fourth, how does each of these sys- *[handwritten: Gender?]* tems look under the lens of gender studies? After coming to terms with many aspects of defilement and sin in the Hebrew Bible, we will find ourselves much better positioned to understand the dynamic between impurity and sin in ancient Judaism.

Throughout this chapter I will offer some correctives and challenges to the biblical scholarship reviewed in the introduction. Still, the ultimate purpose of the schematization is not so much to critique contemporary biblical scholarship as to establish a conceptual framework that will allow for a better understanding of the relationship between sin and impurity in ancient Judaism. We therefore cannot discuss every instance of the use of purity language in the Hebrew Bible, nor can we discuss every facet of the types of purity discerned there. Needless to say, we also cannot discuss the role that purity plays in each biblical document. Our ultimate goal is not to reevaluate biblical impurity law, but rather to reevaluate the dynamic between impurity and sin in ancient Judaism.

Biblical studies today finds itself at odds over the dates of various biblical documents, and one of the current debates concerns the relative and absolute dates of the priestly strands in the Pentateuch. Generally, contemporary scholars recognize two major strands of priestly contributions: the priestly strand, which retains the classic designation P, and the Holiness Code, designated with an H.[1] Leviticus can be divided into two parts, with chapters 1–16 being assigned roughly to P, and chapters 17–

26 to H.[2] Other priestly passages appearing throughout the Pentateuch can also be assigned to one or the other of these strands.[3] We cannot be detained by a discussion of these points, since we are not dealing here with Israelite history as such, but it should be stated that, following Milgrom, the operative assumptions of the present work are (1) that both the priestly strand (P) and the Holiness Code (H) are best seen as distinct sources, and (2) that both strands stem from the preexilic period.[4] Readers who insist on the unity of Leviticus may meet with some initial reluctance to recognize the distinction that will be made between "ritual" and "moral" impurity. Similarly, readers who insist on assigning a postexilic date to P, H, or both may find trouble with the chronology adopted in this work. But none of the arguments presented will require one to distinguish between P and H or to assign either to the preexilic period. Even if Leviticus were a single, postexilic composition, the distinction between two types of defilements would still need to be maintained, and the dynamic between ritual and moral impurity in ancient Judaism would still need to be accounted for.

With these limitations and goals in mind, we turn now to the distinction between ritual and moral impurity in the Hebrew Bible.

Ritual Impurity

Leviticus 11–15 and Numbers 19 describe the contagious but generally impermanent sort of defilement which we will refer to as "ritual impurity." The adjective "ritual" serves to differentiate this type of impurity from "moral impurity," discussed in the next section. It should be noted right from the start that the adjectives "ritual" and "moral" are problematic: The terms do not appear in the texts, and neither one is a category as such in biblical or postbiblical Jewish literature.[5] Moreover, there is the danger, once such a distinction is drawn, that whatever is associated with morality will be evaluated more highly than whatever is associated with ritual. Thus some scholars, such as Neusner and Sanders, opt to shun such adjectives altogether.[6] Nonetheless, despite these concerns, the adjectives are still necessary. The biblical texts use the same terminology of defilement to describe two distinct phenomena, and so unless we supply our own descriptive terminology, confusion about the nature of the relationship between impurity and sin will continue. Thus the fact that the terms "ritual" and "moral" are not in our texts should not stop us from using such adjectives, for scholars of ancient texts ought to articulate the meanings and messages of ancient texts in modern scholarly terms. Moreover, making a distinction between ritual and moral impurity should not be interpreted as taking a first step down the road of antiritualism. By using these terms I am not intending to state that ritual and morality are opposing or mutually exclusive concerns.[7] I am simply trying to drive home the point that there are two kinds of impurity in ancient Israel, one of which is more associated with sin than the other.

The term "ritual" is particularly useful in this regard because this kind of impurity affects the ritual status of persons stricken by it. Ritually impure persons are excluded from participation in certain ritual acts and barred from entering sacred precincts. In certain cases, such persons may affect the ritual status of those around them as well. Moreover, ritual purity is achieved, at least in part, *ritually*, that is by means of sacrifices, sprinklings, washings, and bathings. Rituals, however, are not always sufficient: even after ritual purification, one may remain impure until evening (e.g., Lev. 15:5). Still, rituals frequently play an important role in the transition from impurity to purity, and for this reason also, the term "ritual" is in this context a useful description.   → *Ritual's role in moral purity*

Yet the term "ritual" is not completely unproblematic. Although rituals play an important role in achieving ritual purity, they also play a role—albeit a different one—in the achievement of moral purity. The term "ritual" is not the perfect adjective, but it is better than the commonly used alternatives. Neither of the other two possibilities—"cultic" or "levitical"—is preferable. The term "cultic" is shunned here because, as we will see, the cult center plays an equally important role in both forms of impurity.[8] Moreover, to set cult in opposition to morality seems to make even less sense than opposing ritual to morality. The term "levitical" is avoided here for two reasons. First, both types of impurity are articulated within the book of Leviticus, and neither is articulated solely in that book. Second, neither type of impurity is particularly concerned with Levites. All Israelites—priests and laypersons—had to concern themselves with both types of defilement. The name "Leviticus" is bad enough—we need not perpetuate misnomers.[9]   → *All Israelites were concerned w/ purity*

Finally, by using "ritual" and "moral" we are able to employ terminology that is both parallel and pliable. By isolating two adjectives to modify the noun "impurity," we find ourselves with two categories that at the same time express the difference and interrelatedness of the two types of defilements. They are both defilements, but each of a different sort. A further benefit is the fact that both terms are adjectives with related adverbs ("ritually" and "morally"), allowing for a more felicitous description of substances or sins that may defile in some way. The terminology selected here is not perfect, but these terms are, at least for now, our best options.

Def. Ritual impurity

Ritual impurity results from direct or indirect contact with any of a number of natural sources including childbirth (Lev. 12:1–8), scale disease (Lev. 13:1–14:32), genital discharges (Lev. 15:1–33), the carcasses of certain impure animals (Lev. 11:1–47), and human corpses (Num. 19:10–22). Ritual impurity also comes about as a by-product of certain purificatory procedures (e.g., Lev. 16:28; Num. 19:8).[10] All of these passages can be assigned to the priestly source (P), although Numbers 19 shows signs of being influenced by the ideology of the Holiness Code (H).[11] The durations of these impurities differ, as do the requisite cleansing processes—but the intricacies of these laws are not our concern at this moment.[12] What is our concern is there are three distinct characteristics of ritual impurity. (1) The sources of ritual impurity are generally natural and more or less unavoidable. (2) It is not sinful to contract these impurities. And (3) these impurities convey an impermanent contagion.   *3 characteristics of ritual purity*

1. The sources of ritual impurity are generally natural and more or less unavoidable.[13] That the sources of ritual impurity are natural is quite clear. Birth, death, sex, disease, and discharge are all part of normal life. The only possible exception to this rule is the impurity that is generated by priests in the process of performing purificatory rituals (Lev 16; Num. 19). An impurity that comes about as a result of temple procedures might not seem at first glance to be natural. However, there is nothing unnatural about this impurity either. The cult was, for ancient Israel, part of life.

For whatever reason, certain cultic procedures were believed to defile the priests involved. These were *sacrificial* procedures, activities involving animals, blood, and death — natural things — albeit with some degree of human behavioral control. But the addition of human behavior into the equation does not make this defilement any less natural than the other ritual impurities. Human behavior, after all, plays a role in sexual relations and childbirth as well. Human behavior is part of nature, and in the final analysis, ritual impurity in all its forms is natural.

Ritual impurity is also more or less unavoidable. The "more or less" is important here, because certain contacts are relatively avoidable: in Leviticus 11:43, for instance, Israelites are urged not to defile themselves with certain impure animals.[14] But discharge, disease, and death are, alas, unavoidable. And as has been noted, some impurities are not only unavoidable, but obligatory. Israelites are obligated to bury their dead, though priests are allowed to contract corpse impurity only in certain cases (Lev. 21:1–4). Yet even priests, along with all Israelites, are obligated to reproduce (Gen. 1:28, 9:7). And of course priests are obligated to perform cultic procedures that leave them defiled as a result.

2. It is not a sin to contract these impurities. This idea proceeds logically from the observations drawn above. As Frymer-Kensky, Sanders, and Wright have noticed, it would be impossible, if not absurd, to consider natural processes such as menstruation to be prohibited.[15] Nonetheless, both Sanders and Wright maintain that some or all of these defilements as a general rule are discouraged.[16] But there is no indication that permitted sex is discouraged in any way, that an Israelite man is supposed to avoid coming into physical contact with the mother of his newborn children, or that any Israelite is to avoid contact with the dead. To the contrary, we have noted that many of these things are proper, and some of them even obligatory, even though they are ritually defiling. More problematic for the view that these impurities are to be avoided is the fact that our documents do not contain any warnings against contracting impurity in general, or any advice on how to reduce contact with impurity. If contracting these impurities were indeed discouraged, we should expect to find precautionary measures of some sort. In this regard, a brief comparison with the Zoroastrian impurity system is apt. In Zoroastrianism, impurity and evil are closely identified, and thus impurity is viewed as a source of grave danger. Also, as in ancient Israel, corpses were viewed as a source of ritual impurity. During the process of caring for corpses, Zoroastrians would take a number of precautionary measures in order to reduce the spread of impurity: special dress, the pairing of corpse-bearers, and the presence of a dog.[17] These apotropaic rituals are the kinds of precautions we would expect to find in ancient Israel if ritual impurity were indeed viewed with the degree of danger and misfortune that some suggest.

Priests, of course, must limit their contact with corpse impurity (Lev. 21:1–4), but they are not prohibited from contracting other impurities (Lev. 22:4–7). The primary concern incumbent upon the priests is not to avoid ritual impurity, but to safeguard the separation between ritual impurity and purity (Lev. 10:10).[18] Thus priests are sternly warned against eating sacred food or entering sacred precincts when in a state of ritual impurity (Lev. 7:20–21). Practically speaking, the obligation incumbent upon priests is not avoidance of ritual impurity, but awareness of ritual impurity. By extension, it is not accurate to say that Israelites are encouraged to limit their contacts with ritually impure substances or people. Rather, Israelites are obliged to re-main aware of their ritual status at all times, lest they accidentally come into contact with the sacred while in a state of ritual impurity (Lev. 15:31). As long as they remain aware of their status, there is little chance of danger or transgression.   *Ritual impurity as punishment*

Even though ritual impurity is not sinful, a few biblical narratives view at least one form of ritual defilement as a punishment for moral shortcomings: Moses's sis-ter Miriam was afflicted with "leprosy" when she spoke against her brother's Cushite wife (Num. 12), and the Judean King Uzziah was similarly afflicted when he asserted priestly prerogatives (2 Chron. 26). Yet as both Frymer-Kensky and Douglas have em-phasized, there is nothing within the legal traditions to justify viewing scale disease as a positive indication that the stricken individual has transgressed.[19] As far as both P and H are concerned, the leper is ritually impure, but the leper is not guilty.[20]

There are, though, two ways that ritual impurity can lead to sin. Numbers 19:13 and 19:20 state that the refusal to purify from corpse impurity is a transgression pun-ishable by *karet* (being cut off from the people).[21] The outcome of such a refusal, moreover, is the defilement of the sanctuary. In this case, the defilement of the sanc-tuary is to be understood along the lines laid out by Milgrom in his article "The Priestly 'Picture of Dorian Gray.'" The concern here is not that the direct contact of a ritually impure person defiles the sanctuary ritually, but rather that the wanton sin of refusal to purify, in and of itself, defiles the sanctuary, morally, even from afar.

The second way in which ritual impurity and sin are connected is on a more concrete level. Israelites (priests included) are warned against entering the sancta or coming into direct contact with holy foods when in a state of ritual impurity (Lev. 7:20–21; 15:31; 22:3–7). Clearly, to do so is extremely sinful: the sanctuary will be de-filed, and the sinner is subject to *karet*. Similarly, those directly defiled by corpses, leprosy, or genital flows are banned from entering the Israelite camp (Num. 5:1–4). Possibly the refusal to adhere to this ban would result in *karet*, but the punishment is not specified. Yet accidental violations can be ameliorated: Leviticus 5:1–13 de-scribes the sacrificial procedures that can rectify, among other things, the effects of an accidental defilement.

Despite these prohibitions related to ritual impurity, there is still nothing in-herently sinful about being ritually impure. As long as the prohibitions are adhered to, the impure Israelite — priest or layperson — has done nothing wrong. The ritual purity system concerns itself with the status of an individual vis-à-vis the sacred, and not with an individual's moral status within the community as a whole.

3. The third characteristic of ritual impurity is that it conveys to persons an im-permanent contagion.[22] This is obviously true of the impurity that Israelites contract when they come into contact with people suffering from defiling conditions. The person who comes into contact with a menstruant or someone afflicted with an ir-regular flux contracts a defilement that lasts until sundown (Lev. 15:5, 21). Contact with more severe forms of impurity, like a corpse, can last a week (Num. 19). Being afflicted with a defiling condition can result in an even longer period of defilement. Menstruation lasts roughly a week, but the defiling state left after giving birth lasts, in its less severe form, either 33 or 66 days (Lev. 12). Finally, genital flows, scale dis-ease and house funguses last an unspecified amount of time, but even these forms of impurity are conceived of as impermanent; that is why the biblical tradition records

purificatory procedures. Roughly equal space is devoted, for instance, to the symptomatology of scale disease on the one hand (Lev. 13) and the rituals performed upon its purification (Lev. 14) on the other. Although it is emphasized that such individuals are isolated for the duration of their affliction (Lev. 13:45–46), the paradigm is one of eventual inclusion, not permanent exclusion. Regarding scale disease, this claim is borne out by the biblical narratives, which generally conceive of the disease as impermanent.[23] In the final analysis, we hear of no form of ritual impurity that does not have purificatory procedures, from waiting until sundown, to bathing bodies, washing clothes, and performing sacrificial rites. Even when long-lasting, the status of ritual defilement is an impermanent one.

Moral Impurity

The Bible, however, is concerned with another form of purity and impurity, referred to here as "moral." The term is imperfect, to say the least, but avoiding the term "moral" here only obscures the nature of what is being described: Moral impurity results from what are believed to be immoral acts. We cannot avoid the term "impurity" either. What we will call "moral impurity" results from committing certain acts so heinous that they are explicitly referred to in biblical sources as defiling.[24] Thus describing these acts as impurities is not our choice to make: the biblical sources have explicitly described these sins as impurities. These defiling acts include sexual sins (e.g., Lev. 18:24–30), idolatry (e.g., Lev. 19:31; 20:1–3), and bloodshed (e.g., Num. 35:33–34).[25] These three sinful behaviors are also frequently referred to as "abominations" (תועבות).[26] They bring about an impurity that *morally* — but not *ritually* — defiles the sinner (Lev. 18:24), the land of Israel (Lev. 18:25, Ezek. 36:17), and the sanctuary of God (Lev. 20:3; Ezek. 5:11). This defilement, in turn leads to the expulsion of the people from the land of Israel (Lev. 18:28; Ezek. 36:19).

There are five important differences between moral and ritual defilement. (1) Whereas ritual impurity is generally not sinful, moral impurity is a direct consequence of grave sin.[27] (2) Whereas ritual impurity often results in a contagious defilement, there is no contact-contagion associated with moral impurity. One need not bathe subsequent to direct or indirect contact with an idolater, a murderer, or an individual who committed a sexual sin.[28] (3) Whereas ritual impurity results in an impermanent defilement, moral impurity leads to a long-lasting, if not permanent, degradation of the sinner and, eventually, of the land of Israel.[29] (4) Whereas ritual impurity can be ameliorated by rites of purification, that is not the case for moral impurity;[30] moral purity is achieved by punishment, atonement, or, best of all, by refraining from committing morally impure acts in the first place. (5) In addition to these phenomenological differences, there are also terminological distinctions drawn in the texts themselves. Although the term impure (טמא) is used in both contexts, the terms "abomination" (תועבה) and "pollute" (חנף) are used with regard to the sources of moral impurity, but not with regard to the sources of ritual impurity.[31]

Because moral impurity has no contact-contagion or ritual lustrations, and it does involve serious prohibitions, it is imperative to distinguish between moral and ritual impurity. These distinctions are summarized in the following table.

Impurity Type	Source	Effect	Resolution
Ritual	Bodily flows, corpses, etc.	Temporary, contagious impurity	Bathing, waiting
Moral	Sins: idolatry, incest, murder	Defilement of sinners, land, and sanctuary	Atonement or punishment, and ultimately, exile

The moral impurity of sexual sins is most clearly articulated in the concluding verses of Leviticus 18 (24–30):

(24) Do not defile yourselves [אל־תטמאו] in any of those ways, for it is by such that the nations that I am casting out before you defiled themselves. (25) Thus the land became defiled [ותטמא הארץ]; and I called it to account for its iniquity, and the land spewed out its inhabitants. (26) But you must keep My laws and My rules, and you must not do any of those abhorrent things [תועבת], neither the citizen nor the stranger who resides among you; (27) for all those abhorrent things were done by the people who were in the land before you, and the land became defiled; (28) So let not the land spew you out for defiling it, as it spewed out the nation that came before you. (29) All who do any of those abhorrent things — such persons shall be cut off from their people. (30) You shall keep My charge not to engage in any of the abhorrent practices that were carried on before you, and you shall not defile yourselves through them: I the Lord am your God.

The point of the passage is quite evident: sexual sins defile the sinners and the land upon which their sins have been committed. But in what way are the sinners and the land defiled? As Büchler noted so long ago, there is no hint in Leviticus 18, or in any of the other passages to be discussed in this section, of ritual defilement.[32] The sinners themselves are defiled (v. 24), but not ritually.[33] What decides the matter is that the impurity contracted is conveyed to the land. Ritual impurity, in contrast, is never conveyed to, or contracted from, the land.[34] Indeed, the defilement of the land in this passage does not appear to threaten the ritual status of those who are on it. The effect of the defilement of the land is that the all its residents are subject to exile. The sinners and the land are defiled in Leviticus 18 in the sense that they have been in some way shamefully degraded. The people are supposed to be holy (Lev. 19), but if they sin in such ways, their holiness is no longer possible and, as a result, God's blessings are revoked. The idea that sexual sins defile the people and the land is expressed in Jeremiah 3:1 as well as in a number of other biblical traditions.[35]

The morally defiling force of sexual sins is also articulated in Numbers 5:11–31, which lays out the laws of the ordeal that determines the innocence or guilt of a suspected adulteress.[36] What is revealed by the ordeal is whether the woman is "defiled" or not (5:13–14). Ritual impurity is not of concern here; if that were the concern, the ceremony could never take place in the sanctuary.[37] And since all sexual acts are ritually defiling, at least for a short while (Lev. 15:18), no ordeal would be necessary to determine that status.[38] The concern is, rather, to determine whether the woman has morally degraded herself by committing adultery, that is, whether the woman is morally impure. The language of impurity when used with regard to sexual transgression does not refer to a temporary contagion, but to a permanent debasement.[39]

The defiling force of idolatrous sins is articulated — at least regarding certain idol-atrous acts — in the Holiness Code. Leviticus 19:31 reflects the view that necromancy is a defiling act. Leviticus 20:1–3 views sacrificing children to Molech as an act that defiles the sanctuary and profanes the name of God. More general statements about the defiling force of idolatry can also be found. Jeremiah 2:23 is rather to the point:

> How can you say, "I am not defiled,
> I have not gone after the Baalim"?

Earlier in the same chapter, the prophet articulates the idea that such sins defile the land (2:7). A number of other biblical traditions reflect the same perspective, that the act of idolatry defiles the idolater or the land of Israel.[40] A number of traditions also suggest that idolatry defiles the sanctuary itself, especially when the sin takes place within or in close proximity to the sanctuary.[41] The Holiness Code traditions are the tip of an iceberg: it appears that *all* acts of idolatry were viewed as morally defiling in ancient Israel. But again, there is no indication in these or any other passages that idolatry — or even idols — defile ritually.[42] The defilement of idolatry is moral: the sinners, the sanctuary, and the land are rendered impure by such acts, but no con-tact-contagion is involved.

The defiling force of bloodshed is articulated in Numbers 35:33–34:

> (33) You shall not pollute [לא תחניפו] the land in which you live; for blood pollutes the land, and the land can have no expiation for blood that is shed on it, except by the blood of him who shed it. (34) You shall not defile [לא תטמא] the land in which you live, in which I Myself abide, for I the Lord abide among the Israelite people.

The term "pollute" (חנף), as Büchler correctly argued, is a technical term that articu-lated the defiling force of sins.[43] This term is synonymous with the term "defile" (טמא) only in the latter term's *moral* sense — but it is not used in contexts of *ritual* impurity.

The defiling force of murder, as well as of idolatry, is also clearly expressed in Psalm 106:34–41:

> (34) They did not destroy the nations
> as the Lord commanded them,
> (35) but mingled with the nations
> and learned their ways.
> (36) They worshipped their idols,
> which became a snare for them.
> (37) Their own sons and daughters
> they sacrificed to demons.
> (38) They shed innocent blood,
> the blood of their sons and daughters,
> whom they sacrificed to the idols of Canaan;
> so the land was polluted [ותחנף] with bloodguilt.
> (39) Thus they became defiled [ויטמאו] by their acts,
> debauched [ויזנו] through their deeds.
> (40) The Lord was angry with His people
> and He abhorred [ויתעב] His inheritance.
> (41) He handed them over to the nations;
> their foes ruled them.

The morally defiling force of bloodshed is also reflected in other biblical traditions.[44] And we know quite well that the act of murder does not defile in any ritual way, because murderers were admitted to the sanctuary.[45] Murder, like sexual transgression and idolatry, is morally impure: the sinful behavior defiles the sinner, the sanctuary, and the land of Israel.

Moral impurity is best understood as a potent force unleashed by certain sinful human actions.[46] The force unleashed defiles the sinner, the sanctuary, and the land, even though the sinner is not ritually impure and does not ritually defile. Yet — and this is the source of much confusion — the sinner *is* seen as morally impure.[47]

That idolatry, incest, and murder defile the sinner morally but not ritually can be seen in a number of the traditions cited above. Such is the clear connotation of Leviticus 18:24: "Do not defile yourselves [אל־תטמאו] in any of those ways," and Leviticus 19:31: "Do not turn to ghosts . . . to be defiled by them [לטמאה בהם]." Consider also the statement from Jeremiah quoted above (2:23): "How can you say, 'I am not defiled, / I have not gone after the Baalim'?"[48] Indeed, the moral defilement of the people of Israel by sin is articulated already in Hosea: "Behold, you have fornicated, O Ephraim; / Israel has defiled himself!" (נטמא ישראל).[49] Further confirmation of the fact that these sins defile the sinner in some way can be seen in the narrative and legal traditions that use the term "impure" with regard to women who have, wittingly or unwittingly, been partner to a sexual offense or have been in relations with a foreigner. Thus Dinah is considered defiled subsequent to her victimization (Gen. 34:5ff.).[50] Similarly, the ordeal of a suspected adulteress serves to determine if the woman has defiled herself by so sinning (Num. 5:13ff.). Even a divorced woman whose second marriage ends in either divorce or the death of her husband is considered to have such a status, at least as far as her first husband is concerned (Deut. 24:1–4).[51] In these situations, the woman does not defile ritually, but she is still defiled in that she suffers a permanent and degrading change in status.[52] Sinful acts willingly committed by a woman are, of course, punished, but even unwilled experiences can deprive a woman of the possibility of marrying a priest (Lev. 21:7, 13–14). This legal ramification of moral defilement is significant, for it demonstrates that even though the woman in question is not defiled ritually (and does not defile ritually either, for that matter), she is defiled in a very real way: She has been debased, and her status has been degraded. Wright has claimed regarding these defilements that "the denomination of the people as impure in these verses is a moral reproach rather than a technical description of their ritual condition."[53] This is a moral reproach, to be sure, but it is a reproach with distinct legal ramifications — limitation of marriageability, if not capital punishment — and denotes in a very literal technical way a permanent degradation of status.

Since moral impurity does not produce ritual defilement, such sinners are not excluded from the sanctuary. To the contrary, recall again the case of the suspected adulteress (Num. 5:11–31), who is brought into the sanctuary itself in order to determine her status. Recall too where ancient Israelite murderers sought sanctuary: *in the sanctuary* (Exod. 21:14).[54] Moral impurity does indeed affect the sanctuary (e.g., Lev. 20:3), but its effect does not reach the sanctuary by the entrance of sinners *into* the sanctuary. Moral impurity affects the sanctuary even from afar, in its own way, along the lines drawn by Jacob Milgrom in his article, "Israel's Sanctuary: 'The Priestly Picture of Dorian Gray.'"[55]

We are to understand the effect moral impurity has upon the land in a similar way. A number of the traditions that have been cited so far state that these three sins have the capacity to defile the land of Israel. Among the more explicit traditions to this effect are Leviticus 18:24–30 and Jeremiah 3:1 (sexual immorality); Numbers 35:33–34 (bloodshed); Jeremiah 2:7 and Ezekiel 36:18 (idolatry); and Ezekiel 22:1–4 and Psalm 106:34–40 (bloodshed and idolatry). There is no suggestion in any of these traditions that the land is defiled by these sins in any ritual way.[56] Indeed, in biblical law or narrative the land is never a source of or a means of transmitting ritual defilement. Rather, the land suffers a noncontagious degradation. The ultimate result of this defilement, if it remains unchecked, is the exile of the land's inhabitants. This idea, as we have seen, is clearly expressed in the concluding verses of Leviticus 18, and it is central to the thought of the prophet Ezekiel as well.[57]

It is not only the land of Israel that is subject to this moral defilement; a few biblical traditions refer to the idea that foreign lands were considered to be defiled. Amos 7:17 threatens the insolent Israelites with exile to a polluted land. Joshua 22:19 suggests that the tribal holdings east of the Jordan River are impure from idolatry. In my view, the traditions that refer to foreign lands as impure are to be understood in the context of moral impurity.[58] It is true that according to subsequent rabbinic *halakhah*, foreign lands defile *ritually*,[59] but Büchler is no doubt correct in his insistence that the biblical traditions are not to be seen as evidence for the antiquity of this rabbinic *halakhah*.[60] The biblical traditions are concerned not with ritual impurity but with moral impurity: the noncontagious defilement that results from sin.[61] And it is important to note that the rabbinic traditions explicitly view the *halakhah* in question as a rabbinic innovation.[62] It would appear that foreign lands, like the land of Israel, are subject to moral defilement.

Thus the sources of moral impurity convey a defilement both to the sinners and to the land upon which the sins are committed. As a result of this defilement, the sinners and the land experience a degradation in status. Now it must be asked: Is this condition permanent? The Holiness Code gives no indication of any methods for the removal of these defilements. Ablutions, as we have seen, are not efficacious here. The Day of Atonement service involves the purgation of the altar and shrine, which removes the stain left by sin upon the sanctuary (Lev. 16:11–19).[63] This service also includes other sacrifices which atone for the people (16:20–22). But these sacrifices do not appear to purify grave sinners, or the land upon which the grave sins were committed.[64] Such sinners either live out their lives in a degraded state (like the guilty adulteress) or suffer capital punishment (like apprehended murderers). The land, it appears, likewise suffers a permanent degradation.

The prophet Ezekiel, whose writings have the closest affinity to the Holiness Code, does, however, describe the ultimate purification of sinners (Ezek. 36:16–18, 22–25):

(16) The word of the Lord came to me: (17) O mortal, when the House of Israel dwelt on their own soil, they defiled it with their ways and their deeds, their ways were in my sight like the impurity of a menstruous woman [כטומאת הנדה]. (18) So I poured out My wrath on them for the blood which they shed upon their land, and for the fetishes with which they defiled it .

(22) Say to the house of Israel: Thus said the Lord God: Not for your sake will I act, O House of Israel, but for My holy name, which you have caused to be profaned

among the nations to which you have come. (23) I will sanctify My great name which
has been profaned among the nations. . . .
(24) I will take you from among the nations and gather you from all the countries,
and I will bring you back to your own land. (25) I will sprinkle pure water upon you,
and you shall be purified: I will purify you from all your uncleanness and from all
your fetishes

In the beginning of this passage, we see ideas similar to those in Leviticus 18: The
Israelites are exiled as a result of the defiling force of their idolatrous, murderous, and
sexual sins. But then Ezekiel envisions a miraculous purification of the people, enacted directly by God. The prophet is here building on the simile constructed earlier in the passage, comparing God's rejection of sinful Israelites to the status of a
menstruous woman.[65] By conjuring the image of ritual purification, Ezekiel may be
figuratively describing the ease with which God will be able to bring about a change
in the people's moral status. Just as a menstruating woman can cleanse herself
quickly and easily from her ritual impurity, so too will God purify the people from
the defiling force of their sins. Then again, Ezekiel's vision may have been meant to
be taken more literally: that God will, as the prophet says, purify the people from sin
by dousing them with clean water. Whether Ezekiel envisions a literal purification
of the people by God, or (more likely) is figuratively describing God's power of forgiveness, the fact remains that what is envisioned here is a future hope. Without
God's help, the defilement of the people by sin is permanent. Ezekiel also describes
a process for the purification of the land which has been defiled by the blood that
was shed upon it (Ezek. 39:14–16).[66] But again, this description is part of an eschatological vision. Thus in the end the Holiness Code and Ezekiel converge: the defilement of sinners and the land by grave sin is, for all practical purposes, permanent.

The Dietary Laws: Between "Ritual" and "Moral"

A word must be said at this point about how the dietary laws of Leviticus 11 and
Deuteronomy 14 relate to the schema that has been laid out here. On the one hand,
the book of Leviticus juxtaposes the dietary restrictions with laws of ritual purity; the
dietary laws are presented in Leviticus 11, and the bulk of the impurity laws in
Leviticus 12–15. Indeed this juxtaposition stands to reason, for a number of the dietary restrictions involve issues of purity. This is especially true of the laws dealing
with the defilement conveyed by carcasses of certain impure creatures (Lev. 11:24–
45). And yet, as many have realized, the bulk of the dietary restrictions are not purity
laws per se. The carcasses of prohibited fish and birds are not considered to be ritually defiling, but eating them is nevertheless forbidden.[67] Moreover, ingestion of the
impure foods is not just considered ritually defiling, but is prohibited (e.g., Lev. 11:4).
And to be sure, we hear of no purification procedures that can ameliorate the defilement contracted by ingesting forbidden foods. Hoffmann, for these reasons, included the dietary restrictions in his second, more serious category of defilement
(טומאת הקדושות), which is roughly analogous to what we have called moral impurity.[68] Additional arguments in favor of such a view are (1) that the consumption of
forbidden foods has a deleterious (if not defiling) effect on the person who violates
the law (Lev. 11:43, 20:25),[69] and (2) that this effect appears to be defined in opposi-

tion to holiness (Lev. 11:45, 20:26). More importantly, (3) Leviticus 20:22–26 juxtaposes the violation of these taboos with the expulsion of the people from the land of Israel, and as was noted above, moral defilement leads to exile.

Wright, on the other hand, views the dietary laws as an exception but nonetheless places them under the rubric of "permitted" or "tolerated" impurity, which is roughly analogous to our ritual impurity.[70] Wright justifies his view by noting that the violations of the dietary restrictions are never explicitly viewed as defiling the sanctuary, and violators are not commanded to bring a *chattat* sacrifice or suffer the punishment of *karet*. To this point we would add that even in Leviticus 20, it is not specified that eating impure foods defiles the land of Israel. Even so, I am inclined to favor Hoffmann's view over Wright's: The outright prohibitions of eating certain foods function more like a moral defilement than a ritual one. Still, Wright is no doubt correct to call attention to the difficulty here, and it certainly cannot be said that the dietary laws function on a par with sexual, idolatrous, and murderous sins, which bring about much more severe consequences.

But perhaps the best option is for the dietary laws to seen on their own terms: as a set of restrictions which overlap in some ways with each of the impurity systems laid out here. There is certainly a strong tendency among scholars to treat these laws as their own system, especially when searching for the meaning of these laws. In *Purity and Danger*, Mary Douglas singled out these laws as worthy of their own analysis, and a number of scholars have followed suit, including Eilberg-Schwartz, Walter Houston, and Milgrom.[71] Furthermore, the separation of dietary laws from the laws of ritual purity has at least one clear precedent in ancient Jewish literature: in the Mishnah the dietary laws are dealt with not in the Order of Purities (Seder Toharot), but in the Order of Holy Things (Seder Kodashim).

The food laws are a problematic aspect of purity, worthy of their own treatment. These laws cannot receive their due here, but since they are so exceptional, it is hoped that the lack of focus on them here will not detract too much from this analysis.

Moral Impurity as a Metaphor?

The traditions that illustrate the phenomenon of moral impurity are commonly understood by scholars as either metaphorical or figurative. Neusner's statement to this effect was quoted in the Introduction. But Neusner was hardly the only scholar to suggest viewing as a metaphor what has been called here moral impurity. Similar views have been expressed by Helmer Ringgren, Baruch Levine, and Baruch Schwartz, among others.[72] Even some scholars who recognize the potency of the defiling force of sin do not avoid referring to these traditions as metaphors, including Milgrom and Wright.[73] Despite the force of opinion to the contrary, in my view, the dichotomy between literal and metaphorical language is not very helpful when it comes to understanding the differences between ritual and moral impurity.[74]

To my knowledge, none of the scholars just mentioned states clearly what is meant by the terms "metaphorical" or "figurative." Certainly these terms — especially "metaphor" — are difficult to define, and the phenomena to which they refer are often difficult to isolate.[75] But if the terms cannot be defined at all, then perhaps the best thing to do is drop them from the discussion altogether. At any rate, the philosophical debate on metaphor continues, and no end is in sight. And for better or for worse, the debate has not yet had a substantial impact on the study of biblical and ancient Jewish literature.[76] A reasonable definition of metaphor will be offered here—one that may not be pleasing to all sides in the debate, but that will at least accurately reflect the usage of the term in the scholarship in question.

It appears that the scholars who characterize moral impurity as metaphorical or figurative are using the terms in a rather traditional way. Thus when they claim that the usages are metaphorical, the implication is twofold. First, metaphorical or figurative language is defined in opposition to usage that is literal or technical: metaphorical language is not meant to be taken literally. Second, metaphors involve a degree of transference: a term or phrase that is literally applicable in one case has been transferred to a context to which it is not literally applicable. In sum, metaphorical language is a secondary, nonliteral (or nontechnical) usage that is informed by the prior, literal usage of the language in question.[77] What this boils down to is that when purity language is used metaphorically, then no real defilement or purification is actually taking place.

To illustrate the argument that moral impurity can be understood as non-metaphorical, we return to a key passage from Leviticus (18:24–25):

> Do not defile yourselves in any of those ways, for it is by such that the nations that I am casting out before you defiled themselves. Thus the land became defiled.

Let us focus for the moment on the idea that the land became defiled—a point that many commentators assume to be metaphorical.[78] To say this passage is a metaphor ought to involve two claims, neither of which is correct in our view. First, to say that Leviticus 18 is a metaphor should mean that it is not literal. Second, to say that it is a metaphor should mean that the usage of purity language in this context is secondary.

I fail to see why Leviticus 18:24–25 cannot be taken literally. More specifically, I fail to see why the defilement of land must be metaphorical. If people can be defiled, why not the land? Although few biblical traditions state so explicitly,[79] a number of sources imply or assume that the land of Israel is holy.[80] Among these are the sources that equate the boundaries of the land with the habitation of God,[81] the passages that emphasize God's possession of the land of Israel,[82] and the traditions that emphasize that the obligation to follow certain laws is incumbent upon all the residents of the land of Israel, not just Israelites.[83] The unique status of the land of Israel is bound, at least for the Holiness Code, in the notion that God's dwelling is located in the midst of it: "You shall not defile the land in which you live, in which I Myself abide, for I the Lord abide among the Israelite people" (Num. 35:34). Now if the land of Israel can be holy, the land can be defiled. And as Hoffmann correctly understood almost a century ago, the concept of impurity in the context of grave sins is to be understood in opposition to the idea of holiness.[84] Thus Leviticus 18:24–30 can be read quite literally: the performance of sexual misdeeds defiles the sinners and the land upon which the sins are committed. This defilement is not ritual, to be sure, because ritual impurity conveys an impermanent contagion. The defilement is moral, and what is conveyed is a permanent degradation of status. According to the Holiness

Code, the holy people defile their once-holy land by performing grave sin. The end result is the exile of the people from the land of Israel.

Similarly, I do not see why the defilement of the person by sin is necessarily metaphorical. Wright, even as he recognizes that sin has a defiling effect on the sanctuary, insists that the defilement of the person by sin is not a real defilement. Indeed, he explicitly describes Leviticus 18 and Numbers 5 as metaphorical: "[T]he denomination of the people as impure in these verses is a moral reproach rather than a technical description of their ritual condition . . . ; both P and H use 'impure' as a moral metaphor with reference to sexual sins."[85] As was argued earlier, however, the use of 'impure' in the context of sexual sin is just as technical as the use of the term with regard to ritual impurity. People who commit sexual sins defile their persons, so that they suffer a degradation of their status, the primary legal ramification of this degradation being a decrease in marriageability. People who commit idolatrous sins or murder also defile their persons, the general ramification of this being—as Hoffmann put it—rejection by God.

Thus I see no reason why moral impurity is any more, or less, figurative than ritual impurity. In fact, I see no reason why either type of impurity is any more, or less, real than the other. I certainly cannot understand why the (moral) defilement of the land by blood spilled upon it ought to be a metaphor (Num. 35:33–34), while the (ritual) defilement of a person who merely enters a tent in which there lies a corpse is real (Num. 19:14). To be more accurate, we ought to understand that with both kinds of impurity, we are dealing with perceived effects that result from actual physical processes. In the case of ritual impurity, a real, physical process or event (e.g., death or menstruation) has a perceived effect: impermanent contagion that affects people and certain objects within their reach. In the case of moral impurity, a real, physical process or event (e.g., child sacrifice or adultery) has a different perceived effect: a noncontagious defilement that affects persons, the land, and the sanctuary. In both cases, the impurity is conveyed by contact: ritual impurity is conveyed by direct and indirect human contact, and moral impurity is conveyed to the land by sins that take place upon it.[86] In both cases, moreover, there are practical legal ramifications. The ritually impure person must keep away from sacred things, and in some cases must be barred from certain precincts. The morally impure person may be subject to capital punishment or, in the case of unwitting female partners to sexual misconduct, permanent degradation and fewer options for marriage. When the land has been defiled to a great extent, then its people are exiled. Though the sources and modes of transfer of moral and ritual impurity differ, we are dealing, nonetheless, with two analogous *perceptions of contagion*, each of which brings about effects of legal and social consequence.

We turn now to the second aspect of the definition: metaphors are secondary usages of terminology which has a different primary (literal) use. That moral impurity involves the secondary use of purity terminology is stated or implied by many scholars: Levine refers to "applied concepts of purity," Schwartz speaks of a "transformation," and Wright speaks of "metaphorization."[87] Yet I know of no detailed analysis that establishes firmly the secondary nature of the usage which we refer to as moral impurity. To the contrary, it was noted above that the idea of the defiling force of sin appears in Hosea (5:3 and 6:10), Jeremiah (2 and 3), Deuteronomy (21:23 and 24:1–4), the deuteronomic history (1 Kings 14:24; 2 Kings 16:3), and possibly Amos (7:17), in addition to the Holiness Code and Ezekiel.[88] Now the date of the priestly traditions is a notoriously difficult question, subject to increasing controversy. It is not directly relevant to the work at hand and cannot be taken up here, but what is important to keep in mind is this: Moral impurity is commonly assumed to be a secondary use of purity terminology, and yet the usage appears in prophetic and deuteronomic texts that would, by almost all accounts, be considered earlier than the priestly traditions that attest to the "primary" usage of impurity terminology. This is problematic, to say the least. The bottom line, in my view, is this: We simply cannot know which usage came first. Thus we cannot assume that traditions like Leviticus 18 involve a secondary, metaphorical usage of ritual impurity terminology.

I am not denying that there are metaphorical or figurative uses of purity language in the Hebrew Bible. What I am suggesting is that the usage described here, which has commonly been assumed to be metaphorical, is not. There are indeed a number of passages in the Hebrew Bible in which the language of ritual impurity, or the image of ritually impure persons, is used metaphorically to illustrate the sinfulness of Israelites. Similarly, there are a number of passages in which the language of ritual purity and purification is used metaphorically to illustrate righteousness or atonement. In each of these passages, there is an explicit or implied comparison between ritual impurity or purity on the one hand and sinfulness or righteousness in general on the other. For example, in Isaiah 1:15–17, the Lord states:

(15) And when you lift up your hands,
I will turn My eyes away from you;
Though you pray at length, I will not listen.
Your hands are stained with crime —
(16) Wash yourselves clean;
Put your evil doings
Away from My sight
Cease to do evil;
(17) Learn to do good. . . .

This passage is not concerned with the ritual defilement of sinners, or with the ritual purification of moral defilement. The image of ritual purification here serves, rather, to illustrate the atonement for which the prophet is calling.

And from the perspective of the sinner, we find in Psalm 51 the following prayer for forgiveness:

(4) Wash me thoroughly of my iniquity,
and purify me of my sin;
(5) for I recognize my transgressions,
and am ever conscious of my sin . .
(9) Purge me with hyssop till I am pure;
wash me till I am whiter than snow.

Here too the concern of the passage is not with the morally defiling force of grave sin, but rather with personal atonement from sin in general. The image of purification is used figuratively to illustrate that atonement.[89] What these passages do not state is that ritual purification can serve as a means of removing the defiling force of grave sin. After all, in these passages the washing is done not by the individual sinner, but by God. The real key to understanding these passages is this: The hope expressed is that full atonement from sin could prove to be as easy a matter as purification from ritual impurity. Just as, say, a person who touches the carcass of an impure animal can purify himself or herself quickly and completely, so too does the sinner and prophet hope that God will effect atonement quickly and completely.

In a similar vein, a number of biblical passages compare the status of a sinner to that of a ritually impure person. The following example is from Deutero-Isaiah (64:4–5):

(4) . . . It is because You are angry that we have sinned;
We have been steeped in them from of old,
And can we be saved?
(5) We have all become like an impure thing [כטמא],
And all our virtues like a filthy rag.

The point of this passage is not that sinners are ritually defiling, but that sinners find themselves in a state of rejection by God. A number of biblical passages engage in the same sort of simile, comparing the sinfulness of Israel to ritually impure persons.[90] Some other passages utilize terms of ritual impurity to describe sinful, especially idolatrous, objects.[91] In these passages no form of impurity has been contracted or conveyed, and thus no purification per se is to take place. These passages, by virtue of the juxtaposition of ritual impurity with sinfulness, or ritual purity with righteousness and atonement, are indeed figurative in nature. But this phenomenon is distinct from that seen in the passages analyzed above, which ascribe a nonritual and nonmetaphorical defiling force to certain grave sins.

A Single Symbolic System?

The distinction between ritual and moral defilement having been established, the question that must now be raised is whether the two systems are connected at all. As we saw in the introduction, Mary Douglas at first expressed the view that as an anthropologist she claims "to find in the *totality* of the biblical purity rules a symbolic system."[92] Building explicitly on her work (the first stage of it), Wright has argued that "all the defilement-creating conditions in the priestly legislation are of the same conceptual family and system."[93] Yet Wright goes even further, suggesting that "the whole purity system including tolerated impurities has a moral basis and rationale."[94] As Wright himself notes, this claim echoes themes from Jewish-Hellenistic apologetic literature (especially *Aristeas* and Philo).[95] To be fair, Wright recognizes that his analysis here enters the realm of speculation. Yet the conjectures have been offered, and they must be assessed.

Wright claims to find a fundamental connectedness between the two major components of the purity system as he sees it. He identifies a number of similarities between the two, in addition to the obvious terminological one. According to Wright, the two "share loci of pollution (the sanctuary) and similar ways of removing that pollution (mainly *chattat* sacrifices). This main phenomenological association is complemented by parallels in rules of restriction and exclusion."[96] The fundamental difference between the two types of defilement is the issue of intention. According to Wright, the fundamental connectedness between the two types of defilement justifies viewing the entire "spectrum" of impurity as a symbolic system with a moral basis.

The first objection to be raised is the fact that these similarities are overdrawn. Regarding terminology, the term "defile" (טמא) is, to be sure, used in both contexts. But the verb "pollute" (חנף) is used only in the context of what we have called moral impurity, and the same is true of "abomination" (תועבה). With regard to the loci of impurity, certain sins can defile the land, while no ritual impurity can do so. And even with regard to the sanctuary, Wright's permitted impurities defile the sanctuary on contact, while the prohibited impurities defile it from a distance. With regard to methods of removal, the *chattat* sacrifice is one similarity among many differences. First and foremost among these differences is the fact that ablution does not remove the impurity brought about by sin. In fact, we hear of no method at all for the removal of the defilement of land by sin.[97] And with regard to restriction and exclusion, those who commit sin are not declared to be ritually impure and are not excluded from the sanctuary. Each of these differences is significant, and taken together they demonstrate conclusively that the differences outweigh the similarities when one compares the defiling force of sin to ritual impurity. In my view, it is best to recognize and emphasize the distinctive nature of the defiling force of sin, despite the fact that the systems overlap at some points.

The second objection against the "single-system" argument is the fact that the search for a single symbolic system is not called for by the text itself. The Pentateuch is fully capable of expressing very clearly that one ritual serves as a reminder of some other greater purpose. The Sabbath ritual, for example, serves to remind Israel of either the Exodus from Egypt (Deut. 5:14–15) or the creation of the world (Exod. 20:10–11). More generally, the tassels on Israelites' garments serve to remind the people to obey their laws (Num. 15:37–41). When it comes to the ritual impurity laws, we are never told that these regulations are to serve as behavioral reminders of the morally defiling force of sin. We are simply given the laws of ritual impurity on the one hand, and the notion of moral impurity on the other.

A third problem is that there is a fundamental logical flaw to Wright's argument. Wright has emphasized that the use of impurity language with regard to sin involves metaphorization — the secondary application of language originally used in the context of ritual defilement.[98] Then he argues that morality is the basis of the whole system, and that ritual impurities symbolize moral sin. If we telescope the two claims, we are left with the conclusion that ritual defilement serves to symbolize its own metaphorization. The circularity here is problematic indeed.

It is instructive at this point to bring in the view of D. Z. Hoffmann, who three generations ago also argued that the systems interlock in a symbolic fashion. When commenting on Leviticus 11, Hoffmann suggests that the categories of ritual impurities are analogous to, and therefore symbolize, certain categories of sins.[99] Yet he consistently sees ritual impurity as the symbolic one, never viewing the defilement of sin as metaphorical. Those who are ritually defiled are symbolically impure. Those who committed sin have truly, and permanently, defiled their bodies.[100] It is telling that Hoffmann and Wright can present competing interpretations as to which of the two systems serves as the more symbolic one. This phenomenon is in itself a strong argument for seeing the two conceptions as I have presented them: as *two distinct but analogous conceptions of contagion.*

There can be no doubt, of course, that the two systems overlap in various ways. Yet they overlap with other "systems" in the Hebrew Bible as well. The sacrifices offered by the ritually impure person are part of a larger sacrificial system. The prohibitions that leave the sinner morally defiled are part of a larger system of law and justice. The day devoted to the purgation of the sanctuary is just one of many holy days in the Israelite calendar. And as we saw in the previous section, the purity systems overlap with the dietary laws in various ways as well. The *single* system — if there is one — is Israelite religion as a whole.[101] The systems of impurity should not be associated so closely and at the same time removed too far from their greater context. A full understanding of each of these systems requires one to rely on the resources of the entire Hebrew Bible.[102]

In the end, one cannot eliminate the possibility that the two impurity systems are connected on some deeper level. Yet none of the arguments in favor of such a view is persuasive. Indeed, the impetus behind the search for a single symbolic system seems to come not from the text itself, but from external preconceptions — from either structural anthropology or homiletics. And the results that the search has yielded so far are not convincing. But even more problematic is the fact that in the final analysis, the differences between the two systems outweigh the similarities. It is best, therefore, to take the two systems on their own terms, especially since they are too often confused as it is. For now, it is best to let the emphasis fall on the distinction that ought to be made between ritual and moral defilements.

Gender and the Biblical Impurity Systems

We take up, finally, the issue of gender, in order to shed some light on the ways in which these two systems relate to women, men, and sexuality in general. We do so not only for the sake of taking up a timely theme, but also because as our analysis progresses through the various literatures of ancient Judaism, we will see now and then notably different approaches to some of these issues.

Once it is established that ritual impurity is generally natural, unavoidable, not sinful, and impermanent, it becomes easier to see that the relationship between conceptions of defilement and conceptions of gender is much more complex than what one might at first assume. It is true that traditional Judaism, in both the medieval and modern periods, has been interested in primarily only one source of ritual impurity: that which originates in menstrual blood. And as is well known, of all the Mishnah tractates dealing with ritual impurity, only the tractate dealing with menstrual impurity — tractate Niddah — receives systematic treatment in the Jerusalem and Babylonian Talmuds. But the Hebrew Bible knows of no such selective focus. For a variety of reasons, the menstrual taboo was the only aspect of the biblical ritual impurity system that was maintained for very long after the destruction of the second temple in 70 CE.[103] When we examine the ritual impurity legislation of the Hebrew

HB is even in gender -treatment

Bible, however, we find a system that is rather even-handed in its treatment of gender. In Leviticus 15, regular and irregular genital flows from both men and women are sources of ritual defilement. The menstrual taboo of Leviticus, in order to be properly understood, must be viewed within this broader context.[104] And once the scope is widened, it becomes clear, to quote Howard Eilberg-Schwartz, that ritual impurity is "a state which both genders generate and occupy."[105] Menstrual blood is but one source of ritual impurity, and it is hardly the raison d'être of the biblical impurity system. Indeed, according to Leviticus 15, irregular flows from men or women produce a more severe state of ritual defilement than menstruation does.[106] And in ancient Israelite society, most women of childbearing age were very likely either pregnant or lactating much of the time.[107] Thus ancient Israelite women probably did not find themselves ritually impure on a regular basis as result of the menstrual taboo. Moreover, the other major sources of ritual impurity are clearly gender-blind. "Leprous" impurities affect men and women equally, and the corpses of men and women equally constitute the source of the most severe form of ritual defilement. Systems of ritual impurity can be constructed and utilized for the purpose of subjugating women, but that is not the ultimate purpose of the biblical one.[108] Even if it were, as Mary Douglas's recent work has demonstrated, the biblical system with its "purification for all" attitude would be useless to the task.[109]

Now there is, to be sure, a gender imbalance. Note, for instance, that purification after the birth of a female child takes longer than after the birth of a male child (Lev. 12:2–5).[110] This discrepancy has given rise to various speculations for, literally, millennia.[111] But we ought not be so quick to view this discrepancy as reflecting poorly on women. In fact, the situation is much more complex. There is a degree to which the capacity to defile reflects value.[112] Human corpses, as we have seen, render those who come into contact with them ritually defiled for an entire week (Num. 19:11). And yet the carcasses of quadrupeds, including pigs, convey a ritual impurity that lasts for only a single day (Lev. 11:24–28). This can hardly mean that ancient Israelites valued quadrupeds more highly than they did human beings. By the same token, we cannot assume that the gender imbalance of Leviticus 12:2–5 reflects negative attitudes toward women or girls.[113] In truth, I do not know why women are ritually defiled for a longer period of time after the birth of a daughter than after the birth of a son.[114] But when we take into account all that we have said about ritual impurity — that it is natural, unavoidable, and not sinful — and we add to that the observation that capacity to defile can reflect positive value, then it becomes clear that we cannot simply assume that the prolonged defilement after the birth of a daughter is to be understood as articulating a negative attitude toward women or girls.

Now I am not claiming that the ancient Israelite ritual impurity system was egalitarian — it was not. Very little in ancient Israel was. Women were indeed, for the most part, excluded from ritual life.[115] But in order to understand this exclusion properly, it is essential to keep in mind that ritually impure men were excluded in much the same way as ritually impure women. Indeed, a number of biblical passages problematize masculine impurities more than feminine ones (Exod. 19:15; Deut. 23:10–12). The real question is why ritually *pure* women were excluded from sacred roles in the ancient Israelite cult, but that question is not likely to be answered by an analysis of biblical ritual impurity legislation.

In ancient Israel, then, ritual impurity was perceived to be natural, unavoidable and not sinful, for both males and females. Because the bulk of the laws apply to both men and women equally and assume that all Israelites will become ritually impure from time to time, the system as a whole was not constructed in order to enforce a permanent exclusion of women. And because women were probably only infrequently affected by these taboos, the ritual impurity system would be doing a poor job, if the intent were to subject them. In the final analysis, one cannot build a very strong case in defense of the argument that the biblical ritual impurity laws were legislated for the purpose of subjugating women.

When we turn to examine the notion of moral defilement, however, we find that the gender imbalance looms larger, and particularly when it comes to sexual transgression.[116] The sexual laws of Leviticus 18 and 20 are, first of all, addressed to the men in the community. Moreover, as is well known, there is a double standard here, for a married man can legally have more than one sexual partner, while a married woman legally cannot. There is also the fact that among the morally defiling sins specified in Leviticus is the prohibition of having sexual relations with a woman who is menstruating (Lev. 18:19 and 20:18).

Again, however, we can push the gender imbalance too far. First of all, there are also ways in which these laws are more lenient with regard to women: While male homosexuality is explicitly prohibited, lesbianism is not.[117] But more important, even though the sexual laws are addressed to men, on the whole they apply equally to men and women.[118] Being that these are sexual laws, the prohibitions ultimately shape the behavior of both men and women. Of course, we are still left with the problematic prohibitions of sexual relations during menstruation. On the one hand, because this prohibition focuses on the nature of women's bodies, there is some cause to see it as biased against women. On the other hand, it is important to keep in mind that the prohibition applies equally to men and women (Lev. 20:18). Thus while the situation of menstruation affects women (just as the situation of flux affects men), the prohibition of sex during menstruation affects men and women both. Moreover, there is a degree to which even this prohibition can be seen in a different light. As Ross Kraemer points out, the regulations regarding the menstrual taboo actually empower women, by giving them the opportunity to decline sexual relations by claiming that they are ritually impure.[119]

With regard to the sex laws, both women and men who wittingly commit sexual transgressions are sentenced to death. That is so because in Leviticus 18 and 20, sexual transgression is not primarily a crime of property committed against a husband or father, but an abomination — a crime against God.[120] It is precisely this aspect of the sexual laws that is of interest to us. Like idolatry and murder — crimes that do not discriminate when it comes to gender — the sexual transgressions have the power to defile the land and bring about exile to its inhabitants. Men and women, equally, can perpetrate these crimes. And both men and women equally, if caught, will be punished. Furthermore, the ultimate result of the accumulation of moral impurity — the exile of the people from the land of Israel — is a punishment that affects everyone. Men and women, the children and the elderly, the innocent and the guilty — all will suffer equally the terror of exile.[121] We are left with a problematic interest in menstruation as a potential source for moral defilement, but for the most part, the ancient Israelite system of moral impurity applies equally to men and women.

Summary and Conclusion

In the Hebrew Bible, certain sins defile in a way that is altogether different from — but no less real than — the better-known bodily defilements delineated in Leviticus 11–15 and Numbers 19. These biblical chapters describe what is commonly referred to as "ritual impurity." This defilement results from direct or indirect contact with any one of a number of natural processes, including childbirth, scale disease, genital discharges, the carcasses of certain animals, and human corpses. The durations of these impurities differ, as do the requisite cleansing processes. Nonetheless, the following can be said of ritual impurity: It is natural, more or less unavoidable, generally not sinful, and typically impermanent. It is true that the refusal to purify oneself would constitute a transgression, as would coming into contact with the sacred while in a state of ritual impurity. It is also true that a few biblical narratives view "leprosy" as a punishment for moral shortcomings. But in the end, the following claim still stands: It is not sinful to be ritually impure, and ritual impurity does not result from sin.

The defilement that results from sin, however, is altogether different. This "moral impurity" results from committing certain acts so heinous that they are considered defiling. These acts include sexual sins, idolatry and bloodshed, and they bring about an impurity that *morally* — but not *ritually* — defiles the sinner, the land of Israel, and the sanctuary of God. This defilement, in turn, leads to the expulsion of the people from the land of Israel. Although the sinner's act defiles the land, the sinner does not defile those within his or her physical reach. There is no contact-contagion associated with moral impurity: One need not bathe subsequent to direct or indirect contact with an idolater, a murderer, or an individual who committed a sexual sin. Moreover, there is no purification rite akin to those associated with ritual impurity: moral purity is achieved by punishment, by atonement, or by not committing morally impure acts in the first place. While the sources of ritual impurity convey to persons an impermanent contagion, the sources of moral impurity convey a long-lasting, if not permanent, defilement to sinners and to the land upon which their sins have been committed. Because of these differences, it is imperative to distinguish between moral and ritual impurity.

Moral impurity cannot profitably be understood as either metaphorical or figurative. Even though moral defilement described in Leviticus 18 is of a different sort than the ritual impurity described in Leviticus 11–15, the sinners, land, and sanctuary are defiled by these sins in a very substantial way. This defilement, in turn, brings about tangible results for sinners, the sanctuary, and the land. Sinners are subject to a permanent debasement, if not capital punishment. The sanctuary is subject to defilement along the lines drawn by Jacob Milgrom. Regarding the land, if the defilement becomes severe enough, the people are exiled from it. In the final analysis, the biblical traditions that articulate the concept of moral impurity can and should be taken at face value: sin does indeed defile, in its own way.

As was noted at the beginning of this chapter, a scholarly consensus views Leviticus as a composite work. Leviticus 1–16, roughly, stems from the priestly source

(P), while Leviticus 17–26 (again, roughly) stems from the Holiness Code (H). Thus the two purity systems are articulated in two distinct literary constructs, and perhaps emerged in different milieus. Of course, Leviticus is now a single book, and the Torah was perceived by the Jews who canonized it as a single, integral, work. But this single Torah articulated concerns with two distinct conceptions of defilement, and it did so with overlapping terminology. Despite the potential for confusion, I think we can assume that many Israelites understood well the broad distinctions laid out in this chapter.

At some point, however, this clarity was lost. Ancient Jews — those who lived long after Leviticus was composed and compiled — differed in how they understood what the Pentateuch has to say about impurity. In particular, ancient Jews debated the nature of the relationship between ritual and moral defilement. Chapters 3–6 of this work elucidate these different approaches to ritual and moral impurity taken by various groups of ancient Jews. First, however, it remains to be argued that the idea of moral impurity, which we have now seen in the Hebrew Bible, persists in the Jewish literature of the second temple period. The next chapter will demonstrate that the story of moral impurity does not end with the Holiness Code.

2

Moral Impurity in the
Second Temple Period

*Several impt/
heinous sins
defile.*

The previous chapter demonstrated that a number of biblical traditions express the idea that certain grave sins — especially idolatry, murder, and sexual transgression — have their own distinct defiling force. In this chapter we will see that the biblical idea of moral defilement persists into the second temple period. It is well known that much of ancient Jewish literature is concerned with ritual impurity, but what is not sufficiently appreciated is the fact that ancient Jewish literature also concerns itself with the defiling force of sin. In this chapter, we will study selected passages from the books of Ezra and Nehemiah, the book of Jubilees, the Temple Scroll, the Damascus Document, and other sundry texts. The passages analyzed here have generally, and erroneously, been understood to be concerned with *ritual* impurity. I will argue, however, that they are best understood as articulations of the concept of *moral* impurity.   ⤷ Problem $ solution

Ezra, Nehemiah, and the Expulsion of the Foreign Wives

One of the thornier issues in the history of Judaism in the second temple period is the date of Ezra.[1] Regardless of when Ezra served as a leader of the Jewish people in Jerusalem, the narratives of the books of Ezra and Nehemiah make it clear that both of these figures faced similar social crises. Much to these personalities' dismay, a number of the Jews had married local Gentile women.[2] Both Ezra and Nehemiah urged the dissolution of these marriages. As even a casual reader of these books may notice, the chronology is confusing. Yet whether one or two expulsions took place, and in which order they occurred, is not of concern here. Indeed, it is not directly relevant for us if *any* expulsion occurred at all. Our concern is the ideology behind these books' opposition to marrying foreign women. Is this ideology rooted in any conception of impurity, and if so, which type of impurity is operative?

That purity is a concern of the books of Ezra and Nehemiah can hardly be called into question. Terms of defilement are used with reference to the problem (Ezra 6:21; 9:1, 11–14), and the proposed solution — divorce — is referred to as a purification

43

(Neh. 13:30). This reference has led many scholars to the view that these books considered the foreign wives to be ritually impure, presumably as the result of their status as Gentiles.[3] Indeed, it is commonly assumed that ancient Jews would have considered Gentiles to be a source of ritual impurity. At least as far as the early second temple period is concerned, however, this was not at all the case.[4] But for the moment, let's focus on the case at hand. Regarding the books of Ezra and Nehemiah, even if ritual Gentile impurity were the concern here, these texts address only the status of foreign women. They have nothing to say about the impurity of *all* Gentiles. Second, and more to the point of this chapter, ritual impurity is, in the final analysis, not what lay behind these narratives in Ezra and Nehemiah. The passages in question echo not the priestly traditions relating to ritual impurity, but the Holiness Code traditions related to moral impurity.

This fact can most clearly be seen in Ezra 9:1–3 and 10–12:

(1) When this was over, the officers approached me, saying, "The people of Israel and the priests and Levites have not separated themselves from the peoples of the land whose abhorrent practices [תועבות] are like those of the Canaanites, the Hittites, the Perizzites, the Jebusites, the Ammonites, the Moabites, the Egyptians, and the Amorites. (2) They have taken their daughters as wives for themselves and for their sons, so that the holy seed has become intermingled with the peoples of the land; and it is the officers and prefects who have taken the lead in this trespass." (3) When I heard this, I rent my garment and robe, I tore hair out of my head and beard, and I sat desolate. . . .

[Ezra prays:] (10) "Now, what can we say in the face of this, O our God, for we have forsaken Your commandments, (11) which You gave us through Your servants the prophets when You said, 'The land that you are about to possess is a land unclean [ארץ נדה היא] through the uncleanness of the peoples of the land through their abhorrent practices [בנדת עמי הארצות בתועבתיהם] with which they, in their impurity [בטמאתם], have filled it from one end to the other. (12) Now then, do not give your daughters in marriage to their sons or let their daughters marry your sons; do nothing for their well-being or advantage, then you will be strong and enjoy the bounty of the land and bequeath it to your children forever.'"

The prophetic passage quoted by Ezra in 9:11 is otherwise unattested. But as Büchler pointed out years ago, the passage echoes Leviticus 18 and Ezekiel 36 and thus is an expression of the notion referred to here as moral impurity.[5] The echoes of Leviticus 18 are clear: the abominable acts (תועבות) of the women in question defile the land of Israel and threaten the chances that the people of Israel have of dwelling in their land for perpetuity (9:1, 12). That is to say, the defilement of the land leads to exile, precisely as articulated in the final verses of Leviticus 18.

To be sure, this passage is not merely an echo of Leviticus 18. For one thing, Ezra 9 employs the term *niddah* (נדה) to articulate the moral defilement of sin (9:11). For the most part, this term is used in the Hebrew Bible with reference to menstruation. Just once in the Holiness Code it is used more generally to articulate the moral defilement of sin (Lev. 20:21).[6] That menstrual impurity is the concern of Ezra 9:11 is out of the question: Israelite women too are subject to menstrual impurity, and this impurity does not defile the land. Ezekiel, in 36:17 (quoted in chapter 1) draws a simile between the moral impurity of the Israelites and the ritual impurity of a menstruous woman. The passage in Ezra 9, like Leviticus 20:21, takes this kind of simile one step further. In a usage that becomes increasingly common in some circles in the second temple period, the term נדה is a virtual synonym of "abomination" (תועבה), so that the land defiled by abominations is described as an "impure land" (ארץ נדה).[7] And this usage is particularly apt when it comes to the description of the land defiled by sin. Among the nuances of the term נדה, in both ritual and moral contexts, is the idea of separation.[8] And when the land is morally defiled by sin, Israel will be exiled—that is, separated—from it.

A more serious way in which Ezra 9 diverges from the Holiness Code traditions is that it draws a connection between moral impurity and the prohibition of intermarriage (9:11). While a few pentateuchal traditions ban marriages with certain foreigners, there is no general prohibition of intermarriage articulated in Torah.[9] Interestingly enough, there is not even a limited prohibition against intermarriage in the Holiness Code.[10] Thus with respect to forbidden marriages, the tradition recorded in Ezra 9:11–12 builds not only on the Holiness Code, but also on Deuteronomy 7:1–4, which prohibits marriage with men or women from the seven Canaanite nations. The given reason (7:4) is not that the nations are ritually impure, but that they are idolatrous and will lead astray any Israelites they marry.[11] This fear that intermarriage will lead to idolatry is expressed occasionally in deuteronomic sources.[12] Indeed, this is precisely the snare that trapped Solomon: he was led astray by his foreign wife (1 Kings 11:1–2). But in deuteronomic traditions, this concern is not always operative.[13] In the books of Ezra and Nehemiah, however, the concern is not only operative, but dominant. The fear is that intermarriage will lead to sin, just as it did for Solomon (Neh. 13:26).

Again, the validity of such claims is not our concern. It is not important for our purposes whether the foreign wives were indeed sinful and, if so, in what way. What is important is the perception of that sinfulness, and its perceived effect. The women were clearly perceived as a moral threat to the local populace (Ezra 9:1, 11; Neh. 13:26). Presumably, the threat was that the women would cause the Israelites to commit idolatry (Neh. 13:26). Thus in the passages quoted above, it is the foreign wives' idolatry that is defiling the land of Israel and threatening the moral purity of the community of Judah.[14] It is precisely because of this source of moral impurity that the marriages were opposed by Ezra and Nehemiah.

The idea that Gentiles—especially Canaanites—were wont to engage in morally defiling behavior was not new. This idea was clearly articulated in Leviticus 18. What is new in Ezra and Nehemiah is the view that the moral impurity of Gentiles is inherent. This view indeed contradicts the general trend of the Holiness Code, which extends to the Gentile populace of the land the prohibitions that prevent moral impurity (e.g., Lev. 18:26; Num. 35:15). Obviously, the assumption of the Holiness Code is that the moral impurity of local Gentiles is not inherent: otherwise the code would not bother to obligate the stranger to follow these commands. The books of Ezra and Nehemiah, however, consider local Gentiles to be inherently morally impure. Because these women were sinful by nature, conversion was not an option that either Ezra or Nehemiah entertained.[15] Directly related to the opposition to conversion is another idea expressed in Ezra 9:1 but unknown to either the Holiness Code or the deuteronomic history: the notion of Israel's ethnic/racial purity.[16] This notion too is a development not of the idea of ritual purity, but of the idea of moral purity.

There is one final aspect of the situation that is relevant to the claim being made here. Ritual impurity, as we have seen, is neither permanent nor sinful, yet the impurity problematized here is both permanent and sinful. If ritual impurity were the concern, we would expect to see some possibility of ritual purification, but that is not the case. The only "hope" (Ezra 10:2) for Israel, as far as the books of Ezra and Nehemiah are concerned, is the expulsion of the foreign wives.[17] This cannot be a question of ritual impurity, but it certainly can be an extension of the notion of moral impurity. In the end, there is nothing in these books to make us think that the foreign wives were considered to be a source of ritual defilement. Ezra, Nehemiah, and their supporters were opposed to intermarriage not because the foreign women were impure in any ritual sense, but because the foreign women were inherently morally impure as a result of their alleged sinful behavior.[18]

The discoveries at Qumran now allow us to demonstrate that the conception of moral defilement as articulated in Ezra–Nehemiah had some direct influence on subsequent generations. One of the so-called "non-canonical Psalms" from Qumran (4Q381) includes the following passage (frg. 69, lines 1–2):[19]

בראותו כי התעיבו עמי [הא]ר[ץ ...
... היתה] כל הארץ לטמאה בנדת טמאה ...

.. when He saw that the peoples of [the la]nd acted abominably
.. all the land [became] impure in impure defilement

This passage alludes quite clearly to Ezra 9:11, quoted previously. And just as in Ezra 9, here too the residents of the land have defiled it with their impure behavior. That this verse alludes directly to the book of Ezra can be confirmed by the fact that other verses in the same composition allude to other passages in Ezra–Nehemiah. Indeed, the work as a whole is permeated with various allusions to Scripture.[20] On linguistic and literary grounds, Schuller dates this psalm collection to the late Persian or early Hellenistic period.[21] The text is too fragmentary to justify our analyzing it any further, but we can make the claim that some late Persian or early Hellenistic period Jewish author—and presumably some community of Jews—was reflecting on the concept of moral defilement as articulated in Ezra–Nehemiah.

Jubilees

Scholarly consensus dates Jubilees to the second century BCE, although there is some disagreement about whether the book was produced in the middle or toward the end of that century.[22] There is even more disagreement regarding the book's social provenance. In particular, it remains unclear whether or not the document was produced in sectarian circles.[23] But since it will be seen that the views on impurity and sin expressed in Jubilees are largely the same as those expressed in Ezra and Nehemiah, the question of the book's sectarian nature will not be of great importance to us. Whether the book represented the view of many Jews or of only a few, there is nothing particularly sectarian about the attitudes expressed in Jubilees toward impurity and sin.[24]

Are we shifting focus away from ritual purity?

Jubilees is a book that is very much concerned with purity, and yet ritual purity is the concern of only a few of its passages. Jubilees 3:8–14 echoes some of the childbirth purity laws of Leviticus 12:2–5, and Jubilees 32:13 declares that the second tithe becomes impure after one year has passed. Still, it is fair to say that there is no great concern in Jubilees with ritual purity per se. The extensive narrative of Abraham's death, for instance, does not include any mention of corpse impurity or any reminders of the need to be concerned with that taboo. Moral impurity, however, is Jubilees's constant concern. → *Land focus?*

The following passages are representative of the ideology of moral defilement as expressed in Jubilees:[25]

(22:16) Now you, my son Jacob, remember what I say and keep the commandments of your father Abraham. Separate from the nations, and do not eat with them. Do not act as they do, and do not become their companion, for their actions are something that is impure, and all their ways are defiled and something abominable and detestable. (17) They offer their sacrifices to the dead, and they worship demons. They eat in tombs, and everything they do is empty and worthless. (18) They have no mind to think, and their eyes do not see what they do; and how they err in saying to [a piece of] wood: "You are my God"; or to a stone "You are my Lord, you are my deliverer" [They have] no mind.
(19) As for you, my son Jacob, may the most high God help you and the God of heaven bless you. May he remove you from their impurity and from all their error.
(20) Be careful, my son Jacob, not to marry a woman from all the descendants of Canaan's daughters, because all of his descendants are [meant] for being uprooted from the earth . . .
(22) There is no hope in the land of the living for all who worship idols and for those who are odious. For they will descend to Sheol and will go to the place of judgment. There will be no memory of them on the earth. As the people of Sodom were taken from the earth, so all who worship idols will be taken. . . .
(30 13) It is a disgraceful thing for the Israelites who give or take [in marriage] one of the foreign women because it is too impure and despicable for Israel. (14) Israel will not become clean from this impurity while it has one of the foreign women or if any one has given one of his daughters to any foreign man. (15) For it is a blow upon blow and curse upon curse. Every punishment, blow, and curse will come If one does this or shuts his eyes to those who do impure things and who defile the Lord's sanctuary and to those who profane his holy name, then the entire nation will be condemned together because of all this impurity and this contamination.

In these passages, Jews are encouraged to shun Gentiles lest they learn the Gentiles' morally impure ways. In the first passage, the defiling force of idolatry is quite clearly articulated.[26] In the second passage, the impure behavior is not specified, but it has the power to defile the people (cf. Jubilees 16:5) and the sanctuary of God (cf. Jubilees 23:21). Elsewhere in Jubilees, similar sentiments are expressed with regard to murder and especially sexual transgression.[27] Indeed, throughout Jubilees, the terminology of defilement is juxtaposed to the terminology of sin, and, to a lesser degree, innocence is expressed as purity.[28]

Shun so as to not learn

The similarities between these passages in Jubilees and the Holiness Code traditions that concern moral impurity are overwhelming.[29] Again the concern is with idolatry, incest, and bloodshed. This concern, moreover, is expressed with evocative terminology, in the tradition of the Holiness Code.[30] And again, these abominations defile the land of Israel[31] and the sanctuary of God.[32] And just as in the Holiness Code, there are none of the classic signs of ritual defilement. Sin does not cause an impermanent contagion, and the defilement cannot be rectified by ritual purification. Just as in the Holiness Code, moral impurity has consequences that are much more dire than those caused by ritual impurity. Yet Jubilees foresees a doom even worse than exile. In Jubilees, the ultimate result of this defilement is untold havoc — obliteration from the face of the earth. If the people defile themselves, they will not just end up exiled, they will end up like the inhabitants of Sodom (22:22).[33]

Jubilees also diverges from the Holiness Code traditions in its evaluation of Gentile behavior. As in Ezra and Nehemiah, the moral impurity of Gentiles is deemed to be inherent, and therefore intermarriage is prohibited (30:7).[34] Indeed, not only is intermarriage prohibited, but it appears to have become a source of moral defilement in its own right, presumably because of the fear that it leads to idolatry (30:8–9, 13–14). And Jubilees does not stop with intermarriage: All Jewish–Gentile interaction is to be shunned (22:16). It is often suggested that ritual impurity is the concern of these passages, and that Jubilees considered Gentiles to be a source of ritual defilement.[35] Yet the concern here is not that Gentile persons are ritually defiling,[36] but that Gentile behavior is morally abominable, because Gentiles practice idolatry (22:17–22) and perform sexual transgressions (20:3–7). For this reason, Abraham urges his descendants to remain separate from them — even to refrain from eating with them.[37] Jubilees's use of purity language in these and similar passages thus reflects not the ritual purity laws of Leviticus 11–15, but the moral impurity prohibitions applied to all Israel in the biblical traditions quoted in chapter 1. Indeed, ritual impurity surfaces only now and then in book of Jubilees. Moral impurity, however, is one of Jubilees's central themes.

The Temple Scroll

The date of the Temple Scroll (11QT)[38] remains an open question. While Yigael Yadin dated it to the time of John Hyrcanus (134 BCE), other scholars have offered dates ranging from the fifth century BCE to the reign of Herod the Great.[39] Making matters even more complicated, a number of scholars now view 11QT as a composite.[40] Since the date and nature of this composition are uncertain, it remains unclear what the relationship was between 11QT and the sect at Qumran.[41] Yadin viewed the scroll as the Torah of the Essenes, but other scholars dispute this claim.[42] There are, indeed, some significant differences between 11QT and the other sectarian literature, and one of these will be noted below.[43] What is more problematic for Yadin's view is that whereas sectarian literature quotes the Pentateuch frequently, there are no quotations of 11QT in the sectarian literature from Qumran.[44] Thus it is not likely that the connection between 11QT and the sect is as direct as Yadin thought. In my view, it is best to assume that 11QT had, to use Geza Vermes's term, a "prehistory." Most likely, 11QT stemmed from a group similar but not identical to the sectarians of Qumran.[45] Any discussion of 11QT, however, is necessarily tentative. Despite all that has been preserved — the Temple Scroll is the largest of the Dead Sea Scrolls — we only have at our disposal roughly half of the original document.[46]

Nearly seven columns of the Temple Scroll are devoted almost exclusively to ritual purity regulations (XLV:7 to LI:10).[47] As one might expect, given both the general interest in the document as a whole and the importance of purity to the document, there is no dearth of studies devoted to illuminating the ritual purity law of the Temple Scroll.[48] Contemporary scholarship, however, has not yet noted the fact that the notion of *moral* impurity is also present (though by no means prevalent) in the Temple Scroll. *— Moral purity is also present in 11QT*

Regarding *ritual purity,* some of 11QT's laws cohere with those found in the Torah, while many others do not.[49] Indeed, the generally innovative nature of much of the scroll's legislation cannot be denied, and that is no less true of 11QT's purity law. Like the ritual impurity legislation contained in Ezekiel 40–48,[50] the impurity law of 11QT strengthens older prohibitions and adds prohibitions that appear to be altogether new (e.g., the exclusion from the temple of males under 20 years old).[51] The scroll also introduces sources of impurity that are unknown in earlier literature (e.g., the notion that blind people are ritually defiling).[52] The scroll also introduces a new locus of sanctity in what is referred to as "the city of the sanctuary" (XLV:11– *Heightened* 12).[53] In respect to these stringencies, we could describe 11QT's approach to ritual *degree of* impurity as "expansive": The scroll's legislation seeks to keep more people at a greater *ritual purity* distance from the sacred.[54] Moreover, the Temple Scroll repeatedly emphasizes that those who had immersed in water in order to purify themselves ritually still had to wait until sunset before being considered ritually pure once again (e.g., XLIX:19–21 and LI:2–5). In this respect, 11QT articulates a view that is in rabbinic sources attributed to the Sadducees.[55] Finally, the scroll introduces a new step in the purification process, what Milgrom has called "first day ablutions" (XLIX:17–19).[56] A number of these innovations and stringencies are paralleled in the sectarian literature from Qumran.[57] *Sadducee view*

But there is one important, and hitherto unnoticed, way in which the impurity legislation of 11QT does not cohere with that of the other sectarian literature of *Qumran* Qumran. At Qumran, as will be seen in chapter 3, there is a nearly complete identification of what we have called ritual and moral impurity, with the result that sin *→ Complete* was considered to be a source of ritual impurity in its own right. But interestingly *identification* enough there is not the slightest hint of this notion in the Temple Scroll. To the contrary, the references to the defiling force of sin that can be found in 11QT for the most *of ritual &* part echo ideas made explicit in Scripture. Thus with regard to *ritual* impurity, 11QT *moral* tends to agree with the sectarian literature from Qumran, but with regard to *moral* *impurity* impurity, it tends to agree with the Hebrew Bible.

Immediately after the conclusion to the section of the scroll that deals with purity law comes the following passage (LI:11–15):[58]

> (11) You shall appoint judges and officers in all your towns, and they shall judge the people (12) with righteous judgement. And they shall not show partiality in justice, and shall not take a bribe, and shall not (13) pervert justice, the bribe perverts justice, and subverts the cause of the righteous, and blinds (14) the eyes of the wise, and causes great guilt, and defiles the house because of the sin of (15) iniquity

The important aspect of the passage for us here is the fact that line 14 specifies that bribery "defiles the house" (ומטמא הבית). In his commentary on the passage, Yadin assumes that the point being made is that one who takes a bribe would defile the sanctuary, if he or she chose to enter it.[59] Yadin cites, as parallels, two passages from the early medieval Jewish translations of the Hebrew Bible into Aramaic (the Targumim), each of which speaks of the exclusion of sinners from the sanctuary (Targ. 2 Sam. 5:8 and Targ. Song 6:6). Yet as we have seen in chapter 1, the exclusion of sinners from the sanctuary is nowhere explicitly articulated in the Hebrew Bible. To the contrary, we noted a number of traditions — among them the laws dealing with a suspected adulteress (Num. 5:11–31) and with murderers (Exod. 21:14) — that permit, and even enjoin, the entrance of sinners into the sanctuary.[60] As we will see, the exclusion of sinners from the sanctuary is not commonplace in rabbinic thought either. What is important to note here is that the exclusion of sinners from the sanctuary is also not articulated in this passage from 11QT. The point of the passage is not, as Yadin suggested, that persons who take bribes defile the sanctuary (ritually) upon entering it, but that the act of bribery, *in and of itself*, defiles the sanctuary, *morally*.[61]

Once this point is granted, the question then arises: Whence comes the idea that bribery defiles the sanctuary? It has long been recognized that the Temple Scroll's legal innovations are rooted in scriptural exegesis. Trying to account for 11QT's interpretive technique, Yadin spoke of the scroll's "harmonization" of earlier biblical traditions.[62] Milgrom tried to be a bit more specific and used the term "homogenization" to refer to 11QT's tendency to extend the scope of earlier legislation by melding together disparate biblical traditions.[63] Swanson, in turn, has rejected Milgrom's notion of homogenization and speaks of 11QT's use of supplementary texts to comment on base texts.[64] Clearly, the common denominator here is exegesis, and it behooves us to try and figure out the exegetical reasoning that leads 11QT to the view that bribery is morally defiling.

In the Holiness Code, the Israelites are commanded not to "render an unfair decision [לא־תעשו עול במשפט]: do not favor the poor or show deference to the rich; judge your kinsman fairly" (Lev. 19:15). Later on in the same passage, the same introductory phrase (לא־תעשו עול במשפט) introduces the command to have equal weights and measures (Lev. 19:35). Now in Deuteronomy 25:15–6, a similar prohibition is couched in these terms:

> (15) You must have completely honest weights and completely honest measures, if you are to endure long on the soil that the Lord your God is giving you. (16) For everyone who does those things, everyone who deals dishonestly, is abhorrent to the Lord your God.

These passages have been mentioned because the tannaitic interpretation of them does something quite remarkable, moving in the same direction as the passage from 11QT quoted above. The tannaitic commentary on Leviticus (the Sifra) 19:15 states:[65]

> We learn from this verse that the judge who perverts justice [המקלקל את הדין] is called deceitful [עול], hated, shunned, banned, and an abomination [תועבה]. And he causes five things: [he] defiles the land, profanes the name [of God], causes the withdrawal of the divine presence, brings the sword down upon Israel, and exiles him [Israel] from his land.

We see here that the Sifra considered deceit to be a source of moral defilement. This idea is also expressed elsewhere in tannaitic sources.[66] In my view, these passages are the true rabbinic parallels to 11QT LI:11–15, not the targumic passages cited by Yadin. In these parallels, moreover, we get a possible — even likely — explanation for how 11QT came to view bribery as morally defiling. It was a process of creatively applying one to another the biblical verses quoted above, so that the concepts of deceit, abomination, and moral defilement were all brought together into a single chain of thought. Deceit is referred to in Deuteronomy 25:16 as an abomination, and we know from Leviticus 18 and elsewhere that abominations are morally defiling. And bribery, of course, is a form of judicial deceit. Harmonizing — or "homogenizing," to use Milgrom's term[67] — these biblical traditions, 11QT LI:11–15 reaches the conclusion that bribery is morally defiling. It is intriguing that in this case the tannaim and the Temple Scroll meld together disparate biblical traditions in a similar way, with a similar result. But what is important here for our purposes is the fact that 11QT views bribery as morally defiling. Thus in this respect, the Temple Scroll has slightly expanded upon the biblical notion of moral defilement.

There are a few additional passages in the Temple Scroll in which the notion of moral impurity is reflected, although these passages are more obscure. Within the section of the scroll devoted to ritual purity law we find the following isolated warning: "And you shall not defile your land" (XLVIII:10–11).[68] This statement is physically separated from its context by a *vacat* (an empty space on the manuscript) on each side. The warning may articulate the concern that improper burial, or failure to perform burial at all, defiles the land.[69] Alternatively it is possible that the phrase articulates a concern with the defiling force of bloodshed.[70] A further reference to the defilement of the land is found in 11QT LXIV:10–13, which echoes Deuteronomy 21:23 and articulates the concern that the hanged criminal — or the hanged criminal's body — is a potential source for the defilement of the land. The fact that these passages speak of the defilement of the land and are concerned with behavior leaves it clear that they ought to be understood as reflections of the biblical notion of moral impurity. Further than that, we cannot discern precisely what their concern is. But neither of these passages seems to break any new ground. Rather, they simply reiterate notions of moral impurity made explicit in the Hebrew Bible.

With regard to moral impurity, the Temple Scroll deviates from the earlier biblical traditions only in the identification of a new source of moral defilement (bribery). In other respects, its treatment of moral impurity does not diverge from what we find in the Pentateuch: Certain sins morally defile the land and sanctuary. This stands in stark contrast to the Temple Scroll's treatment of ritual impurity, which, as is noted above, is undeniably innovative. Its lengthy treatment of ritual impurity law mandates new prohibitions and strengthens older ones, but its treatment of moral impurity is much more in line with the Hebrew Bible. Indeed, the truth is that the Temple Scroll is really not that interested in moral defilement. Only a few references could be positively identified in the entire document. Interestingly enough, the extant material does not yield even one reference to the morally defiling nature of sexual or idolatrous sins.[71] Regarding its treatment of ritual and moral defilement, the Temple Scroll finds its mirror image in Jubilees.[72] Jubilees is greatly concerned with the defiling force of idolatry and sexual sins, but not so concerned with ritual impurity per se. The Temple Scroll, by contrast, is greatly interested in ritual impurity legislation, but not so interested in moral impurity.[73] What the two books share is that in neither is any fusion of the two ideas presented. Just as in the Pentateuch, in Jubilees and the Temple Scroll, two distinct types of defilement are noted, and no attempt is made to integrate them.

↳ Two distinct systems, again

The Damascus Document

We turn now to a text whose date and provenance are, relatively speaking, more secure than those of Jubilees and the Temple Scroll. The Damascus Document (CD) is commonly dated to late in the second or early in the first century BCE.[74] Since the discovery of at least ten distinct copies of the work at Qumran, it has also been commonly recognized that the Damascus Document is somewhat directly related to the community at Qumran.[75] Indeed, CD uses some typically Qumranic expressions: The document, for instance, speaks of the Teacher of Righteousness (I:11). Yet there are also a number of discrepancies between CD and other sectarian literature from Qumran. Foremost among these are the peculiar allusions to Damascus occurring throughout CD; no such allusions appear in other sectarian works. There are also various *halakhic* (legal) disagreements, notably between CD and the Community Rule (1QS).[76] A number of suggestions have been put forth to try to account for these discrepancies on the one hand, and the obvious connections between CD and the sectarian scrolls on the other. Some have seen the text as stemming from pre-Qumranic Essenes, and others have suggested that the text stems from Qumran but was intended for either potential members or sectarians who did not dwell at the site.[77] The question of the precise relationship between CD and the sectarian literature from Qumran is well beyond the scope of this study; the problem is mentioned here as partial justification for turning to the Damascus Document in this chapter rather than in chapter 3, which focuses on the sectarian literature of Qumran and its distinctive approach to ritual and moral impurity. It will be argued here that a problematic passage from CD (IV:12–V:11) can best be understood not as a reflection of the sectarian approach to impurity and sin taken at Qumran, but rather as a reflection of the more standard conception of moral defilement that is being traced in this chapter.

No great attempt will be made here to characterize the approach to impurity and sin taken in the Damascus Document, because I discern no single approach in this document. The passage discussed in this section appears to reflect the more general notion of moral defilement delineated in chapter 1. Yet other passages in CD (noted in chapter 3) do appear to reflect the approach to impurity and sin that is particular to the Qumran community. True to the complex — and, very likely, composite[78] — nature of the Damascus Document, the approach to defilement and sin taken there can for now be described only as eclectic.

Our concern centers on CD (MS A) IV:12 to V:11, which involves an exegesis of Isaiah 24:17:[79]

> (IV:12) . . . But during all those years, (13) Belial will run unbridled amidst Israel, as God spoke through the hand of the prophet Isaiah, son of (14) Amoz, saying, "Fear and a pit and a snare are upon you, O inhabitant(s) of the land" [Isa 24.17]. This refers (15) to the three nets of Belial, of which Levi, the son of Jacob, said (16) that he [Belial] entrapped Israel with them, making them seem as if they were three types

of (17) righteousness. The first is unchastity [זנות], the second is arrogance, and the third (18) defilement of the sanctuary [טמא המקדש]. He who escapes from this is caught by that and he who is saved from that is caught (19) by this.

At this point, as many commentators recognize, there is a break in the text,[80] but it becomes clear that the theme has not been dropped. Indeed the text goes on to assert that some group that the sect opposes — the "builders of the barrier" (בוני החיץ) — is caught up in two of these snares (IV:19–V:1).

(19) . . . "The builders of the barrier," who walked after ṣw — the ṣw is the preacher (20) of whom it is said, "they shall surely preach" [Micah 2:6] — are caught by two [snares]. By unchastity, [namely,] taking (21) two wives in their lives, while the foundation of creation is "male and female he created them" [Gen. 1:27] (V:1) And those who entered [Noah's] ark went two by two into the ark.

The first snare in which this other group is caught is the snare of unchastity (זנות). The second, as we will see, is defilement of the sanctuary. Unchastity is then defined in IV:20–21 as "taking two wives in their lives" (לקחת שתי נשים בחייהם). It is debated whether this complaint articulates a prohibition against some or all of the following: polygamy, divorce, remarriage after divorce, or remarriage even after the death of a spouse.[81] This debate is beyond the scope of this work, but I tend to think that the concern here is with both polygamy and remarriage after divorce: The prohibition against "taking two women in their lives" permits taking a second if the first has died.[82] Whatever the correct interpretation of this phrase is, it is relatively clear what is meant by "unchastity" (זנות): some violation of marriage law relating to having more than one wife, either at the same time or in some improper sequence. The concern here is not that the first or second marriage would have been improper under any circumstance. It is the circumstance of multiplicity that renders the second marriage forbidden. In other words, the concern here is infidelity, not incest.

This distinction between infidelity and incest is important for a proper understanding of the next few lines of the text. In V:6–9 the text takes up the second of the two snares in which the opponents of the sect are caught (recall that, according to IV:20, these opponents are trapped in only two of the three snares mentioned in the initial exegesis of Isaiah 24:17):

(6) . . And they also continuously polluted the sanctuary by not (7) separating according to the Torah, and they habitually lay with a woman who sees blood of flowing; and they marry (8) each one his brother's daughter or sister's daughter. But Moses said, "To (9) your mother's sister you may not draw near, for she is your mother's near relation" [Lev. 18:13].

At first glance the passage is rather confusing. What do the sexual sins mentioned here — incest and cohabitation with a menstruant — have to do with defilement of the sanctuary? Indeed, a number of commentators have found the juxtaposition of sanctuary defilement with sexual transgression in this passage to be baffling.

One view, represented by Philip Davies, argues simply that the text makes no sense. Davies claims that the passage "condemns as defilement of the sanctuary an activity which really has nothing to do with the sanctuary at all."[83] Elsewhere Davies more forcefully claims that the charge of sexual sin "is so ill-fitted to the general accusation that we must seriously doubt whether Temple defilement is a crucial issue in this case rather than a mere stereotype."[84]

A second view was articulated early in this century by Louis Ginzberg, to the effect that only part of the text makes sense. Ginzberg claims that the defilement of the sanctuary in V:6 refers to "a ritual transgression, and then only in a limited sense."[85] He goes on to say that the sinners in question "defile the Temple in that they permit intercourse with a זבה, and so they enter the Sanctuary in a state of uncleanness."[86] That is a possible reading, to be sure, but it is not likely. After all, the defilement contracted by such an act is impermanent (Lev. 15:24), so the problem would be not that they violate the prohibition, but rather that they refuse to purify, or fail to wait until they are fully purified. Also, if the concern were ritual impurity, it is unclear why the text focuses on intercourse: Ritual impurity can be contracted by nonsexual contact as well. Most important, however, this interpretation does not account for how the second sin — incest — fits into the picture. Indeed Ginzberg suggests that incest does *not* fit into this picture, and he views V:7–11 as a second example of the first snare, unchastity.[87]

I suggest, however, that we need not follow Davies and view the text as entirely nonsensical. Nor need we assume, with Ginzberg, that there is some jumbling of the sequence here. I suggest, rather, that the passage be understood as a somewhat straightforward — albeit a bit choppy — articulation of the doctrine of moral defilement. The two sexual sins — sexual contact with an impure woman, and incest — are listed as examples of sanctuary defilement precisely because these sexual sins can defile the sanctuary, *morally.*

A number of points can be raised in defense of this argument. First, it has long been noted that Holiness Code traditions figure prominently in CD. Indeed, as J. Murphy O'Connor has shown, almost all of the precepts listed in columns VI to VIII have parallels in the Holiness Code.[88] Therefore we should not be surprised to find reflections of the idea of moral defilement here.

Second, the passage is concerned not with sources of ritual impurity in general, but with two sexual sins that were believed to be morally defiling. The first sin — cohabitation with a woman in a state of flux — is clearly related in some direct way to the Holiness Code's prohibition of cohabitation with a menstruant (Lev. 18:19).[89] This sin is already considered to be a source of moral defilement in the Holiness Code.

Regarding the incest prohibition, that the concern here is the morally defiling force of sexual sins is equally clear. Indeed, the passage contains within it an unmistakable allusion to Leviticus 18, a passage concerned with the morally defiling force of sexual sins. Of course, the passage from CD interprets Leviticus 18:13, and it expands the prohibition to apply not only to men and their aunts, but also to men and their nieces.[90] But the expansion of the prohibition does not bring us beyond the realm of moral defilement. The second snare in which the opponents are caught is the moral defilement of the sanctuary, which is brought about by at least two types of sexual misdeeds: cohabitation with a woman in a state of flux, and violation of the laws of incest.

The claim that this passage from CD is concerned with the morally defiling force of sexual sins finds further justification in the next few lines of the text (V:9–12):

> (V:9) . . . Now the precept of incest is written (10) from the point of view of males, but the same [law] applies to women, so if a brother's daughter uncovers the nakedness of a brother of (11) her father, she is a [forbidden] close relationship. They also polluted their holy spirits, and with a tongue of (12) blasphemies, they   . .

Immediately upon concluding its brief discussion of sexual sins, the text takes up again the theme of defilement. This juxtaposition strongly suggests that, in the author's mind, the theme of defilement was never so completely dropped as Davies would have us believe. It's just that the defilement spoken of here is not ritual impurity, but moral impurity.

For even further justification for seeing in CD columns IV to V an articulation of the doctrine of moral defilement, we turn back to the beginning of the passage. Recall that the passage opens with an exegesis of Isaiah 24:17. In order to evaluate fully the concerns of this passage from CD, it is important to note that Isaiah 24:17 is extracted from a passage whose larger context is concerned with the desolation of the land that is caused by Israel's sin. Furthermore, the passage uses language reminiscent of the Holiness Code: "For the earth was defiled [והארץ חנפה] under its inhabitants." (24:5). Both conceptually and terminologically, Isaiah 24 is related to the idea of moral defilement. This fact further justifies the claim that the Damascus Document's exegesis on Isaiah 24:17 also articulates the doctrine of moral defilement.

Only one question remains. It has been argued that CD IV to V speaks of sanctuary defilement precisely because the sexual sins discussed there are viewed as sources of moral impurity. But then one must ask, why are the sins that constitute the first snare — polygamy and remarriage after divorce — not included in the category of morally defiling sins? It is important to note that one would be hard-pressed to find scriptural support for the idea that either polygamy or remarriage after divorce is morally defiling. Indeed, one would be hard-pressed to find scriptural support for the idea that either polygamy or remarriage after divorce is prohibited at all.[91] In fact, the discussion of "unchastity" (זנות) in CD IV:20–V:6 alludes not to the sexual prohibitions of the Holiness Code, but rather to verses in Genesis that purportedly praise monogamy (Gen. 1:27 and 7:7–9) and to the deuteronomic law of the king (17:17), which precludes his taking too many wives (IV:20–V:6):

> (IV:20) . . By unchastity, [namely,] taking (21) two wives in their lives, while the foundation of creation is "male and female he created them" [Gen. 1:27].
> (V·1) And those who entered [Noah's] ark went two by two into the ark. And of the prince it is written, (2) "Let him not multiply wives for himself" [Deut 17.17]. And David did not read the sealed book of the Torah which (3) was in the Ark [of the Covenant], for it was not opened in Israel since the day of the death of Eleazar (4) and Joshua and the elders. For [their successors] worshipped the Ashtoreth, and that which had been revealed was hidden (5) until Zadok arose, so David's works were accepted, with the exception of Uriah's blood, (6) and God forgave him for them.

We can now see why CD makes a distinction between two types of sexual sin. The first snare, "unchastity" (זנות), which includes polygamy and remarriage after divorce, falls short of the biblical monogamous ideal. But this sin does not, presumably, violate the sex laws of Leviticus; if it did, CD would allude to them. Since the sin does not violate that code, it does not result in the moral defilement discussed in Leviticus 18:24–30. The second snare, however, involves sexual sins of different nature. Since Leviticus explicitly views both incest and sexual contact with a menstruant as morally defiling, these sins are referred to in CD as "sanctuary defilement." It is true that Leviticus views these sins as defiling the land, not the sanctuary, but we will see in the next section that the view of sexual sins as a source of sanctuary defilement was common in the late second temple period.

Considering all the arguments offered, it appears best to view CD IV:12–V:11 as an expression of the doctrine of moral defilement. Even though the text is corrupt, and traces of its rather protracted development are in evidence, the general sequence of ideas is both sound and sensible.

Sin and the Sanctuary in Other Sundry Texts

It has been argued throughout this chapter that the idea of moral defilement was very much alive in the second temple period. In the previous section, it was argued that a problematic passage from the Damascus Document can best be understood when the phrase "sanctuary defilement" is taken as a reference to the idea of moral impurity. But there is an irony here: While there are biblical references to the idea that, say, idolatry defiles the sanctuary (e.g., Lev. 20:1–3), there are no biblical statements to the effect that sexual sins defile the sanctuary. Nonetheless, as we will see presently, the idea that sexual sins have the capacity to defile the sanctuary is a common concern in the Jewish literature of the second temple period. In this section, we will examine a few texts from 1 Enoch, the Testaments of the Twelve Patriarchs, and the Psalms of Solomon. There may well be other references in the extant literature, but these examples ought to suffice to make the point that sexual sins were perceived to defile the sanctuary, morally.

One of the earliest extrabiblical Jewish texts that has a particular interest in the defiling force of sexual sins is "The Book of Watchers" (1 Enoch 1–36),[92] a work based in part on Genesis 6:1–4. This biblical passage contains a curiously brief notice concerning illicit sexual relationship between divine angels and the daughters of humankind, which resulted in the birth of giants. In 1 Enoch's expanded version of the narrative, some 200 heavenly angels descend to earth under the leadership of an angel named Semyaza (1 Enoch 6). They take wives for themselves and teach the women various crafts, including magic, incantation, and astrology (7:1). Soon enough, the offspring of these relationships — the giants — bring about all sorts of evil in their own right (7:2–6). The angels are ultimately punished for having initiated illicit relationships with the women of the earth, thereby having brought about earthly chaos (chs. 9–10). Of concern to us are the following aspects of the narrative. First, the watchers are said, more than once, to have defiled themselves by having sexual relations with the women (9:8, 10:11, 12:4, 15:3).[93] This defilement brings about not an impermanent state of contagion, but a state of permanent degradation (14:4–5). Second, as a result of having so defiled themselves, the watchers are banished from the heavens (14:5). We can therefore say that according to the Book of Watchers, the watchers have defiled themselves morally by committing sexual misdeeds.

The dynamic of defilement and exclusion articulated in 1 Enoch does not, to be sure, conform perfectly with the biblical idea of moral defilement as spelled out in chapter 1. For instance, in 1 Enoch there is no explicit reference to the defilement of the land—a key aspect of the Holiness Code's conception of moral defilement. Yet according to 10:7, the sin of the watchers does have some sort of deleterious effect on the land, so that it requires some sort of purification (10:20). Presumably, the biblical idea of the earth's defilement by sin does lurk somewhere in the background. 1 Enoch also lacks reference to the defilement of the sanctuary, but since the entire narrative takes place long before the sanctuary is built, this stands to reason. A further difference is the fact that the defiled sinners are not exiled from the land but are banished from heaven. But we must keep in mind that in this document, the ones who defiled themselves are not human beings, but angels. The angels' banishment from heaven can be seen as analogous to the exile with which the Israelites are threatened in the Holiness Code. Thus in its own particular way, the Book of Watchers also articulates the idea of moral defilement: The watchers engage in sexually defiling behavior, which leads to their permanent degradation and their exile from Heaven.

While almost all of the texts discussed in this chapter are the subjects of controversy when it comes to date and provenance, the Testaments of the Twelve Patriarchs are particularly problematic.[94] It is even questioned whether they are Jewish or Christian in origin.[95] And when one takes into account the related Hebrew and Aramaic documents that have emerged from Cairo and Qumran, the situation becomes even more complex.[96] Parts of the Testaments are clearly Christian in origin and therefore come from the first century CE at the earliest. Yet the Qumran manuscripts related to T. Levi, for instance, can be dated on paleographical grounds to the second century BCE.[97] Michael Stone convincingly dates the Aramaic Levi Document—a work related to T. Levi and preserved in Qumran and Genizah fragments—to the third century BCE.[98] Again, for our purposes, we can only note the presence of these difficulties and then go on to discuss the passages concerned with the defiling force of sins.

Many passages in the Greek Testaments of the Twelve Patriarchs use the language of defilement when discussing sin, and more often than not the sin is sexual in nature.[99] Yet the bulk of these passages do not go beyond using the terminology of defilement in the context of sin, or the terminology of purification in the context of avoidance of sin. A few passages do go further, however, articulating specific aspects of the idea of moral impurity: that these defilements lead to exile.

The clearest articulation of the idea of moral defilement can be seen in T. Levi 14:5–15:1:[100]

> (14 5) " . . . You will rob the Lord's offerings; from the portions allotted to him you will steal; and before sacrificing to the Lord you will take for yourselves the choicest pieces and share them like common food with whores (6) You will teach the Lord's commandments for your own personal gain. You will pollute married women and defile the virgins of Jerusalem, and you will be united with prostitutes and adul-

teresses. You will take Gentile women as wives and purify them with a form of purification contrary to the law; and your unions will be like Sodom and Gomorrah in
ungodliness.(7) And you will be full of self-importance on account of the priesthood
and set yourselves up against other men; and not only so, but you will think yourselves of more importance than the commandments of God, and you will mock at
holy things and make cheap jokes about them.
(15:1) And so the temple, which the Lord will choose, will be laid waste because of
your uncleanness, and you will be carried off as captives by all the Gentiles."

This passage ought by now to appear as a rather straightforward articulation of the
idea of moral defilement.[101] Other passages in the Testaments make substantially
the same point. Consider, for example, T. Levi 9:9: "Be on guard against the spirit
of promiscuity, for it is constantly active and through your descendants it is about to
defile the sanctuary."[102]

Admittedly, these passages are ambiguous on one rather crucial point. It is not
clear whether the sins committed defile the sanctuary directly or whether the sins —
which surely are defiling in some way — bring about some divine punishment, part
of which is the desolation of the sanctuary by Israel's enemies. Note the sequence of
events in T. Asher 7:1–2:

(1) Do not, children, be like Sodom which did not recognize the Lord's angels and
perished for ever. (2) For I know that you will sin and be handed over to your enemies, and your land will be desolated and your holy places destroyed, and you will
be scattered to the four corners of the earth and be dispersed and despised like water that is useless, until the Most High looks with favour on the earth.

Here defiling sins lead to exile, just as in the Holiness Code. In T. Asher, however,
the defilement of the sanctuary is not brought about directly by the accumulation of
sin. There is no 'Dorian Gray' image. Rather, the destruction of the sanctuary is
brought about by the enemies of Israel, who have come into the land in accordance
with God's will in order to punish the Israelites. Of course, we are dealing here with
texts that were translated in antiquity, and probably poorly transmitted as well.
Certainty on these points is well beyond our reach. Even so, it is clear that the
Testaments are, on the whole, aware of and concerned with the morally defiling force
of sexual sins. T. Levi is particularly concerned with this moral defilement, and it is
T. Levi that articulates most clearly the idea that sexual sins bring about the defilement of the sanctuary.

That T. Levi articulates these ideas becomes even more important when we recall that within the passage from the Damascus Document discussed above, there is
a direct allusion to a text that is very likely related to T. Levi (CD IV:14–17):

(14) . This [Isa. 24:17] refers (15) to the three nets of Belial, *of which Levi, the son
of Jacob, said* (16) that he [Belial] entrapped Israel with them, making them seem as
if they were three types of (17) righteousness.

The extant Greek versions of T. Levi contain no such passage, nor for that manner
do any of the other Levi documents at our disposal. Still it has been proposed that
CD is alluding here to the Aramaic Levi Document but that the allusion has been
obscured by subsequent scribal errors.[103] Indeed, the Aramaic Levi Document and

the Damascus Document are concerned with similar issues. The former, as preserved at both Qumran and Cairo, does use the language of impurity with regard to sin, and it seems that the sins in question are sexual in nature.[104] If it could be demonstrated conclusively that the Damascus Document made use of the Aramaic Levi Document, that connection could even further justify the claim that the former is also concerned with the defiling force of sexual sins. But even if that cannot be demonstrated conclusively, the fact remains that all of the Levi documents at our disposal are concerned with the idea of sin as a defilement of some sort, and T. Levi explicitly articulates the idea that sexual sins defile the sanctuary.

Further evidence that the idea of sexual sins defiling the sanctuary was current in the second temple period can be seen in the Psalms of Solomon. This collection is commonly dated to the first century BCE and is generally believed to have been composed in Hebrew.[105] A number of its passages are concerned with the defiling force of sin, and a few of them articulate very clearly the concern that sexual transgression defiles the sanctuary.[106]
Consider the following passage (1:7–8):

(7) Their sins were in secret, and even I did not know.
(8) Their lawless actions surpassed the gentiles before them;
they completely profaned [ἐβεβήλωσαν] the sanctuary of the Lord.

The phrase "the gentiles before them" recalls Leviticus 18:27, which states that the Canaanites were expelled from the land because of their sexual misdeeds.[107] The Psalms of Solomon here is not discussing sexual sins, at least not explicitly or exclusively. The previous verses (4–6) are concerned primarily with greed. Yet the ultimate sin — the worst sin, as far as Psalms of Solomon 1 is concerned — was committed in secret. This secret sin is probably not another instance of greed. The image of a sin committed in secret brings to mind sexual sins, and this conclusion is confirmed when we compare Psalms of Solomon 4:5 and 8:9, both of which describe sexual misdeeds committed in secret. Moreover, Psalms of Solomon 8:9 describes an incestuous sin, again forging a link with Leviticus 18. We therefore see in the passage above an articulation of the concern that had become rather common by the first century BCE: that sexual sins have the capacity to defile the sanctuary.[108]

Evolution

I noted at the beginning of this section that the biblical traditions dealing with the defiling force of sexual sins focus primarily on the effect sexual sins have on the land, not on the sanctuary. Yet in the second temple period, references to the moral defilement of the sanctuary by sexual sins becomes commonplace. We have seen the notion articulated in the Testament of Levi, the Psalms of Solomon, and the Damascus Document. All of this evidence testifies to the vitality of the idea of moral impurity in the second temple period. The concern with the defiling force of sin was very much of interest, and there was even a development of the idea, somewhat akin to what Milgrom has called homogenization: The biblical tradition describes sexual sin as defiling (Lev. 18:24) and describes idolatry as defiling the sanctuary (Lev. 20:3). By the second temple period, these traditions have been melded into the concern that sexual sins defile the sanctuary.

Summary and Conclusion

The main goal of this chapter has been to demonstrate that the concern with the defiling force of sin is expressed in a number of second temple period Jewish texts. The distinction drawn here between ritual and moral impurity can be helpful in the interpretation of a number of passages from the Jewish literature of this period. The texts that articulate these ideas include, in rough chronological order, Ezra–Nehemiah, 4Q 381, 1 Enoch, Jubilees, the Temple Scroll, the Damascus Document, the Testament of Levi, and the Psalms of Solomon. These texts were composed throughout the period in question, and while a number of them are believed to be tied in some way to Qumran or some similar sect, none can be exclusively identified with any single known sect.

For the most part, these texts reiterate the idea of moral impurity as expressed in Scripture, particularly the Holiness Code. Yet there are a number of innovations and developments in the Jewish literature of the second temple period. Some texts introduce new sources of moral defilement: for example, the Temple Scroll views bribery as a source of moral defilement, and the Damascus Document expands the category of sexual sins. Also a number of texts were concerned with one particular result of the moral impurity of sexual sins: The fear that sexual sins defile the sanctuary is articulated in the Testament of Levi, the Psalms of Solomon, and the Damascus Document. And some of these texts propose legislation to curtail moral defilement: Both Ezra–Nehemiah and Jubilees oppose intermarriage, because the moral impurity of Gentiles is deemed to be inherent. Finally, the ultimate consequence of the defiling force of sin in the texts of the second temple period is usually exile, but Jubilees, for instance, threatens Israel with utter destruction.

Even where these texts do not disagree, we can sometimes discern significant shifts in emphasis. Most notably, while Jubilees is deeply concerned with moral impurity and only somewhat concerned with ritual impurity, the Temple Scroll is, to the contrary, very much concerned with ritual impurity and only somewhat concerned with moral impurity. And a number of the texts that we looked at were concerned only with certain aspects of the idea of moral defilement. Many expressed the concern that sexual sins defile the sanctuary, while fewer were concerned with the morally defiling force of idolatry and murder.

Yet all of the texts examined in this section share one thing, in addition to the concern with moral defilement: None confuses or integrates ritual and moral impurity in any way. Just as in the book of Leviticus itself, in each of these texts, if both types of impurity are discussed, they are juxtaposed without any attempt to integrate them.

Thus we have seen that the idea that sin has its own distinct defiling force persists into the second temple period. That Jewish texts of that period were concerned with *ritual* impurity needs hardly to be established; in this respect, Neusner's *The Idea of Purity in Ancient Judaism* remains unsurpassed. But now we can clearly see that *both* types of defilement were among the concerns of Jews living in the second temple period. We are ready, therefore, to move on to the next stage: an analysis of the ways in which ancient Jews answered the question of how these two distinct types of defilement relate to one another.

RITUAL AND MORAL IMPURITY
IN ANCIENT JEWISH LITERATURE

Part II: Introduction

The previous two chapters established the distinction between ritual and moral impurity and demonstrated that the idea of moral impurity is articulated not only in the Hebrew Bible but also in a number of Jewish texts from the second temple period. It does not need to be established here that the idea of *ritual* impurity is articulated in Jewish texts of the second temple period; no one familiar with the Temple Scroll or the Rule of the Community, to say nothing of Josephus, Philo, the New Testament, or rabbinic literature for that matter, would dispute that point.[1] Thus, given the conclusions of chapter 2, it can be claimed that Jewish literature from the second temple period deals with both types of defilement: ritual and moral.

It has been noted that the Hebrew Bible — and the book of Leviticus in particular — juxtaposes discussions of ritual and moral impurity without giving any indication of the nature of the relationship, if any, between these two kinds of defilements. Unfortunately, we cannot know how Israelites responded to this state of affairs. However, we can infer, on the basis of the sources we are about to analyze, that some Jews living in the second temple period were either dissatisfied with, or confused by, the biblical legacy. How are these two types of impurity related to one another? Are they to be identified to some degree? Or ought we clearly to separate the two? If sin is described as a source of impurity, does it defile ritually? In the remainder of this work, we will see that these were significant questions in the second temple period, ones that were answered differently by various groups of Jews. Philo, the sectarians at Qumran, the tannaim, and early Christians all had different answers to these questions.

After a brief discussion of Philo, the remaining chapters will be devoted to the ways in which the sectarians at Qumran, the tannaim (early rabbinic sages), and early Christians dealt with the relationship between ritual and moral impurity, and more generally the relationship between impurity and sin. These four are selected not because they were the only Jews or Jewish groups who left us their views on impurity or sin in general. Indeed, a great many other Jewish texts, as we saw in chapter 2, deal with the defiling force of sin. But I believe that these four were the only ones to leave

63

[handwritten: The main question is how they relate]

us clear answers to the question of how ritual and moral impurity were understood to relate to one another. ✳

We will proceed programmatically. We start with Philo, because his treatment of ritual and moral impurity is both brief and clear. We go then to Qumran, which holds a position between Philo and tannaitic literature: the Qumran corpus is comparatively brief, and its attitudes towards impurity and sin are relatively clear. We then examine tannaitic literature, which is much vaster, and yet contains fewer clear statements about the issue at hand. Finally we turn to the New Testament. This is to be treated last, despite the fact that it predates much (but not all, in my mind) tannaitic literature, because it will be argued that a proper understanding of the tannaitic approach to purity allows for a greatly enhanced understanding of the debate between Jesus and the Pharisees with regard to ritual purity.

Impurity and Sin in Philo's Thought

The Jewish-Hellenistic philosopher par excellence was Philo of Alexandria (c. 10 BCE–45 CE).[2] Philo's approach to impurity and sin is not only important for our discussion, but distinctive. Furthermore, it is rather clear as well. Philo is the one ancient Jewish author who tells us precisely what he thought of the relationship between ritual and moral impurity. It is Philo's clarity on this issue that justifies our dealing with his work only briefly.

In his treatise *Special Laws* (1: 256–261), Philo works out a relationship between ritual and moral impurity that could not be clearer:[3]

> We have described to the best of our ability the regulations for sacrifices and will next proceed to speak of those who offer them. The Law would have such a person pure in body and soul, the soul purged of its passions and distempers and infirmities and every viciousness of word and deed, the body of the things which commonly defile it. For each it devised the purifications which befitted it For the soul it used the animals which the worshiper is providing for sacrifice, for the body sprinklings and ablutions of which we will speak a little later.

Here Philo posits that there is an analogical, or allegorical, relationship between ritual and moral impurity.[4] According to Philo, the ritual impurity that results naturally and affects our bodies should teach us to direct our attention to the moral impurity that results from sin and afflicts our souls. As is the case in the Pentateuch, for Philo ritual impurity is resolved by ritual purification, while moral impurity is resolved by sacrificial acts of atonement.

Just as it was for Plato before him, purification of the soul is a major concern for Philo.[5] Again and again in his works, Philo expresses the concern for the purification of the soul from passions and various sins.[6] In this respect too, Philo's approach is similar to that of the Hebrew Bible,[7] for the Pentateuch also articulates the notion that sin can morally defile the sinner's person, even without ritually defiling the sinner's body (Lev. 18:24). But whereas the biblical notion of moral defilement focuses on idolatry, incest, and murder, Philo speaks much more generally in these passages about the defilement of the soul by all sorts of sins. And in the Hebrew Bible, the primary concern is that sin can defile the land, while Philo puts his emphasis on the defiling effect that sin has on the soul.[8] We will find, especially in chapter 6, that other ancient Jews also emphasized the effects that moral defilement has on the individual sinner, as opposed to the community of Israel as a whole.

Another nonscriptural aspect of Philo's view is his explicit analogy between ritual and moral impurity. As I argued in chapter 1, the Hebrew Bible does not articulate any such analogy.[9] Extending from his analogy, another important aspect of Philo's approach is the consistent and explicit prioritization of the concern for moral purity. For Philo, just as the soul is more important than the body, the purification of the soul is of greater consequence than purification of the body.[10] Indeed, it is the purification of the soul that is the prerequisite for immortality.[11] That is not to say that the laws of ritual impurity are to be ignored. To the contrary, what Philo says with regard to circumcision would apply to the laws regarding ritual impurity as well:[12]

> Nay, we should look on all these outward observances as resembling the body, and their inner meanings as resembling the soul. It follows that, exactly as we have to take thought for the body, because it is the abode of the soul, so we must pay heed to the letter of the laws.

Even so, the prioritization of the soul over the body, and thus the prioritization of moral purity over ritual purity, remains clear.[13]

In Philo's analogical approach to ritual and moral defilement, ritual impurity is not sinful, nor does it necessarily come about as a punishment for sin. Ritual impurity is for Philo, just as it is in Scripture, natural and often unavoidable.[14] Philo offers explanations of the ritual impurities that frequently involve moral lessons, but he does not cast blame on those who are ritually defiled.[15] Nor does he bestow inherent merit on those who are ritually pure.[16] For Philo, ritual impurity is not sinful, but it is a living reminder, by analogy, of the fact that sins defile the soul. By the same token, the moral defilement that afflicts the soul does not result in any ritual defilement. Sinners, according to Philo, ought to be excluded from the sanctuary,[17] but not because they are ritually defiling. Sinners are excluded from the sanctuary because their sins make them unworthy of encountering the sacred. That is, they are excluded from the sanctuary not because they have ritually impure bodies, but because they have morally impure souls.

Moral defilement in Philo's thought is by no means metaphorical, it is simply nonphysical. But it is after all the nonphysical world that is the true reality for Philo.[18] If anything, for Philo it is *ritual* impurity that is the metaphor.[19] At any rate, for Philo, as in Leviticus, there are two types of defilement. The (middle-)Platonic body/soul dualism that is so central to Philo's thought allows the philosopher to correlate the two ideas while at the same time maintaining the distinction between them.

Philo was anticipated, in a way, by Pseudo-Aristeas. In an extended treatment of Jewish dietary regulations (§§ 128–171), the author reflects as well on the purification of the soul and the defiling force of sin (§ 139):[20]

> In his wisdom, the legislator . being endowed by God for the knowledge of universal truths, surrounded us with unbroken palisades and iron walls to prevent our mixing with any of the other peoples in any matter being thus kept pure in body and

soul, preserved from false beliefs, and worshipping the only God omnipotent over all creation.

Assuming the author to be an observant Diaspora Jew, it is not at all surprising that he was keenly aware of the social ramifications of Jewish dietary laws. Still there is something strikingly to the point about this comment, which immediately follows a passage denigrating Gentile idolatry (§§ 134–138). The thrust of the argument, therefore, is that Jewish dietary laws serve to prevent Jews from participating in Gentile idolatrous practices. Later it is argued that these laws also serve to prevent the Jewish people from engaging in defiling sexual practices as well (§ 152). In addition to noting the social ramification of these laws, the author also discusses the symbolism inherent in the dietary restrictions. The prohibition of carnivorous birds translates into reluctance to "achieve anything by brute force" (§ 148). The split hoof "is a sign of setting apart each of our actions for good" (§ 150). And animal rumination is seen as analogous to human remembrance of God, the latter ought to be just as constant as the former (§§ 144–145). The laws are not just symbols, however: Like the fringes to be worn on garments (Num. 15:38–39), the dietary laws are to serve as constant behavioral reminders of God's Law. Moreover, the animals that are forbidden do not just represent or remind us of defilement, these animals actually do defile (§§ 164–166).

Toward the end of his treatment of the purity laws, *Aristeas* notes that impiety defiles the sinner (§§ 165–166):

> The species of weasel is unique: Apart from the aforementioned characteristic, it has another polluting feature, that of conceiving through its ears and producing its young through its mouth. So for this reason any similar feature in people is unclean; people who hear anything and give physical expression to it by word of mouth, thus embroiling other people in evil, commit no ordinary act of uncleanliness, and are themselves completely defiled with the taint of impiety. .
> [μιανθέτες αὐτοὶ παντάπασι τῷ τῆς ἀσεβείας μολυσμῷ].

It is not exactly clear, however, whether sin defiles the body or the soul. Nor is it clear what relationship, if any, this moral impurity has to what we have been referring to as ritual impurity. In fact, what is missing from the entire passage is any discussion of ritual purity law per se; nothing in this passage from *Aristeas* deals with the impermanent defilement resulting from contact with the sources of ritual impurity such as corpses or menstrual blood. What this passage does do is draw symbolic and practical connections between the biblical dietary laws and the idea that sins defile the sinner. Since no discussion of the ritual purity laws per se is evident, it is not possible to discern what *Aristeas* thought of the relationship between ritual and moral purity. It is therefore not possible to trace Philo's analogical approach to ritual and moral impurity back to *Aristeas*. Nor is it possible, simply by comparison to *Aristeas*, to argue that Philo's view was a common belief of Alexandrian Jewry.

3

Impurity and Sin in the Literature of Qumran

We turn in this chapter to the literature from Qumran. The focus will be on the texts that were not only unearthed at Qumran, but also generally recognized to have been composed by the group that settled there. Since our main concern is the approach taken toward impurity and sin in the sectarian documents, we will concentrate on those sectarian documents that treat these themes. Thus the analysis will focus most closely on the Community Rule (1QS), a major theme of which is the defiling force of sin. Other texts that will be examined include the Habakkuk Pesher (1QpHab), the Thanksgiving Scroll (1QH), the War Scroll (1QM), the Damascus Document (CD),[1] and some of the more fragmentary texts that were discovered in Qumran Cave Four, including the recently published *halakhic* letter, 4Q Miqsat Ma'aseh ha-Torah (4QMMT). Because the question of the identity of the sect remains a subject of scholarly debate, the descriptions of the Essenes by Philo, Josephus, and other classical authors will not be considered as evidence of Qumran sectarian practice.[2]

It has long been noticed that the Qumran sectarians associated sin with impurity in some way.[3] Even so, the scholarly treatment of the question has been both imprecise and insufficient, and there is agreement only on the most general point: that there is some association between impurity and sin at Qumran. Thus many important questions remain. Does sin defile ritually or morally? Is it the land, the sanctuary, or the person that is affected by the defiling force of sin? Is the approach taken to impurity and sin at Qumran distinctive and new, or is it largely similar to the approach taken by ancient Judaism in general? It is the goal of this chapter to answer as many of these questions as possible, by examining pertinent literature from Qumran in light of the conceptual framework and historical analyses presented in the previous chapters.

We will first note how a few trends that were identified in the previous chapters are also in evidence in the literature from Qumran (first section of the chapter). We will then turn to an analysis of what is most distinctive about the approach taken to ritual and moral impurity at Qumran: the nearly complete integration of the two once distinct ideas into one single conception of impurity that has both ritual and moral connotations (second section). Finally (third section), we will try to account for Qumran's innovative approach to ritual and moral impurity. In so doing, we will also consider a few general questions concerning the history of the sect, with the hope that the present analysis may shed some light on these questions too. By the end of this chapter, the differences between what is expressed in sectarian literature and what is expressed in the literature discussed earlier ought to be clear. Contrasts with the tannaim and early Christians must wait until later in this work.

Previous Trends Continued at Qumran

Moral Impurity in the Nonsectarian Dead Sea Scrolls

In chapter 2 it was noted that a number of texts composed by Jews in the second temple period articulate the concern, first expressed in the Hebrew Bible, that grave sins produce an impurity that results in the defilement of the land of Israel and the sanctuary of God. While there is no one-to-one correspondence between the Qumran finds and the second temple Jewish literature that expresses these ideas, it is noteworthy that so many of the texts discussed in that chapter can be tied to the sect at Qumran in some way, albeit indirect. Scholars knew of 1 Enoch and Jubilees long before scrolls started turning up at Qumran. Because multiple copies of each turned up among the manuscript finds, we can now assume that these documents were of some importance to the sect, even while most agree that they were almost certainly not composed there.[4] Scholars also knew of the Damascus Document before the discovery of additional copies at Qumran, and as has been noted, many scholars still believe that the document stems from the prehistory of the Qumran sect. Yet judging from the fact that at least ten copies of this work have been identified among the Qumran finds to date, we can presume that the Damascus Document too was of great import to the sect.[5] Unlike CD, the Temple Scroll was unknown before its discovery at Qumran, and even now only two copies have been unearthed. But the Temple Scroll too can likely be described as pre-Qumranic composition that was of great interest to the Qumran sectarians. Thus much of the literature reviewed in chapter 2 was of interest to the Qumran sectarians. There are exceptions of course: Not all of the ancient Jewish documents that are interested in the defiling force of sin have turned up at Qumran. In this category we could include the Psalms of Solomon and the Testament of Levi. In the end, however, the correspondence between the extant ancient Jewish texts that are interested in the defiling force of sin on the one hand and the Qumran finds on the other is remarkable. I believe it can therefore be stated with some degree of confidence, even before we examine the Qumran sectarian documents, that the sectarians at Qumran were probably more interested in the question of the defiling force of sin than were other contemporary Jews. Moreover, there may well be some linear connection here between the third- and second-century BCE Jews who composed 1 Enoch, Jubilees, the Damascus Document, and the Temple Scroll, and the second- and first-century Qumran sectarians.[6] For that reason, the possibility that the interest in the defiling force of sin was among these connections ought to be entertained.

Sin and the Sanctuary in the Habakkuk Pesher

In addition to the passages from the quasi-sectarian literature examined in chapter 2, at least one passage from the sectarian literature from Qumran articulates the idea that certain grave sins defile the sanctuary, morally. In the Habakkuk Pesher[7] (1QpHab) XII:6–9, the following commentary is offered for Habakkuk 2:17:[8]

> (6) "... On account of the bloodshed of (7) the town and violence [done to] the land" [Hab 2:17], the interpretation of it: the "town" is Jerusalem, (8) where the Wicked Priest committed abominable deeds [מעשי תועבות] and defiled [ויטמא] (9) God's sanctuary. And "violence [done to] the land" [refers to] the cities of Judah, where (10) he stole the wealth of the poor ones.

According to this indictment, the wicked priest committed abominable deeds and defiled God's sanctuary. These charges are vague indeed. What were these abominable deeds? In what way did the wicked priest in question defile the sanctuary?

We should begin, perhaps, with a more general question: Who was this wicked priest? Unfortunately, there is no agreement among scholars as to the identification of this priest. Almost every high priest of the Hasmonean period has been suggested as a candidate.[9] Indeed, when we consider the ritual and moral standards of the Dead Sea sectarians on the one hand, and the behavior of the Hasmonean high priests on the other, one encounters an embarrassment of riches: There was a whole slew of wicked priests. But in addition to debating the identity of the wicked priest, scholars now debate whether the Habakkuk Pesher was concerned with a single wicked priest at all. Indeed, an important element of the so-called "Groningen Hypothesis"[10] of Qumran origins is the suggestion that 1QpHab deals with a series of more or less wicked priests, in chronological order, from Judah the Maccabee to Alexander Jannaeus.[11] These questions are beyond the scope of this work but are mentioned here to underscore the fact that it would be extremely precarious to try to interpret the above passage of 1QpHab in light of any incident in the lifetime of a specific high priest known to us from 1 Maccabees or Josephus.

Because the wicked priest of 1QpHab XII cannot be identified, in order for us to determine the nature of the charges raised here against the wicked priest, we must limit ourselves to what can be extracted from the passage. We start with the first part of the charge, the performance of abominable acts (מעשי תועבות). The immediate context gives no clue other than the juxtaposition of abominable acts with the defilement of the sanctuary (to which we will return). The larger context (XII:9–10) makes it clear that stealing from the poor was among the evil deeds performed by this priest. Indeed, the Habakkuk Pesher as a whole is concerned with the thieving avarice of the wicked priest(s); the charge is raised in almost every pericope from column VIII to the end of the extant manuscript.[12] Thus it is safe to assume that the greed of the wicked priest(s) was indeed a serious concern for the author of the Habakkuk Pesher.

But is greed the essence of the charge that the high priest committed abominable deeds? This is indeed one possibility, and it is strengthened when one takes into account 1QpHab VIII:8–13, which exegetes Habakkuk 2:5–6. This is the only other passage in the Habakkuk Pesher that speaks of abominable deeds, and we find that this passage too juxtaposes a charge of greed with the performance of abominable deeds:

> (8) . . . The interpretation of it concerns the Wicked Priest, who (9) was called by the true name at the beginning of his course, but when he ruled (10) in Israel, he became arrogant, abandoned God, and betrayed the statutes for the sake of (11) wealth He stole and amassed the wealth of the men of violence who had rebelled against God, (12) and he took the wealth of peoples to add to himself guilty sin. And the abominable ways (13) he pursued with every sort of unclean impurity.

The key aspect of the passage for our concern is found in the last two lines (12–13), where the wicked priest in question is accused of pursuing "abominable ways" (דרכי ת[ו]עבות) "with every sort of unclean impurity" (בכול נדת טמאה).

In this passage we see, for the second time in 1QpHab, the juxtaposition of theft with abomination. It could be that the point of this passage is that the wicked priest committed theft and, perhaps, sexual abominations — and this possibility cannot be excluded. Indeed the passage employs not only the term "abomination" (תועבה) but also, like Ezra 9:11 and Leviticus 20:21, the term *niddah* (נדה). As we have seen, these terms were previously used with some frequency to convey the morally defiling force of sexual sin. But it is not likely that these terms refer here to sexual sins. In the next major section we will see that the terms נדה and תועבה are used throughout the Qumran corpus with reference not to any sin in particular, but to grave sin in general.[13] Thus it is, in fact, precarious to try to isolate the referent of the charge of abomination raised in 1QpHab VIII and XII at all. At Qumran, as will be seen, these terms could refer to almost any sinful behavior. But despite the wide use of these terms in the rest of the sectarian corpus, the fact remains that in the Pesher Habakkuk, the charge of abominable behavior is raised twice, and both times that charge is juxtaposed with the charge of theft. Indeed, it seems likely that the author considers theft to be the prime example of the defiling behavior of the wicked priest(s).[14] It is therefore worth pursuing the possibility that there is some connection between the two charges.

But whence comes the idea that avarice is an abomination? If we view the wicked priest's thieving avarice as an aspect of his arrogance, then everything begins to fall into place. Line 10 of 1QpHab VIII alleges that the wicked priest became arrogant (רם לבו). Brownlee has already identified some likely biblical inspirations for the idea that arrogance was abominable: Ezekiel 16:49–50 juxtaposes Sodom's haughtiness with her performance of abominations. Proverbs 16:5 is even more to the point: "Every haughty person is an abomination [תועבה] to the Lord."[15] What we add to Brownlee's analysis at this point is this: On the basis of these passages, it is possible that the author of 1QpHab has come to view arrogance — or more precisely, the greedy behavior that results from it — as an abomination. That is to say, the author of 1QpHab has possibly come to view arrogance as a source of what we have called moral impurity. If true, this would account for the juxtaposition of the charges of greed and abomination in Pesher Habakkuk VIII and XII.[16]

It is worth recalling here the analysis of 11QT LI:11–15 offered in "Temple Scroll" section of chapter 2. There it was argued that the Temple Scroll views bribery as a source of moral defilement, and it was suggested that the idea was based on an exegesis of Deuteronomy 25:13–16. What is being suggested here with regard to the Pesher Habakkuk is very similar. One possible explanation of 1QpHab XII:6–9 is that the author has come to view avarice as a source of moral defilement, and that view could very well be based on an exegesis of Proverbs 16:5.

The possibility that the general charges raised in 1QpHab XII were meant to involve even more serious crimes cannot be ruled out. As we saw in chapter 1, bloodshed is a source of moral defilement (Num. 35:33) that is commonly referred to as an abomination (e.g., Ezek. 22:1–12).[17] Bloodshed is also among the specific charges raised against the wicked priest(s) throughout the Pesher (X:9–10; XI:4–6). Thus because of the vague nature of the charges in 1QpHab VIII and XII, we are left with the following possibilities: that the abominations committed by the wicked priest(s) were acts of avarice or bloodshed, or that the charge of abomination refers, as it does elsewhere in the Qumran corpus, to grave sinfulness in general.

The next question regards the nature of the second charge raised against the wicked priest of 1QpHab XII: the defilement of the sanctuary. It is necessary first to entertain the possibility that what the priest has done is violate some norm of ritual purity, so that the sanctuary has become ritually defiled. This possibility cannot be dismissed out of hand, especially when one considers the serious questions of ritual purity law raised in 4QMMT (this document will be discussed later in this section). Yet the possibility is even greater, I think, that something other than the ritual defilement of the sanctuary is meant. The juxtaposition of abominable acts with the defilement of the sanctuary is, to my mind, enough to justify entertaining the possibility that the concern here is with the *morally* defiling force of the grave sins performed by the wicked priest. And the use of the term "abomination" (תועבה) underscores the possibility of such a connection, for this term is used generally in contexts of moral impurity, or sin in general, but not ritual defilement. As noted in "Moral Impurity" in chapter 1, in the Bible the term תועבה is used most often with regard to the sources of moral defilement: murder, idolatry, and forbidden sexual unions. But the term is applied to other sins as well, such as deceit (Deut. 25:15–16) and arrogance (Prov. 16:5). It seems likely that 1QpHab viewed avarice and arrogance as sources of moral defilement, and it is therefore distinctly possible that such is the force of the charge raised against the wicked priest of 1QpHab XII: The wicked priest has committed morally impure acts (abominations) and has by so doing defiled the sanctuary.

Moral impurity, as was argued in chapter 1, need not be conveyed to the sanctuary by direct contact. Thus while Brownlee, for instance, correctly points to passages such as Numbers 35:33 and Psalm 106 as inspirations for the charges raised against the wicked priest, he errs in stating that the defilement of the sanctuary would take place when the wicked priest entered it.[18] Bloodshed would indeed render the wicked priest impure (morally), but that defilement would affect the sanctuary anytime, not merely upon the priest's entry into the sanctuary. The error here is the idea that sinners are sources of ritual defilement; we have seen that this is not necessarily the case (recall that case of the suspected adulteress). It is possible, of course, that this text does articulate such a notion, since other Qumran literature will explicitly state that sinners are a source of ritual defilement (see the next major section). But in this case, I think the force of the charge against the wicked priest is not that it is bad for the High Priest to sin, because he could then defile the sanctuary *ritually* by entering it, but that it is bad for the High Priest, of all people, to be responsible for the *moral* defilement of the sanctuary that results from the performance of grave sin.

What we have seen here is this: Despite the fact that the Pesher Habakkuk is undoubtedly a sectarian work, it appears to articulate ideas about impurity and sin that are pretty much in line with what we have already seen: that the performance of grave sin has the power to defile the sanctuary, morally.

Impurity and Sin in 4Q Miqṣat Maʿaseh ha-Torah

We turn now to another text that can be tied to the Qumran sect in a rather direct way, but which also nonetheless articulates an approach to impurity and sin that is not necessarily distinctive to Qumran: the newly published document from Qumran Cave Four, 4Q Miqṣat Maʿaseh ha-Torah (4QMMT).[19] As will be seen, despite the fact that 4QMMT is greatly concerned with ritual impurity, the document — at least what we have of it — has very little to say about the defiling force of sin. Since we do not yet have a complete copy of the work, any analysis is necessarily inconclusive, but because of the notoriety of this text, and its presumed importance for determining the identification of the Qumran sect, it is worthwhile to include here a few comments about how the document treats the themes we are tracing.

The significance of 4QMMT can hardly be overstated. Although the document has not and will not provide the final word on the identity of the sect, 4QMMT will still contribute greatly to our knowledge of the history of the Qumran sect, because it is believed to stem from a very early period in the sect's history.[20] While the six extant manuscripts can be dated to the early and middle parts of the first century BCE, it is generally agreed that the composition itself stems from the middle of the second century BCE. Qimron supports this view with a number of lexical, literary, and historical arguments.[21] Intriguingly enough, the document seems to refer to the formation of the sect as a recent event: "[And you know that] we have separated ourselves from the multitude of the people." (C 7–8).[22] And despite the fact that the document refers to this separation, the letter maintains a conciliatory tone. While the later sectarian documents such as 1QM and 1QS articulate a radical, even spiteful, dualism, 4QMMT's tone is accurately described by Qimron as "eirenic."[23] All this suggests that the break between the authors[24] and the addressees was not yet seen as permanent at the time the letter was originally sent. In turn — along with other lexical and literary arguments — this points to the mid-second century BCE as the date of composition.[25] This dating also makes 4QMMT significant for the history of ancient Jewish law as whole: Most *halakhic* literature is widely believed to be much later indeed.[26]

In the third section of the previous chapter, we analyzed the approach taken to impurity and sin in what is most likely a protosectarian document, the Temple Scroll (11QT). As we will see, the approach to impurity and sin in 4QMMT is largely similar.[27] To start with the most general comparison, both works are concerned with legal praxis, and though the Temple Scroll is much greater in size than 4QMMT, a relatively significant portion of each work is devoted to issues of ritual impurity.[28] More specifically, on a number of legal disputes, 4QMMT and 11QT are in agreement.[29]

And important for our concerns is the fact that a few of the agreements between 11QT and 4QMMT concern issues of ritual impurity. Like the Temple Scroll, 4QMMT rejects the purity of the *tebul yom*: according to 4QMMT B 13–17, the priests who prepare the red heifer for the purification from corpse impurity are ritually impure until sunset.[30] Thus, in this case, both 11QT and 4QMMT advocate the position attributed to the Sadducees in M. Parah 3:7.[31] Also, like the Temple Scroll, 4QMMT is concerned with the danger that blind people may defile the sacred.[32] Although there are some points of disagreement between these texts,[33] these similarities are striking, and they argue strongly for some degree of connection between them.

These (and other) agreements between 11QT and 4QMMT on specific points of law are not the only similarities. These two documents also take a similar approach to purity issues.[34] First, both documents advocate some ritual purity legislation that is more stringent than what we hear of in the Pharisaic-rabbinic tradition. The rejection of the purity of the *tebul yom*, the concern that the blind will defile the sacred, and a generally strict attitude toward exclusions from sacred space — in all these respects, the legislation of these documents can be described as relatively stringent compared with both the Pentateuch and tannaitic sources.[35] Second, it is now well known that both 11QT and 4QMMT advocate some legal positions that were, according to rabbinic sources, advocated by Sadducees.[36] Third, it was noted in chapter 2 that 11QT articulates what can be called an "expansive" approach to the realm of the sacred.[37] The same can be said of 4QMMT: It appears that 4QMMT considers the entire city of Jerusalem to have the sanctity of the biblical war camp.[38] Thus both documents appear to expand the realm of the sacred, in comparison with the Pentateuch: Both texts are interested in keeping more people farther away from the sanctum. In this regard, both documents can be said to be following in the line of Ezekiel 40–48.[39]

One further point of comparison can be made. Both 11QT and 4QMMT are texts that are tied to the Qumran sect in some way — the latter more directly than the former, in my view — and neither text articulates the distinctively Qumranic approach to impurity and sin. Despite all the stringent attitudes toward exclusion and ritual defilement that *are* articulated in 4QMMT, there is no indication in the extant fragments of this document that the authors considered sin to be ritually defiling, or that they otherwise integrated the previously distinct ideas of moral and ritual impurity. In fact, there is no indication that they had a dispute with their addressees concerning the defiling force of sin. In a way, one could draw a contrast between 11QT and 4QMMT on this point, because as we saw in chapter 2, 11QT does at a few points articulate the previously known idea of moral defilement, and it even expands the notion in a way, by viewing bribery as a source of moral impurity. 4QMMT, on the other hand, does not raise the issue of moral defilement at all. In truth, however, this is not much of a contrast. 4QMMT is a terse polemic, and the issues raised in it are subjects of controversy. Thus 11QT's relatively standard treatment of the notion of moral impurity and 4QMMT's avoidance of the issue are, in a way, parallel. What is more, neither document expresses any awareness of the integration of moral and ritual impurity that is characteristic of the Rule of the Community.

This is, of course, an argument from silence. Since we do not have at our disposal a complete version of 4QMMT, or of 11QT for that matter, it is a particularly precarious argument from silence. Nonetheless, the silence in this case is, I believe, meaningful. 4QMMT articulates a number of concerns with ritual impurity, but none relating to moral impurity. Its silence with regard to moral impurity becomes even more striking when one recalls that it does appear to address purity issues with regard to Gentiles. Although this is not always the case, discussions of moral impurity often go hand-in-hand with discussions of the behavior of Gentiles (e.g., Lev. 18, Ezra 9, and Jubilees 22). But while 4QMMT does discuss the status of Gentiles, the issue of moral impurity is not raised at all.

At least two of the *halakhot* in 4QMMT deal with the status of Gentiles — more precisely, the grain and sacrifices of Gentiles. 4QMMT B 3–5 presents a ruling dealing with Gentile grain. The text is poorly preserved, and even the restored topic — "concerning the sowed gifts of the new wheat grains of Gentiles" — is doubtful.[40] Nonetheless, it is generally agreed that there is some concern here with the purity of Gentiles' grain. 4QMMT B 9–11 contains another poorly preserved ruling dealing with the offerings of Gentiles. This one apparently prohibits sacrificial offerings from Gentiles altogether.[41]

How are we to evaluate these traditions? Were such sacrifices limited or even banned because 4QMMT considered Gentiles to be impure in some way? When dealing with such laws, one needs to distinguish between exclusions based on ritual impurity and exclusions based on class.[42] According to Josephus, for instance, all women, whether ritually impure or not, were excluded from entering the temple beyond the court reserved for them.[43] From this law we learn that an exclusion from the sacred is not necessarily tantamount to a declaration that those who are excluded are ritually impure.[44] On the other hand, rabbinic law permits the offerings of Gentiles, even as it decrees that Gentiles are to be considered ritually impure.[45] From this we learn that even those who are not fully excluded from the cult could still be considered ritually impure. In short, while categories of those excluded from the temple and those considered ritually impure overlap, they are not identical. Exclusions from the temple are also determined on the basis of status and class. Thus, despite 4QMMT's concern with the sacrifices of Gentiles, it cannot be said with certainty that the authors considered Gentiles to be ritually impure.[46]

What is notable for our purposes is this final point: Not only is 4QMMT unaware of the inherent ritual impurity of Gentiles, it appears to be equally unaware of their inherent moral impurity. It cannot be said with certainty that the authors of 4QMMT considered Gentiles to be inherently morally impure. It is certainly possible that they did, but the idea is not explicitly articulated, even when the subjects of Gentiles and their offerings are raised. As we will soon see, a number of sectarian texts are indeed concerned with the morally impure behavior of Gentiles and nonsectarian Jews. These texts are also concerned with the power of that morally impure behavior to render those outsiders ritually defiling. But the idea that nonsectarians behave in a necessarily morally impure manner and are as a result ritually impure is absent from both 11QT and 4QMMT. This silence is one more thing that these two texts share when compared with sectarian documents such as 1QS.

In this section we have seen that the literature of Qumran has some degree of continuity with what came before it. First, we noted that among the Qumran finds there are a large number of copies of the nonsectarian or protosectarian works identified in chapter 2 as having an interest in the defiling force of sin. This fact suggests, at the very least, that the Qumran sectarians were aware of and interested in the traditional concept of moral defilement. Second, we noted that the Pesher Habakkuk raises charges against the wicked priest which can be interpreted as a straightforward articulation of the idea of moral defilement: The wicked priest has performed evil deeds and is thereby responsible for the moral defilement of the sanctuary. Third, we noted that 4QMMT articulates a number of sectarian *halakhot* regarding ritual purity, without articulating what is distinctively sectarian: the integration of ritual and moral impurity into a single conception of defilement. It is to this distinctive aspect of the sectarian literature from Qumran that we now turn. *4QMMT doesn't define this*

The Identification of Ritual and Moral Impurity at Qumran

In the sectarian literature from Qumran, we see, for the first time in ancient Jewish literature, an articulated response to the question of the relationship between ritual and moral impurity. Of course our question was not asked of the sectarians in our terms, and we will therefore not find any single phrase or statement in the Qumran literature that answers the question fully. On the other hand, subtlety is not one of the characteristics of the sectarian literature from Qumran. Therefore, we can see all too easily how the sectarians would have answered our question if we somehow had the opportunity to ask it. I will try now to describe in some detail the approach taken to impurity and sin at Qumran. What will emerge from the analysis is this: At Qumran the once distinct concepts of ritual and moral impurity were merged into a single conception of defilement. That is, what we see at Qumran is not merely an association between ritual and moral impurity, but a basically complete identification of ritual and moral impurity.

There are, as I see it, five ways in which the identification of ritual and moral impurity manifests itself in the sectarian literature of Qumran. First, very frequently, sins — and not just those enumerated in Leviticus 18, but all sins — are described as impurities. Second, outsiders, who by definition sin, are assumed to be ritually pure. Third, insiders are not to sin, and those who do are likewise considered defiling. Fourth, initiation involves not only moral repentance, but ritual purification. Finally, instances of ritual defilement among insiders seem to be assumed to result from sin: The ritual purification of insiders involves repentance too. The first four of these notions can most clearly be seen in The Rule of the Community (1QS), but they are in evidence also in the Damascus Document (CD),[47] The Thanksgiving Scroll (1QH), and the Pesher Habakkuk (1QpHab), as well as other documents. The fifth notion can most clearly be seen in 4Q Purification Ritual (4Q512) and is in evidence elsewhere too.

Sin as Defilement

The use of impurity terminology in the context of sin is, of course, not an innovation of the Qumran sectarians. Scripture itself uses the terminology of impurity with regard to sin, both literally in the sense of moral defilement, and also on occasion in figurative ways (see "Moral Impurity as a Metaphor?" in chapter 1). As was demonstrated in chapter 2, a number of ancient Jewish texts refer to the power of certain sins to defile sinners, the land of Israel, and the sanctuary of God. But as we will see presently, there is something very distinctive about the way in which this terminology is employed with regard to sin at Qumran.

In 1QS columns III–IV, the ways of good and evil are clearly contrasted. In IV:10–11, the way of the Spirit of Deceit is described in these terms:[48]

ורוב חנפ קצור אפים ורוב אולת וקנאת זדון מעשי תועבה ברוח זנות ודרכי נדה בעבודת טמאה
ולשון גדופום עורון עינים ...

(10) great hypocrisy,[49] fury, great vileness, shameless zeal for abominable works in a spirit of fornication, filthy ways in impure worship, (11) a tongue of blasphemy, blindness of eyes.

When in the end of days the Spirit of Deceit meets its end, those once under its power are to be purified from "all the abominations of falsehood and from being polluted by a spirit of impurity" (IV:21–22; מכול תועבות שקר והתגולל ברוח נדה). Similar descriptions of sin as defilement can be found elsewhere in 1QS (IV:5; V:19), as well as throughout the Qumran corpus, as we will see.

At this point it must be stated that these passages are not concerned with violations of ritual purity law, strictly speaking. It is clear from the context that they are not referring to matters such as the debate about the status of the *tebul yom*. The last four words 1QS IV:10 are, "filthy ways in impure worship" (דרכי נדה בעבודת טמאה); there is no way to understand this phrase except to assume that the language of ritual impurity (טמאה and נדה) is being used to describe not specific violations of ritual purity law, but grave sinfulness in general. – *Abominable worship is grave sin.*

Then exactly what kind of sins are of concern here? It would appear that 1QS is not all that discriminating in this regard. One term that shows up rather frequently to refer to evil in general is "deceit" (עול, e.g., III:19, 21; IV:9). It is important to note that deceit is referred to as an abomination (IV:17). The Community Rule's juxtaposition of deceit and abomination is also noteworthy because, as we have seen, there is a scriptural basis for this idea (Deut. 25:16): "For everyone who does those things, everyone who deals dishonestly [עול], is abhorrent [תועבה] to the Lord your God." In the Hebrew Bible, of course, the passage is meant to illustrate God's hatred of deceit, and in the Temple Scroll and the tannaitic midrashim, as we have seen, it is understood to mean that deceit produces moral defilement.[50] But for the sectarians, a number of developments have taken place. First, deceit as abomination is no longer just a question of moral impurity, as it is in the Temple Scroll and the tannaitic midrashim. Deceit in 1QS is both morally abominable (IV:9–10) *and* ritually defiling (IV:21; VII:17–18).[51] What is more, 1QS appears to understand the meaning of the term in the widest sense possible. It is not just specific deceitful acts that are viewed as morally defiling, as in the Temple Scroll and the tannaitic midrashim. In 1QS, the concepts of evil and deceit overlap and interchange: The phrase "the people of deceit" is synonymous with "sons of darkness" (III:21; VIII:13). It is for this reason that the people of truth—the sectarians—are to separate themselves from the people of deceit (V:1–2, 10; VIII:13), just as what is defiling is to be kept separate from what is pure (e.g., 1QS VI:25; cf. CD VII:3). The idea of deceit,

widely understood as a source of both moral and ritual impurity is one of the linch-
pins of 1QS.

An important and distinctive aspect of the passages noted so far is the fact that a
term previously associated primarily with what we have called moral impurity —
"abomination" (תועבה) — is used in the sectarian literature much more widely, and
with reference, it would appear, to all sorts of sin. In the Hebrew Bible the term is
used primarily with regard to sexual, idolatrous, and murderous sins, and secondar-
ily (and metaphorically) with regard to sinfulness in general.[52] In the Qumran corpus, the term תועבה consistently refers to grave sin in general. Consider the following passage from the Thanksgiving Scroll (1QH XIX [XI]:10–11):[53]

... ולמען כבודכה טהרתה אנוש מפשע להתקדש

... לכה מכול תועבות נדה ואשמת מעל

(10) . For your glory, you have purified man from sin, so that he can make himself holy (11) for you from every impure abomination and blameworthy iniquity.

The shift back and forth here from sin to abomination and back to sin again makes
it clear, I think, that the term "abomination" (תועבה) is meant to refer not to a restricted set of sins, but, as suggested by context, to sinfulness in general. Usage of the
term תועבה to refer to sinfulness in general can be seen elsewhere in the Qumran
corpus as well. One can compare 1QS IV:21 "abominations of falsehood" (תועבות
שקר) and 1QpHab VIII:12–13 and XII:8, quoted earlier.

Another purity term that is used widely in these passages is the term *niddah* (נדה),
which in the Hebrew Bible is used primarily with regard to menstruation (e.g, Lev.
15).[54] Of course, figurative use of this term can also be found in Scripture. Ezekiel,
for instance, states that the sinful ways of Israel have made the people like a menstruating woman in the eyes of God (Ezek. 36:17), and Lamentations compares the
solitude of the conquered city of Jerusalem to the isolation of a menstruant (Lam.
1:8). On occasion the term is used in Scripture with regard to moral impurity as well:
Leviticus 20:21 uses it to express the abominable nature of an incestuous relationship.
As we saw in chapter 2, נדה is employed in a moral impurity context in Ezra–
Nehemiah (Ezra 9:11).[55]

In the sectarian literature from Qumran, however, the usage of the term נדה is
much less restricted.[56] A good example can be seen in the passage from 1QS IV:10
quoted above: "shameless zeal for abominable works in a spirit of fornication, filthy
ways in impure worship" (וקנאת זדון מעשי תועבה ברוח זנות ודרכי נדה בעבודת טמאה). The
phrase takes Ezekiel's simile one step further. Ezekiel 36:17 compares Israel's ways to
that of a menstruant (כטמאת הנדה היתה דרכם לפני). Indeed, 1QS employs the same simile in V:19–20 (וכול מעשיהם לנדה לפניו). But in 1QS IV:10, quoted above, there is no
simile: The term נדה itself connotes Israel's sinfulness. The same shift is in evidence
in the Damascus Document. Like Ezekiel 36, CD II:1 compares Israel's sinfulness
to a menstruant: "their works were like an impurity before him" (ומעשיהם לנדה לפניו).
But the document later speaks of Israel's sinfulness as impurity itself (III:17): "Rather,
they wallowed in human sin and in the ways of impurity" (והם התגוללו בפשע אנוש
ובדרכי נדה).

These passages are by no means the only examples from the Qumran literature
of the use of the term נדה to refer to sinfulness in general. In 1QS IV:5, the principle

of the Spirit of Truth involves "a glorious purity, loathing all impure idols" (טהרת כבוד מתעב כול גלולי נדה). And when ultimately, the spirit of humankind is purified (1QS IV:20–22), God

> (20) . . . will purify by his truth all the works of man and purge for himself the sons of man. He will utterly destroy the spirit of deceit from the veins of (21) his flesh He will purify him by the Holy Spirit from all ungodly acts and sprinkle upon him the Spirit of Truth like waters of purification [כמי נדה], [to purify him] from all the abominations of falsehood and from being polluted (22) by a spirit of impurity [מכול תועבות שקר והתגולל ברוח נדה].

While the usage of the term נדה in the expression "waters of purification" reflects a standard biblical usage (cf. e.g., Num. 19:9), the second usage in the passage is a further example of the phenomenon we are tracing: the use of the term נדה to refer to grave sins in general.

Further examples can be seen in the following passages:

1QS XI:14–15: "purify me of human impurity" (יטהרני מנדת אנוש).

1QM XIII:5: "may they [the spirits of Belial] be cursed for all their service of unclean impurity!" (וזעומים המה בכול עבודת נדת טמאתם).

1QH IV (XVII):19: "because I wallowed in impurity" (כי בנדה התגוללתי).

1QH IX (I):22: "foundation of shame, source of impurity, oven of iniquity, building of sin" (סוד הערוה ומקור הנדה כור העון ומבנה החטאה); cf. XX (XII):25.

1QH XIX (XI):11: "every impure abomination and blameworthy iniquity" (תועבות נדה ואשמת מעל).

4Q Purification Ritual (512) frgs 29–32, VII:9: "purified me from impure immodesty" (ותטהרני מערות נדה).

In all of these passages, the term נדה is used in a way that is characteristic of the sectarian literature of Qumran: The term describes moral sinfulness.[57]

It is important to compare these usages with what we find in the Temple Scroll, which is widely considered to be protosectarian, and with what we find in 4QMMT, which is widely considered to stem from the formative period of the Qumran sect. It is interesting that the Temple Scroll uses these terms (נדה and תועבה) exclusively within the semantic range tolerated by Scripture itself. Indeed, we can be even more specific: These terms in 11QT are restricted to usages that have precise analogues in the Pentateuch. Thus "abomination" (תועבה) is used in 11QT XLVIII:6 with reference to unpermitted food (cf. Deut. 14:3); in LII:4–5 (twice) with regard to the sacrifice of a maimed or pregnant cow (cf. Deut. 17:1); in LX:17–21 (three times) with regard to the idolatrous behavior of Gentiles (cf. Deut. 18:9–12); and finally in LXVI:14–17 (twice) with regard to prohibited sexual practices (cf. Lev. 18 and 20). In each of these cases, there is an explicit scriptural analogue to the usage.

The same is true of the Temple Scroll's use of the term *niddah* (נדה): In XLIX:18 the term is used with regard to the water of purification (cf. Num. 19:20), and in LXVI:13 it is used with reference to a prohibited sexual practice (cf. Lev. 20:21). In XLV:10 and XLVIII:16–17 the phrase "menstrual impurity" (נדת טמאתם) is used with regard to the ritually defiling force of genital emissions (the same phrase is used with reference to a menstruous woman in Lev. 18:19).[58] Although this last phrase is used in the Qumran corpus with regard to sin (e.g., 1QpHab VIII:12–13; 1QH XIX [XI]:11; 1QM XIII:5), the use of the phrase in the Temple Scroll is analogous again to its use in the Pentateuch: it refers only to the ritually defiling force of genital discharges.

We turn now to 4QMMT. The term *niddah* (נדה) does not appear in the extant fragments of this work. The term "abomination" (תועבה) is used in C 6–7, and although the passage is fragmentary, it is clear that the usage in question is based on Deuteronomy 7:26. Thus once again we can draw a close comparison between 11QT and 4QMMT: Both use these terms only within the semantic ranges allowed by the Pentateuch. Once again we can draw a clear contrast between the approach taken to impurity in 11QT and 4QMMT and that taken in, for example, 1QS. In the full-blown sectarian literature from Qumran, as we have seen, the terms נדה and תועבה are commonly used to refer not to ritual or moral defilement in particular, but to sins in general. And this difference in linguistic usage is related to a greater difference in ideology. In the full-blown sectarian literature from Qumran, sin in general is viewed as a defilement in a way, as we will see, that is much more developed. But this distinctively sectarian approach to impurity and sin is nowhere in evidence in either the Temple Scroll or 4QMMT.

Before we turn again to the later, sectarian texts, one other point ought to be made. We noted above in the discussion of 4QMMT that some scholars have emphasized the significance of a number of parallels between Qumran sectarian law on the one hand, and traditions attributed to the Sadducees in rabbinic literature on the other. Indeed, these parallels are striking and undeniable. But we can point now to one very important difference between their approaches to purity. The Qumran sectarians were greatly concerned with the defiling force of sin — and, as we will see, the *ritually* defiling force of sin. Yet I know of no ancient Jewish source, rabbinic or otherwise, that would lead us to believe that Sadducees considered sin to be a source of ritual defilement.

Sinful Outsiders as Ritually Defiling

The passages analyzed above, which refer to sin as defiling, are not metaphorical.[59] This fact can be seen quite clearly since the documents that describe outsiders' sins as impure also assume those outsiders to be ritually defiling.[60] This is the second way in which the identification of impurity and immorality manifests itself at Qumran. Outsiders[61] were not permitted to eat of the community's pure food, lest they ritually defile it (1QS V:13–14):

...אל יבוא במים לגעת בטהרת אנשי הקודש כיא לוא יטהרו

כי אם שבו מרעתם כיא טמא בכול עוברי דברו ...

(13) . . [The outsider] must not enter the water in order to touch the purity of the men of holiness. For they cannot be purified (14) unless they turn away from their wickedness, for [he remains] impure among all those who transgress His words.

Compare III:4–6, which also precludes the possibility that an unrepentant outsider[62] could become ritually pure:[63]

... לוא יזכה בכפורים ולוא יטהר במי נדה ולוא יתקדש בימים
ונהרות ולוא יטהר בכול מי רחצ טמא טמא יהיה כול יומי מואסו במשפטי
אל לבלתי התיסר ביחד עצתו ...

(4) . . . He [the one who refuses to enter the covenant of God; cf. II:25–6] cannot be purified by atonement, nor cleansed by waters of purification, nor sanctify himself in streams (5) and rivers, nor cleanse himself in any waters of ablution. Impure, impure is he, as long as he rejects the judgments of (6) God, so that he cannot be instructed within the Community of his [God's] counsel.

It is not only the outsiders' deeds and bodies that are impure, but their property as well (V:19–20; cf. CD VI:14):

... וכול מעשיהם לנדה
לפניו וטמא בכול הון[ו]ם . . . .

(19) . . . and all their works are unclean (20) before him, and all their property is impure.

→ Innovation → even Gentiles

That the deeds, bodies, and even property of outsiders were considered by the sectarians to be ritually impure seems clear.

But then we must ask, who were these outsiders? It is indisputable that the scroll is speaking, at the very least, of nonsectarian Jews. The real question is whether the sectarians would have lumped all outsiders—Jews and Gentiles—into a single category where ritual impurity is concerned. This question is rather difficult to answer, despite the wealth of Qumranic material relating to ritual impurity. The fact remains that one would be hard-pressed to find an unambiguous legal pronouncement in the sectarian literature of Qumran to the effect that Gentiles were considered to be ritually impure.[64] Yet there is some evidence that they *were* so considered: Both Hannah K. Harrington and Christine E. Hayes have recognized the lack of definitive proof but argue nonetheless that Gentiles were considered to be ritually impure at Qumran.[65] While I accept the conclusions of their recent studies, I base my conclusion on a different argument.

key point

One piece of evidence is what Josephus says of the Essenes: that they bathed after contact with outsiders (*Jewish War* II:150).[66] But as was noted at the beginning of this chapter, we cannot involve ourselves here with the question of the identification of the Qumran sectarians with the Essenes. So for the sake of argument, we turn to evidence from the Qumran literature.

We need to consider the fact that the sectarians believed that proselytes were to be excluded from the temple.[67] The key texts to this effect include 11QT XXXIX:5–7, XL:6, and 4QForilegium 3–4. These texts have been analyzed in sufficient detail elsewhere.[68] What is important here is this: In the final analysis, the issue of the status of proselytes within the sectarian community has very little to do with the question of the ritual purity status of outsiders. First, proselytes, by definition, are no longer outsiders, and thus it is precarious to try to determine the status of outsiders at Qumran from what we know about the status of proselytes. Even more to the point is the fact that the exclusion of proselytes from the temple most likely reflects their postconversion status within the community, and not their preconversion condition of ritual impurity.[69] As I have argued already,[70] exclusions from the sanctuary are not by any means based entirely on conceptions of purity. Status plays an equally important role (e.g., in the case of women). As Hayes recognizes, the exclusion of proselytes from the temple in the sectarian literature from Qumran is very likely a reflection of the belief that converts were of a lower status than born Israelites.[71] In end, these passages from the Qumran texts are related to the question of the impurity of Gentiles only indirectly.[72]

We consider, finally, the evidence of comparison: the fact that Ethiopian Jews considered Gentiles to be ritually defiling, a point that Harrington notes in her discussion of the impurity of Gentiles.[73] It was once commonly believed that Ethiopian Jewish praxis represented a primitive (i.e., ancient) form of Judaism.[74] Recent scholarship, however, argues convincingly that it would be precarious indeed to call into evidence the ritual of Ethiopian Jews when trying to determine the practice of ancient Jews.[75] With regard, in particular, to the Ethiopian Jews' conception of outsiders as ritually impure (the laws of *attenkugn*), and the relevance of that information for the issue of ritual Gentile impurity in ancient Judaism, the following points are important to bear in mind: (1) The Ethiopian Jews themselves trace their distinct purity laws (including the laws of *attenkugn*) only back to the fifteenth century.[76] (2) From what we can reconstruct of the history of Ethiopian Judaism, it becomes quite clear that their religious traditions, like those of all other peoples, evolved over time.[77] Thus it is extremely problematic — if not completely "untenable," as Steven Kaplan puts it[78] — to try to determine ancient Jewish practice by calling into evidence the practices of Ethiopian Jewry.

Yet there is little doubt in my mind that the sectarians considered Gentiles to be a source of ritual impurity. Persuasive evidence can be found, however, not in the references noted above, nor by comparison with the practices of Ethiopian Jews. The evidence is to be found, rather, in the Qumran texts that deal more generally with sin and its defiling force.

The sectarians clearly considered Jewish nonmembers to be ritually defiling, and this view was related to the nonmembers' alleged sinfulness — this, as was argued above, is the plain meaning of 1QS III:4–6 and V:13–14. The sectarians can be presumed to have considered Gentiles to be sinful as well. Consider the following phrase from the extant fragments of the Pesher Nahum (4QpNah frgs. 3–4, III:1):[79]

הגוים בנדתם [ובש]קוצי תועבותיהם . . .

the nations because of their impurity [and because of] the [fi]lth of their abominations.

It appears that the sins of Gentiles are on a par with those of nonsectarian Jews: Both groups' sins are a source of defilement to the sectarians just the same.

To these observations we must add one other. The sectarians were dualists. There were, in their view, two fundamental social categories: the sons of light, and the sons of darkness. By "sons of light," they were referring, as is nearly universally recognized, to themselves. By "sons of darkness," they were referring, it seems, to everyone else. That would include, necessarily, not only nonsectarian Jews, but all Gentiles as well.

That the scope of sectarian anthropology included *all* humanity, and not just

Jews, is quite clear. The Rule of the Community frequently refers to God's creation of all humankind, and of the division of all humankind into these two categories (1QS III:13, 17–19):

(13) It is for the Master to instruct and teach all the Sons of Light concerning the nature of all the sons of man,
(17) . . He created the human for the dominion of (18) the world, designing for him two spirits in which to walk until the appointed time for his visitation, namely the spirits of (19) truth and deceit.

That God created *all* humankind, and that *all* humankind is under the power of one spirit or the other is articulated elsewhere in 1QS and throughout the Qumran corpus.[80] Finally, the War Scroll catalogs the sons of darkness and makes it quite clear that the enemies in question are Gentile nations (1QM I:1–2; II:9–14). Thus when the sectarians speak of the sinful impurity of the sons of darkness (1QM XIII:4–5) or of the abominable behavior of those under the spirit of deceit (1QS IV:10–11), it is fairly safe to infer that they had in mind all outsiders, nonsectarian Jews as well as Gentiles. Therefore, the selections from 1QS quoted earlier in the "Sin as Defilement" section should be understood as referring to all outsiders, both Gentiles and nonsectarian Jews. And the meaning of these passages is this: The sectarians considered all outsiders to be ritually defiling, as a result of their morally sinful behavior.

Sinful Insiders as Ritually Defiling

Despite their dualism and predeterminism, the sectarians recognized that sin was not exclusively in the domain of the sons of darkness. Members too could sin. And what happened when they did? It appears that the identification of ritual and moral impurity at Qumran knew no boundaries. The sins of insiders, too, were believed to bring about ritual defilement.

According to the Rule of the Community, insiders who transgress are, like outsiders, banned from the community's pure-food (טהרת רבים).[81] That is, sinful insiders, just like outsiders, were considered to be ritually defiling. This idea is articulated in the following passage from 1QS (VI:24–25), which introduces the section of the document often referred to as the penal code (VI:24–VII:25):[82]

(24) . . . If a man among them is found who lies (25) about property, and he knows [his deception], he shall be excluded from the midst of the pure-food of the Many [for] one year, and be fined one fourth of his food.

The penal code legislates similar punishments for a whole host of crimes, ranging from blasphemy, which is punished by permanent banishment, to interrupting a fellow's speech, which results in a ten-day punishment. For some crimes (e.g., speaking angrily against a priest; VII:2–3), it is stipulated that the guilty party is both to be excluded from pure-food and to suffer a reduction in rations. For other crimes, (e.g., speaking angrily but unintentionally against a priest; VII:3), only the reduction of rations is stipulated. For still other crimes (as in the above-mentioned prohibition of interrupting a fellow's speech; VII:9–10), only the duration of punishment is stipulated. In these cases (VII:9–11), it is not stated whether the duration of time refers to a reduction of rations or an exclusion from pure-food, or both.[83]

The question here is this: How are we to understand the text when only one of the two punishments is stipulated? One approach is taken by Lawrence Schiffman, who sets forth a compelling argument that the penal code stipulates punishments with consistent precision.[84] Noting how, in the passage quoted above, the banishment is introduced by the verb "exclude" (בדל) and the fine with the verb "punish" (ענש), Schiffman argues that these two verbs continue to have precisely those meanings throughout the penal code. He argues that because a few laws are explicit in stipulating both an exclusion and a fine, when only a fine is mentioned we then ought not assume that an exclusion too is intended. The other possibility is that the code employs ellipsis that for stylistic reasons, unnecessary repetition is avoided. According to this approach, which is taken by Licht and Newton, all of the sins in the penal code are to be punished with both a fine and exclusion.[85]

If we were to adopt Schiffman's approach, it would not be accurate to say that the sectarians recognized the ritually defiling force of all sins committed by insiders, for only some sins in the penal code are said to be punishable by exclusion from pure-food. At the very least, though, the Qumran sectarians did recognize the ritually defiling force of the sins that are punished in this way, for that would be the reasonable justification for banning these sinners from the pure-food. Thus no matter what, we can still say that the sectarians recognize the ritually defiling force of the following sins: lying about property (VI:24–25), speaking angrily against a priest intentionally (VII:2–3), insulting a fellow member intentionally (VII:4–5), slandering a fellow member (VII:15–16), and dealing treacherously with the truth (VII:18–21). And of course, the crimes of blasphemy (VII:1–2) and slander (VII:16–17) result in permanent banishment and thus would also presumably be considered ritually defiling. In addition, it is generally recognized that the phrase "and excluded" is to be restored in VI:27, which would mean that the crimes of stubbornness and impatience delineated in VI:25–26 would also be believed to defile the sinner ritually.

It is important to note that none of these sins has anything to do with the violation of ritual purity norms.[86] Moreover, they are not sins that were considered to bring about moral defilement in the Holiness Code (idolatry, incest, murder). We pointed above to passages from the Temple Scroll and the Pesher Habakkuk that consider acts of bribery and theft to be sources of moral impurity,[87] and it was suggested that this view finds its base in the scriptural passages that refer to these crimes as abominations.[88] This tendency has become full-blown in the penal code of the Rule of the Community, with the result that all sorts of acts of deceit and arrogance have come to be understood as sources of defilement. And because the Rule of the Community recognizes no distinction between ritual and moral impurity, these moral sins were considered to bring about ritual impurity. *Conflate and tighten*

But then the question arises, if *only* those sins for which banishment from the pure-food is explicitly stipulated were considered to bring about ritual defilement, then what of the others? Why were some sins considered defiling but not the rest? The answer, I believe, is that *all* these sins were considered defiling, and the punishment of banishment is to be understood as stipulated even where it is not explicitly stated. As has been noted, for a number of the sins, the only thing specified is the duration of the punishment, not the nature of the punishment itself. Consider the following passage (VII:9–10): "(9) . . . Whoever speaks during his fellow's speech (10) ten days." Clearly, something needs to be filled in here. But what? Schiffman suggests that what is intended is a ten day reduction of rations. He identifies a trend in the penal code to "abbreviate progressively," by which he means that those passages specifying only a duration of punishment have in mind only the punishment spelled out in the more detailed passage that immediately precedes the law in question.[89] Thus in the passage quoted above, we are to understand that what is intended is a reduction of rations for the period of time specified.

This is certainly one possibility, but I am not sure that the terminology in the code is that consistent, especially once we recognize that a number of the clauses fail to specify the nature of the punishment altogether. Since the passage just quoted exhibits ellipsis, why can't we suppose that any number of the punishment clauses leave out one factor or another? Moreover, the problems of interpreting the penal code do not stop here. It is generally recognized that the penal code of the sect is some sort of composite and may well be a liturgical summary of a much larger criminal code.[90] Making matters more complex, the manuscript itself exhibits both gaps and corrections.[91] Thus when we confine ourselves to the code itself, discerning exactly what punishments are intended for the crimes listed remains problematic.

There are, however, two passages in the Qumran corpus that appear to state explicitly that *all* sins of insiders are punished with banishment from pure-food. In my view, both Licht and Newton are correct in interpreting the punishments of the penal code in light of these more general statements of principle.[92] The first passage is in the Rule of the Community itself (VIII:16–18):

> (16) . . . No man of the men of the Community of the covenant of (17) the Community, who strays from any one of the ordinances deliberately may touch the pure-food of the men of holiness (18) nor know any of their counsel, until his works have become purified from all deceit by walking with those perfect of the Way

The other passage is from the Damascus Document IX:16–23:

> (16) . Any trespass committed by (17) a man against the Torah, which is witnessed by his neighbor — he being but one — if it is a capital matter, he shall report it (18) before his eyes with reproof to the Examiner. And the Examiner shall write it down with his hand until he does it (19) again before one who again reports it to the Examiner. If he is again caught in the presence of one, (20) his judgment is complete. And if they are two and they testify about (21) different things, the man shall only be separated from the purity, provided they are (22) reliable. And on the day when a man sees it, he shall make it known to the Examiner And concerning property they shall receive two (23) reliable witnesses, while one is sufficient to separate [him from] the purity

The first passage is clear enough, stipulating separation from the pure-food for any violation of the communal norms. The second passage is somewhat more difficult, but it seems that the separation from the pure-food referred to in line 21 is the default position: Regardless of whether there is sufficient testimony to carry out complete judgment, the accused is to be separated from the pure-food, presumably because the accused is ritually impure as a result of sin. Of course, if two witnesses concur, or even if one witness reports the same testimony twice,[93] then even a more severe punishment is to be enacted, above and beyond the separation from the pure-food. Along with with Licht and Newton, I believe that the penal code of the Rule of the Community ought to be read in light of these passages. Thus we find that the sectarians did indeed believe that the moral sins of insiders brought about ritual defilement.

Repentance Requires Purification

The identification of sin with defilement at Qumran leads to an equally strong identification between atonement and purification. This is the fourth way in which the identification of moral and ritual impurity is manifest at Qumran: repentance from sin and purification from defilement have become mutually dependent. According to the sectarians, moral repentance is not efficacious without ritual purification, and ritual purification without moral repentance is equally invalid.

That repentance would be described in terms of ritual purification is by no means new. A number of biblical traditions speak of moral repentance in terms of ritual purification. In chapter 1 (section on "Moral Impurity as a Metaphor?") we examined, among other passages, Isaiah 1 and Psalm 51. This phenomenon, as far as the scriptural passages are concerned, is best understood as metaphor: The image of purification is used figuratively to illustrate God's redemptive power. Since as far as ancient Israel was concerned, sin did not bring about ritual defilement, there was no need to incorporate rituals of purification into the process of atonement.

A number of passages in the sectarian literature can be seen simply as a continuation of the trend seen in Scripture: The image of purification is used figuratively to describe God's power to effect atonement. This is especially true of the Thanksgiving Hymns (1QH), many of which contain petitions for purification from sin.[94] There can be no doubt that this usage is scripturally based: 1QH VIII (XVI), for instance, takes much of its inspiration from Psalm 51.[95] Yet even with this degree of continuity, there is also some change. The image appears with greater frequency in 1QH than in the book of Psalms.[96] But also, as we saw in the first two parts of this section, 1QH — and indeed many of the scrolls — describes sin as a defilement with much greater frequency and with much more seriousness than what was seen in Israelite and earlier Jewish literature. Despite a degree of continuity between 1QH and, for example, Psalm 51, there can also be no doubt that at Qumran, the concept of purification from sin was no longer a figure or a literary motif, but an integral part of sectarian ritual.

We noted above that the sectarians believed sinners to be ritually defiling. As 1QS II:25–III:12 makes clear, sinners will continue to be ritually impure until they repent:

> (4) . He [the one who refuses to enter the covenant of God; cf. II.25–26] cannot be purified by atonement, nor cleansed by waters of purification, nor sanctify himself in streams (5) and rivers, nor cleanse himself in any waters of ablution. Impure, impure is he, as long as he rejects the judgments of (6) God, so that he cannot be instructed within the Community of his [God's] counsel.

But when sinners do repent, then purification and admission into the community become possible (III:6–9):

> (6) . . . For it is by the spirit of the true counsel of God that the ways of man — all his iniquities — (7) are atoned, so that he can behold the light of life. It is by the Holy Spirit of the Community in his [God's] truth that he can be cleansed from all (8) his iniquities. It is by an upright and humble spirit that his sin can be atoned. It is by humbling his soul to all God's statutes, that (9) his flesh can be cleansed, by sprinkling with waters of purification, and by sanctifying himself with waters of purity.

For the community that viewed sin as a source of ritual defilement, the completion of atonement is effected by ritual purification.

Just as it has long been noticed that sin and defilement were associated at Qumran, it has also long been noticed that atonement and purification were similarly identified.[97] For the most part, however, the descriptions of this association have been, in my view, imprecise. In one of the most thorough descriptions of this association, David Flusser states that at Qumran, moral repentance was the prerequisite for ritual purification.[98] Indeed, he notes that the Rule of the Community states so explicitly (V:13–14):

. . . כיא לוא יטהרו

כי אם שבו מרעתם כיא טמא בכול עוברי דברו . . .

(13) . . . For they [sinful outsiders] cannot be cleansed (14) unless they turn away from their wickedness, for [he remains] impure among all those who transgress His words.

Flusser's claim that atonement is a precondition for purification cannot be refuted, and it is frequently quoted or referred to,[99] but I believe that his formulation is incomplete as it stands. It is not enough to say that atonement is the precondition for purification, because that formulation obscures the fact that for the sectarians, both requirements are necessary and neither alone is sufficient. As was seen in 1QS II:25–III:12, ritual purification is the culminating step of the process of atonement; thus atonement is not complete without purification. That is why the sinful outsiders and the backsliding insiders are excluded from the pure-food of the community not just until they have atoned, but until they have atoned *and* purified themselves anew. No matter how sincere the sinners' atonement may be, they are not readmitted until the time-bound process of purification is complete. As Newton points out, the ritual impurity of the sinners prevents their being admitted (or readmitted), until they have been purified.[100] Atonement is required for (re-)admission to the community, but it is not sufficient, and purification is equally insufficient if atonement has not taken place. What we ought to say then is not that one requirement is the precondition for the other, but that they are mutually dependent conditions, both of which must be met. Just as impurity and sin have become identified, so too have purification and atonement.

Purification Requires Repentance

The final illustration of the identification of ritual and moral impurity at Qumran is the converse of the above. It is not only the case that the sectarians believed sin to be ritually defiling and that purification was part of the atonement process; they also believed that manifestations of ritual defilement were in some way sinful. It is for this reason that penitential formulae find a place in 4Q 512 (Ritual of Purification).[101] For instance, in the following selection, a petition for repentance is incorporated within a blessing that is presumably to be recited upon purification from menstrual impurity (frgs. 29–32, VII:8–9):[102]

[וברך וענ]ה[ואמר ברוך אתה] אל ישראל אשר [

[הצלתי מכו]ל פשעי ותטהרני מערות נדה[יכפר לבוא]

(8)   . And he will bless. He will start speaking and say: May you be blessed, [God of Israel, who] (9) [forgave me all] my faults, and purified me from impure modesty /and atoned/ so that I can enter. . .

The penitential tone of this blessing is undeniable.[103] The same penitential tone is evident in another relatively well-preserved passage which contains blessings to be recited, apparently, upon purification from corpse impurity.[104] The entire document is fragmentary, and the interpretation of even the relatively well-preserved passage quoted above is uncertain,[105] but there is enough here to indicate that this blessing is to be recited upon the performance of some ritual of purification. There is enough here as well for us to see that for the sectarians, purification and atonement were conceptually intertwined.[106]

The same conceptual conjoinment of purification and atonement appears to lurk behind 4Q 274 (Tohoraᵃ).[107] This document contains a number of intriguing purity laws, the main thrust of which is the idea that the various categories of defiled people must be separated not only from those who are pure, but from each other as well. In other words, in addition to being separated from the community, lepers and menstruants must stay separate from each other as well. What is important for our concern is the fact that in this document too there is some evidence that the sectarians assumed ritual defiling disorders to come about as a result of sin. Consider the following passage (lines 1–4):[108]

(1)   . . [Let him not] begin to cast his supplication. In a bed of sorrow shall he lie and in a seat of sighing shall he sit. Apart from all the impure shall he sit and at a distance of (2) twelve cubits from the purity when he speaks to him; toward the northwest of any dwelling place shall he sit distant by this measure. (3) Anyone of the impure who touches him shall bathe in water and wash his clothes and afterwards he may eat, for this is what he said, "'Impure, impure' (4) shall he call out all the days [when the plague is upon him]."

The passage is not simple to understand. Indeed, it is not clear exactly what defilement the impure person has contracted. Joseph Baumgarten believes that the text concerns the impurity of genital fluxes (*zab* impurity, Lev. 15:1–15). His argument is based on the fact that the text is concerned with the bed and seat of the impure person — an allusion, in his view, to Leviticus 15:4.[109] Milgrom, on the other hand, focuses on lines 3–4: "'Impure, impure, shall he call out . . . '", which is a clear allusion to Leviticus 13:45–46 — the laws of the leper.[110] Either way, the text clearly states that the impure person is to sit alone in his sorrows until his purification. Thus although there is a disagreement about who is being purified in this text, it cannot be denied that there is a penitential formula here.

. . .

These last texts complete the picture. At Qumran, sin was considered to be ritually defiling, and ritual defilement was assumed to come about because of sin. Sinners not only had to atone, but also had to cleanse themselves of the ritual impurity their sins produced. Insiders who sinned were assumed to be ritually impure, and insiders who were ritually impure had to atone. In short, what were, in the Hebrew Bible, the independent concepts of ritual and moral impurity have become, at Qumran, fully intertwined. What we are left with, intriguingly, is a conception of defilement that is not unlike that of Zoroastrianism: What is evil is impure, what is impure is demonic, and foreigners are impure.[111]

Sin, the Land, Exile, and the Sectarians

It is most unfortunate, from my point of view, that no Qumranic exegesis of Leviticus 18:24–30 (or a similar passage) has yet surfaced. It is my hunch, however, that the identification of ritual and moral defilement at Qumran can be understood as a further example of the process that Jacob Milgrom has referred to as "homogenization."[112] In the Hebrew Bible, ritual and moral impurity were distinct phenomena. At Qumran, however, the sources of one were perceived to produce the effects of the other, and vice versa.

There is, unfortunately, no way for me to prove this point without a Qumranic exegesis of a passage such as Leviticus 18:24–30. There is, however, in addition to what has already been pointed out, evidence that the sectarians were greatly influenced by the biblical traditions that articulate the idea of moral defilement. It has long been noticed that both the Holiness Code and the book of Ezekiel exerted a strong influence on the Qumran sectarians.[113] That fact in itself makes it likely that the concept of moral impurity, which is so clearly articulated in both the Holiness Code and Ezekiel, would have a profound influence at Qumran. We can go even further, because the sectarian literature from Qumran not only is interested in the defiling force of sin, as we have seen, but is interested also in the larger dynamic of moral impurity as articulated in the Holiness Code: that sin defiles the land and leads to exile.

In chapter 2 I identified a few sources discovered at Qumran that articulate the idea that grave sin defiles the land of Israel. These included 4Q 381, a noncanonical and nonsectarian psalm, and a few passages from the Temple Scroll (11QT), which, as I argued, is best seen as stemming from the sect's prehistory. There is, unfortunately, less evidence for this notion to be found in the undisputedly sectarian texts. Still there is some evidence that the sectarians considered the land of Israel to be impure.

The Rule of the Community is aware of the idea that the sins of the people can have a deleterious, and probably defiling, effect on the land of Israel. It is precisely for this reason that the council of the community (עצת היחד) will, at the end of time,[114] "atone for the earth and repay the wicked their punishment" (לכפר בעד הארץ ולהשב לרשעים גמולם; VIII:6–7). The idea that the land needs to be atoned for is echoed later in 1QS (VIII:10;[115] IX:4) and elsewhere in the Qumran corpus (1QSa I:3).[116] It should be rather obvious by now that these passages are reflections of the biblical traditions, such as Numbers 35:33, that articulate the idea of the moral de-

[handwritten: Atone & purify take on synonymous meaning]

filement of the land by sin.[117] The use of the term "atone" here—we might expect "purify"—is not problematic, for, as we have seen, the sectarians did not separate the concepts of atonement and purification. Thus what we see in these passages is another reflection of that age-old eschatological hope for the purification of the land of Israel from the defilement caused by Israel's sin. *[handwritten: —How? → atonement]*

The other hint we have that the sectarians considered the land of Israel to be defiled in some way is the fact that they viewed themselves as living in exile. Exile, according to the standard notion of moral defilement as articulated in the Holiness Code and Ezekiel, comes about as a direct result of the defilement of the land. A number of sources indicate that the sectarians considered themselves to be living in exile already (e.g., CD VI:5; 1QS VIII:13; 1QpHab XI:6; 1QM I:2). But how could the sectarians, living at Qumran, consider themselves in exile? Of course, exile could have been a metaphor, symbolizing their physical removal from the greater Jewish polity, but there is good reason to think that they considered themselves to be truly in exile at Qumran. *[handwritten: → why don't borders fully cohere?]*

The precise delineation of the borders of the land of Israel was an issue that was never fully settled; the various biblical traditions do not cohere fully (cf. Num. 34:1–12; Deut. 11:24; Joshua 12–19; Ezek. 47:13–20). But it is interesting that the priestly traditions—Numbers 34 and Ezekiel 47—agree that the Jordan River was the eastern boundary. What this means is that for a number of traditions, Qumran would have been on the boundary of Israel. There is even scriptural justification for the idea that the Dead Sea, in particular, was on the boundary of Israel (2 Kings 14:25):

> And it was he [Amaziah] who restored the territory of Israel [גבול ישראל] from Lebo-hamath to the sea of the Arabah, in accordance with the promise that the Lord, the God of Israel, had made through His servant, the prophet Jonah son of Amittai

Frank Moore Cross, among others, has argued that "Damascus" in the Damascus Document is a code word for the settlement of Qumran.[118] I am persuaded by his view, and I wish to add only one point. It remains unclear why "Damascus" would be a good code word for Qumran. Of course, CD VII:14–17 allows us to see that, for the sectarians, the idea of exile to Damascus was rooted, at least in part, in Amos 5:26–27: "And I will exile Sikkuth your king . . . to Damascus." I suggest that the key to the "Damascus" code is this: Qumran, just like Damascus, is on or just beyond the boundary of Israel. While Numbers 34:10–11 presumably includes Damascus within the boundaries of Israel, Ezekiel 47:17–18 does not. The view of Syria as being on the boundary of the land of Israel is also noted in rabbinic sources (e.g., M. Ohal. 18:7; T. Kel. B. Q. 1:5). We have just cited sources that would put Qumran on the boundary of Israel. What this all boils down to is the notion that the sectarians believed that they lived in exile, at Qumran. Was this self-imposed exile related in some way to the idea that the land of Israel had become defiled by sin? The juxtaposition, in 1QS VIII, of the themes of atonement for the land and exile from the land certainly raises the possibility of such a connection, but it remains only a possibility.

Of course, the removal of the sectarians from society to Qumran need not be explained by the idea of the defilement of the land. If the analysis and schematization here of the sectarian literature are correct, then something striking emerges. Various disputes over ritual impurity can already be seen in the protosectarian 11QT and the early sectarian 4QMMT. Yet these documents lack the full-blown sectarian dualism that is indicative of 1QS, 1QpHab, 1QM, and 1QH. Furthermore, these later documents share another common idea: that sins render sinners ritually defiling. This idea is not articulated in 4QMMT or 11QT. What this indicates is that the disputes over the *tebul yom*, the scope of temple sanctity, and other ritual purity matters may well have precipitated some dispute between the sect and the surrounding Jewish polity. The purity issue that solidified that schism, however, could well have been the same issue that separates 1QS from 11QT: the defiling force of sin. I am not certain which came first — the interest in the defiling force of sin or the schism — but the fact remains that the idea of the ritually defiling force of sin necessitates, justifies, and reinforces the physical separation of the sectarians from the larger Jewish polity. If you believe in the maintenance of purity, and you believe that sin and sinners are defiling, you have little choice but to remove yourself from that society that you consider to be irredeemably sinful.[119]

Summary and Conclusion

In the sectarian literature from Qumran, a distinctive approach to the question of the relationship between ritual and moral impurity was articulated: Ritual and moral impurity were melded into a single conception of defilement, which had both ritual and moral ramifications. Thus the sectarian approach to purity was quite different from that articulated in the Hebrew Bible, where moral impurity and ritual impurity remained distinct: Sin did not produce ritual impurity, sinners were not ritually defiling, and sinners did not need to be purified. At Qumran, sin was considered to be ritually defiling, and sinners had to purify themselves. At Qumran, moreover, the association between ritual and moral impurity went even further. In the Hebrew Bible, ritual impurity was not considered to be sinful; at Qumran those who became ritually impure had not only to purify themselves, but to atone as well. In addition to melding together ritual and moral impurity, at Qumran the scope of moral impurity also widened considerably. In the Hebrew Bible, moral impurity was produced by idolatrous, murderous, and sexual sins; at Qumran, impurity was produced by all sorts of sin.

   This analysis has also demonstrated that with regard to purity issues, one can trace a clear evolution of ideas in the literature associated with the sect. The Temple Scroll was viewed here as protosectarian, and it articulated ideas that are pretty much in line with Scripture: No integration of ritual and moral impurity was in evidence, nor was any distinctively Qumranic use of ritual purity terminology. The same can be said of 4QMMT, which appears to stem from the formative period of the sect. The situation of the Damascus Document (CD) is more complex; this text may well be a composite, and it articulates some ideas that are fully in line with previous Jewish literature and others that are more distinctively sectarian. However, when it comes to the documents of undoubtedly sectarian origin, like 1QS, 1QM and 1QH, we see the full integration of ritual and moral impurity into a single conception of defilement. For this reason, the "systemic" method advocated by some scholars — whereby a single purity system is discerned in diverse Qumran texts — is to be called into question. The differences noted here between, for instance, 11QT and 1QS, serve as a reminder of the need to analyze these sources diachronically.

In addition to being aware of developments in sectarian thought, we must also remember that even within the sectarian corpus, there can be shifts in emphasis and differing concerns. The main example we have seen here of this phenomenon is the fact that at Qumran, the anti-temple polemic proceeds on two levels. There is the idea articulated in 4QMMT, and even already in 11QT, that the current temple is ritually defiled as a result of a failure by the priests in power to follow the correct ritual purity law. In other texts, however, the anti-temple polemic functions on a different level altogether. The concern expressed in CD and 1QpHab is that the temple has been defiled morally, by the performance of grave sin.

A significant portion of the scholarly literature on ancient Judaism focuses on the differences between the sectarians and the tannaim regarding the scope and locus of ritual impurity. As we have seen in this chapter, however, one of the most significant disagreements between the sectarians and other contemporary Jews was not about the locus of impurity (temple or community), or about the scope of impurity (how far from the temple the ritually impure must remain). Rather, the key disagreement we have seen here regards a source of impurity: whether or not, and in what way, sin defiles the sinner, the sanctuary, and the land of Israel.

How the tannaim dealt with these questions will be explored in the next chapter.

4

Ritual Impurity and Sin
in Tannaitic Literature

The next two chapters focus on the relationship between impurity and sin in the literature of the *tannaim,* the rabbinic sages of the first two centuries of the Common Era.[1] Two chapters are devoted to this topic for two reasons. First, tannaitic literature is much vaster than either the Qumran corpus or the New Testament. Second, as will be seen shortly, the material divides itself well into two parts. There are two major aspects of the way in which impurity and sin are treated in tannaitic literature. The first, the subject of this chapter, is the way in which tannaitic *ha-lakhah* (the legal tradition) addresses the relationship between *ritual* impurity and sin. Once it is understood how it answers this question, a second question arises: How did the tannaim deal with the issue of moral impurity, in particular the biblical verses that clearly articulate that notion? This is the subject of chapter 5.[2]

The sages whose legacy is our concern here — the tannaim — composed and transmitted legal and exegetical traditions, much of which has been preserved in what can be referred to as the tannaitic corpus, which includes the Mishnah, the Tosefta, the early rabbinic sources (baraithot) preserved in the Babylonian and Jerusalem Talmudim, as well as the tannaitic midrashim.[3] The best-known of these "tannaitic"[4] midrashim are: the Mekhilta d'Rabbi Ishmael (on Exodus), the Sifra (on Leviticus), and the two Sifres (on Numbers and Deuteronomy).[5] Like the Mishnah and the Tosefta, these tannaitic midrashim were all composed in Hebrew in the land of Israel. The material in them is attributed to the sages who lived in the first two centuries of the common era, up to and including the time of the publication of the Mishnah, at approximately 200 CE.[6] Beyond this, the dates of the tannaitic midrashim are subject to controversy.[7]

An even greater controversy concerns the proper methodology for the study of these tannaitic texts.[8] In order to situate the methodological assumptions of the present work within contemporary approaches, I will draw a brief contrast between the approach taken here and the most clearly delineated approach in the field today. According to Neusner's "literary-documentary" approach, each rabbinic text is an organic whole, articulating a clear argument or philosophy. Once discerned, this argument or philosophy can be attributed with certainty only to that document's final redactors (attributions to named authorities are viewed as of little or no value). Thus one can describe a Judaism of the Mishnah, a Judaism of Leviticus Rabbah, and so on. Only after the documentary analysis is complete can something greater than the Judaism of an individual text be described.[9]

The method adopted here is quite different and is rooted in the "source-critical" approach taken in the works of J. N. Epstein, S. Friedman, and D. W. Halivni, as well as some of the early work of Neusner.[10] We will assume that the documents are composites, preserving some earlier materials in form or content.[11] Attributions to named authorities, therefore, are to be taken seriously, though not blindly accepted.[12] We will also assume that these texts are interconnected in ways that defy generalization, so that in order to understand and evaluate properly any specific pericope, one must study the various traditions synoptically, although chronology and the nature of the documents themselves cannot be ignored.[13] Finally, we will recognize the likelihood that behind these texts as we have them is a complex of oral tradition.[14] That is not to say that the content of any of these texts is prerabbinic, pharisaic, or even earlier, but the possibility that any particular tradition echoes earlier ones must be entertained, especially when genuinely pretannaitic parallels to that tradition can be identified in other ancient Jewish literature.

From time to time in this chapter, the analysis of tannaitic source material will be illustrated by parallels, commentaries, and discussions culled from the later, *aggadic* midrashim[15] (e.g., Midrash Rabbah) and the amoraic layers of the Jerusalem and Babylonian Talmud.[16] For the most part, these texts will serve a secondary purpose, as aids to understanding the tannaitic sources.

This chapter will describe the approach taken to impurity and sin in tannaitic *halakhah*. The tannaitic approach to purity is characterized, in my view, by the "compartmentalization" of the notions of ritual and moral impurity, and of ritual impurity and sin more generally. The tannaim are indeed, as Büchler argued,[17] familiar with the notion of the defiling force of sin (discussed in chapter 5). Yet almost without exception, the tannaitic discussions of ritual impurity law are devoid of any reference to the defiling force of sin. Similarly, tannaitic discussions of laws dealing with sin, status, and atonement are kept separate from issues of ritual impurity. What we will see is that the tannaim exerted a great effort to avoid any confusion on this point: Defilement and sin are separate concerns. In the fist section we will turn to the fact that in tannaitic *halakhah*, ritual impurity retains an overall similarity to what is articulated in the Torah: ritual impurity is natural and unavoidable, generally not sinful, and typically impermanent. In the second major section we will examine more closely the claim that the tannaim "compartmentalized" ritual and moral impurity, by demonstrating the notably guarded way in which they deal with potentiallly problematic aspects of ritual impurity legislation. In the third and final section we will direct our attention to a related phenomenon: the fact that in tannaitic *halakhah*, the issues of sin and atonement are generally kept distinct from issues of defilement and purification.

Ritual Impurity from Leviticus to the Tannaim

An important general observation is that there is a great deal of difference between the ritual impurity legislation of the Pentateuch and that of the tannaim.[18] Most obvious is the difference in sheer volume. The legislation of the Hebrew Bible takes up roughly half a dozen chapters: Leviticus 11–15 and Numbers 19. The tannaitic system, by contrast, is articulated in an order of Mishnah, an order of Tosefta, large portions of the tannaitic midrashim, including approximately a quarter of the Sifra, and a number of talmudic passages as well. Within this great amount of material, there appear new — or, rather, extrabiblical — sources of ritual defilement, such as idols and Gentiles. There are new modes of transferring ritual impurity, such as *maddaf* (the transference from a person with flux or menstrual impurity to certain objects even though those objects remain above, not below, the impure person).[19] There are also legal issues that are discussed at some length in Scripture — such as the purification of earthenware vessels (Lev. 11:32–35; 15:4–6, 22; Num. 19:15) and the spread of corpse impurity within a tent (Num. 19:14–15) — that are developed well beyond what one might at first expect: Mishnah tractate Kelim (dealing with the purity of vessels) takes up thirty chapters, and Mishnah tractate Ohalot (dealing with the spread of corpse impurity within a tent) takes up eighteen.[20]

The best systematic comparison of scriptural impurity law with that of the tannaim remains the final volume of Neusner's *History of Mishnaic Law of Purities*. Neusner emphasizes again and again that the mishnaic purity system is strongly based on its scriptural foundation,[21] but with equal frequency, he points out aspects of the mishnaic system that are innovative.[22] One such tannaitic innovation, according to Neusner, was to shift the focus of purity concerns away from the temple and toward the table.[23] Another was the recognition of the power of human intention.[24] According to Neusner, the all-encompassing power of human intention can particularly be seen, for example, in the tannaitic law regarding immersion pools, whereby purificatory power is bestowed not only on running water, but on water collected by people for the purpose of purification from ritual impurity.[25]

Neusner has been criticized on this point by Jacob Milgrom and Hannah K. Harrington, who both demonstrate that a number of ostensibly tannaitic innovations are actually implied or even made explicit in the Hebrew Bible. Milgrom has argued — convincingly, I believe — that the issue of human intention is central not only to the mishnaic mode of thinking, but to the priestly mode of thinking as well.[26] And Milgrom and Harrington have argued, persuasively, that the purificatory power of collected water is evident in Scripture as well.[27]

I agree with Milgrom and Harrington insofar as they emphasize the scriptural basis of the tannaitic purity system, but I continue to agree with Neusner that scriptural exegesis does not necessarily unfold in inevitable ways.[28] Clearly, tannaitic legislation is based to a great extent on Scripture, but Scripture in itself did not determine the way in which it was interpreted by the tannaim. When faced with exegetical decisions, the tannaim exercised *choice*.

We will compare the general characteristics of ritual impurity in the Pentateuch and tannaitic sources. Despite the tremendous amount of legal development and systematization — allowing the tannaim to devote an entire order of the Mishnah to a topic dealt with in merely a few chapters of the Bible — it will be seen that much has remained the same. By looking at the ways in which the tannaim chose to interpret the biblical purity system, we will learn something about their attitudes toward the relationship between impurity and sin.

Chapter 1 argued that the Pentateuch juxtaposes two distinct conceptions of defilement, without indicating how one relates to the other. We then saw in chapter 3 that the Qumran sectarians integrated these two conceptions, so that the sources of either one were perceived to produce the effects of the other. In contrast to the sectarians at Qumran, the tannaim chose to interpret Scripture in such a way as to keep ritual impurity and sin as distinct from each other as possible. As a result of this effort, the general characteristics of ritual impurity in tannaitic *halakhah* remain very similar to those in the Hebrew Bible. But as we saw in chapter 3, the general characteristics of ritual impurity in the sectarian system are in many ways distinct from those in the Hebrew Bible. Precisely because the distinctions between ritual and moral defilements that were maintained in the Hebrew Bible disappear at Qumran, one cannot say that the overall characteristics of ritual impurity at Qumran are the same as in the Hebrew Bible. But since the tannaim maintain the distinctions that the sectarians rejected, these characteristics of ritual impurity in the tannaitic system are congruent with those in the biblical system.

In chapter 1, it was suggested that ritual impurity in the Hebrew Bible can best be seen as (1) natural and more or less unavoidable, (2) generally not sinful, and (3) conveying a typically impermanent contagion. Despite the great differences between ritual impurity law in the Pentateuch and in tannaitic literature, these general characteristics are equally descriptive of ritual impurity in both sources.

1. By and large, the sources of ritual impurity are the same in tannaitic law as in the Pentateuch. The first chapter of Mishnah tractate Kelim serves as a kind of introduction to the Order of Purities (Seder Toharot) and presents a prioritized list of the sources of ritual impurity (Kelim 1:1–4):[29]

> (1) The fathers of impurity. a [dead] creeping thing, male semen, whoever has contracted impurity from a corpse, a leper in the days of reckoning, and Sin-offering water too little in quantity to be sprinkled, [these] convey impurity to people and vessels by contact and to earthenware vessels by overhang, but they do not convey impurity by [being] carried.
>
> (2) They are exceeded by carrion and by Sin-offering water sufficient in quantity to be sprinkled, for these convey impurity to whomever carries them, so that s/he, too, conveys impurity to garments by contact, but the garments do not become impure by contact [alone].
>
> (3) They are exceeded by him that has intercourse with a menstruant, for he conveys impurity to what lies beneath him in like degree to that above him.   .

And so forth, until we reach the corpse (1:4), which is the most potent source of ritual impurity. It is important to note that the list is not comprehensive. Reference is not made to the ritual impurity that is caused by childbirth, or that, according to tannaitic sources, results from contact with idols. Perhaps the latter was left out because tannaitic sources consistently view the ritual impurity of idols as a postbiblical innovation, and thus of a lower priority than the sources of impurity clearly listed in the Torah. The absence of birth is a greater mystery, perhaps explained by the fact that, with the exception of marriage, the Mishnah and Tosefta do not devote much effort to life-cycle events.[30]

Despite the absence of birth from M. Kelim 1:1–4, the general description of ritual impurity as natural and more or less unavoidable is just as true for the tannaitic sources as it is for the Hebrew Bible. Death, disease, and discharge are simply a part of life, perfectly natural and normal processes and events. What is ritually impure is not, as Neusner says, "disruptive of the economy and the wholeness of nature."[31] To the contrary, the sources of ritual impurity are, by and large, part and parcel of the "wholeness of nature."

Moreover, just as in the Pentateuch, ritual impurity in tannaitic sources is in many cases not only natural and unavoidable, but even obligatory. In tannaitic *halakhah*, priests continue to contract ritual impurity from the performance of certain cultic rituals, which are no less obligatory in the Mishnah than they were in the Pentateuch (M. Kel. 1:1; M. Par. 4:4).[32] The biblical obligation to marry and procreate persists into tannaitic Judaism (M. Yeb. 6:6), but of course sexual union still leaves both partners to the act ritually defiled (Lev. 15:18; M. Kel. 1:1; Sifra Metzorah Perek 6). The obligation to bury the dead also persists and becomes increasingly important. Indeed, even though the biblical limitations on priestly contraction of corpse impurity (Lev. 21:1–4) are maintained in tannaitic *halakhah* (M. Naz. 7:1), the burial of the dead becomes so important a concern that these limitations are waved in certain cases, even for the High Priest. According to M. Nazir 7:1, the High Priest who stumbles upon a neglected corpse is to defile himself ritually and bury it. There is then a debate in the passage on whether a Nazirite or the High Priest ought to bury the neglected corpse if the responsibility fell on both in the same instance. The image of a High Priest defiling himself to bury a neglected corpse highlights the fact that in tannaitic Judaism, ritual impurity is something that is natural and unavoidable, and from time to time even obligatory.

2. By extension, just as in the Pentateuch, in tannaitic *halakhah*, ritual impurity is also not sinful. It is never articulated or assumed anywhere in the Mishnah that a person has sinned in any way merely by contracting any form of ritual impurity. For the most part, ritual impurity is contracted by behaviors that are — like death, disease, and discharge — natural and unavoidable. The one sinful behavior that does produce ritual defilement in tannaitic sources is precisely the same sin that produces it in the Hebrew Bible. It remains forbidden for a man to have sexual intercourse with his wife while she is menstruating. Intercourse during menstruation is both ritually defiling (M. Kel. 1: 3) and forbidden (M. Ker. 1:1; see section on "*Niddah*" in this chapter), just as in Scripture (Lev. 15:24; 18:19). In addition to this one sinful act that is both sinful and ritually defiling, there is at least one way in which ritual impurity can result from sin: as in the Pentateuch, there are reflections in tannaitic sources of the idea that certain ritual defilements, especially "leprosy," may come about as a punishment for certain sins. This issue will be taken up in detail later. Generally speaking, however, just as in Scripture, in tannaitic sources ritual impurity is not sinful.[33] To quote Neusner's judgment: "Not a single line in the entire Mishnah treats cultic uncleanness as in and of itself a representation of sin. An unclean person is not a sinner, therefore not wicked."[34]

Of course, if one disregards ritual impurity regulations, then certain transgressions may in the end be committed. Leviticus 5:1–13 delineates the sacrificial rituals to be performed by an individual who contracted some form of ritual impurity and subsequently forgot that he or she was impure.[35] This passage is understood in tannaitic sources to refer to a situation in which an individual accidentally came in contact with sancta when in a state of ritual impurity. Such sins, which would include, for example, entering the temple in a state of ritual impurity, are collectively referred to in tannaitic sources as "the ritual defilement of the sanctuary and its sancta" (טומאת מקדש וקדשיו).[36] These sins are, to be sure, related to ritual impurity. But provided one follows the rules, one ought to be able to contract ritual impurity and eventually purify oneself, all without having ritually defiled the sanctuary or any other holy things. In order to avoid committing such sins, one need not avoid ritual impurity at all times, one must simply remain aware of one's status vis-à-vis the ritual purity system. *— Just be cognizant of status.*

Finally, it is important to emphasize that to a large degree, the ability to contract ritual impurity is not viewed in tannaitic sources as something categorically bad by any means. To the contrary, the ability to contract and convey ritual impurity is viewed at times as a prerogative.[37] As I have discussed elsewhere, Gentiles are generally considered in tannaitic sources to be exempt from contracting ritual impurities.[38] On the other hand, it is sacred writings that have the capacity to defile the hands (M. Yad. 3:5), while secular writings do not. As the sages say in M. Yadaim 4:6, "their impurity is in accordance to our love for them" (לפי חבתן היא טמאתן).

3. Just as in the Pentateuch, ritual impurity in the Hebrew Bible conveys to persons and some objects an impermanent contagion. That this is true is patently obvious to any reader of M. Seder Toharot. Just like Scripture, the tannaitic sources describe fixed durations of ritual defilement and provide methods of ritual purification. Indeed, it could be argued that the tannaitic sources reduce the power of ritual impurity in comparison with the Torah.[39] The value of these claims is not directly relevant here; what we note here is simply that the general characteristics of ritual impurity are much the same in tannaitic sources and in the Hebrew Bible.

We have noted the complexity of the relationship between tannaitic *halakhah* and its scriptural base. While Scripture has a tremendous influence over tannaitic *halakhah*, it does not in itself determine, or generate, its tannaitic interpretation. Both the tannaim and the Qumran sectarians received the same Pentateuch, and yet their conceptions of impurity were quite different. The Qumran sectarians interpreted Scripture in such a way as to meld together the concepts of ritual and moral defilement. The tannaim, however, maintained the distinctions and, as we will see in chapter 5, interpreted Scripture in such a way as to compartmentalize ritual and moral defilement. Thus while many tannaitic *halakahot* relating to ritual impurity are like "mountains hanging by a hair" (M. Hag. 1:8), with many rules based on scanty scriptural support, the general conception of ritual impurity in tannaitic *halakhah* is hardly dangling by a hair. It is both deeply rooted in Scripture and, all things considered, roughly commensurate with contemporary scholarly readings of the biblical approach to ritual impurity.

Ritual Impurity in Tannaitic *Halakhah*

We turn now to the main theme of this chapter: the compartmentalization of ritual impurity and sin in tannaitic literature.[40] The term "compartmentalization" calls attention to the fact that the tannaim exerted great effort to maintain the distinctions between ritual impurity and moral impurity, and more generally between ritual impurity and sin. On the most general level, the tannaitic compartmentalization of impurity and sin can be seen clearly in the structure, language, and content of the Mishnah itself: No tractate is devoted to the defiling force of sin. Similarly, sins and their defiling force are completely absent from the major "essays" on ritual purity found in tannaitic sources (e.g., M. Kel. ch. 1; M. Hag. chs. 2–3). Indeed, the entire Mishnah, more than one sixth of which is devoted to ritual purity, does not contain a single discussion or ruling concerning the defiling force of idolatrous, incestuous, or murderous sins. It is even rare, though not unheard of, for the terms "impure" (טמא) and "pure" (טהור) to be used in the Mishnah in contexts other than that of ritual impurity and ritual purification.[41] Idols—but not idolatry—are considered to be ritually defiling in rabbinic literature, and this case will be examined in some detail below.

The phenomenon of compartmentalization can be also seen in the ways in which the tannaim deal with situations that have the potential to blur the distinctions they wish to maintain. For instance, how do they interpret biblical passages that juxtapose impurity and sin? As we will see in chapter 5, their use of such passages is limited, and their interpretations of them are carefully constructed so as to avoid confusion regarding the defiling force of sin. And how do the tannaim deal with sinful violations of ritual impurity law on the one hand and violations of the moral impurity prohibitions on the other? Again, we will see that they are very careful to drive a wedge between—to compartmentalize—ritual and moral impurity. This section focuses on tannaitic ritual impurity law and on the ways in which sin does and does not figure in at various points.

Negaim: *"Leprosy" and Sin in Tannaitic Sources*

Of all the forms of ritual impurity, perhaps none is associated more with sin in tannaitic sources than the ritual impurity that results from "leprosy."[42] However, there is no explicit articulation of the notion of leprosy as a punishment in the Mishnah. To be sure, the Tosefta, the Sifra, and some later collections do preserve traditions to the effect that ritually defiling afflictions come about as a result of sin. Yet the treatment of these defiling afflictions[43] in tannaitic sources remains perfectly in line with the effort to keep impurity and sin as separate concerns: As we will see, in tannaitic sources the "leper" is not inherently sinful. Nor for that matter is the sinner inherently "leprous." Indeed, the idea that "leprosy" can be a punishment for sin has nothing to do with ritual impurity at all. The punitive value of these afflictions lies not in the fact that they are defiling, but in the fact that they are painful. The idea of "leprosy" as a punishment is, in fact, but just one aspect of a much larger tannaitic effort to understand many human diseases and sufferings as divine punishments for sin.[44] In tannaitic theology, because God is all-powerful and just, almost all human sufferings are tied in some way to sinful behavior.[45]

So despite the tannaitic effort to compartmentalize impurity and sin, there are indeed a few tannaitic sources that assume some moral dimension to the appearance of "leprous" afflictions. In M. Keritot 2:3, defiling afflictions come up in the context of sin. M. Negaim 12:6 addresses a situation of a house afflicted on a wall that is common to two dwellings. The wall must be torn down, an act that affects the unafflicted house sharing that wall as well. "Woe to the evil doer, and woe to his neighbor," the Mishnah emotes. Yet despite the recognition of a moral dimension to the appearance of these afflictions, the tannaitic sources remain neutral with regard to the moral status of the individual who contracts this impurity. It is not assumed that the individual has sinned in any way. One cannot find in the entire Mishnah tractate Negaim a single clear allusion to the biblical narrative traditions that view such ailments as punishments for slander (e.g., Num. 12:1–16). Indeed, the working assumption in the tractate is that any Jewish person could be afflicted, even learned students of Torah and righteous people.[46] And while children are exempt from certain afflictions, they are not exempt from them all.[47] Yet Gentiles, who are by no means free of sin, do not contract ritual impurity on account of such afflictions, whether on their bodies (M. Neg. 3:1), their garments (11:1), or their houses (12:1). No direct relationship can be discerned between sin and the appearance of defiling afflictions.

The diagnosis of the afflictions, moreover, depends not on any determination of guilt, but solely on the identification of symptoms by a priest. The purification of the afflicted individual depends not on atonement or payment of restitution, but on the disappearance of the affliction and the performance of the requisite rituals. The Mishnah even suggests that if these rituals cannot be performed as required, then the individual cannot be purified. Since purification requires that the once-afflicted individual be daubed with sacrificial blood on the corners of the hand, foot, and ear (Lev. 14:14), it is said—though the point is disputed—that the individual who for some reason lacks these body parts remains ritually impure in perpetuity.[48] Thus, in this disturbing case, the maimed individual could remain ritually impure for life, even after the disappearance of the affliction. Of course, there is no reason to suppose that the Mishnah considered maimed individuals to be inherently guilty of any sins. The individuals afflicted with these defiling disorders are ritually impure, but they are not inherently guilty.

Further confirmation that for the tannaim defiling afflictions and sin do not necessarily cohere can be seen in M. Negaim 7:4. According to this anonymous tradition, one who removes marks of an affliction is guilty of violating a prohibitive commandment. A similar tradition appears in Tosefta Negaim 3:1, which also specifies the punishment for such a crime: forty lashes. But what prohibitive commandment has been violated? Presumably we find the answer in the toseftan tradition, as well as in Sifre Deuteronomy § 274,[49] both of which quote Deuteronomy 24:8: "In cases of skin affliction be most careful to do exactly as the levitical priests instruct you." The inference drawn from the passage is that removing signs of a defiling affliction would certainly not be in agreement with any priestly instruction. Since the person has not done what the priest has instructed, he has violated the law. Whether or not the Mishnah is based on a similar exegesis of Deuteronomy 24:8, all three traditions agree that the Israelite who removes the marks of leprosy has done something terribly wrong. What is also striking is that this Israelite who has acted presumptuously,

↳ THs in w/ Jesus

in violation of the Torah, is deemed to be ritually pure nonetheless, provided that the act of removal precedes the act of diagnosis by a priest. The tannaitic treatment of this issue is perfectly in line with the general tannaitic approach to ritual impurity and sin: sin and ritual impurity are distinct concerns, even when the sin involves wrongfully changing one's own status vis-à-vis ritual impurity.

The Mishnah, as we have seen, does not directly associate defiling afflictions with sin and does not even clearly allude to the biblical traditions that make such associations. There are nonetheless a few tannaitic traditions to the effect that "leprous" impurities could appear as punishments for certain sins. There is only one such tradition in the Tosefta, and it is paralleled in the Sifra and Sifre Deuteronomy.[50] While a number of the tannaitic passages are related to each other in some way, there are some independent traditions as well. The idea that defiling afflictions come about as a result of sin continues to appear, and even develops somewhat, in the Babylonian Talmud and Leviticus Rabbah.

We start with Tosefta Negaim 6:7:

> How are afflictions examined? . . .
> [The afflicted person] comes to the priest, and the priest says: "Go and investigate yourself, and repent, for afflictions [נגעים] come about only as a result of slander, and leprosy [צרעת] comes about only as a result of arrogance, and the Lord does not judge humans except in clemency.
> Behold, the [afflictions] appear on his house. If s/he repents, it will require removal [of the afflicted stone]; if s/he does not, it will require demolition [of the entire house].
> Behold, the [afflictions] appear on his [or her] clothing. If s/he repents, they will require tearing; if not, they will require burning.
> Behold, the [afflictions] appear on his [or her] body. If s/he repents, it will leave him [or her], if not, "he shall dwell apart; his dwelling shall be outside the camp" [Lev. 13:46].
> R. Shimon ben Eleazar said in the name of R. Meir: [Afflictions] appear also for arrogance [גסות הרוח], as we find in the case of Uzziah.

According to this text, the impurities discussed in M. Negaim come about as a result of sin. Indeed, according to the words of the priest, these afflictions come about only as a result of sin. But even in this text there is no one-to-one correspondence between sin and defilement. It is not suggested here, or anywhere else in tannaitic literature, that a slanderer would be considered defiling *unless* he or she has been afflicted with some ritually defiling disorder.[51] Even though repentance in this tradition will impact upon the severity of the defilement, repentance is not tantamount to purification. Nor, for that matter, is it even necessary. Purification is not denied to the guilty and unrepentant, it is just prolonged.

As far as the view of the Tosefta itself on these matters, it is difficult to judge. The passage above is the only tradition in the Tosefta that articulates the view that defiling afflictions are punishments for sin.[52] It is important to keep in mind that the idea we are tracing here — that defiling afflictions come about as a punishment for sin — is not articulated in T. Negaim 6:7 directly by a rabbinic sage. Rather, the anonymous tradition puts the words "afflictions appear only as a result of slander" into the mouth of the priest. It is important to note that in tannaitic texts, the role of the voice of wisdom is rarely played by a priest.[53] To be sure, named authorities do appear in the passage quoted here, but the statement attributed to R. Meir, through R. Shimon ben Eleazar, is much more guarded. The named tannaim themselves do not say that these afflictions come about *only* as a result of some sin. The statement attributed to R. Meir, rather, asserts merely that afflictions can come about as punishments for certain sins.[54] Moreover, even the words of the priest are less clear on that matter than they may at first appear. Even as the statement associates afflictions with sin, at the same time it serves to emphasize the difference: "Go and investigate yourself, and repent," the priest says. The priest has the power to declare someone ritually impure or pure, but he does not have the power to determine whether or not the individual has in fact sinned.

The tradition as it appears in the Sifra is different in form but substantially similar in content.[55] Indeed, some of the phrasing is identical, but the Sifra states the biblical precedents for its theme: the fact that both Miriam and Uzziah were punished with leprosy for their sins. The parallel tradition that appears in Sifre Deuteronomy is very brief.[56] Commenting on Deuteronomy 24:9, the Sifre, like the Sifra, asks "what has one to do with the other?" Then it states simply—without putting the words into the mouth of a priest—that afflictions come about only as a result of slander.[57]

These traditions, though rare, are by no means surprising, even though the idea cannot be found in the Mishnah. The tannaim, after all, must grant the central thesis of these traditions—that afflictions can come about as a result of slander and arrogance—because that thesis is clearly expressed in Scripture. What is more, all three traditions—even that which appears in the Tosefta—clearly have these biblical precedents in mind. Thus it is not at all surprising that this notion appears in tannaitic sources. If anything, what is interesting is that it does not appear in the Mishnah and appears so rarely in the Tosefta and the Sifra. It's also important to note that the tannaitic sources contribute very little that is new. The theme of these passages—that defiling afflictions can come about as punishments for sins—is articulated clearly in Scripture and is simply reiterated by the tannaim.[58]

An additional independent tradition attributed to R. Yosi ha-Glili appears in Sifre Numbers.[59] This tradition, based on Numbers 5:1–4, suggests that defiling afflictions and fluxes appeared in Israel only when Israel began to sin. Although the tradition is relevant, it is hardly surprising. Again, while this tannaitic tradition posits some correspondence between the phenomena of sin and defiling afflictions, there is no direct relationship between sinners and ritual defilements, or between atonement and purification.

When one is evaluating these traditions, it is important to keep in mind that viewing defiling afflictions as possible punishments for certain sins is very different from seeing sin in itself as a ritual defilement. In tannaitic literature, sinners are not ritually defiling *unless* they have been struck with such an affliction. And despite Tosefta Negaim 6:7, it is not assumed that these afflictions strike only sinners. The fact that the tannaim can discuss defiling afflictions to such an extent in Mishnah tractate Negaim without coming to the idea of sin shows that they were surely able to conceive of afflictions that come about naturally, not as a result of sin. Indeed, we have noted that the Mishnah entertains the possibility that a Torah scholar would be afflicted, and the Sifra entertains the same possibility.[60] Moreover, even when a bona fide sinner has been struck with a defiling affliction, the impurity disappears not upon repentance, but only upon purification. And there is no suggestion in any of these documents that purification is in any way dependent upon repentance.

In the final analysis, the tannaim accept the thesis put forth by Scripture, that defiling afflictions can come about as a result of sin. Yet they go no further. As far as they are concerned, there are no legal ramifications that result from the fact that the afflicted individual may have sinned. The sinner is not ritually impure unless he or she has been afflicted. The sinner becomes ritually pure again upon ritual purification, with or without atonement. And there is no assumption that an afflicted individual is a sinner. Thus while the narrative traditions of the Hebrew Bible that connect defiling afflictions with sin are echoed by the tannaim, no law is derived from them. Thus it is apparent that these traditions are echoed in tannaitic literature not for their legal substance, but to reiterate the moral lesson that slander and arrogance are hateful to God. In other words, these traditions are *aggadot*: passages of moral/theological concern that do not, strictly speaking, have any legal force.[61] The restraint with which the tannaim approached these biblical traditions is characteristic of their compartmentalizing approach to impurity and sin in general. To appreciate the significance of the tannaitic effort to separate ritual impurity from sin in this regard, we need only recall the degree to which such ideas were integrated by the Qumran sectarians.

In the literature of the amoraic period, the idea that ritually defiling afflictions may come about as punishments for sins is reiterated and even expanded somewhat. Traditions preserved in the amoraic layers of the Babylonian Talmud and in Leviticus Rabbah (a midrashic text that likely emerged in the amoraic period) draw a direct connection between defiling afflictions and a number of sins. In Leviticus Rabbah[62] we find the following tradition associating defiling afflictions and sin.

Commenting on Leviticus 14:2 ("This is the law of the leper"), Leviticus Rabbah 16:1[63] quotes Proverbs 6:16–19:

(16) Six things the Lord hates;
seven are an abomination to Him:
(17) A haughty bearing,
a lying tongue
Hands that shed innocent blood,
(18) A mind that hatches evil plots,
Feet quick to run to evil,
(19) A false witness testifying lies,
And one who incites brothers to quarrel.

The Proverbs passage gives cause to associate impurity with sin — note the use of "abomination" in 6:16. But Leviticus Rabbah is not satisfied with such a loose association between these sins and defiling afflictions. The midrash provides explicit scriptural support for the view that these sins are punished with defiling afflictions. And the exegesis here is hardly far-fetched. Most involve straightforward readings of Scripture. That the sin of "evil tongue" can be so punished is learned from the case of Miriam. That the sin of murder can be so punished is learned from the case of

Joab, who murdered Abner and whose family was to be cursed with defiling afflictions (2 Sam. 3:28–30). A similar tradition appears in the Babylonian Talmud, tractate Arakhin 16a, and a lengthier treatment, discussing ten sins, appears elsewhere in
Leviticus Rabbah.[64]

One can discern in these amoraic traditions some expansion of the idea that we
are tracing. First, the impurity of flux becomes more and more associated with defiling afflictions, a connection based perhaps on the juxtaposition of the two in
Numbers 5:2.[65] Second, these traditions present a greater number of sins as possible
causes of defiling afflictions. The tannaitic sources spoke of slander and arrogance,
but these amoraic sources list seven (in the case of B. Arakhin) and ten (in the case
Lev. Rabbah 17:3), and other traditions speak of an even greater number.[66] In
Leviticus Rabbah, the notion that defiling afflictions are connected to sin is even justified by wordplay: The phrase "this is the law of the leper" (תורת המצרע) is interpreted
as "the law of the one who brings forth wickedness" (תורת המוציא רע).[67]

Despite these developments, however, the overall approach is substantially similar to that taken in the tannaitic sources: that defiling afflictions may come about as
punishments for sins. Again, it is not assumed that sinners are ritually impure, that
those who are ritually defiled have sinned, or that atonement is necessary in the purification process. In one sense, perhaps, the later traditions are even more limited
in scope than their tannaitic predecessors: While the tannaitic sources flirt with the
idea that these defilements come about *only* as a result of sin, the amoraic sources
state simply that they may come about as a result of sin. And again there is no direct
relationship between the sins and the appearance of defiling afflictions.[68]

Amoraic sources entertain the possibility that any number of calamities, not just
defiling afflictions, may come about as punishments for slander. On B. Shabbat 33a
and b, a few baraithot (tannaitic traditions quoted in the Talmuds) understand some
fatal choking disease (אסכרה) as a punishment for slander, and of course the Mishnah
itself (M. Arakhin 3:5) suggests that slander (המוציא שם רע) was the cause of the
Israelites' wandering in the desert for forty years. On the other hand, defiling afflictions are not seen only as punishments. In B. Berakhot 5b, a brief baraitha is quoted
to the effect that defiling afflictions are meant to inspire atonement (אינן אלא מזבח
כפרה). The anonymous discussion of the baraitha even concludes that defiling afflictions can in some cases be "chastisements of love" (יסורין של אהבה) — afflictions
that serve not to punish the guilty, nor to push backsliders back in line, but to test the
righteous. There are also traditions that view the afflictions that strike houses as a
blessing. According to Leviticus Rabbah 17:6, the leprosy that struck Israelite houses
forced them to bore holes in dwellings built by Canaanites, allowing them to find
buried treasure. The clear implication is that defiling afflictions were not viewed as
categorically bad.

One additional point must be reiterated: Even when these texts recognize that
defiling afflictions can come about as punishments for certain sins, the punitive
value of these afflictions is not the fact that they defile. It must be kept in mind that
these texts emerge during a period when the temple is long gone, and the practical
ramifications of ritual impurity were rather limited. The punitive value of the afflictions is the fact that they are ailments and thus at the very least bothersome, if not
terribly painful. The defiling force of these afflictions is secondary in most of these

Not sin & defilement, but Sin & Punishment

discussions. Thus even when there is a causal relationship between ritual impurity and sin, the real connection is not between sin and defilement, but with sin and punishment. And as we have already suggested, these traditions are probably best understood as part of the larger tannaitic effort to directly relate human suffering with divine punishment.

In the final analysis, there is nothing surprising in the amoraic traditions either. Even though the catalog of sins that can be punished with defilement is expanded, it is still limited to what can be scripturally justified. Even the list of ten sins presented in Leviticus Rabbah is based on careful, considered exegesis. There is no radical "metaphorization" of these afflictions even in the later rabbinic literature.[69] What we find in these amoraic sources, rather, is fairly consistent with what we find in their tannaitic predecessors: the reiteration of a theme articulated in Scripture. The theme is reiterated in order to present a moral lesson: God hates slander, arrogance, and other such sins. For the amoraim, certain sins *may* result in defiling afflictions, but they may not. The amoraim take up the moral lesson that Scripture itself presents: afflictions — defiling and otherwise — may come about as a result of sin. Just like their tannaitic predecessors, the amoraim affirm this thesis and go no further.

Niddah: *Women, Menstruation, and Sin*

Impurity Concern

Traditional Judaism has been particularly concerned with one form of impurity: menstrual defilement. In one way, the selective focus on menstruation begins to surface in the amoraic period: the only tractate in Mishnah Seder Toharot that is subjected to thoroughgoing amoraic treatment in the Jerusalem and Babylonian Talmuds is tractate Niddah.[70] This selective focus eventually led to specific stringencies: At different times, and in various places, the concern with menstrual impurity has led some Jewish communities to demand the physical isolation of the menstruant and even her exclusion from the synagogue. As far as we can tell, these stringencies appear to be medieval in origin.[71] There are, to be sure, scattered hints here and there that the medieval practices had an ancient basis. Some point to Josephus, *Antiquities* III:261, as testifying to the social isolation of menstruants in the first century CE,[72] but this passage does not testify that women were banished from their houses.[73] It is also common to point to the practices of the Samaritans, Karaites, or Falashas,[74] but we have already given sufficient cause to exclude such evidence from consideration when trying to determine the practice of Jews in the ancient period. The assumption that the practices of these groups did not develop over time is naive.[75] There is also a cryptic reference in M. Niddah 7:4 to בית הטמאות, which, depending on how it is vocalized, could be taken to mean either "house of impurities" or "house of impure women."[76] Either way, the reference is hardly unambiguous evidence for the ostracization of menstruants. The Tosefta parallel to this passage, T. Niddah 6:15, less ambiguously refers to bath houses, which could indeed be what is meant in the Mishnah passage as well. As Sanders, Cohen, and others have argued, too much has been made over the reference to בית הטמאות in M. Niddah 7:4.[77] What is more, rabbinic literature throughout assumes that the menstruant will remain at home, performing many of her domestic tasks.[78] Historians must always be wary of anachronism, particularly when it comes to understanding tannaitic attitudes toward menstrual impurity, for the tannaitic sources simply do not articulate the medieval concern for the isolation of menstruants.[79]

When we focus on the tannaitic sources themselves, however, we get a very different picture. Chapter 1 argued that the relationship between conceptions of defilement and of gender is more complex than what one might assume.[80] The same can be said of tannaitic impurity law. As we will see, it can readily be concluded that the tannaitic sources related to menstrual impurity are remarkably consistent with the claim that the tannaim "compartmentalized" impurity and sin.

We start by noting points of continuity with Scripture. Although the specifics of tannaitic purity law regarding the menstruant incorporate much that is not explicitly legislated in Scripture, we see again a continuity in terms of overall perspectives. Like their biblical foundation, the tannaitic sources do not single out women as particularly impure, nor view menstruation as something sinful. Indeed, menstrual blood is just another source of ritual defilement pure and simple, one among many, some of which originate in men, others in women, and most of which affect men and women equally. Unlike the Talmuds, the tannaitic sources devote roughly equal energy to all the major forms of defilement.

It has been argued that the mere placement of tractate Niddah in Mishnah Seder Toharot reflects poorly on women, if only for the fact that Niddah finds its place among tractates named for *things*, such as tents, pots, and pools (tractates Ohalot, Kelim, and Mikvaot).[81] But in Seder Toharot, the menstruant is no more objectified in tractate Niddah than the man with a flux is objectified in tractate Zabim. If women are objectified by the perception that menstruation defiles, it is only to the same extent that all Jews, men and women, are objectified by the ritual impurities that affect them. Furthermore, even with regard to the menstrual taboo, the determinative category in tannaitic impurity legislation is not gender, but Jewish identity. According to the M. Niddah 7:3, the menstrual taboo applies only to Jewish women: the bloodstains of Gentile women were not defiling. As Paula Fredriksen astutely points out, this would not be the case if gender were the determinative concern here.[82]

It is also claimed by some that tannaitic interest in the menstrual impurity is motivated not by concern with the ritual impurity of women, but "entirely from their concern with the cultic purity of *men*."[83] This is also not entirely accurate. The primary concern of tannaitic impurity law is maintaining the ritual purity of the sanctuary and other holy things, such as priestly dues. These are subject to ritual defilement by men as well as women. Women themselves are, of course, directly affected by these exclusions.[84] According to M. Kelim 1:8, menstruants were excluded from the Temple Mount altogether, while ritually pure women were admitted at least as far as the Women's Court.[85] In order to understand properly the tannaitic approach to the menstrual taboo, one must recognize that for the tannaim, menstruation was just one of many sources of ritual impurity, and that the tannaim appear to be interested equally in the ritual impurity of (Jewish) men and women.

In both the Hebrew Bible and tannaitic sources there is one way in which the menstrual taboo differs from the other ritual impurities. Not only is cohabitation with a menstruant considered to be a severe source of ritual defilement in the Bible (Lev.

15:24), but the act is also explicitly prohibited among the other sexual sins that bring about moral defilement (Lev. 18:19; 20:18). Thus with regard to the menstrual taboo, the stakes are much higher than they are with regard to the other sources of ritual impurity. If a man knowingly cohabits with his menstruating wife, he is subject to *karet* (M. Ker. 1:1), and if both knowingly sin, they are both subject to *karet*.[86]

It is precisely because of this added danger that tannaitic sources speculate on the punishments that will befall women who fail to observe these regulations. The classic source is M. Shabbat 2:6:

> For three transgressions do women die in childbirth· for not being careful with regard to menstruation, with regard to *ḥallah*, and with regard to lighting the [Sabbath] lamp.

Similar traditions can be found elsewhere in rabbinic literature.[87] Some of them even go as far as to view these commandments (and the threats related to their violation) as punishments visited upon women of all time, due to the sin of Eve.[88]

M. Shabbat 2:6 threatens women who violate the menstrual impurity, claiming that they could suffer death in childbirth. While this idea appears to be a juxtaposition of ritual impurity and sin, the situation is in fact complex. M. Shabbat 2:6 is concerned not with the violation of ritual impurity law, but with the prohibition of cohabitation during menstruation. And the text does not deal exclusively with impurity laws by any means. The passage singles out three sinful acts, and does so for a reason. The commandments mentioned here are incumbent upon all Israel, men and women.[89] The performance of these rituals, however, depends upon women:[90] women light the Sabbath lights (M. Shab. 2:7), women were the ones who baked the bread (M. Ket. 5:5), and, as M. Niddah assumes throughout, women were responsible for determining their own status with regard to menstrual impurity. Yet if the woman fails in her duty, her husband can be directly affected: he can cohabit with his menstruous wife, eat bread from which *ḥallah* was not taken, or come home from synagogue to a house in which no Sabbath lights have been kindled (thus compelling him, perhaps, to light a lamp on the Sabbath). Thus the common denominator of the sins singled out in M. Shabbat 2:6 is that in these three situations, a recalcitrant wife has the power to make a transgressor of her husband. That is why the woman who violates these laws is threatened with such punishments.

It is important to recognize, however, that there is another side to all this, which reflects positively on women. As Wegner points out, one can see in M. tractate Niddah the tannaitic recognition of the personhood of women.[91] Tannaitic law assumes that women will learn complex rules (M. Nid. 8:1–2) and that they can be trusted to follow them (M. Nid. 2:4). And because of modesty concerns, only women can make the final decisions in any questionable situation.[92] Tannaitic law relating to menstrual impurity does not assume that women are inherently sinful. To the contrary, it assumes that women follow the regulations in good faith. Ross Kraemer points out an irony, which we have noted in chapter 1. The regulations regarding the menstrual taboo actually empower women, by giving them the opportunity to decline sexual relations by claiming that they are ritually impure.[93]

It remains to be noted, finally, that M. Shabbat 2:6 and the passages related to it have no legal force. It is not as if the tannaitic sages expected midwives to be their hangmen, or assumed that their own wives must have sinned if they had miscarried or died in childbirth. These passages are meant, rather, to persuade women to follow the laws delegated to them. Just as we saw regarding the tannaitic treatment of defiling afflictions, when the tannaim juxtapose impurity and sin (which they very rarely do) the juxtaposition has no legal ramifications; these juxtapositions take place in the realm of *aggadah*. Although these *aggadot* may be displeasing to the modern eye, their primary purpose — as with many other *aggadic* juxtapositions of sin and punishment in tannaitic and rabbinic sources — is to encourage Israel to observe the commandments of God.

With regard to impurity and sin, the tannaitic discussions of menstrual impurity in the Mishnah, Tosefta and Sifra are devoid of any suggestion that menstruation is sinful. Indeed, the tannaim are notably — and in comparison with the sources analyzed thus far, even uniquely — restrained. I know of no instance in tannaitic literature in which the sages use the term *niddah* (נדה) in a way other than its technical senses (except when quoting Scripture). Thus the tannaim use the term with regard either to menstruation or to the "waters of purification" (מי נדה) described in Numbers 19.[94] Chapter 3 noted that the Qumran sectarians were wont to use the term נדה with reference to sins, especially of the idolatrous and sexual sort.[95] Also there are some scriptural precedents for such usage, including the simile in Ezekiel 36:17 (Israel's ways were in God's sight like the impurity of a menstruous woman), the use of the term to mean "abomination" in Leviticus 20:21, and the use of the term for "idol" in 2 Chronicles 29:5. Compared with the Qumran corpus, the tannaitic use of the term נדה is notably restricted. And in this one respect, the tannaim are even more restrained than Scripture. When we keep in mind the various scriptural uses of the term נדה, we can plainly see that the tannaim chose to ignore the wider semantic potential of the term נדה, and that they have consciously restricted its use to refer to the ritual status of menstruants or the purification water described in Numbers 19.

One question remains: Why have medieval and modern Jewish communities paid more attention to the menstrual defilement than to other sorts of ritual impurity? And why, of all the tractates in the Mishnah dealing with impurity, does only Niddah receive thoroughgoing treatment in the Talmuds? We cannot answer these questions fully here.[96] Even the question regarding the structure and content of the Talmud brings us well beyond our chronological focus, since it was shaped centuries after the tannaitic period. It is important to note, however, that part of the answer is to be found in the dynamic that has been explained in this section. In the Hebrew Bible and in tannaitic sources, the menstruant is both a source of ritual impurity and a potential partner to a grave sin: Sexual relations between a man and a menstruating woman bring about both ritual (Lev. 15:24) and moral defilement (Lev. 18:19). The maintained and even heightened interest in menstrual defilement, even when the ritual impurity system itself has long ceased to function, is no doubt due to the fact that a married couple is prohibited from having sexual relations while the woman is menstruating. Because the ritual purifications here also mark the time when a married couple may once again engage in sexual relations, these regulations remained in force, even while others fell by the wayside. Here too we find some continuity with the biblical tradition. As chapter 1 argued, in the Hebrew Bible the genders are treated rather equally vis-à-vis ritual impurity, but somewhat less equally with regard to moral impurity. After the fall of the temple in 70 CE, that inequality regarding moral impurity brought about an inequality regarding ritual impurity, resulting in a selective focus on the ritual impurity of women, well into the amoraic period.

The Pharisaic Ḥavurah

The compartmentalization of ritual impurity and sin in tannaitic sources can also be clearly seen in another place where ritual impurity figures prominently, in the rules regarding the Pharisaic *havurah* (חבורה).[97] According to a number of tannaitic sources—especially Tosefta Demai, chapter 2, parts of which will be examined here—in the first centuries of the Common Era there was a voluntary association of fellows who chose to eat their common food in a state of ritual purity.[98] The nature of their relationship with the Pharisees remains unclear, but it is certain that one cannot simply identify Pharisees with these associates.[99] Yet it is likely that those who were associates in the pretannaitic period were Pharisees as well.

Sanders has recently denied the authenticity of these reports.[100] He asks, "Did the Pharisees eat ordinary food in purity?" and his answer is "No." Among his key arguments is the supposition that eating ordinary food in ritual purity would be impossible, since any observant (and married) Pharisee would be ritually impure nearly all the time.[101] Sanders must here assume that the Pharisees did not have the notion of the *tebul yom*, which would allow a person ritually defiled from, say, permitted sexual relations, to be become ritually pure for most practical purposes immediately after bathing, without waiting for the sun to set. But if one supposes the antiquity of the notion of the *tebul yom*, Sanders's argument begins to unravel.[102] And as we have seen, the discoveries from Qumran all but definitively prove that the notion of the *tebul yom* was current in the pretannaitic period.[103] Thus Sanders's argument is overstated. We cannot, of course, prove that there was such an association in the Pharisaic and tannaitic periods, but the claim that some did chose to live this way is reasonable enough. Even if the association did not exist, the tannaitic sources relating to the *havurah* are intriguing in that they are fully in line with the tannaitic approach to impurity and sin.

We now turn to selections from the classic source, Tosefta Demai, chapter 2:

> (2) He who imposes upon himself four things is accepted to be an associate. not to give heave offering or tithes to an outsider [עם הארץ]; not to prepare his pure food in the house of an outsider; and to eat even ordinary food in purity. . .
>
> (10) If one who comes to impose upon himself the obligations of an associate has previously acted according to them in private he is accepted; otherwise he is first taught and afterwards accepted. R. Simon b. Yohai says: he is in any case accepted and then taught as he goes along
>
> (11) And he is accepted first with regard to "wings"[104] and is afterwards accepted with regard to pure food. If he only imposes upon himself the obligations concerning wings, he is accepted; if he imposes upon himself the obligations concerning pure food but not those concerning wings, he is not considered reliable with regard to pure food.

(12) Until when is a man accepted? The school of Shammai say: for fluids thirty days, for clothing twelve months. The school of Hillel say. for either thirty days.

The structural similarities here between the Pharisaic association and the Qumran sect are obvious, although they are not close enough to justify any identification between the two groups.[105] We see a similar terminology, and an analogous, gradual form of initiation. Also, of course, the groups share a common ideal: the maintenance of ritual purity. Yet what is different is also significant. Compared with those of 1QS, the rules of the associates are notably sober. There is no great concern in the tannaitic sources with the initiate's past or even present moral behavior, and there is no association between ritual purification and moral atonement. Presumably, known sinners would not have been admitted to the *havurah*.[106] Thus we can state that righteousness was a prerequisite for membership in both the *havurah* and the Qumran sect.[107] But, as we saw in chapter 3, righteousness was a prerequisite for joining the Qumran sect because sin was viewed by the sectarians as a source of ritual defilement. There is no reflection of this notion in the tannaitic sources relating to the *havurah*.

In the tannaitic sources, the exclusion of certain sinners is not based on the idea that sin produces ritual impurity, but rather, sinners would not have been admitted for the simple reason that they could not be trusted. Tax collectors — the epitome of dishonesty — were barred from participation in the association, at least as long as they served in that capacity.[108] The mid-second-century sage R. Yehudah suggests that those who rear small cattle, who are loose with vows and laughter, and who contract corpse impurity are not to be accepted (M. Dem. 2:3).[109] Only the last of these conditions deals with ritual impurity; in actuality all of them relate primarily to trustworthiness.[110] Rabin is likely correct that R. Yehudah is concerned here with priests who contract corpse impurity, in violation of the Torah.[111] Those frivolous with vows or too inclined toward humor obviously cannot be taken at their word. And those who rear small cattle were, along with tax collectors, considered to be invalid as witnesses.[112] Thus trust turns out to be the bottom line in all of the concerns raised about potential membership. This stands to reason. After all, the purity of the association was dependent upon the trustworthiness of the individual members. If, however, there was any concern here with the ritually defiling force of moral sins, we would expect to see references to atonement and purification — as we find in 1QS — but we find nothing of the sort. Moreover, while the associates did view nonmembers as ritually defiling, the outsiders' ritual impurity resulted not from the commission of some grave sin but simply from the fact that the outsiders did not take upon themselves the same purity obligations that the associates had. It is important to note that there is no evidence that the associates considered Gentiles, who also committed idolatry, to be inherently ritually impure. The members of the Pharisaic *havurah*, like the tannaim, separated the issue of ritual impurity from that of moral sin. Again, when it comes to the defiling force of sin, we see a wide gulf separating the view of the tannaim from that of the Qumran sectarians.

Sin, Status, and Atonement in Tannaitic *Halakhah*

In the previous section, it was established that regarding issues relating to ritual impurity, tannaitic sources are very careful to separate — to compartmentalize — the concerns of impurity and sin. In this section we will consider the same phenomenon from a different angle. We will look at topics relating to sin, status, and atonement. These issues could well have been related to ritual impurity, had the tannaim chosen to relate them. But as we will see the tannaim carefully chose not to do so.

Sin, Sex, and the Sotah

We noted in the introduction to the previous section that sin as a topic is not addressed in Mishnah (or Tosefta) Seder Toharot, and sinful behavior is not viewed as a source of ritual defilement anywhere in tannaitic literature. Certain sins are viewed as sources of *moral* impurity, but otherwise, sins are not viewed as ritually defiling, and ritual defilement is not viewed as sinful.

Among the strategies used by the tannaim to reinforce the distinction between impurity and sin is careful use of terminology. We have already noted that the tannaitic use of the term *niddah* (נדה) is notably restrained. Whereas the Qumran sectarian literature frequently uses the term with regard to sin, and Scripture does so on occasion, the tannaim generally restrict their use of the term to its technical sense of menstrual defilement, and they do not use it as an adjective describing sin.

A similar phenomenon can be seen in the tannaitic avoidance of the term "abomination" (תועבה). The term barely appears at all in tannaitic sources,[113] and when it does, it is either in a quotation from Scripture (e.g., M. Avodah Zarah 1:9)[114] or in a midrashic passage commenting on a scriptural verse that uses the term (e.g., Sifre Deut. § 99).[115] This observation is important because it is not as if the tannaim did not have the occasion to use the term. As we saw in chapter 1, the term is used in the Hebrew Bible to refer to all sorts of sins, though most often in relation to the sources of moral defilement: idolatry, incest, and murder. And while there are very few discussions of moral defilement per se in tannaitic literature, there is no dearth of discussion of the sins that are perceived to produce moral defilement. Indeed, a tractate of Mishnah, Tosefta, and the Talmud is devoted to idolatry (Avodah Zarah), and murderous and sexual sins are addressed also throughout the corpus. Considering the frequency with which the term תועבה is used in Scripture (which the tannaim clearly had at their disposal) and in the Qumran corpus (which testifies to the continued use of the term in the first few centuries before the Common Era), the tannaitic avoidance of the term is notable indeed.

The restricted nature of the tannaitic use of impurity terminology with regard to sin can also be seen in the use of the term "defile" (טמא). Almost every time the term is used, it is in regard to ritual impurity. In the tannaitic midrashim, the term טמא is used also with regard to the less frequently discussed concept of moral impurity (see chapter 5), but there is one usage of the term that is related to moral defilement and that is manifest, although rarely, even in the Mishnah. From time to time in tannaitic sources the term טמא is used with regard to a woman who has been raped or who has committed adultery. Yet the sense conveyed in these cases is not to be understood as ritual impurity. Rather, it is a permanent change in status caused by the act perpetrated by or upon the woman. The incident may well affect the woman's status regarding marriageability, particularly if her husband or potential husband is a priest. It is that change in status that is conveyed by the statement that the woman is impure.[116] The woman is not considered to be ritually impure, however, despite the use of the term טמא.

M. Ketubot 2:5–6 delineates some laws pertaining to women whose sexual history affects their current status with regard to marriageability. Biblical law insists that priests marry virgins or widows (Lev. 21:7), and tannaitic law follows suit (cf. M. Ket. 2:9). Among the scenarios discussed in M. Ketubot 2:5–6 is the status of a woman who was captured by enemy forces and perhaps raped during her captivity.[117] A woman who admits to her captivity and claims that she was not raped is trusted, provided, ironically, that there are no valid witnesses to her captivity.[118] The logic works as follows. The woman's admission of captivity is completely voluntary, because there are no witnesses. Yet that admission threatens to invalidate her capacity to marry a priest or even resume relations with her priestly husband. Thus her voluntary admission validates her testimony that she was not raped, because if she were going to lie, she could just deny that she was captured altogether. As the tannaim put it, "the mouth that prohibits is the mouth that permits." Now — and here the irony is manifest — if her testimony regarding her captivity comes to be corroborated by valid witnesses, then her claim that she was not raped is no longer accepted as valid testimony (unless of course, that claim too is corroborated by valid witnesses).

What is important for our purposes is a phrase that appears now and again in the passage. In the Mishnah, the woman testifies, "I have been captured, but I remain pure" (נשביתי וטהורה אני).[119] Clearly, ritual impurity is not the concern here, for ritual impurity is not an issue that pertains to marriageability. Context allows nothing but the understanding that "pure" connotes that the woman has not been raped, just as, as will be seen momentarily, the term "defile" can connote that a woman has been raped or has committed a sexual sin.

Consider the following passage (M. Ter. 8:12):

So too if Gentiles say to [a group of] women· "Hand over one of you and we will defile her [ונטמאה] and if you do not, we will defile all of you," they are all to defile themselves, and they are not to deliver to them one Jewish person

The passage in question immediately follows a similar passage where Gentiles threaten to defile priestly dues. Nonetheless, in this passage, it is clear again that the issue at stake is not ritual defilement, but sexual sin (again, rape). Whence comes this usage? The term טמא with regard to rape has clear scriptural precedent in the narrative of Dinah (Gen. 34:5ff). Also the use of the term to connote the disqualification of a woman with respect to her husband is precedented in Deuteronomy 24:4, which forbids a man to remarry a woman he divorced, if in the interim she was married to any other man.[120] In M. Ketubot 2:5–6 and the other passages just cited, the tannaim use the terminology of purity and impurity in ways very similar to these scriptural precedents.

This alternative usage of purity terminology in tannaitic sources is most evident with regard to the rules of the suspected adulteress (Num. 5:11–31) which are delineated in the Mishnah, Tosefta, and Talmud (tractate Sotah) and in the tannaitic midrashim to Numbers 5.[121] The terminology of impurity is used throughout these sources with reference to the determination of the woman's status: if the *sotah*, as the suspected adulteress is called in rabbinic sources, has committed adultery, as her husband suspects, then she is impure; if she has not, then she is pure (e.g., M. Sot. 1:5). Yet it is evident that the *sotah* was not considered to be ritually impure, for the *sotah* is admitted into the sanctuary. According to M. Sotah 1:5, the suspected adulteress is brought somewhere within the vicinity of the Nicanor Gate,[122] which was on the eastern side of the court (*azarah*)[123] and presumably divided the court of Israel from the court of Women. Thus the suspected adulteress was brought either into the court of Israel or very close to it. Either way, she was brought into and beyond the court of Women, while ritually impure women — *niddot* and *zabot* — were excluded from the Temple Mount altogether (M. Kel. 1:8).

Once the rite was administered, the woman was immediately removed from the court, lest she defile it (M. Sot. 3:4). Here, for the first time in the tractate, we see the concern that the *sotah* may ritually defile the sanctuary. But the concern is only indirectly indirectly related to the woman's guilt. It is related more to the fact that the rite (or the excitement caused by the rite) threatens to cause the woman either to menstruate or bleed irregularly — or perhaps even die — and any of these eventualities would cause the sanctuary to be ritually defiled.[124]

So why do the tannaim describe the *sotah*'s innocence or guilt by using the terms of "impure" (טמא) and "pure" (טהור)? The reason is not hard to find: It is that the scriptural passage that details the rite of the suspected adulteress (Num. 5:11–31) also uses the terms טמא and טהור throughout, and the content of this scriptural passage looms large in the tannaitic sources. We noted in chapter 1 above that as far as Numbers is concerned, the suspected adulteress is not ritually impure. The same is true of the tannaitic sources.

We have seen all along that the relationship between the tannaitic sources and its scriptural base defies simple description. This is no less true when it comes to the tannaitic use of purity terminology with regard to sin and sex. For the most part, such usages are avoided in tannaitic sources, and as a result, *niddah* (נדה), which is used primarily with regard to ritual impurity in the Hebrew Bible, but occasionally with regard to moral impurity, is used in tannaitic sources only with regard to ritual impurity. The term "abomination" (תועבה), which is used primarily with regard to moral impurity in the Hebrew Bible, is avoided as much as possible in tannaitic sources. The same is true of the term "pollute" (חנף). The one usage that continues is the use of טמא with regard to sexual sins perpetrated by or upon women. It is probably impossible for us to know why the tannaim tolerated this usage. But for what it is worth, it is interesting to note that when טמא is used in tannaitic literature to connote the sexual status of a woman, it is used primarily in reporting or commenting upon the statements made not by sages, but by common people. That is, most instances of this usage occur when the tannaim characterize the ways in which common people speak to each other.[125] Because the tannaim use these terms in this sense so rarely, one gets the sense that they would have preferred to avoid this usage too but were compelled otherwise by common convention.

Regardless of how we account for the intermittent use of the term טמא to refer to the sexual status of women, the fact remains that the tannaitic use of impurity terminology with regard to sin is an extremely rare phenomenon. And there is no usage in tannaitic sources that does not have a scriptural — indeed, Pentateuchal — base. What is more important is that there are usages in the Pentateuch that cannot be found in tannaitic sources. The tannaitic effort to restrict their use of such terminology in these contexts is, I believe, the result of a conscious effort to avoid juxtaposing issues that they wished to compartmentalize.

Avodah Zarah: *Idols, Idolatry, and Impurity*

As was noted in chapter 1, there is no reason to assume that idols were considered ritually defiling in the Hebrew Bible, although as we have seen, idolatry was considered a source of moral defilement,[126] as it is in most ancient Jewish literature. The concern in ancient Jewish literature is not with the ritually defiling force of idols or idolaters, but with the morally defiling force of idolatrous behavior.[127] As we will see in chapter 5, the tannaim too concern themselves with the morally defiling force of idolatrous behavior. What we are addressing here is the fact that, according to tannaitic *halakhah*, idols have become a source of *ritual* defilement.

The idea of the idol as ritually defiling is hardly central to the tannaitic conception of ritual impurity. There are very few discussions of the ritual impurity of idols in M. Seder Toharot (we have already noted its absence from M. Kel. ch. 1). Equally important is the fact that the tractate that covers idolatry (M. Avodah Zarah) is to be found not in Mishnah Seder Toharot, but in Seder Nezikin (the Order of Damages). This fact underscores what becomes clear after a casual reading of tractate Avodah Zarah: For the tannaim, the primary ontological categories relating to idols and idolatry are not pure and impure, but permitted and prohibited.

Nonetheless, the tannaim do consider idols to be ritually defiling. M. Avodah Zarah 3:6 states:

> If a man's house adjoined an idol's shrine, and it fell down, it is forbidden to build it again. What shall he do? He must withdraw four cubits[128] within his own domain and then build again. If there was a wall common to him and the idol's shrine it is deemed to belong half to each; its stones, wood and earth convey impurity as though they were a creeping thing; for it is written, "You shall utterly detest it [Deut 7:26]." R. Akiba says: Like a menstruant, for it is written, "You shall cast them away as a menstruous thing: you shall say to it, 'get away from here'" [Is. 30:22]; as a menstruant conveys impurity by being carried, so too an idol conveys impurity by being carried

A number of important ideas are expressed here. First, it is clear that an idol has become a source of ritual impurity in its own right, although the rabbis argue about the nature of its impurity. In the talmudic discussion of this passage (B. Shabbat 82a–83b), it becomes clear that the rabbis believed that the ritual impurity of an idol derives from a rabbinic decree to that effect.[129] In other words, as far as the talmudic sages were concerned, the ritual impurity of idols was not a biblical law, but a rabbinic one.[130] Indeed, though this view is not articulated in quite that fashion in the Mishnah itself, it does appear that the tannaim viewed the ritual impurity of idols as something of a novelty.

M. Shabbat 8:7 to 9:4 brings up a number of examples of laws for which there is no scriptural "proof" per se, although there is some scriptural "indication" for the law.[131] In this context, the following tradition concerning idolatry is presented (9:1):

> R. Akiba said· How do we know that an idol defiles through carrying? [It is] like the menstruant, as it is said [Is. 30 22], "You will cast them away like a menstruant. 'Out!' you will call to it." Just as a menstruant defiles through carrying, so too does an idol defile through carrying.

One would think that if the tannaim wanted to argue that idols were ritually defiling they could easily find support by reinterpreting any of the verses in Scripture (say, Lev. 20:1–3) that view idolatry as morally defiling. Yet they do no such thing. To the contrary, they generally take the biblical verses articulating the idea of moral impurity at face value: The tannaim, too, view idolatry, incest, and murder as sources of moral defilement, as we will see in chapter 5. Thus as far as the tannaim and subsequent rabbinic sages are concerned, idols defile ritually not because the Torah said so, but because the tannaim said so.

It would appear, from just a casual reading of B. Shabbat 82a–83b, that the talmudic sages were hardly in agreement as to the precise nature of idol impurity: Is it to be compared to the force of a menstruant? A corpse? Or perhaps a Gentile? These and other possibilities are entertained in the talmudic discussion of M. Shabbbat 9:1, leaving the impression that there was hardly a long-standing or well-understood tradition regarding the ritually defiling force of idolatry.

In addition, the defiling force of idols does not appear to be inherent. Generally, idols defile, but there are exceptions. In the situation of the common wall, while the Israelite was prohibited from rebuilding the wall, he or she was not prohibited from living there while the wall was still standing. That the impurity of an idol is affected by circumstance can also be seen in the following (M. Avodah Zarah 3:8):

> None may sit in [an idol's] shadow, but if one has sat there, s/he remains pure; and none may pass under it, and if s/he has done so s/he becomes impure If it encroached on the public way and one passed under it, s/he remains pure.

The concerns of M. Avodah Zarah are not those of the Holiness Code. There is no hint in M. Avodah Zarah that idols pollute the land. Moreover, there is no great concern for the defiling force of idolaters. The concern is simply with the effect that contact with an idol can have on an Israelite.

Perhaps the most important point is this: Even as these sources articulate the ritually defiling force of idols, they nowhere articulate or assume that idolatrous behavior is ritually defiling in any way. Idolatry is punished by *sekilah* (stoning) or *karet* (extirpation), depending on the circumstance.[132] But even though idols are ritually defiling, the act of idolatry is itself viewed in tannaitic *halakhah* as a crime, and not as a source of ritual defilement.

What we have seen here is fully in line with the approach of the tannaim as described it up until now. Had the tannaim recognized a connection between ritual and moral impurity, they might have tried to derive the ritual impurity of the idol from the scriptural passages dealing with the morally defiling force of idolatry. But they do nothing of the kind. In tannaitic *halakhah*, idols are ritually defiling. As we will see in chapter 5, idolatry is morally defiling in tannaitic sources. Yet as related as idols and idolatry are, the moral impurity of idolatry and the ritually defiling force of idols are completely different issues in tannaitic sources.

The Status of Sinners

The compartmentalization of impurity and sin can further be seen in the fact that in tannaitic *halakhah,* sinners are by no means barred from the sanctuary. I have argued that exclusions from the sanctuary are not tantamount to declarations that what is excluded is ritually impure.[133] That is so because exclusions from the sanctuary are based on both purity and status. Thus if sinners *were* barred from the sanctuary, that prohibition could mean one of two things: It could mean that sinners were ritually impure, or it could mean that they were considered to be of some lower status than nonsinners. On the other hand, if sinners were considered to be ritually impure, we would expect that they too would be excluded from the sanctuary, but they are not mentioned in the tannaitic texts that delineate the exclusions from the sanctuary (e.g., M. Kel. 1:8–9).

This argument from silence is bolstered by the laws of the *sotah*, which explicitly enjoin the presentation of a suspected sinner into the sanctuary. Another passage in the Mishnah even more clearly assumes that sinners can be admitted to the sanctuary. M. Bekhorot 7:7 states that an animal that has killed a person is not fit to be offered as a sacrifice or even to be slaughtered for the purpose of food (cf. M. Bekh. 6:12).[134] But this exclusion, as the Mishnah states, is one of a series of exclusions that apply to animals but not to persons. Thus a priest who has killed another person is not disqualified from serving in the temple. This means that a priest who has killed a person is admitted into the sanctuary as well. This is not to say that tannaitic sources treat murder or manslaughter lightly. Murder is a capital crime, and manslaughter too brings punishments. What is important here is the fact that when issues of sin are raised even when it relates to the temple, concerns with ritual defilement are not to be found.

To be sure, there is a status in tannaitic *halakhah* that is directly related to sins that are believed to bring about moral defilement. The child born of certain sinful relationships is known in tannaitic sources as a *mamzer.* The precise definition of a *mamzer* is subject to debate in these sources (M. Yeb. 4:13),[135] but it is clear that a number, though not all, of the sexual relationships prohibited in Leviticus 18 and 20 could result in the conception of a *mamzer.* The *mamzer* suffers in having a low status and few potential marriage partners (M. Kid. 4:1).[136] But the *mamzer* is not inherently impure. Indeed, under certain circumstances, the *mamzer* is even permitted to eat priestly dues (M. Yeb. 7:5). The fact that the *mamzer* is not considered to be ritually impure further underscores the fact for the tannaim, sin and ritual impurity were distinct concerns.

Atonement and Purification

In chapter 3 we saw the degree to which atonement and purification were merged at Qumran. In the tannaitic corpus, however, purification and atonement remain conceptually distinct.[137] Just as ritual impurity is separated from sin, so too is ritual purification kept distinct from atonement. We observed the compartmentalization of purification and atonement in our analysis of the *ḥavurah.* The process of joining the *ḥavurah* involved a gradual acceptance of stringent standards of ritual purity, but it did not involve any formal rituals of repentance, purificatory or otherwise, in stark contrast to the process of joining the Qumran sect.

The tannaitic compartmentalization of purification and atonement can equally be seen in the laws relating to Yom Kippur, the Day of Atonement. What is striking about the rituals for Yom Kippur in tannaitic sources is the complete absence of any purificatory rituals of atonement. There are, of course, purification rituals: The High Priest must immerse himself five times during the course of the day (M. Yoma 3:3). But these rituals are not purifications of atonement. Rather, they are standard rituals of purification that allow the priest to perform the sacrificial rituals of atonement in the temple (cf. M. Yoma 3:2). Considering the degree to which atonement and purification were merged at Qumran and, for that matter, for many other groups in first-century Palestine — Johanine and Christian baptism will be discussed in chapter 6 — it is remarkable that there are no purificatory rituals of atonement performed on Yom Kippur. This contrast is even more remarkable when it is recalled that the biblical description of the rites for the Day of Atonement includes a few passages that juxtapose impurity and sin and purification and atonement (Lev. 16:16, 30).[138] Had the tannaim wanted to incorporate purificatory rituals of atonement into Yom Kippur rituals, they would not have been short of scriptural support.

There is, however, one passage in M. Yoma that juxtaposes purification and atonement, and it is the second half of the last mishnah in the tractate (M. Yoma 8:9):[139]

> This did Rabbi Eleazar Ben Azariah expound· "from all of your sins you shall be purified before the Lord" [Lev. 16:30]. Transgressions between a person and God, the Day of Atonement effects atonement; transgressions between a person and another, the Day of Atonement does not effect atonement, until s/he has appeased his or her fellow.
>
> Rabbi Akiba said: Blessed are you, Israel. Before whom are you purified? Who purifies you? Your Father in heaven, as it is written: "And I will sprinkle pure water upon you, and you will be purified" [Ezek. 36:25]; "The Lord, hope [מקוה] of Israel!" [Jer. 17:13]. Just as the immersion pool [מקוה] purifies the impure, so the Holy One Blessed be He purifies Israel.

At first glance, this passage might appear to contradict the claim that the tannaim compartmentalized purification and atonement. On closer inspection, however, it becomes clear that the passage actually confirms the claim. What is notable is that while Leviticus 16:30 juxtaposes purification and atonement, the legal exegesis of the verse attributed to Rabbi Eleazar does not. The exegesis would have been no different had the sage started with a passage that read "from all of your sins you shall be atoned before the Lord." The exegesis attributed to Rabbi Akiba is slightly more startling, in that it not only quotes verses that juxtapose purification and atonement, but the exegesis itself continues to juxtapose the two. Yet what we see in this passage is really no different from what we have been seeing all along. The juxtaposition of impurity and sin is not unheard of, it is just extremely rare. And when the juxtaposition does appear, it is scripturally based and lacking in legal force. That the usage is scripturally motivated is clear; the shift from "atone" to "purify" begins only after Leviticus 16:30 has been quoted. That the passage lacks legal force is also clear. Indeed, like the final passages of a number of Mishnah tractates,[140] the midrash attributed here to Rabbi Akiba is *aggadic* in nature.

Summary and Conclusion

This chapter has analyzed a good number of tannaitic sources relevant to the issues of ritual impurity and sin and has argued that the tannaitic approach to ritual impurity and sin can be characterized as an effort at "compartmentalization." The tannaim strive to separate the conception of ritual impurity from the conception of sin. Thus ritual impurity remains, as in Scripture, something that is natural, unavoidable, and not sinful. Sin does not produce ritual impurity, and ritual impurity does not render one sinful. Also ritual purification is not a part of the process of atonement. Even when it comes to the Pharisaic *ḥavurah*, the tannaitic sources drive a wedge between sin and ritual impurity, and between ritual purification and atonement. As we have seen, the tannaim are also notably careful with their use of purity terminology. The term *niddah* (נדה) is used by the tannaim only in its technical ritual impurity sense; the terms "impure" (טמא) and "pure" (טהור) are also used reservedly, and the emotive term "abomination" (תועבה) is almost totally avoided in tannaitic *halakhah*.

From time to time, however, impurity and sin are juxtaposed in tannaitic sources: defiling afflictions are viewed as possible punishments for sin, and women who disregard their menstrual impurity are threatened with death in childbirth. The first of these perspectives is deeply rooted in Scripture. The second is not about ritual impurity as much as it is about the sinful situation that could result from the woman's negligence — the possibility that the couple will violate the injunction against sexual relations while the woman is menstruating. More important, in neither case is any legal ramification drawn from the juxtaposition of impurity and sin. Defiling afflictions may come about as a result of sin, but sinners are not assumed to be ritually impure unless they are also afflicted with an affliction. And any person so afflicted, no matter how righteous, is ritually defiling just the same. The purpose of these traditions is not to legislate impurity law, but to teach moral lessons. The overriding concern here is to emphasize that sin will be punished and that human suffering comes about as a result of sin. These traditions are best seen as *aggadot*.

I emphasize this point because I believe that the *aggadah–halakhah* distinction can lead to a better understanding of the more general dynamic between sin and defilement in tannaitic literature. The idea that the "leper" *could* be guilty of slander is just one of those juxtapositions between sin and defilement. The upsetting idea that sinful women could die in childbirth is another. What is true of both of these notions — and, I believe, of virtually all tannaitic juxtapositions of impurity and sin — is that they are *aggadic* in nature. When it comes to *halakhah*, the tannaim do all they can to separate — to "compartmentalize" — impurity and sin. But in the realm of *aggadah* — and, I believe, for the tannaim, *only* in the realm of *aggadah* — juxtapositions of the concepts of impurity and sin are tolerated.

The significance of all this is best seen by comparison, when we realize how different the approach of the tannaim is from that taken at Qumran and by early Christians. But comparison at this point would be premature, for I have yet to analyze the tannaitic approach to moral impurity in any detail. We turn to that issue in the next chapter.

5

Siluk Ha-Shekhinah: Sin, Defilement, and the Departure of the Divine Presence

This chapter will examine the tannaitic treatment of the idea of moral defilement. Chapter 4 demonstrated that in tannaitic *halakhah*, the issues of ritual defilement and sin are compartmentalized as much as possible. Yet tannaitic sources do indeed articulate the idea of moral defilement.[1] These sources, however, have received very little attention in scholarly literature on impurity in rabbinic Judaism.[2] In our analysis of the relevant tannaitic sources, the goal will be to determine the ways in which the biblical conception of moral impurity is understood in tannaitic sources. What are the sources of moral defilement? What are its effects? After considering these questions, we will turn briefly to two further questions. Can we assign a date to any of these tannaitic traditions? Finally, what are the tannaim expressing in their rearticulation of this biblical doctrine?

We will begin by offering some general observations about the tannaitic passages that form the basis of our analysis. The first general observation is that there are very few passages in the tannaitic corpus that articulate the idea of moral defilement. As was mentioned in chapter 4, the idea of moral defilement is not articulated at all in the Mishnah. As we will soon see, the idea is noted only a few times in the Tosefta. There are about a dozen or so traditions in the tannaitic midrashim, and perhaps half that number of related baraithot in the Bavli and Yerushalmi. We barely need to reiterate that *ritual* impurity is a favorite topic of the tannaim, and there is no dearth of tannaitic sources dealing with issues of transgression either. Nonetheless, the idea of moral impurity is infrequently articulated in the tannaitic corpus.

The second general observation is that the bulk of the tannaitic passages that discuss moral defilement are midrashim on scriptural verses dealing with moral impurity. That is, most of the tannaitic sources we will examine involve exegesis on scriptural passages such as Leviticus 18:24–30 and 20:1–3.[3] This claim holds true not only for the relevant traditions that appear in the tannaitic midrashim, but also for the few traditions that can be found in the Tosefta and the Talmudim. Thus, despite their rarity, most of the tannaitic traditions we wish to analyze are easy enough to find. Identify a biblical verse that articulates the idea of moral impurity, find the tannaitic commentary on that verse, and very likely one will then find a tannaitic articulation of the idea of moral defilement. But I think we learn something from all this: The tannaim were not greatly interested in contributing much to what the Hebrew Bible itself has to say on moral impurity. If they were inclined to expand upon the notion at all, we might expect it to come up more frequently.

The third point to be made regarding these passages is that they typically artic- ulate a rather literal reading of the biblical verses. Where the Torah states that the performance of grave sins defiles the land and leads to exile, we will see that the tan- naitic commentaries are generally satisfied with taking Scripture at face value. In the first section of chapter 4 it was argued that while many of the specific rulings re- garding ritual impurity have changed and developed as we move from Scripture to tannaitic literature, the overall conception of ritual impurity remains more or less consistent. The same can be said of moral impurity. As we will see in the next two sections, the tannaim introduce new sources of moral impurity and systematize its effects. But what remains striking is the similarity: In both the Hebrew Bible and tan- naitic sources, grave sins bring about a nonritual sort of defilement that defiles the sinner, the sanctuary, and the land of Israel and that leads ultimately to the exile of the people from the land.

The Sources of Moral Impurity in Tannaitic Literature

In the Hebrew Bible, moral impurity is brought about by the sins of idolatry, incest, and murder. For the most part, the sources of moral defilement in tannaitic litera- ture are precisely the same, although there are some exceptions.

Just as the final verses of Leviticus 18 constitute one of the clearest articulations of the idea of moral defilement in the Hebrew Bible, so too the Sifra's commentary on that passage constitutes one of the clearest articulations of the idea of moral de- filement in tannaitic literature (Sifra Aharei Mot, Perek 13: 16, 19 [ed. Weiss, pp. 86b– c]):[4]

> (16) "Do not defile yourselves in any of those ways" [Lev. 18 24a]: whether in all of them, or any of them. "For it is by such that the nations defiled themselves" [24b]. these are the Egyptians. "That I am casting out before you" [24c]· these are the Canaanites. "Thus the land became defiled" [25a]. this teaches us that the land be- comes defiled by these things. "And I called it to account for its iniquity" [25b]: as soon as I open the account book, I seize it all. "And the land spewed out its inhabi- tants" [25c]. just like a person who vomits his food . .
> (19) "For all those abhorrent things were done by the people who were in the land before you" [27a]. this teaches us that the land is defiled by these things. "So let not the land spew you out just as it spewed out the nation that came before you" [28]· this teaches us that the land is subject to exile on account of these things.

There are a number of striking features to this passage. First, this exegesis is anony- mous (unattributed) and undisputed, as are a great many of the passages analyzed in this chapter (attributions and disputes will be noted when they do occur). Second, the tannaitic reading of Leviticus 18:24–30 is literal: The incestuous sins delineated in Leviticus 18 are understood to defile the land, with the result that the land "spews out" its inhabitants. The fact that the defilement originates in sin and affects the land leaves little doubt that we are dealing here not with ritual impurity but with moral impurity. Indeed, neither here nor in any of the other passages we will discuss do the tannaim state or even suggest that idolatrous, incestuous, and murderous sins bring about ritual defilement. A number of other tannaitic traditions also attest to the idea of the morally defiling force of sexual sins.[5]

By being so literal in their exegesis of Leviticus 18, the tannaim have restricted the application of the idea of moral defilement. Notably, they apply the force of Leviticus 18 only to the Canaanites and the Egyptians.[6] In Ezra and Jubilees, passages like Leviticus 18 were taken to mean that all Gentiles at all times were inherently sinful and inherently morally impure, but the tannaim do not articulate that idea here (on Gentiles in tannaitic sources, see excursus 1 at the end of this chapter). Indeed, the treatment of intermarriage and conversion in tannaitic sources is more sober and restrained than what we find in Jubilees and Ezra. In fact, Sifra Aharei Mot Perek 13:18 explicitly brings converts and their wives within the scope of the sexual prohibitions. If Gentiles were considered inherently morally impure, conversion would not be possible, for it could not be expected that converts would follow these laws. In tannaitic sources, however, no one is inherently morally impure, and conversion remains a possibility. Despite this significant disagreement, there is a degree to which Ezra, Jubilees, and the tannaim agree: All accept that the performance of grave sin has the capacity to defile the land of Israel.

Elsewhere the tannaim express similar ideas about idolatry and bloodshed. The tannaitic recognition of the morally defiling force of idolatrous sins is articulated clearly in the tannaitic commentary on Leviticus 20:1–3 (Sifra Kedoshim, Parashah 10:8 [ed. Weiss, 91c]):

> "And so defiled My sanctuary and profaned My holy name" [Lev. 20:3c]: this teaches that [Molech worship] defiles the sanctuary, profanes the Name, causes the Divine Presence to depart, brings the sword upon Israel, and exiles them from their land.

The effects brought about by the morally defiling force of idolatry will be analyzed in greater detail in the next section. The important thing to note here is that in the Sifra, idolatry, like incest, brings about not a ritual defilement but a moral defilement. Other tannaitic sources also articulate the idea of the morally defiling force of idolatrous sins.[7]

On the issue of idolatry, it is interesting to compare once more the tannaitic view with that taken in Jubilees. On the one hand, there is a vast gulf between the isolationist, anti-Gentile rhetoric of Jubilees and the more sober legal literature of the tannaim. On the other hand, there is a certain degree of agreement, for both affirm the literal meaning of the Holiness Code: Idolatrous and adulterous sins defile the land and the sanctuary, leading to exile and the departure of God's presence (see Jubilees 23:18–21). This agreement, however, is overshadowed by a significant difference in emphasis. The moral impurity of idols and idolatry is a major theme of Jubilees but a small footnote in tannaitic literature.

Just as there is no clear articulation of the defiling force of murder in Leviticus, so too there is no statement to that effect in the Sifra. For a clear statement on the defiling force of murder, we can turn to the tannaitic commentary on Numbers 35:33–34 (Sifre Num. § 161 [ed. Horovitz, p. 222]), which reads in part:

"You shall not defile the land in which you live" [Num. 35:34a]: Scripture states that bloodshed defiles the land and causes the Divine Presence to depart; and it was due to bloodshed that the temple was destroyed.

Again, the dynamic falls under the rubric of what I have been referring to as moral defilement: a more or less permanent defilement of the land that leads to exile. Although we cannot be certain of this conclusion, it may well be that the tannaim had a particular interest in the morally defiling force of murder.[8] I suggest this first of all because a number of the tannaitic traditions articulating the idea of the morally defiling force of bloodshed deal with bloodshed exclusively.[9] And a portion of those passages, like the selection quoted above, appear to draw a connection between bloodshed and the destruction of the temple.[10] For what it is worth, the only articulations of the notion of moral defilement in the Tosefta both relate to the morally defiling force of bloodshed.

The two toseftan traditions are in fact one: The following narrative as preserved in T. Yoma 1:12 (MS Vienna) appears in a substantially similar form in T. Sheb. 1:4:[11]

It happened that when two priests of equal rank were running up the ramp, one pushed the other within four cubits [of the altar]. The other took a knife and stabbed the first in the heart.
R. Zakok came and stood on the steps of the hall and said, "Hear me, house of Israel, our brothers Behold it is said, ' If someone is found lying in the open . . . your elders and magistrates shall go out and measure the distances. . .' [Deut. 21:1–2]. Let us go and measure [and determine] for which a heifer must be brought, for the sanctuary, or for the courts." They all moaned in tears after him.
But afterwards, the father of [the slain] boy said to them· "Brothers, may I[12] be your expiation! [My] son still convulses, and so the knife has not been defiled."[13] This teaches that the impurity of a knife was a more serious matter to Israel than bloodshed
And so it is written, "Moreover, Manasseh put so many innocent persons to death that he filled Jerusalem from end to end [with blood]" [2 Kings 21:16]. From this they said that for the sin of bloodshed the Divine Presence departed [נעלית], and the sanctuary was defiled.

This important and difficult narrative has a choppy feel to it and would appear to be constructed of diverse elements. The fact remains, however, that the versions preserved in the manuscripts and printed editions of T. Yoma and its parallels differ only in minor details; The general content and sequence of the statements remain the same.[14]

The most detailed analysis of the meaning of this passage is Neusner's.[15] Neusner views it as a black-and-white tannaitic criticism of a morally bankrupt priesthood.[16] Though the narrative does indeed offer a trenchant critique of Jewish society in Jerusalem before 70, I am not so sure the tradition is exclusively antipriestly. First of all, the one rabbinic figure in the narrative — an unidentifiable R. Zadok[17] — is hardly the voice of reason. His homily (which we will turn to in a moment) is quite problematic. That the story is not exclusively antipriestly can further be seen in the fact that its moral does not direct its accusation against the priests, but either against an unspecified "them," or, as many versions have it,[18] against Israel as a whole. Finally, the prooftext (2 Kings 21:16) has nothing to do with priestly sinfulness, but deals with with the sinfulness of King Manasseh. Whatever this passage may be, it is clearly not a polemic directed exclusively against the priesthood.

Neusner refers to R. Zadok's speech as a "sarcastic homily."[19] It is a homily to be sure. Indeed, the entire pericope is a homily — or, rather, an *aggadah*. But I am not so sure R. Zadok's homily is sarcastic, or at least I do not think we are supposed to think that R. Zadok was intentionally being sarcastic. What is clear, however, is this: R. Zadok's response to the murder is really rather preposterous. On top of caring more about the ritual than the crime, the ritual discussed hardly applies to the situation. In the story the murderer is known, while the biblical law applies to a case where the murderer is not known.[20] Moreover, the biblical law applies to a case where the corpse is found dead between two villages. Why anyone would think this would apply to the sanctuary itself is difficult to understand.[21] Clearly, R. Zodok's homily is presented as a parody.

In this narrative, the tannaim accuse the generation of Jews who lived before the destruction of the temple of misplaced priorities: On the whole, they paid too much attention to ritual impurity and too little to grave sins such as bloodshed. The misplaced prioritization is illustrated both in R. Zodok's homily, which gives priority to the ritual of Deuteronomy 21, and in the father's brief speech, which leads directly to the accusation that Israel considered the ritual impurity of a knife to be more important than bloodshed. Because of these misplaced priorities, the passage argues, God withdrew the Divine Presence and brought about the destruction of the temple.

There is another important aspect of the views attributed in this passage to the Jews who lived prior to the destruction of the temple. Neither R. Zadok nor the father of the priest — to say nothing of the many silent priests — betray any familiarity with the idea of moral defilement. To be sure, they know something about ritual impurity. They also seem to know that murder does not produce ritual impurity: No one in the story is concerned that the killer might defile the sanctuary ritually. What they all have forgotten — and what the story itself comes to remind us of — is the fact that murder does indeed defile the sanctuary, morally.

The bulk of the passages in the tannaitic corpus dealing with moral impurity discuss the defiling force of idolatry, incest, and murder, but these are not the only sources of moral defilement in tannaitic literature. A number of sources entertain the idea that deceit (עול) is a source of moral defilement.[22] In Leviticus 19:15, the Israelites are commanded not to "render an unfair decision" (לא-תעשו עול במשפט). The Sifra on Leviticus 19:15 reads as follows (Sifra Kedoshim, Perek 4:1 [ed. Weiss, pp. 88d–89a]):

> We learn from this verse that the judge who perverts justice [המקלקל את הדין] is called unjust [עול], hated, shunned, banned, and an abomination [תועבה]. And he causes five things. [he] defiles the land, profanes the Name [of God], causes the withdrawal of the Divine Presence, brings the sword down upon Israel, and exiles them from their land

If we had not already discussed this passage in chapter 2, the idea that deceit could find a place alongside murder as a source of moral defilement might be rather jarring. How is deceit to be compared to murder? On further reflection, however, judicial deceit — at least in the case of a capital crime — comes very close to murder indeed. And our passage from Leviticus does seem to have capital crimes in focus. Leviticus 19:16 states: "Do not 'profit by' the blood of your fellow."

But the notion of judicial deceit as a source of moral defilement is justified not only by this conceptual link between judicial deceit and murder. There is, as we saw in chapter 2, a scriptural basis for this idea as well. Deuteronomy 25:16 articulates a prohibition very similar to that in Leviticus 19:15, but with — for our purposes — one essential difference: Deuteronomy refers to judicial deceit as an abomination.[23] It is likely that this verse lies behind the Sifra's analogy — a *gezerah shavah* of sorts[24] — between abomination and judicial deceit. Since idolatry and deceit are each referred to as an "abomination" (תועבה), both are to be seen as sources of moral defilement.

Confirmation that the tannaim were thinking along these lines can be seen in the Sifre on Deuteronomy 25:16, where we find a substantially similar, though truncated, articulation of the idea that deceit is a source of moral defilement.[25] Even clearer confirmation that deceit becomes a source of moral impurity by a *gezerah shavah* based on the term "abomination" can be seen in the Mekhilta de-Rabbi Ishmael Yitro 9 (ed. Horovitz-Rabin, p. 238). Commenting on Exodus 20:18 — "and Moses approached the cloud where God was" — the Mekhilta discusses Moses's humility. While humility serves to enhance God's presence on earth, arrogance has the opposite effect:

> But all those who are arrogant [גבה לב] cause the land to be defiled and the Divine Presence to depart, as it is written, "Every arrogant person is an abomination to God" [Prov. 16:5]. Idolatry is referred to as an abomination, as it is written: "Do not bring an abomination into your house" [Deut. 7:26]. Just as idolatry defiles the land and causes the Divine Presence to depart, [so too whoever is arrogant causes the land to be defiled and the Divine Presence to depart]

In a sense, this text has nothing to do with deceit at all, except to the degree to which we can view acts of judicial deceit as acts of arrogance.[26] It is notable that this text considers arrogance to be a source of moral defilement — an idea we have seen already in the Habakkuk Pesher.[27] But this text is also interesting in that it allows us to recover precisely the logic that is left unarticulated in the Sifra and the Sifre. Just as the Mekhilta here uses Proverbs 16:5 as the basis for a *gezerah shavah* to reach the conclusion that arrogance is a source of moral defilement, so too we can imagine the tannaim using Deuteronomy 25:16 as the basis for a *gezerah shavah* to reach the conclusion that deceit is a source of moral defilement.

The tannaim were not alone in viewing judicial deceit as a source of moral defilement. There is, as we saw in chapter 2, a striking parallel to these traditions in the Temple Scroll, which states that bribery "defiles the house" (LI:11–15). This is to be understood, as I argued, that bribery is a source of moral defilement. It is likely that we have here another example of 11QT's homogenization, whereby Leviticus 19:15 and Deuteronomy 25:16 — as well as Deuteronomy 16:18–21 (which forms the basis of this 11QT passage) — have congealed into the idea that judicial bribery is a source of moral defilement. The tannaitic sources come to the same conclusion, although in that case by a *gezerah shavah* on the word "abomination" (תועבה). It is important to note that the similarity in the results reached by 11QT and the tannaim under-

scores the similarity of method: both "homogenization" and *gezerah shavah* are pow-
erfully pliable tools of analogical exegesis. When we have only the results of exegesis, it may not be possible to determine which of these two methods has been used.

We also find the idea of deceit as defilement in much of the sectarian literature
from Qumran. Indeed, this idea is a *leitmotif* of the Community Rule (1QS).[28] Yet
whereas in the Temple Scroll and in tannaitic sources deceit is understood only as a
source of moral defilement, at Qumran, deceit, like all sin, is understood as ritually
defiling as well. Despite the agreement between 11QT and the sectarian literature
from Qumran on certain issues of ritual defilement (e.g., the *tebul yom*), on the question of the relationship between sin and defilement, the Temple Scroll and tannaitic
sources are generally in agreement against the sectarian literature from Qumran.

Another source of moral impurity in tannaitic literature is blasphemy (קללת ה׳). This
idea, too, is articulated only rarely. The clearest statement to this effect can be found
in the Sifre to Deuteronomy 23:10 (§ 254 [ed. Finkelstein, p. 280]):[29]

> "When you go out as a troop against your enemies" [Deut. 23:10a]: When you go
> out, go out in a camp . . . "be on guard against anything bad [ונשמרת מכל דבר רע]"
> [Deut. 23:10b]: I could understand this to mean that Scripture here refers to puri-
> ties, impurities, and tithes. But Scripture states· "unseemly [ערוה]" [Deut. 23.15] [to
> indicate that Scripture has sexual sin in mind]. But I only have here sexual sin. How
> do I know that idolatry, murder, and blasphemy [קללת ה׳] are also included?
> Scripture states: "be on guard against *anything* bad." By "be on guard," I could sup-
> pose that Scripture has in mind purities, impurities, and tithes. But Scripture states:
> "unseemly [ערוה]." Just as a distinguishing characteristic of sexual sin is that the
> Canaanites were exiled on account of it, and it causes the departure of the Divine
> Presence, so [we include here] all activity on account of which the Canaanites were
> exiled, and which brings about the departure of the Divine Presence.

Whence comes the idea that blasphemy (קללת ה׳) is a source of moral defilement?
Again, the Sifre does not state explicitly how the tannaim reached this conclusion.

This idea about blasphemy is probably based on a reading of Deuteronomy
21:22–23, which prohibits leaving the body of an executed criminal out for display.
An impaled body, Deuteronomy 21:23 states, is "an affront to God" (קללת אל׳). The
stated reason for this command is that the body, if not properly and hastily buried,
will defile the land: "lest you defile the land which the Lord God has given you."

The Midrash Tannaim to Deuteronomy accepts Deuteronomy 21:23 at its face
value: failure to bury the corpse defiles the land.[30] And, typically, the midrash also
notes that the act causes the Divine Presence to withdraw. Midrash Tannaim actually puts all this in the form of a *qal va-homer* (an a fortiori argument): if refusal to
bury the corpse defiles the land and causes the Divine Presence to withdraw, how
much more so would idolatry, incest, and murder? Once one has read the Midrash
Tannaim to Deuteronomy 21:23, one might wonder if Sifre § 254 means to say that
blasphemy is morally defiling at all. Is it possible that when the above-quoted passage from the Sifre speaks of the defiling force of קללת ה׳, it intends to state that an
unburied impaled body defiles the land?

That is indeed one possibility. The second possibility — the stronger one by far —
is that the Sifre does in fact mean to say that cursing God in general is a source of

moral impurity. Generally the phrase קללת ה׳ is used in the tannaitic corpus to mean blasphemy. At least some tannaitic exegetes of Deuteronomy 21:23 have allowed that understanding of it to color their interpretation. Accordingly, the Sifre to Deuteronomy 21:23 understands the scriptural verse to mean that the hanged person is one who cursed God: "Why was this person hanged? Because he committed blasphemy."[31] A passage in the Temple Scroll appears to take the same approach to Deuteronomy 21:23.[32] Once the deuteronomic passage is read this way, then it is possible to take the second half of verse 21:23 ("lest you defile the land . . .") and connect it not with exposing the impaled body, but with the sin for which the criminal was impaled: cursing God. It is by this route that *some* tannaim arrived at the idea of blasphemy as a source of moral defilement. Apparently, others disputed this reading of Deuteronomy 21:23 and, along with the Midrash Tannaim, understood the passage in a way more commensurate with most contemporary translations: that the defilement of the land is brought about by the failure to bury the impaled body. But despite this disagreement, the traditions preserved in the Sifre and the Midrash Tannaim agree upon something significant: Deuteronomy 21:23 was understood to articulate that some behavior brings about moral defilement.   _ The impl. point.

In order to appreciate fully the tannaitic approach to moral defilement, we must recognize that the tannaim did not act on every opportunity to introduce new sources of moral defilement. They could have found new sources of moral impurity by using various analogical exegetical tools. They frequently chose, however, *not* to act on such opportunities. Indeed, when faced with scriptural juxtaposition of impurity and sin, the tannaim now and again offered interpretations that made use of restrictive exegesis, thereby excluding moral impurity from the situation.

The tannaitic exegesis of Numbers 19:13 provides an instructive example (Sifre Num. § 125).[33] The biblical passage states that one who refuses to purify from corpse impurity will defile the sanctuary: "Whoever touches a corpse . . . and does not purify himself, defiles the Lord's tabernacle." Presumably, the original concern here was that the refusal to purify would bring about the (moral) defilement of the sanctuary, whether or not the sinner chose to enter the sanctuary.[34] Yet the tannaitic sources chose not to understand it this way. The tannaim state quite clearly that this defilement is of a ritual sort. They view this situation as a case of טומאת מקדש וקדשיו— the ritual defilement of the sanctuary or sacred things by a person who did not know or forgot that s/he was ritually impure. In the tannaitic understanding of corpse impurity, the Israelite who refuses to purify defiles the sanctuary ritually if (and only if) that person chooses to enter the sanctuary. It would have been very easy for the tannaim to view the refusal to purify as a sin that produces moral impurity, but they chose otherwise. ► Changed Moral impurity to ritual impurity

Another example can be seen in the tannaitic treatments of Deuteronomy 14:3: "do not eat any reviling thing" (תועבה). In the "Dietary Laws" section of chapter 1, we discussed the status of the biblical food laws vis-à-vis the idea of moral impurity, and we concluded that while there is some overlap, food laws were most likely not viewed as sources of moral defilement. In this respect, the tannaitic approach to the same question is not so surprising. The tannaitic exegesis of Deuteronomy 14:3 in Sifre Deuteronomy § 99[35] has nothing to do with moral impurity at all, and that is precisely the point. And yet the (unnamed) sages in the passage articulate a *gezerah shavah* very similar to that seen above in Mekhilta de-Rabbi Ishmael Yitro 9. In this case, the use of the term "abomination" in Deuteronomy 14:3 is compared to the use of the same term in Deuteronomy 17:1, and both are understood to refer to consecrated animals that are considered unfit due to some blemish (פסולי המקדשין). Had the tannaim wished to consider violations of the dietary laws as sources of moral defilement, they could have found ample justification by drawing an analogy between the use of "abomination" in Deuteronomy 14:3 and of the same term in any of the many passages dealing with moral defilement. But again, they chose not to consider the food laws to be a source of moral defilement.

A final example of this kind of restrictive exegesis can be seen in Sifra Aharei Mot Perek 4, which comments on Leviticus 16:16 (ed. Weiss, 81 c–d):

> (1) "Thus he shall purge the Shrine of the impurities and transgression of the Israelites, whatever their sins; and he shall do the same for the Tent of Meeting" [Lev 16:16]: I could include here three impurities: the impurity of idolatry, as it is written, ["because he gave of his offspring to Molech] and so defiled My sanctuary and profaned My holy name" [Lev. 20:3]; the impurity of sexual sins, as it is written, "lest you engage in any of the abhorrent practices that were carried on before you, and you shall not defile yourselves through them" [Lev. 18:30]; the impurity of bloodshed, as it is written, "You shall not defile the land in which you live, in which I Myself abide" [Num 35:34]
>
> (2) Is it possible that this goat makes atonement for these three impurities? Scripture states "of their impurities" and not "all their impurities" Just as we find that Scripture separates the defilement of the Sanctuary and its holy things from the rest of the impurities, here too Scripture separates only the defilement of the Sanctuary and its holy things, the words of R. Yehudah.
>
> R. Shimon says. the point is proven from the text itself as it is said, "Thus he shall purge the Shrine of the impurities of the Israelites" — of the impurities pertaining to the Shrine.

In the first paragraph, some anonymous tannaim grapple with the reference, in Leviticus 16:16, to the fact that the priest on the Day of Atonement is to purge the shrine "of the impurities and transgressions of the Israelites." The juxtaposition of sin with defilement leads the sages to entertain the possibility that all three sources of moral defilement are meant. This suggestion is bolstered by an appeal to the classical scriptural references to moral defilement. Then, in the second paragraph, this interpretation is rejected. The concern of Leviticus 16:16, rather, is with the defilement of the sanctuary and sacred things (טומאת מקדש וקדשיו). Two different arguments for this case are presented, one by R. Yehudah and a second by R. Shimon. Rabbi Yehudah's argument is based on a typical rabbinic method of restrictive exegesis: focusing on the preposition translated as "of" ("*of* the impurities"), it can be argued that the verse refers not to *all* impurities, but just to *some* impurities. When Scripture singles out one impurity from others in such contexts, R. Yehudah continues, it has the ritual defilement of the sanctuary and sacred things in mind. R. Shimon's argument is based on the juxtaposition of the Hebrew words "sanctuary" and "impurity" ("and he will purge the Shrine of their defilements . . ."). Of course, whether we follow R. Yehudah or R. Shimon, the overall effect is the same. The verse from Leviticus

juxtaposes impurity and sin. The tannaim could have determined that moral impurity was of concern here; this possibility is entertained and rejected. Alternatively,
they could have determined that ritual impurity generally speaking is the concern,
but this possibility is not even entertained. The Sifra, however, faced with an otherwise unaccounted for juxtaposition of sin with impurity makes it clear that the impurity in question is not moral impurity or ritual impurity in general, but rather a
specific type of sin that is related to ritual impurity: the ritual defilement of the sanctuary and sacred things (טומאת מקדש וקדשיו).[36]

This example differs from the first two, in that the restrictive exegesis here does
not serve to allow the tannaim to avoid the creation of a new source of moral impurity. Yet the passage is relevant, both for its similar restrictive approach and for the
fact that it betrays the motive behind the other two passages: in all three, the tannaim
strive to preserve the distinctive qualities of the conception of moral impurity. Moral
impurity, in the tannaitic view, is produced only by grave sin. Thus while arrogance
and deceit can — with scriptural justification — be added to the list, food laws and
other less weighty violations cannot.

For the most part, the sources of moral defilement in tannaitic literature are the same
as they were in Scripture: incest, idolatry, and murder. Judicial deceit, which is also
referred to as an abomination, is added to the list in the Sifre and the Sifra, and cursing God is added in one passage in the Sifre. These additions are scripturally justified, and they really do not bring us too far from the original three: judicial deceit,
at least in a capital crime, is conceptually akin to murder; and cursing God is not so
far from idolatry, especially since Leviticus 20:3 states that idolatry profanes the name
of God. In the final analysis, regarding the sources of moral defilement in the Hebrew
Bible and tannaitic sources, the similarities are much greater than the differences.

The Effects of Moral Impurity in Tannaitic Literature

In the Torah, the clearest statement on the effects of moral defilement is, again,
Leviticus 18:24–30, which states that sin defiles the land and eventually leads to the
exile of the people. Another way in which the tannaitic treatments of moral defilement diverge from the Holiness Code is that the tannaitic sources, almost without
exception, introduce an intermediate step: sin defiles the land, leading to the departure of the Divine Presence ("Siluk ha-Shekhinah"[37]), which in turn leads to exile.

The tannaitic midrashim are commonly divided into two groups, based on a
number of differences in style and exegetical technique (although many exceptions
to the schema have been suggested).[38] The first group (often associated more closely
with the school of R. Akiba) includes the Mekhilta de-Rabbi Shimon Bar Yohai, the
Sifra, and the Sifre Zutta to Numbers and the Sifre to Deuteronomy. The second
group of texts (often associated more with the school of R. Ishmael) includes the
Mekhilta de-Rabbi Ishmael, the Sifre to Numbers, and the Midrash Tannaim on
Deuteronomy. The distinction is mentioned here because the issue of moral
impurity is dealt with differently by the two "schools" of tannaitic midrash. In the
"Akiban"[39] texts (particularly the Sifra and Sifre Deuteronomy), a number of tradi-
tions — such as Sifra Kedoshim, Perek 4:1, quoted earlier — state that moral impurity

brings about five things: "[it] defiles the land, profanes the Name, causes the Divine Presence to depart, [which] brings the sword upon Israel, and exiles them from their land."[40] In the "Ishmaelian" texts, however, presentation of the idea is typically more abbreviated: the sin is said to "defile the land and cause the departure of the Divine Presence" (מטמא את הארץ ומסלק את השכינה).[41] It is this shorter expression of the idea that appears in the Tosefta and the Talmudim.

The differences between the longer and shorter expressions are interesting and important, although the overall effect of moral defilement as expressed in both forms is pretty much the same. The Akiban and Ishmaelian midrashim share the idea that the defilement of the land causes the departure of the Divine Presence, which in turn leads to exile. To be sure, there is a great variety in tannaitic and amoraic opinions regarding the nature and movements of the Divine Presence.[42] A number of sources maintain, for instance, that the Divine Presence goes into exile with the people of Israel.[43] And at least one authority questions whether the Divine Presence ever descended or ascended at all.[44] We cannot, therefore, speak of unanimity in regard to any of these ideas, but there would appear to be some consensus. No tannaitic source that I know of denies or disputes the main thrust of the traditions that we are analyzing here: that grave sins bring about the departure of the Divine Presence.

Whence comes the idea that sin causes the departure of the Divine Presence? In part, the notion emerges from the Holiness Code traditions themselves: Recall Numbers 35:34: "You shall not defile [לא תטמא] the land in which you live, in which I Myself abide, for I the Lord abide among the Israelite people." The pentateuchal traditions concerned with moral defilement also appear to be concerned with the maintenance of God's presence among the people.[45] It thus stands to reason that the defilement of the land might lead to the withdrawal of the *Shekhinah*. But what does not necessarily stand to reason is the sequence of events: that the departure of the Divine Presence is an intermediate step that precedes exile. The scriptural justification for this sequence can be found in Ezekiel 8–11. In chapters 8 and 9, the prophet is taken to Jerusalem to observe the abominable acts (תועבות) of the Israelite people. Then in chapter 10, he dramatically describes his vision of the withdrawal of the Divine Presence (כבוד ה׳) from the sanctuary of God. It is in chapter 11 that God says the following to the people of Israel:

> (6) Many have you slain in this city; you have filled its streets with corpses. (7) Assuredly, thus says the Lord god: The corpses that you have piled up in it are the meat for which it is the pot; but you shall be taken out of it. (8) you feared the sword, and the sword I will bring upon you — declares the Lord God (9) I will take you out of it and deliver you into the hands of strangers, and I will execute judgments upon you. (10) You shall fall by the sword; I will punish you at the border of Israel. And you shall know that I am the Lord.

Strictly speaking, Ezekiel describes not God's *Shekhinah*, but God's *Kavod*. But in Avot de-Rabbi Natan A 34, for instance, the tannaim speak of the *Shekhinah*, while many of the verses quoted (including Ezek. 10:4) speak of God's *Kavod*. Thus it is likely that Ezekiel 8–11 serves as the basis for the sequence of events as assumed in our tannaitic sources: the defilement by sin brings about the departure of the Divine Presence.

It is intriguing that moral defilement is viewed by the tannaim as bringing about the departure of the Divine Presence. It is precisely in this aspect of moral defilement that we see yet another example of the ways in which the tannaim have separated — compartmentalized — the concepts of ritual and moral defilement. While moral defilement brings about the departure of the Divine Presence, we are told a number of times in tannaitic sources that ritual defilement does not cause the departure of the Divine Presence. Sifre Naso ∫ 1 reads in part:[46]

> ". . in whose midst I dwell" [Num. 5:3]. how dear are the Israelites, for even though they are [ritually] impure, the Divine Presence [dwells] among them.

The text goes on to quote other passages concerning God's dwelling among the Israelites and then quotes a statement of R. Yosi ha-Glili, to the effect that Israelites suffer from ritually defiling discharges and afflictions on account of their sinfulness. We have already noted this passage in our discussion of the tannaitic belief that ritual defilement can come about as a punishment for sin.[47] I mention this passage here only to underscore our understanding of what is quoted above. When the tannaim state here that the Divine Presence can dwell among the Israelites despite their impurity, it is clear that the tannaim have *ritual* impurity in mind.[48] The scriptural text on which the exegesis is based (Num. 5:1–4) deals with ritual defilement, as does the statement by R. Yosi ha-Glili. Correctly understood, the passage quoted asserts that the ritual impurity of the Israelites does not pose a threat to God's dwelling among the people (unless, of course, the Israelites enter the sanctuary while they are ritually impure).[49] According to the tannaim, God dwells with the Israelites despite their ritual impurities. To understand the significance of that statement, we must keep in mind the other tannaitic traditions being discussed here. As far as the tannaim are concerned, the departure of the Divine Presence is brought about by moral impurity, but not by ritual impurity.

We now turn to the effects of moral defilement as articulated in the Sifra and the Sifre Deuteronomy. A typical statement on its effects can be found in the Sifra on Leviticus 20 (Kedoshim, Parashah 10:8 [ed. Weiss, 91c]):

> "And so defiled My sanctuary and profaned My holy name" [Lev. 20:3c]: this teaches that [Molech worship] defiles the sanctuary, profanes the Name, causes the Divine Presence to depart, brings the sword upon Israel, and exiles them from their land.

The first two results brought about by moral impurity find their origin in the biblical verse that this passage sets out to expound. According to the plain meaning of Leviticus 20:3, Molech worship brings about the defilement of the sanctuary and the profanation of the name of God. Interestingly, the other tannaitic sources that identify the five results of moral defilement begin the list not with the defilement of the sanctuary, but with the defilement of the land.[50] But we ought not make too much of this difference. Although no passage in the Pentateuch states that idolatry defiles the land,[51] a number of tannaitic sources nonetheless do state that idolatry defiles the land.[52] We have already seen (in chapter 2) that there was a good deal of fluidity with regard to the effects of moral impurity on the land and the sanctuary. In particular a number of sources from the second temple period expressed the concern that

sexual sins bring about the moral defilement of the sanctuary, even while the biblical basis of these traditions (Lev. 18) focuses on the effect these sins have upon the
land of Israel. The same fluidity is evident in the tannaitic sources as well. According
to Numbers 35:34, bloodshed defiles the land. But T. Yoma 1:12, for instance, articulates the notion of moral defilement by saying that bloodshed brings about the departure of the Divine Presence and the defilement of the sanctuary. There is reason
for this fluidity: The sanctuary of God is located at the sacred heart of the land of
Israel (M. Kel. 1:6–9). We cannot therefore distinguish too strongly between these
results of moral impurity, for the defilement of the land will lead to the defilement
of the sanctuary. And because these sins are committed on the land, and they defile
the sanctuary even from a distance, we can presume, I think, that for the tannaim
the land served as the conduit by which the sanctuary was defiled by sin.[53]

We have now accounted for four of the five results of moral impurity mentioned
in the Sifra and the Sifre Deuteronomy: The first two — the defilement of the land
or sanctuary and the profanation of God's name — find their basis within the Holiness
Code traditions upon which the tannaitic notion of moral defilement is based. The
third — the departure of the Divine Presence — is based, as we have already seen, on
the imagery of Ezekiel 8–11. The fifth result — exile — also finds its basis in the
Holiness Code traditions (e.g., Lev. 18:28). So we are left with the fourth result of
moral defilement: that the sword will be brought upon Israel. It stands to reason, of
course, that war will precede exile. In the biblical narrative, the exile of the
Canaanites and the subsequent exile of the Israelites, both of which are connected
to sin, are brought about violently. But we can do even better than this in discerning
the scriptural basis of the tannaitic use of the word "sword" in these passages. If we
look again at Ezekiel 11:6–9, we will see that the direct connection between the
sword and exile is stated. With regard to this connection between sin, sword and exile, we can also see the same sequence of events in the Holiness Code (Lev. 26:30–
33):

> (30) I will destroy your cult places and cut down your incense stands, and I will heap
> your carcasses upon your lifeless fetishes. I will spurn you. (31) I will lay your cities
> in ruin [חרבה] and make your sanctuaries desolate, and I will not savor your pleas-
> ing odors. (32) I will make the land desolate, so that your enemies who settle in it
> shall be appalled by it (33) And you I will scatter among the nations, and I will un-
> sheath the sword against you. Your land shall become a desolation and your cities a
> ruin.

According to the Sifra on this passage (Behukotai Perek 6:4–6 [ed. Weiss, p. 112a]),
some tannaitic authorities understood the phrase "I will spurn you" (וגעלה נפשי אתכם)
to refer to exile, while others understood it to refer to the departure of the Divine
Presence. Either way, the tannaim who commented on this passage were clearly
thinking of the events brought about by the moral defilement of the land.

The use of a nonpentateuchal source such as Ezekiel underscores another important aspect of these passages that we have examined. They are *aggadot*.[54] We are
also alerted to the *aggadic* nature of these traditions by the term *Shekhinah*, which
appears in *aggadah* but not *halakhah*.[55] Perhaps, too, the difficulty in determining
the hermeneutic methods used in these sources is related to their *aggadic* nature.[56]

I have said that for the tannaim, the sources of moral impurity do not convey ritual impurity. That being the case, there are no *halakhic* ramifications of the idea of moral defilement. This is in marked contrast to the sectarians at Qumran, for whom the defiling force of sin did have *halakhic* ramifications, such as exclusion from the pure-food of the community.

This is not to say that moral impurity was not real or consequential for the tannaim. Moral impurity and its results, especially exile, were both real and consequential. But the concept was not *halakhic* in that the doctrine had no impact on issues of civil justice, ritual purity, or personal status. Thus we find no extended discussions of moral impurity that resemble the treatment of ritual impurity in Mishnah-Tosefta Seder Toharot. With regard to moral impurity, there are no discussions of minimum measures, modes of transfer, or situations of doubt. How much idolatry does it take to defile the land? What happens if when a person is murdered no blood spills on the ground? What happens if a man has sexual relations with a woman who thinks she was widowed but in fact her husband is still alive? Has the land been defiled? These kind of questions constitute the warp and woof of the tannaitic treatment of ritual impurity, but they are not even posed with regard to moral impurity, precisely because moral impurity is not an *halakhic* concept, but an *aggadic* concept.

The five results of moral defilement—the defilement of the land or sanctuary, the profanation of the Name, the departure of the Divine Presence, and then sword and exile—all find their basis in biblical traditions related to moral impurity. Three of them—defilement of the land, profanation of the Name, and exile—find their basis in the Holiness Code passages related to moral impurity. But for the others, in particular the image of the departure of the Divine Presence, the tannaim presumably drew upon passages from Ezekiel. What is so interesting is how systematized it has all become: The five results can be brought about by any of the sources of moral impurity—even deceit—and not just those sources, such as Molech worship, that are connected to these results in the Holiness Code traditions. For the present, I know of no better way to describe the exegesis involved here other than to use Milgrom's term "homogenization." It would appear that all of the sources and all of the results of moral defilement as explicitly stated in the Torah have congealed.

The Date of the Doctrine of Moral Defilement

The question we must now ask is, when did all this come about? At what point in the history of ancient Judaism did the ideas expressed in the tannaitic sources emerge? On the one hand, we could argue that the tannaitic systematization of the idea of moral impurity is late: The notion is not articulated in the Mishnah, but it does appear in the Sifre and the Sifra, which are generally considered to have emerged in the amoraic period. Indeed, if we were to follow the "literary-documentary" methods, we would be bound to come up with that conclusion. Yet we ought not make too much of the Mishnah's silence on this matter. First of all, the Mishnah does seem to assume a similar dynamic: M. Avot 5:9 states that exile comes about as a result of three sins: idolatry, incest, and murder. The defilement of the land and the departure of Divine Presence are not mentioned, but the general dynamic is there just the same.

Two other factors are important in trying to date the ideas expressed in the sources examined in this chapter. First, almost all of the tannaitic sources that have been analyzed in this chapter are anonymous and undisputed.[57] Second, as I have been arguing throughout, there is very little in the tannaitic doctrine of moral defilement that is not stated rather clearly in Scripture itself. Indeed many of these traditions simply reiterate or paraphrase biblical verses. There are, of course, points where the tannaitic sources diverge from Scripture, as when the Sifra considers deceit to be a source of moral defilement. But what is remarkable about that instance is that other ancient Jewish literature (such as the Temple Scroll) diverges from Scripture in similar ways.

Thus we have a set of undisputed anonymous traditions that largely cohere with what is contained in earlier ancient Jewish literature, and even Scripture itself. Alternatively, we could say that the idea of moral defilement is an aspect of biblical and ancient Jewish theology that has been accepted by the tannaim.

If the tannaim inherited the idea, is it possible that the Pharisees too believed in the doctrine of moral defilement? It is indeed possible, for the same reasons, although we cannot be certain. We do have an articulation of the idea that moral defilement brings about the departure of the Divine Presence that can be reliably dated to the first century CE. Moreover, the author of this passage refers to himself as a Pharisee. In his autobiographical work, Josephus claims to have been a Pharisee (*Life* 12), though some have doubted the sincerity of this claim.[58] But whatever his ideological background, Josephus juxtaposes moral sin with the defilement of the sanctuary (*Jewish War* V:402), and he asserts that God has, as a result, fled from the midst of the sinful people of Israel (V:412).[59]

One final point should be noted: We have no reason to believe that the Sadducees and Pharisees disputed the nature of moral impurity, or the nature of the relationship between ritual and moral impurity. Thus it would certainly be precarious to claim that the notion was Pharisaic in any exclusive sense. But since the idea of moral impurity is found in the Hebrew Bible, in Jewish literature of the second Temple period, and in tannaitic sources, it does seem likely that many first-century Jews, Pharisees included, also accepted the idea.

The Meaning of the Doctrine of Moral Defilement

We turn now to the next question. Why? What is the point of this doctrine, and why do the tannaim adhere to it? Milgrom, in his Anchor Bible Leviticus commentary, offers the following analysis of the *chattat* sacrifice (Lev. 4:1–35), and his comments pertain to the biblical conception of moral impurity as well. Recalling Oscar Wilde's novel, Milgrom speaks of the priestly *Picture of Dorian Gray*. "Sin may not leave its mark on the face of the sinner," Milgrom writes, "but it is certain to mark the face of the sanctuary; and unless it is quickly expunged, God's presence will depart." Simply put, he observes, the *chattat* sacrifice articulates the idea of collective responsibility.[60]

The doctrine of moral impurity, in both the Hebrew Bible and tannaitic literature, can be understood similarly. The Divine Presence cannot or will not abide in a land defiled by idolatry, murder, and sexual sin. By defiling the land, these acts threaten the sanctity that is the prerequisite for God's presence among the Israelite people. Even though many Israelites may not have committed such sins, the results come about just the same. Sin brings the defilement of the land, which leads to the departure of the Divine Presence.[61] This in turn brings about sword and exile. These are severe punishments that affect everyone equally: The Divine Presence departs not just from the sinners, but from the land of Israel and all its inhabitants. The message of this communal punishment is collective responsibility. Abraham Joshua Heschel's formulation of prophetic theology is, I think, apt: "few are guilty, all are responsible."[62] Communal responsibility is one of the ideals of the doctrine of moral impurity. → very, very Impt!!

There is another communal issue involved here as well. I have argued that the dynamic between sin and impurity was very much at issue among ancient Jews. The juxtaposition of sin and impurity is in Scripture, and ancient Jews struggled to make sense of it. At Qumran, sin was considered to be a source of ritual impurity (chapter 3). That idea is very much connected to their sectarian ideology: If you view the constant maintenance of ritual purity as a desideratum, and you view sin as a source of ritual defilement, and you view most of your neighbors as sinners, then you have little choice but to remove yourself from the general populace that you view as sinful. And if you view sin as a source of ritual defilement, you also have little choice but to ostracize or banish the sinner.   *Reason for Sectarianism*

Every time the tannaim insist that sin produces moral impurity, they are simultaneously emphasizing that sin does *not* produce ritual impurity. Each of the tannaitic traditions dealing with moral impurity is carefully constructed so as to avoid any confusion between ritual and moral impurity. By maintaining this distinction, even though they reject neither impurity, the tannaim are articulating a distinctively non-sectarian ideology of impurity. As the Introduction noted, Mary Douglas has spoken of the biblical ritual purity system as one in which impurity is defanged: The system does not serve to isolate sinners or to subordinate castes.[63] This idea, of course, is in great contrast to that of Qumran, where purity laws do serve to draw and highlight boundaries along socioethical lines. Compared with these two systems, the tannaitic approach is more like that of Leviticus and less like that of Qumran. In tannaitic literature, too, impurity is defanged. And here lies the irony: it is by drawing and maintaining strict boundaries between ritual and moral impurity — by "compartmentalizing" them — that the tannaim are able to articulate an ideology of impurity that does *not* draw strict boundaries along socioethical lines. — very interesting

Re - Read

Summary and Conclusion: Impurity in Tannaitic Judaism

We have reviewed a number of tannaitic traditions relating to the biblical doctrine of moral defilement. We have noted some developments, but to a great extent there is considerable similarity between the Holiness Code and tannaitic sources. In both, sin produces its own distinct kind of defilement that affects the land of Israel and leads to exile. Indeed, this idea is essentially an aspect of biblical theology that is adopted in whole by the tannaim. Of course the tannaim add their own terminology and focus on the image of the departure of the Divine Presence. Even so, the similarities are much greater than the differences. It has recently been argued — and this cannot be denied — that Scripture looms large in the tannaitic treatment of ritual impurity.[64] To that point I add this: The scriptural notion of *moral* impurity also leaves its mark on the tannaitic corpus.

The system of moral impurity — and I do think we can call it that — may well have been systematized in a way akin to what Milgrom has called "homogenization." There are reflections of this homogenized moral impurity within the Temple Scroll itself, the homogenizing document par excellence. This fact underscores how difficult it is to discern precisely what the tannaitic contribution to the idea of moral impurity was. The tannaim may well have inherited many of these ideas from previous generations.

Where we do see difference is between the tannaim and the earlier Qumran sectarians. At Qumran, the concepts of ritual and moral impurity were closely identified. The tannaim, however, compartmentalized ritual impurity and sin and thereby separated the notions of moral and ritual impurity. What this boils down to is this. For the sectarians, sin as defilement had distinct *halakhic* ramifications. For the tannaim, however, it was an *aggadic* concept. By maintaining the distinctive, *aggadic* nature of moral impurity, the tannaim were able to rearticulate the ethical messages of the Holiness Code. At the same time, the tannaim and perhaps their Pharisaic predecessors, were thereby able to avoid articulating a sectarian, separatist, ideology of impurity like that of Qumran. The possibility that some groups of ancient Jews did articulate a non-sectarian ideology of impurity is, unfortunately, poorly appreciated, especially in contemporary New Testament scholarship, as we will see in the next chapter.

Excursus 1: Gentiles and Gentile Lands

We turn here to a brief consideration of some important and complex questions concerning the ritual and moral impurity of Gentiles and Gentile lands in tannaitic sources. We have noted that idols have become sources of ritual impurity in tannaitic *halakhah*.[65] So too have Gentiles and Gentile lands. As was the case with idols, as far as the ritual impurity of both Gentiles and Gentile lands are concerned, tannaitic sources view these conceptions as innovations.[66]

In spite of these claims, a number of scholars maintain that Gentiles were widely considered to be ritually defiling in prerabbinic times.[67] Indeed, the thrust of Alon's "The Levitical Uncleanness of Gentiles" is the claim that the ritual impurity of Gentiles was "one of the early Halakhot."[68] Following Alon, a number of scholars have maintained that ancient Jews would have considered Gentiles to be ritually impure as a matter of course.[69] A number of these scholars bolster their claims by referring to passages such as Jubilees 16 and 30. Yet as was demonstrated in chapter 2 of this work, the bulk of the (non-Qumranic) passages in ancient Jewish literature that juxtapose Gentiles and impurity refer not to the status of Gentiles vis-à-vis the ritual impurity system, but rather to the fact that Gentiles are idolaters and for that reason a source of moral defilement. When the distinction between ritual and moral impurity is kept in mind, then the bulk of the evidence adduced by Alon and his followers falls by the wayside. What becomes striking is the fact that the tannaitic claim that ritual Gentile impurity came about as the result of a tannaitic decree coheres with the fact that there is no evidence for the notion in pretannaitic Jewish literature. Therefore, we have little reason to doubt the veracity of the tannaitic claim that the notion of ritual Gentile impurity was a something of a novelty

We can now offer essentially the same argument with regard to Gentile lands. According to a number of rabbinic sources, the ruling concerning the ritual impurity of Gentile lands also came about as the result of a tannaitic decree.[70] Yet scholars tend to doubt the veracity of these claims, arguing that the idea goes back to biblical times.[71] Such scholars root their argument in those few biblical verses that speak of the impurity of foreign lands (e.g., Amos 7:17) We noted some of these passages in chapter 1, where I argued that the ostensible biblical precedents for the idea of the ritual impurity of Gentile lands actually testify not to their *ritual* impurity but to their *moral* impurity [72] The idea that foreign lands are *ritually* impure, therefore, has no real biblical precedent. With little or no evidence for the notion of the ritual impurity of Gentile lands in prerabbinic sources, perhaps with regard to this issue too the rabbinic claim that the idea is new ought to be taken seriously

Going back to the idea of the impurity of Gentiles themselves, there is one further observation that needs to be offered here. There is in fact a tradition recorded three times in the Babylonian Talmud that appears to reflect the idea of Gentiles as morally impure. These passages are not tannaitic — in each case the tradition is attributed to a Palestinian sage of the amoraic period, Rabbi Yohanan. These traditions, moreover, do not explicitly attribute moral impurity to Gentiles. Yet the tradition is conceptually related to the idea of moral impurity, and it needs to be discussed briefly (B. Yeb. 103b):[73]

> Rabbi Yohanan said· "When the serpent came upon Eve, he injected lust [זוהמא] into her. The people of Israel, who stood at Mount Sinai, their lust departed. The Gentiles, who did not stand at Mount Sinai, their lustfulness did not depart.

What is so fascinating in this passage is the assumption that all humankind was at some point infected with an inherent "lust," referred to here as זוהמא, a term that has not yet been found in ancient Jewish texts articulating the notion of moral defilement. According to Buchler, the terminological shift here is not so relevant, the important point being that the tradition attributes a nonritual sort of defilement to Gentiles.[74] To a certain degree, Büchler is correct· It is significant that these passages do not assign any ritual impurity to Gentiles. Yet the passages do not exactly attribute any moral impurity to Gentiles either, and to my mind this point too is significant. The difference is not only terminological, but conceptual, and the latter fact adds greater significance to the terminological difference than Büchler was willing to grant. Moral impurity, as we defined it, refers to the capacity of certain sins to produce a nonritual sort of defilement that affects sinners, the land, and the sanctuary of God This moral impurity is not by any means something that Israel cannot contract or convey. To the contrary, a great number of sources in the Hebrew Bible and rabbinic literature assume that the Jewish people has contracted, and can again contract, moral impurity Moreover, Israel has suffered, and can again suffer, the consequences of this moral defilement. Yet in the passage quoted above, the "lust" is attributed to Gentiles and not to Jews Whatever it is that Rabbi Yohanan has in mind, it is not, strictly speaking, the idea of moral impurity as we have understood it here [75] Thus once again we see a difference between rabbinic literature on the one hand and the Jewish literature from the second temple period — the books of Ezra and Jubilees in particular — that articulated the idea of the inherent moral impurity of Gentiles. And all the more so do we see a difference between rabbinic literature and the sectarian literature from Qumran, which attributed a fused conception of ritual and moral impurity to outsiders. In tannaitic sources, and in posttannaitic rabbinic literature as well, Gentiles were considered ritually impure, but they were not considered to be inherently morally impure.

6

Ritual and Moral Impurity
in the New Testament

In this chapter, the focus shifts to the New Testament. I will not analyze every aspect of impurity in the New Testament,[1] but simply point out some ways in which
the analysis presented thus far can shed light on some problems facing contemporary New Testament scholarship. In particular, the distinction between ritual and
moral impurity will help provide clarity to a scholarly discussion regarding purity in
the New Testament that is, unfortunately, too often lacking in specificity. Also the
recognition that there were different ancient Jewish approaches to the relationship
between moral and ritual impurity will shed some light on some of the central personalities of the New Testament, including John the Baptist, Jesus, and Paul.

Misunderstandings of ancient Jewish conceptions of ritual impurity continue to surface in New Testament scholarship, despite the fact that a number of accurate descriptions of it have been available for some time. A few of these clear descriptions
are even addressed directly to New Testament scholars, including Sanders's *Jewish
Law from Jesus to the Mishnah* and Paula Fredriksen's "Did Jesus Oppose the Purity
Laws?" We cannot here review all of the scholarship, nor can we trace all the errors,
but in order to illustrate the claim, I will point out a number of misconceptions in
some recent studies on impurity in the New Testament. It is interesting that these
misperceptions generally appear in New Testament scholarship but not in scholarship on ancient Judaism. Yet although scholars of ancient Judaism generally understand impurity better, they have not paid due attention to what New Testament
sources can tell us about it. These facts highlight what has been claimed throughout: that the study of impurity in ancient Judaism has been impinged by the boundaries that separate the scholars who focus on the different literatures covered in this
work.

One erroneous trope in contemporary scholarship is the assumption that purity
and status were closely identified in ancient Judaism. I have argued both here and
elsewhere[3] — as have others[4] — that one must distinguish between, say, exclusions
from the temple based on ritual impurity and exclusions based on class or status.

Ritual impurity is generally conceived to be impermanent, but class is, generally speaking, a rather permanent condition. In the Hebrew Bible and ancient Jewish literature, a person's status is generally determined by factors that have nothing to do with ritual impurity per se. Thus, for instance, the *mamzer*,[5] who has the most restricted range of marriageability and therefore the lowest status among Jews in tannaitic *halakhah*, is not necessarily more or less ritually impure than anyone else. On the other hand, priests may — indeed, *must* — become ritually impure now and again, whether in order to bury their deceased relatives or to perform those sacrificial procedures — like that outlined in Numbers 19 — that render priests ritually defiled. Nevertheless, one can point to a number of instances where contemporary New Testament scholars confuse impurity and status and assume that the status of outsiders, women, or members of lower classes would be determined with regard to purity and impurity.[6] This general confusion leads to more specific errors, such as the assumptions that Gentiles were widely considered to be impure,[7] that blind or lame priests were ritually defiling,[8] or that women were considered to be impure all of the time.[9] None of these claims is true, and all of these errors are rooted in the confusion of purity and status. – Errors

Another erroneous trope in the scholarship is undue emphasis on what could be called the "locative" approach to ritual impurity. Years ago, Mary Douglas helpfully pointed to the definition of dirt as "matter out of place" in her discussion of the nature of ritual defilement.[10] This definition of dirt is apt, but it is also misleading when applied too strongly to the impurity system of ancient Israel. Conceptions of space certainly play an important role in the system, but place is hardly the determining factor. A corpse, for instance, is ritually defiling wherever it may be, be it in a street (not the proper place for a corpse) or buried in a cemetery (the proper place for a corpse). Nonetheless, Malina, Neyrey, and Rhoads put undue emphasis on the issue of place in their definitions of what is pure and impure.[11] – Not always 'out of place'

A third erroneous trope in much of this literature is the blind identification of impurity and sin, and this brings us back to our main theme. It is not uncommon to stumble across statements that sinners were considered impure and that, by extension, those who associated with sinners were violating norms of purity.[12] There are actually two errors in such assumptions. The first error is the assumption that sinners were ritually impure. The second is that it is prohibited for Israelites to contract ritual impurity.[13] As I have argued, Israelites are almost always permitted to become ritually impure, and it is often obligatory to do so. Thus even if sinners were considered to be a source of ritual defilement, contact between the righteous and sinners would not necessarily violate norms of ritual purity.

With regard to this issue, a number of scholars have recognized that sin and ritual impurity were generally considered to be separate issues in the Hebrew Bible and much of ancient Jewish literature.[14] But there is more to be said on this issue. It is not enough just to say that impurity and sin are distinct. The first thing that must be recalled from our analysis is that while *ritual* impurity generally has very little to do with sin, certain grave sins do in fact produce their own distinct type of defilement — *moral* impurity. As was demonstrated in chapter 2, the idea of moral impurity appeared now and again in ancient Jewish literature throughout the second temple period. And as was shown in chapter 5, the idea of moral impurity can also be seen in the literature of the tannaim. Thus we cannot by any means assume that the conception of moral impurity had little or no impact on the New Testament. To the contrary, we must keep the idea of moral defilement in mind in order to understand properly many of the references to impurity in the New Testament. New Testament scholarship, just like scholarship on ancient Judaism, has yet to recognize the distinctive nature of moral defilement.[15]

This point then leads to another problem. As we saw in chapters 3 and 4, different groups of ancient Jews disputed the nature of the relationship between impurity and sin. Thus it is not really accurate to claim that impurity and sin were distinct concerns for all ancient Jews. For some, that was no doubt the case. For the Qumran sectarians, however, that was not at all the case; sin and impurity had a great deal to do with each other. What needs to be recognized is that the relationship between defilement and sin in ancient Judaism was the subject of sectarian debates. Precisely because we can trace a significant disagreement about as important a question as the defiling force of sin, we cannot simply refer to ancient Jewish Palestine as a "Purity Society."[16] Any number of distinct attitudes competed for the dominance that none actually achieved until well into the rabbinic period. Those New Testament figures — John, Jesus, and Paul — who played a key role in laying the foundations of early Christianity may have agreed with some groups and not others, or they may have paved their own paths with regard to this issue. If we believe these figures said anything about impurity at all, they must be seen not *against* this background, but *within* it.

I could point out still other errors, but I think the need for this review has been adequately justified.[17] As we turn to the New Testament itself, we will keep in mind the distinction between ritual and moral impurity and also recognize that ancient Jews differed on the issue of the defiling force of sin. In so doing, we will better understand a number of aspects of the New Testament.

The Baptism of John

For the sake of clarity, I take the structure here from the flow of the New Testament narrative and thus begin with John the Baptist. Unfortunately, John is a figure shrouded in mystery.[18] On the one hand, we are fortunate to have diverse sources at our disposal, with accounts in the synoptic Gospels, the Gospel of John,[19] and the testimony of Josephus.[20] On the other hand, all of these sources are tendentious: the Gospels very likely strove, as John P. Meier asserts, "to 'make John safe' for Christianity."[21] And Josephus's testimony regarding John cannot be blindly accepted either. Scholars generally agree that this account is authentic, even while agreeing that his account of Jesus has been heavily edited by pious Christian scribes.[22] But even if Josephus's account of John is authentic, whether or not Josephus described John's religious message accurately is another question.[23] Keeping these methodological questions in mind, our concerns are these: In light of the present analysis of ancient Jewish conceptions of defilement and sin, how is John's baptism to be understood? More specifically, how is it to be understood in relation to the purificatory rituals performed by the Dead Sea sectarians on the one hand and the tannaim on the other?

In order to answer these questions, we must first characterize as best as possible John's baptism. According to the information in the Gospels and Josephus, John's baptism appears to be a ritual of moral purification, with eschatological overtones. The ritual was performed, perhaps only once,[24] on Jews who were influenced by John's preaching. And despite the initiatory character of the rite in Christianity, it does not appear that those baptized by John constituted a coherent group. As we will see, this combination of characteristics sets John's baptism apart from other water rites known from Qumran and tannaitic sources.

John, according to the Gospel of Mark 1:4, preached "a baptism of repentance for the forgiveness of sins" (βάπτισμα μετανοίας εἰς ἄφεσιν ἁμαρτιῶν).[25] Indeed one thing that almost all sources, including Josephus, agree upon is that baptism was conceived by John as a ritual of atonement.[26] Yet Josephus goes out of his way to emphasize that for John, repentance was the prerequisite for the ritual: The "consecration" of the body (ἁγνεία τοῦ σώματος) would be performed by John only upon an individual who already had purged his or her soul of sin (ἄτε δὴ καὶ ψυχῆς δικαιοσύνη προεκκεκαθαρμένης).[27] But I am not so sure we should put too much emphasis on Josephus's argument here.[28] I will grant that John would not have performed his baptism on an individual whom he did not feel to be repentant. Presumably, the ritual was meant to effect some sincere and lasting change undertaken by the baptized.[29] But one cannot deny that there was some power to the ritual itself. Considering that the Gospels and Josephus both emphasize the importance of baptism to John, it is reasonable to assume that John did not consider repentance in itself to be sufficient for fully effecting atonement. Indeed, almost all Jews would have agreed that atonement was effected by sincere repentance *and* rituals of atonement of one sort or another.[30] If John rejected this consensus and believed that personal repentance alone was fully effective, then his baptism would not have been necessary. Yet both repentance and baptism were considered necessary, and neither alone was sufficient.[31] Josephus, I believe, tells only half the story by overemphasizing the prerequisite of repentance over the power of the ritual itself to effect atonement.[32] Thus in the end, I think the emphasis ought to be where the New Testament sources place it: John's baptism was a ritual of atonement.[33]

The second aspect that the gospel evidence emphasizes is that John's baptism had an eschatological motive behind it. According to Matthew 3:2, John's cry was "Repent, for the kingdom of heaven is at hand" (Μετανοεῖτε, ἤγγικεν γὰρ ἡ βασιλεία τῶν οὐρανῶν). On a number of occasions, the gospel sources testify to the eschatological nature of John's message.[34] The call for repentance, the coming doom, and the atoning power of the baptismal rite all come together into a single coherent program.[35] One problem with emphasizing the role played by eschatology in John's mission, however, is the fact that Josephus says nothing at all about it. Yet it is difficult to know what to make of what Josephus does not tell us. As Meier points out, Josephus does not discuss Essene eschatology either, an omission that is certainly glaring if the Essenes and the Qumran sectarians are to be identified on some level.[36] Also, despite the efforts among some contemporary New Testament scholars to downplay the importance of eschatology for understanding the historical figure of Jesus, almost all New Testament scholars recognize the centrality of eschatology to the message of John the Baptist.[37]

That John's baptism has atoning and eschatological aspects seems clear enough. What is much less clear is the degree to which it is to be understood as a purificatory ritual.[38] This is indeed a complex question. If John's baptism were to be understood as purificatory, I would want to be able to point to explicit descriptions of the rite as purificatory, and I would want to be able to understand what kind of defilement—ritual or moral, bodily or otherwise—the rite is meant to purify. It is interesting that the synoptics do not explicitly speak of John's baptism as purificatory. There is a reference in the fourth Gospel (John 3:25) to a controversy between the Baptist and other Jews concerning "purification" (περὶ καθαρισμοῦ), but it is still not so clear that John's baptism per se was understood as purificatory. This passage says that John's baptism roused controversies regarding purification, which is not the same thing as stating that John himself understood his baptism as purificatory. It could be that he viewed it in some other way and that John 3:25 tells us that the Baptist's opponents were concerned with issues of purification.

The one source that speaks most clearly of John's baptism as purificatory is Josephus. We noted above that Josephus describes the rite as a "consecration" of the body (ἁγνεία τοῦ σώματος), which is to follow a "purification" of the soul (ἅτε δὴ καὶ ψυχῆς δικαιοσύνῃ προεκκεκαθαρμένης). Josephus's description brings to mind Philo's approach to ritual and moral impurity, which was analyzed in the introduction to Part II of this book where it was argued that Philo viewed ritual impurity as the physical analogue of moral impurity. According to Philo, the ritual impurities that affect human bodies serve as symbolic reminders of the moral sins that defile the soul.[39] In Josephus's account, John appears to take a similar approach: The baptism purifies the body, but it is atonement that cleanses the soul. Yet there is a difference. For Philo, it is clear that ritual purification purifies the body from ritual defilements such as that brought on by contact with a corpse, and that atonement cleanses the soul from sin. Josephus, however, does not state clearly what it is that John's baptism purifies the body from. There are three possibilities. (1) John's baptism could have served to purify people from ritual defilements simply speaking. (2) John could have agreed with the Qumran sectarians, believing that sin rendered people ritually defiling. Thus baptism would serve to ritually purify the sinner's body from the ritual defilement that results from sin. Or (3) John's baptism could have had nothing to do with ritual purity at all.

It is highly unlikely that his baptism served simply to purify individuals from the standard ritual defilements.[40] We have already noted that it may have been a ritual that was to be performed, at least ideally, only once.[41] Even if John allowed for repeat performances, it is unlikely that it could have been frequent enough for the maintenance of ritual purity. Since it was a rite apparently administered by John alone, in a remote location, frequent repetition would hardly be efficient. Yet ritual purification in the Hebrew Bible, in the literature from Qumran, and in tannaitic sources would have to be repeated often, because one cannot help but come into contact with sources of ritual impurity. Indeed, it was obligatory to become ritually defiled, at least on occasion, to bury the dead and to procreate. Even if performed more than once, John's baptism was most likely not repeated enough for the effective maintenance of a state of ritual purity. Another argument against viewing John's baptism as a ritual purification is that none of the sources indicate that he had any particular concerns with ritual defilement. I do assume that, like most first-century Jews, John had concerns of some sort with ritual impurity,[42] yet none of the sources indicate any such concerns that would go along with his special concern with baptism. John calls on his followers to repent but does not ask them to stay away from corpses or any other sources of ritual impurity. Without such concerns, it is difficult to comprehend why John would advocate a distinctive rite of ritual purification.

It would be easier to understand John's baptism as a ritual purification if it could be argued that he viewed sin as ritually defiling. Yet I know of no reason why we ought to assume that John held this view.[43] In this respect, Josephus's evidence again becomes important. Josephus does view John's baptism as purificatory, but he gives us no indication that the ritual was meant to purify the body from defilement caused by sin. To the contrary, he strongly suggests the opposite: The ritual symbolizes what should already have transpired—the purification of the soul from sin. Even when John's baptism is described as purificatory, it is not suggested that sins render the pre-baptized sinner ritually defiled.

What is more, there is no indication that either John or any of his followers behaved in a way to suggest that they considered sin or sinners to be ritually defiling. If they had such concerns, we would expect that they, like the Qumran sectarians, would have kept physically separate from outsiders, and that they would have purified themselves again after engaging in such contact. John himself lived in the desert (Mark 1:2–6),[44] but he does not appear to have expected those whom he baptized to stay with him there. To the contrary, it would appear that his followers returned to their homes and presumably resumed physical contact with other sinners. Had John or his followers considered sin and sinners to be ritually defiling, and if the point of baptism was to remove such defilement, we would expect either that John and his followers would have kept physically apart from sinners, or that they would have frequently repeated baptism. Since neither appears to have been the case, it is not likely that John viewed sin as a source of ritual defilement. Thus it is equally unlikely that his baptism purified individuals from ritual defilement caused by sin.

This difference is just one of many that one could point to separating John from the Qumran sectarians. There are of course some similarities—an emphasis on repentance, a focus on eschatology, the use of water rituals, and interest in the Spirit[45]—but these are too general to be illuminating. Many Jews had these concerns.[46] It is also intriguing that the Community Rule (1QS) makes use of Isaiah 40:3, the voice calling in the wilderness, as do the gospel accounts of John the Baptist.[47] Still the differences between John and the Qumran sectarians are many and more significant, and worth noting here. Regarding Isaiah 40:3, the gospel accounts of John the Baptist punctuate the verse in accordance with the Septuagint, whereas the Community Rule's version is in accordance with a (proto-)Masoretic text. And of course, for the sectarians, the verse justified their establishment of a commune in the desert—something that John never did. Joan Taylor correctly concludes: "If the same text is used, but with a completely different hermeneutical emphasis, this shows in fact that the two groups were not related."[48] Indeed, while the Qumran sect was a coherent community located in a specific locale, John was a wandering loner.[49] Perhaps most important is the difference highlighted by the role of John himself. At Qumran, the frequently repeated lustrations that had both a purificatory and atoning function could be performed on an individual basis. By all accounts, however, John's baptism was to be administered by John himself.[50] All of this increases the likelihood that the other contrast I drew is apt: While we have many reasons to believe that the Qumran sectarians viewed sin as ritually defiling, we have no reason to assume that John and the sectarians would have agreed. To the contrary, our evidence regarding John the Baptist does not compel us to think that he would have considered sin to be a source of ritual defilement. Thus we have no reason to believe that his baptism is to be understood as a purification for ritual defilement.

Once it is understood that atonement and eschatology were central to John's baptism, and that ritual purification was not, then the wide gulf separating his baptism from the ritual purifications described in tannaitic literature becomes rather clear. As I argued in chapter 4, the tannaim compartmentalized the issues of ritual impurity and sin and thereby separated the notions of atonement and purification. For the tannaim, repeated ritual purifications would have been the norm, and there is no indication that the tannaim bestowed repentant or eschatological significance upon ritual purification. John's personally administered baptism of atonement, by contrast, was meant not to purify ritually individuals from sin or defilement, but to change the status of individuals once and for all.[51]

A tannaitic ritual that has often been compared to John's baptism is one commonly referred to as Jewish proselyte immersion. In tannaitic *halakhah*, and in traditional Jewish law to this day, male and female converts to Judaism are required to undergo a ritual purification as part of the conversion process.[52] This would appear to be a one-time purificatory ritual that changes the status of the individual in question. For that very reason, a great deal has been written on the nature of the relationship between John's baptism and Jewish proselyte immersion.[53] But is there a connection between these rituals? Historically speaking there is a great problem here. While we have many sources that pertain to conversion to ancient Judaism — detailed descriptions abound in Josephus, Philo, and the New Testament — there is no evidence of the practice of Jewish proselyte immersion that can be reliably dated to even the first century CE, let alone to a time preceding that of John the Baptist.[54] There are other reasons as well to separate John's baptism from Jewish proselyte immersion. First and foremost, John's baptism was performed on Jews, and Jewish proselyte immersion is performed on Gentiles. Second, John's baptism has a strong eschatological motive, while Jewish proselyte immersion does not. Third, the atonement aspect of John's baptism is also absent from Jewish proselyte immersion. The tannaim were reticent to associate any ritual purification with atonement. In the final analysis, John's baptism cannot be understood as either a development from, or as an analogue to, Jewish proselyte immersion.[55]

How then do we account for John's baptism, if it is not to be compared to the rites performed at Qumran or by the tannaim? In my view, John's baptism can best be understood as its own distinct development from the trends that we have been tracing throughout this work. We find in John's baptism the articulation of a different relationship between ritual and moral impurity than those we have seen thus far.

There are a good number of passages in the Hebrew Bible that speak of ritual purification in contexts of atonement. We have discussed some of these passages — including Isaiah 1:16–17 and Ezekiel 36:16–22 — in chapter 1.[56] There are other passages as well, such as Jeremiah 2:22 and Psalm 51:7–9. These passages comprise an odd lot — no one explanation can account for them all — but one thing about them is clear. In the Hebrew Bible, water rituals were not used for the removal of moral impurity strictly speaking. Murderers, adulterers, and idolaters could not hope to purify themselves morally by undergoing ritual purification. In the Hebrew Bible, the imagery of ritual purification is used in a broader sense, as a metaphorical illustration of God's capacity to effect atonement. This is the nature of passages like Psalm 51:7–9 and Ezekiel 36:16–22. Other passages suggest that it is the Israelites who need to purify themselves from sin, in order to effect their own repentance. This is the nature of passages like Jeremiah 2:22 and 4:14 and Psalms 73:13. But none of this mitigates the fact that the main way in which atonement is ritually effected in the Hebrew Bible is through sacrificial rituals of atonement, like those described in Leviticus 16.

What has any of this to do with John's baptism? John, as a latter-day prophetic figure,[57] appears to have concretized the metaphors one finds in passages such as Isaiah 1:16 and Psalm 51:9. John insisted that in order to atone for sin, one had to undergo a baptism — a rite whose practice ancient Jews were more likely to associate with ritual purification. Thus John sets out on a path that is different from that followed at Qumran and by the tannaim. The Qumran sectarians merged the conceptions of ritual and moral impurity, so that sin was seen as defiling and purification was required for atonement. The tannaim strove to separate these things as much as possible. John's path went somewhere in between. Because John advocated baptism as a ritual of repentance, he clearly did not compartmentalize ritual impurity and sin. But because he did not apparently view sin as a source of ritual defilement, he did not merge the conceptions of ritual impurity and sin. As far as we can tell, John did not consider sinners to be ritually defiling and thus probably did not conceive of his baptism as purificatory in the ritual sense. But he did view his baptism as an effective means of atonement. This approach would have set him apart from many other Jews — including, probably, the Pharisees — who would not have agreed that atonement could be effected by ritual immersion. Also John's interest in moral impurity seems focused not on the land or the sanctuary, but — as with Philo — on the individual sinners themselves. In the end — keeping in mind that any interpretation of John the Baptist must remain tentative — we come to understand that John's baptism worked as a ritual of moral purification, effecting atonement by purifying individuals from moral defilement. With this understanding, it should come to no surprise that his baptism occasioned controversy among ancient Jews with regard to ritual purification (John 3:25).

The Historical Jesus, Impurity, and Sin

It is difficult to exaggerate the degree of current interest in the historical Jesus, on the part of both scholars and the general public. So great is popular curiosity and scholarly output that one can easily find any number of recent books on the figure of Jesus, and even books *about* recent books on the figure of Jesus.[58] And there is certainly a bewildering array of contemporary images of Jesus, from John Dominic Crossan's depiction of Jesus as a Jewish peasant Cynic to Geza Vermes's presentation of Jesus as a Galilean *Hasid*. But we cannot here get involved in disputes about Jesus research or about the overall image of Jesus. What is relevant to us are the current debates on Jesus's relationship to Jewish law, and those regarding Jesus's attitudes toward impurity in particular.

Jesus and the Law

It should come as no surprise that the nature of Jesus's relationship to Jewish law is a hotly debated issue, since the Gospels leave us with a varied picture. On the one hand, Matthew's Jesus declares unambiguously, toward the beginning of the Sermon on the Mount, that "not one letter, not one stroke of a letter, will pass from the law until all is accomplished" (Matt. 5:18). On the other hand, Mark would have us understand that Jesus declared all foods pure (Mark 7:19b), thus abrogating the food laws of Leviticus 11 and Deuteronomy 14. As we will see, Mark 7:19b is widely recognized to be a secondary gloss. And the Sermon on the Mount contains all sorts of adaptations, interpretations, and other modifications of the law that Matthew's Jesus claims to have fully upheld. On the question of Jesus and the law, a simple yes or no will just not do.

To illustrate briefly the state of the question, I will note two very different approaches to the question of Jesus and the law, both of which involve discussions of purity. One school of thought, best represented by the work of E. P. Sanders, defends the view that Jesus in fact had no major conflict with his contemporaries over Jewish law. In Sanders's words, "The synoptic Jesus lived as a law-abiding Jew."[59] Thus, Sanders argues, Jesus did not abrogate either the biblical food laws or ancient Jewish practices concerning ritual impurity.[60] Interestingly, the view defended by Sanders is also advocated in a great number of the classic works on Jesus by Jewish scholars. As Sanders notes, Jewish scholars have "maintained with remarkable consistency that [Jesus] did not consciously set himself against the Torah of Moses."[61]

For the sake of illustration, I pit against Sanders's approach that of Marcus J. Borg, whose depiction of Jesus rests to no small extent on the idea that Jesus rejected traditional Jewish conceptions of purity and holiness. In Borg's words:[62]

> The purity system, with its sharp social boundaries generated closed commensality. — But Not
> The open commensality of Jesus subverted these boundaries, and embodies a radically inclusive social vision.
> . . . Jesus replaced the "politics of purity" with a "politics of compassion."
> . . . In short, the evidence is very strong that Jesus mounted a pointed critique of the purity system of his day . . . for a figure like Jesus, who spoke of the kingdom of God and who attracted a following, to ignore purity made a strong statement. It was a challenge to a social world organized as a purity system. Purity was not a question of piety, but of society.

There are other important differences between Sanders's and Borg's interpretations of Jesus,[63] but for our purposes we remain focused on their dispute regarding impurity.

As Paula Fredriksen has already pointed out, Borg's thesis is based on a number of unfortunate misunderstandings of Jewish approaches to ritual impurity.[64] Following Malina and Neyrey, Borg erroneously assumes there to be direct relationships between purity and status, and between impurity and sin.[65] But this fact in itself does not mean that Borg's overall thesis is wrong. If we take out Borg's misunderstandings of impurity in ancient Judaism, we would find ourselves left not with a vision of Jesus in agreement with his contemporaries, but rather with a very altered vision of Jesus in conflict with them. Indeed, ironically, Borg's other mistakes allow us to resuscitate parts of his argument. He does not express concern with the notion that we have referred to here as moral impurity. Thus, by extension he does not realize that the defiling force of sin was an issue in first-century Judaism. But if we reread Borg's works, keeping these facts in mind, we could easily conceive of a Jesus who has not rejected *the* contemporary Jewish approach to purity — there was no such thing — but a Jesus who has taken a side in an ongoing debate *among* ancient Jews about how ritual and moral impurity were supposed to relate to each other. When we replace Borg's "replacement" with a "shift in emphasis," we could conjure a picture of Jesus that is at once more accurate than Borg's vision of Jesus against Jewish society as well as Sanders's vision of Jesus in consonance with the Pharisees. *— Adapting Borg*   ✳

At this point it is worth asking another question. Is it even possible to conceive of a Jesus who rejected the ritual impurity laws altogether? Although in my view such a Jesus does not emerge from our sources, one must grant that it is possible to conceive of such a Jesus. While purity laws were an important part of biblical and post-biblical Jewish tradition, we do know of groups of Jews who, at various times in antiquity, rejected purity laws or even all Jewish law, without necessarily rejecting their Jewish identity. This description would hold true for the "extreme allegorizers" described by Philo,[66] as well as for the radical reformers who played a key role in the events leading to the Maccabean revolt.[67] Granted, of course, that the extreme allegorizers lived in Egypt, and the radical reformers lived hundreds of years before Jesus's birth, we still cannot deny the possibility that some who upheld such views found a place within the diversity of first-century Palestine. Indeed, many scholars assume that Paul — who spent a significant amount of time in the land of Israel, not even a generation after Jesus — rejected all such purity practices (Rom. 14:14) without ever rejecting his Jewish identity (Phil. 3:4–6).[68] By all accounts, Judaism even in the land of Israel in the first century CE was marked by great diversity. We cannot, therefore, come to questions of Jesus and the law with any prior suppositions; it *is* possible to conceive of a first-century Palestinian Jew rejecting Jewish law, in part or in whole. *— Spectrum of Jesus & the law*

That being the case, I still find it highly unlikely that Jesus rejected Jewish law in any truly radical way. The reason, however, is not that such an approach would be impossible for a first-century Jew, but rather that the status of Jewish ritual law was highly debated in early Christian communities. We can see evidence of controversy regarding its observance in the New Testament itself in texts such as Acts 15 and Paul's letter to the Galatians. Indeed one thing we learn from John Chrysostom's distasteful diatribes against the Jews is that even in the Diaspora in the fourth century CE, the voluntary observance of Jewish law by Gentiles remained an issue that church leaders had to contend with.[69] Had Jesus clearly abrogated Jewish law — if Jesus's statements on law were unambiguously against observance — this situation would not have come about.   *often words not clear* ✳

The question that remains is: Did Jesus engage in controversies with his contemporaries over the substance and practice of Jewish law? I believe the answer is "yes." Moreover, I believe that when we apply what we have observed about ancient Jewish attitudes toward impurity and sin to what we can infer from the synoptic Gospels about the historical Jesus, then the nature of at least one aspect of Jesus's conflict with his contemporaries will come into sharper focus.

Jesus and the Pharisees in Mark 7:1–23

In the seventh chapter of the Gospel of Mark, Jesus disputes with scribes and Pharisees. When they accused Jesus of disregarding "tradition" by eating with un-washed hands, Jesus responds with the famous saying (7:15): "there is nothing out-side a person which by going in can defile [κοινῶσαι], but the things that come out of a person are what defile."[70] We will presently consider the authenticity and then the meaning of this saying, but first we must note that it appears in a wide variety of forms in New Testament literature.

Of course, the parallel in Matthew contains a formulation very close to that in Mark 7:15 (Matt. 15:11), but Mark 7 contains further formulations of the same principle. Upon leaving the crowd, Jesus then restates the principle to his disciples (Mark 7:18–19a): " . . . whatever goes into a person from outside cannot defile, since it en-ters, not the heart but the stomach, and so passes on." This statement is followed by a further narrative clarification (19b): "Thus he declared all foods pure" (καθαρίζων πάντα τὰ βρώματα). The section then closes (7:20–23) with yet another restatement of the principle:

> (20) And he said: "It is what comes out of a person that defiles (21) For it is from within, out of the human heart, that evil intentions come: fornication, theft, mur-der, (22) adultery, avarice, wickedness, deceit, licentiousness, envy, slander, pride, folly (23) All these things come from within, and they defile"

Although Mark presents the latter two versions as reformulations of 7:15, it could well have been the other way around, with 7:15 a reformulation of the principle stated in verses 18–19. Moreover, the second two formulations are divided by what appears to be a secondary explanation, or gloss. Verse 19b spells out what to many is the ramifi-cation of verse 15: the declaration of all foods as clean. But if one considers 19b sec-ondary, then verses 18–19a and 20–23 possibly preserve two halves of what was orig-inally a single version of the saying contained in 7:15. Indeed, in Matthew, we find a single saying (15:16–20) that contains both parts of what is expressed in Mark 7:18–19a and 20–23. Additional early formulations can be found in Matthew 23:25–26,[71] in the Gospel of Thomas,[72] and in a well-known papyrus fragment of an unknown gospel.[73]

This is not the place to examine the question of how the Gospels of Matthew and Mark relate to one another historically (what is known as the "synoptic prob-lem").[74] Although I am generally persuaded by the notion of Markan priority, the problem with this chapter is complex enough that no simple solutions will do: Our Mark did not copy our Matthew, nor did our Matthew copy our Mark. Thus the pos-sibility remains that the Markan version was edited later, and therefore early mate-rial may be more visible even in the Matthean version. But the fact is that New Testament scholarship is almost unanimous in granting authenticity to the content —

if not the form—of what Jesus is recorded to have said in Mark 7:15.[75] Even the generally skeptical "Jesus Seminar" believes that Jesus probably said something like the saying preserved in Mark 7:15.[76] Thus what we need do is briefly consider the arguments of those who would reject its authenticity.[77]

Generally speaking, the opposition takes the view that Mark 7:15 is too radical a statement for any first-century Jew to have uttered.[78] To a large degree, the issue revolves around the relationship between Mark 7:15 and what is stated in Mark 7:19b ("thus he declared all foods pure"). As was noted, many scholars believe 7:19b to be an explanatory gloss.[79] There is near unanimity among scholars that the statement and its explanation could not reflect the views of the historical Jesus. Thus there would seem to be two choices: (1) the statement is authentic and the explanation secondary, or (2) because the explanation cannot be separated from the statement, neither is authentic, because a statement clearly rejecting the food laws is too radical to have been uttered by Jesus himself.

It is actually rather clear that Jesus could not have uttered both Mark 7:15 and 7:19b, because no such statement is alluded to in subsequent Christian conflicts over food laws, such as those recorded in Acts 15 and Galatians 2.[80] But only the explained, expanded, and "radical" version of the principle presented in Mark 7:15 would have aided Paul in these conflicts. Mark 7:15 may not originally have meant what 7:19b says it means. If that is the case, then the absence of the statement from the Pauline controversies regarding food laws (Acts 15 and Galatians) should not be so surprising and does not constitute a strong argument for inauthenticity.[81]

Mark 7:15, even in its immediate context, is not nearly as radical as some have made it out to be.[82] In Mark 7, Jesus's disciples are eating with unwashed hands.[83] If one ignores the explanatory gloss in 7:19b ("thus he declared all foods pure"), the entire passage can be understood as a discussion of hand washing, not the food laws.[84] This is precisely how the parallel in Matthew would have it. In Matthew, the dispute from beginning to end concerns not the food laws, but the issue of eating with unwashed hands.[85] If Jesus rejected the food laws, he would be rejecting an aspect of the Torah itself. But if Jesus rejected the Pharisaic requirement of hand washing, he would still be well within the bounds of opinions held by law-observant first-century Jews.[86]

The fact is that Mark 7:15 need not be read as an outright rejection of anything, even just hand washing, let alone the food laws. As James D. G. Dunn argues, "the 'not . . . but' antithesis need not be understood as an 'either . . . or,' but rather with the force of 'more important than'."[87] This interpretation can best be seen in Mark 2:17, where Jesus says, "I came not to call the righteous, but sinners."[88] Here if the "not . . . but" structure is to be understood as an "either . . . or," then the verse would mean that Jesus wished to associate *only* with sinners. Jesus's disciples were not all sinners, and in fact they are on occasion depicted as being alarmed at Jesus's more challenging teachings and actions (e.g., Matt. 7:28–29). The "not . . . but" structure of Mark 2:17 connotes a shift in priorities away from what would have been assumed. This is how Matthew 15:11 and Mark 7:15 are to be read as well. Jesus here suggests that his followers would be better off if more attention were paid to what comes out of the mouth than what comes in. Mark 7:15 does not necessarily suggest an abrogation of ritual practice any more than 2:17 suggests an exclusion of righteous people from Jesus's following.

Once it is granted that the statement constitutes not a rejection but a prioritization, then it also becomes clear that in order to understand properly the statement as a whole, we must pay attention to both halves of it. A proper understanding of Mark 7:15 must explain not only why Jesus gives less importance to the defiling force of what comes into the mouth, but also why Jesus gives more importance to *the defiling force* of what comes out.

To my mind, the most fascinating part of the pericope is not what is in Mark 7:15, but what is in 7:20–23: Jesus's list of the things coming out of a person that defile the person. Because each item of this list will be of importance to us, the English text of the passage is printed again, along with the Greek:

(20) ἔλεγεν δὲ ὅτι τὸ ἐκ τοῦ ἀνθρώπου ἐκπορευόμενον ἐκεῖνο κοινοῖ τὸν ἄνθρωπον· (21) ἔσωθεν γὰρ ἐκ τῆς καρδίας τῶν ἀνθρώπων οἱ διαλογισμοὶ οἱ κακοὶ ἐκπορεύονται, πορνεῖαι, κλοπαί, φόνοι, (22) μοιχεῖαι, πλεονεξίαι, πονηρίαι, δόλος, ἀσέλγεια, ὀφθαλμὸς πονηρός, βλασφημία, ὑπερηφανία, ἀφροσύνη· (23) πάντα ταῦτα τὰ πονηρὰ ἔσωθεν ἐκπορεύεται καὶ κοινοῖ τὸν ἄνθρωπον.

(20) And he said. "It is what comes out of a person that defiles. (21) For it is from within, out of the human heart, that evil intentions come: fornication, theft, murder, (22) adultery, avarice, wickedness, deceit, licentiousness, envy, slander, pride, folly. (23) All these things come from within, and they defile."

The Matthean parallel has a shorter list of vices that is substantially similar (15:19):

ἐκ γὰρ τῆς καρδίας ἐξέρχονται διαλογισμοὶ πονηροί, φόνοι, μοιχεῖαι, πορνεῖαι, κλοπαί, ψευδομαρτυρίαι, βλασφημίαι.

For out of the heart come evil intentions, murder, adultery, fornication, theft, false witness, slander.   *Clear narrative intention* ← *The Temple*

What is so striking about these lists is the degree of conceptual correspondence between what Jesus views as defiling and the sins that were generally conceived by ancient Jews to be sources of moral defilement. This is extremely significant, because I believe we are to understand that Jesus viewed these sins as *morally* defiling.

[margin note: Sins as moral defilement food laws are ritual, sort of.]

Both the Matthew and Mark versions have Jesus interested in the defiling force of murder and sexual sins.[89] In addition, by both accounts, Jesus is interested in the defiling force of sins that fall under the rubric of "deceit." Matthew's list contains "false testimony" and Mark's contains, following the NRSV, "deceit" itself (δόλος). As we have seen, deceit was considered a source of moral impurity in both the Temple Scroll and tannaitic sources, and it was understood as a defilement at Qumran as well.[90] Following the NRSV, both lists also contain "slander," but the Greek term (βλασφημία) can also be translated as "blasphemy," which was considered to be a source of moral defilement in tannaitic literature (see chapter 5).[91] Two elements that appear in both lists are clearly new. The first is theft, which we have not yet seen as a source of moral defilement. The second is "evil thoughts." Here we may well be able to see the innovation of Jesus or early Christian thought (cf. Matt. 5:27–28). In the rest of Mark's list, we see some references to other sins that are by now familiar, including avarice and envy.[92] Finally we find other very general terms thrown in as well (e.g., "wickedness").

The correspondence between these lists and what ancient Jews generally considered to be sources of moral defilement is not one hundred percent. Nonetheless, the overlap is surprisingly high. I do not know whether we can presume to say that the content of these lists goes back to Jesus himself, but we can say that nothing in Mark 7:20–22 puts Jesus in radical opposition to first-century Jewish attitudes toward impurity. Nor does anything in these lists argue that they derived from either Diaspora synagogues or Greek philosophical schools.[93] There is an undeniable degree of correspondence between these lists and others in early Christian, especially Pauline, literature. We cannot preclude the possibility that Mark 7:20–22 and Matthew 15:19 have been influenced by such writings.[94] But that possibility does not in itself mitigate the claim being made here. The fact remains that what is expressed in these passages fits well within the range of ancient Jewish attitudes toward impurity. These verses depict Jesus as emphasizing the *morally* defiling force of what Jews living in the land of Israel in the first century CE commonly believed to be morally defiling sins. Therefore, we have no reason to discount the possibility that the general content of these passages is an accurate and authentic reflection of Jesus's actual teaching.

But Jesus in Mark 7:20–22 is not only saying that these sins are morally defiling. The passage in that case would be unremarkable. But the passage — and probably Jesus's original teaching on the subject — was indeed remarkable, even if not radical. I have argued that the "not . . . but" formula in these chapters is to be understood as a prioritization of the latter term over the former. Thus what Mark 7 and Matthew 15 attribute to Jesus is the idea that attention to moral purity is more important than attention to ritual purity. That is, Jesus here is addressing himself to the relationship between ritual purity and moral purity, and clearly he prioritizes moral purity over ritual purity. Jesus's position here, in a way, recalls Philo's prioritizing of moral purity over ritual purity. Yet there is one important difference: Jesus nowhere defends ritual purity as a symbol of moral purity. Philo's prioritization of moral purity over ritual purity still provides a symbolic justification for the lesser partner of his pair, whereas Jesus's teachings on the subject do not. I remain convinced that Jesus did not reject these laws himself; too much gospel evidence testifies that these laws did remain important to him.[95] But the fact that Jesus did not defend even the symbolic value of ritual purity laws, while he placed them in a position subordinate to other laws, may well have played a role in allowing early Christianity to move in the direction that it ultimately did.

The position attributed to Jesus in Mark and Matthew also differs in no small way from that of the later tannaim. The tannaim compartmentalized impurity and sin. Mark 7:15 indicates that Jesus — like the Qumran sectarians, and probably like John the Baptist as well — did *not* compartmentalize impurity and sin. For Jesus, a discussion of ritual impurity led — inevitably perhaps? — into a discussion of sin. That in itself is an important difference between Jesus and the later tannaim. The fact that Jesus is depicted as downplaying the importance of ritual impurity only serves to widen that gulf.[96]

One further difference can be observed. I argued in chapter 5 that for the tannaim, the idea of moral impurity was a communal concept. When the tannaim do discuss matters of moral impurity, they focus not on the status of individual Jews within the polity of Israel, but on the status of the people of Israel as a whole in relationship to God. Tannaitic sources do not deny that moral impurity affects individuals, but their primary concern is with how moral impurity affects the land and the sanctuary. The moral impurity sayings attributed to Jesus, however, are concerned first and foremost with the status of the individual. They virtually ignore the effect of moral defilement on the land and sanctuary. —or do they?

In this respect, Jesus's approach, perhaps like that of John the Baptist, can be compared to that of Qumran, which also seems particularly interested in the status of individual members with regard to moral purity. But there are important differences between Jesus and Qumran as well. Whereas the Qumran sectarians viewed sin as a source of ritual defilement, there is no sense in these passages that Jesus viewed sins as ritually defiling. Jesus's concern was, strictly speaking, with the morally defiling effect that sin can have on individual sinners.

If we approach Mark 7:1–23 from another direction, the observations made in chapter 5 about tannaitic literature allow us to speculate on the Pharisaic side to this debate, and thus on the origin of the disagreement between Jesus and the Pharisees. I suggest that the Pharisees, like the tannaim after them, compartmentalized ritual and moral impurity. The evidence for this claim, admittedly, is not as strong as I would like. Still the overall continuity observed in chapters 2 and 5, from the Hebrew Bible through some ancient Jewish literature and to the literature of the tannaim, certainly raises the possibility that the predecessors of the tannaim and the tannaim themselves agreed that (1) certain sins had a morally defiling force and (2) the morally defiling force of sin was an issue separate from ritual impurity. It is also important to recall that the tannaitic sources relating to the Pharisaic *ḥavurah* also operate on the assumption that ritual impurity and moral sin are distinct issues.[97] Finally, if this analysis is correct—to argue in a circular fashion—the Jesus–Pharisee dispute of Mark 7 adds further credence to the claim that the Pharisees compartmentalized ritual and moral impurity. While no Pharisee would argue that sin is acceptable, a Pharisee would not agree with Mark 7:15, for the simple fact that what comes out of the mouth does not ritually defile. In the Pharisaic perspective, sins render people guilty, not ritually impure. →Jesus changes the discussion

Impurity and Sin in the Writings of Paul

When we turn to the figure of Paul, we are both more and less fortunate than when studying the historical Jesus. We are more fortunate in having a number of letters composed by Paul himself. Even though scholars continue to debate the authenticity of some Pauline epistles, it is widely agreed that Romans, 1 and 2 Corinthians, Galatians, 1 Thessalonians, Philippians, and Philemon were composed by the apostle himself.[98] We are also fortunate in that we can glean more biographical information about Paul from the book of Acts.[99] Where we are less fortunate is in the fact that Paul's writings are among the most difficult to understand in the New Testament.

The difficulty of Pauline prose is only one part of the problem. The Pauline corpus, even the undisputedly authentic parts of it, is marked by statements that appear contradictory. Especially problematic are the statements regarding the law in Romans and Galatians.[100] Has Paul's view changed over time? Has Paul's view been influenced by the specific social situation in the community to which he is writing? Have his letters been subject to later interpolations? In order to understand fully any one of Paul's letters, one must face these and other questions, but we cannot address them here.[101] Rather, we will deal with Paul's letters as a whole — not out of a conviction that Paul was a systematic theologian or a remarkably consistent thinker with regard to all matters of importance to him, but rather because the authentic Pauline corpus as a whole presents a relatively consistent picture of his concerns vis-à-vis impurity and sin.

Though currently overshadowed by widespread interest in the historical Jesus, the historical figure of Paul was, just a short time ago, all the rage.[102] The literature on Paul and the law is vast, but ritual impurity, for the most part, plays a less prominent role than in the literature concerning Jesus and the law.[103] This is appropriate, for, as we will see, ritual impurity law is not of great concern in the Pauline corpus. Almost all agree that Paul did not require his Gentile followers to adhere to Jewish ritual law. The real question, it seems, is whether Paul's teaching involved a rejection of the entirety of Jewish law or just many or all of its ritual aspects.[104] Either way, ritual impurity law would appear to be of little importance to Paul and the communities to which he wrote his letters. The issues of greater concern for Paul — as Sanders points out — were the Sabbath (and other "special days"), diet, and circumcision.[105]

One ritual impurity issue that has been raised now and again with regard to Paul and the social situation of the communities in Asia Minor is the notion of the ritual impurity of Gentiles.[106] It is most often raised with regard to the incident at Antioch described in Galatians 2 and the apostolic decree recorded in Acts 15.[107] These texts, however, have little to do with ritual impurity per se. They address issues of greater social significance, such as circumcision (Acts 15:1), and Jewish laws that applied to both Jews and Gentiles, such as rules regarding idolatry and sex (15:20).[108] Yet some scholars have assumed that Jewish–Gentile interaction at Antioch would have been hindered by ritual impurity laws.[109] As I have argued here and elsewhere, however, it ought not be assumed that Jews considered Gentiles to be a source of ritual defilement.[110] Moreover, even if Jews considered Gentiles to be ritually defiling, it would not necessarily be unlawful for Jews to associate with Gentiles, for it was not considered sinful to contract ritual impurity. The assumption that a notion of ritual Gentile impurity played a significant role in the dynamic of Jewish–Gentile relations in the Diaspora cannot be sustained and thus is not directly relevant to an understanding of either Galatians 2 or Acts 15.[111]

Yet some notion of impurity must have been of concern to Paul, for he frequently urges his followers to shun it (e.g., Rom. 6:19).[112] Indeed, he expresses his concerns with defilement throughout his letters, and certainly his community was expected to maintain some standard of purity.[113] But what were Paul's specific concerns? He does not appear to be concerned with ritual impurity at all. Indeed, he seems unconcerned with his followers' diet (Rom. 14:14 and 1 Cor. 8), let alone ritual impurity in general. As we will see, when Paul does raise concerns with purity and impurity, he does so in a moral context, thereby indicating that that what remains important to him is not biblical or postbiblical ritual impurity laws, but the biblical and ancient Jewish notion of moral impurity.

Consider, for example, the following passage from Romans (1:21–25):[114]

> (21) For although they [the wicked] knew God they did not honor him as God or give thanks to Him, but they became futile in their thinking and their senseless minds were darkened. (22) Claiming to be wise, they became fools; (23) and exchanged the glory of the immortal God for images resembling mortal man or birds or animals or reptiles. (24) Therefore God gave them up in lusts of their hearts to impurity, to the dishonoring of their bodies among themselves, (25) because they exchanged the truth about God for a lie and worshiped and served the creature rather than the Creator, who is blessed forever! Amen.

This passage is fascinating in its own right, and the reader may sense some similarity to a selection from the Talmud discussed in excursus 1.[115] What is important for our purposes is the use of the term "impurity" (ἀκαθαρσία) with regard to sins (1:24). In this passage, it seems to refer to sexual sins. Since idolatry leads to impurity (1:23–24), idolatry itself cannot be the impurity mentioned. And the impurity is directly related to misuse of the body (1:24). Indeed, as we will see, other passages in the Pauline corpus clearly juxtapose impurity with sexual sin.[116] Still it may be important that idolatry is an issue here as well. At any rate, when we find idolatrous and sexual sins juxtaposed with defilement, we ought to consider whether the passage is reflecting the ancient Jewish conception of moral impurity.

We find another juxtaposition of impurity and sexual sin in Romans 6:19:

> For just as you once presented your members as slaves to impurity and to greater and greater iniquity, so now present your members as slaves to righteousness for sanctification.

That ritual impurity is the concern of this passage is out of the question. Even if Paul's followers were once slaves to ritual impurity, how could they ever hope not to be unless their bodies began to function in a radically different way? The sources of ritual impurity, recall, are natural and unavoidable. In this passage, Paul juxtaposes impurity and sin and draws a contrast between defilement and righteousness. His concern is for his followers to maintain *moral* purity by shunning the sinful behavior which, according to the Hebrew Bible and ancient Jewish literature, was perceived to be morally defiling. What is surprising is that a number of commentators assume that the terms used and ideas expressed here — sin as defilement — find their origin in Jewish-Hellenistic literature.[117] Such ideas are expressed in Jewish-Hellenistic literature, as we saw in chapter 3, but what is too often overlooked is the fact that the idea of grave sin as defilement can be traced *through* Jewish-Hellenistic literature, and back to the books of Leviticus and Numbers.

The same argument pertains to a number of other passages in the Pauline corpus, where Paul employs the term "impurity" (ἀκαθαρσία) when discussing the moral sins that his followers are to shun (Gal. 5:19–21):[118]

> (19) Now the works of the flesh are obvious: fornication, impurity, licentiousness, (20) idolatry, sorcery, enmities, strife, jealousy, anger, selfishness, dissensions, factions, (21) envy, drunkenness, carousing, and things like these.

Similar juxtapositions of defilement and sin can be found in 2 Corinthians 12:21 and elsewhere in the Pauline and deutero-Pauline corpus.[119] The immediate juxtaposition of "impurity" with "porneia" in Galatians 5:19 confirms the suspicion that when Paul uses terms of defilement in juxtaposition with sin, he has sexual sins in mind. But even if we cannot be so specific, it is quite clear that "impurity" in these contexts is a moral sin, and thus it stands to reason that Paul's concern is with defilement of the moral, not ritual, sort. The lists of vices in these and other Pauline passages are generally compared to vice lists in Greco-Roman philosophical literature.[120] I do not deny the comparison altogether by any means, but I do think that in order to understand fully Paul's approach on such matters, we must recall that there is a greater ancient Jewish and biblical background to Paul's juxtaposition of sexual and idolatrous sin with defilement, and that is the notion of moral impurity.

Of course, according to some Jews — in particular, the Qumran sectarians — sin was not only morally defiling but also *ritually* defiling, so is it not possible that Paul considered grave sin to be both ritually and morally defiling? It is possible, but I do not see any evidence in support of such a view. Grave sinners are, to be sure, excluded from Paul's communities. This is the thrust of 1 Corinthians 5:1–13.[121] The person guilty of incest cannot abide within the new community. What is more, Paul urges his followers not even to eat with an insider who "is sexually immoral or greedy, or is an idolater, reviler, drunkard, or robber" (1 Cor. 5:11; cf. Eph. 5:3–7). And Paul colorfully illustrates his point by drawing an analogy with leaven: "do you not know that a little yeast leavens the whole batch of dough?" (5:6). Paul's point would appear to be that the integrity — the *moral purity* — of the community can be threatened by the continued presence of grave sinners.[122] But exclusion from social contact is not in itself a sign that concerns of *ritual* defilement are in force. Exclusion can be the result of moral impurity as well. The exile of the morally impure Canaanites (Lev. 18:24–30) is an exclusion of sorts. And without a doubt, the Jubilees passages discussed earlier in chapter 2 articulate the notion that the righteous are to shun those whose ways are morally impure. Moreover, the Hebrew Bible itself calls for the exclusion of grave sinners from the community (e.g., Lev. 18:29).[123] These are precisely the concerns expressed in 1 Corinthians 5. Paul wants his followers to shun moral impurity and to exclude from the community[124] those who fail to do so. Paul's concerns with exclusions are not reflective of any concern with ritual impurity.

The same can be said of a rather problematic passage in the Pauline corpus, 2 Corinthians 6:14–7:1, which exhibits a number of conceptual and lexical affinities with the literature of Qumran.[125] The contrasts between light and darkness and between Christ and Belial recall the apocalyptic, dualistic themes of the Community Rule, the War Scroll, and the Damascus Document. Moreover, the passage clearly does not fit well into its immediate context. Yet as Newton argues, there is little in the passage that does not relate in some way to what we can find elsewhere in the Pauline corpus.[126] And of course the possibility remains that the apostle himself made use of preexisting literary or liturgical sources.[127] At any rate, whatever the original source of this passage, the concern here too is that moral sinners must be kept apart from the new community of believers. One rather striking concern for our purposes is the call to be cleansed "from every defilement of body and spirit" (7:1: καθαρίσωμεν ἑαυτοὺς ἀπὸ παντὸς μολυσμοῦ σαρκὸς καὶ πνεύματος). At first reading, it sounds as if Paul wants his followers to maintain standards of moral *and* ritual purity, a notion that would make the passage sound less Pauline and more like

Qumran. But whether the passage is Pauline or not, I do not think the concern here is with ritual impurity at all. We see elsewhere in the Pauline corpus the recognition that moral impurity, especially sexual sins, have an effect on the bodies of the sinners (Rom. 1:24; 6:12; 1 Cor. 6:16–20). That is the concern of 2 Corinthians 7:1, and indeed the entire passage is concerned not with ritual defilement but moral defilement.

If Paul had been concerned with the ritually defiling force of sins, we would expect to see frequently repeated rituals of purification being performed upon casual contact with sinful outsiders, but we see nothing of the sort. To the contrary, the one purificatory rite that figures centrally in the Pauline corpus — baptism — is most likely not repeated frequently, and perhaps performed only once.[128] This fact stands in stark contrast to frequent ritual purification in, for instance, tannaitic sources. If Paul's baptism is to be understood as a purificatory rite, it is to be so understood in the same way as John's baptism: as a ritual of atonement, with eschatological connotations, that, among other things, purifies the initiate from moral impurity.[129] This understanding of baptism as the ultimate purification from moral defilement is clearest in 1 Corinthians 6:9–11:

> (9) Do you not know that wrongdoers will not inherit the kingdom of God? Do not be deceived! Fornicators, idolaters, adulterers, male prostitutes, sodomites, (10) thieves, the greedy, drunkards, revilers, robbers — none of these will inherit the kingdom of God. (11) And this is what some of you used to be. But you were washed [ἀπελούσασθε], you were sanctified, you were justified in the name of the Lord Jesus Christ and in the Spirit of our God.

For Paul, as for John the Baptist before him, individuals could hope to rid themselves of moral defilement through the ritual of baptism.[130] Following both John the Baptist and Jesus, Paul's emphasis on moral purity may well be related to heightened eschatological concerns.[131] It is distinctly possible that Paul's understanding of baptism in this respect has been influenced by his understanding of Jesus's death as a salvific event which effected atonement for Israel (e.g., Rom. 3:24–25).[132] Indeed, throughout Romans 6:1–23, Paul associates baptism with Jesus's death.[133] But how he understood the connection between Jesus's death, baptism, and atonement is by no means clear.[134] What I do think is clear, however, is that the purity achieved by Paul's baptism is of the moral, not ritual, sort.

The persistence of the notion of moral defilement in Paul's writings can also be seen in other ways. As Newton argues, Paul came to view the community of believers by analogy to the sanctuary of God.[135] Paul states as much in 1 Corinthians 3:16: "Do you not know that you are God's temple and that God's Spirit dwells in you?" As Newton argues, the influence of this notion can be felt elsewhere in Pauline writings, such as in 2 Corinthians 6:14–17:1 discussed earlier.[136] Paul's view of the new community as a temple coheres well with his concern that moral defilement would violate the integrity of that community. The effect of moral impurity is felt in the new community in the same way as it was perceived, by Jews, to affect the temple. Paul also repeatedly expresses his belief that the spirit of God rests upon the new community (Rom. 8:9).[137] When we recall that the tannaim believed that God's *Shekhinah* would depart from the temple defiled by sin, one must also wonder: Is it possible that Paul believed in a similar idea, that God's Presence — or Spirit — would be removed from a sinful community?) Is that what lay behind the reference to God's Spirit dwelling among the community in 1 Corinthians 3:16?[138] I suspect that Paul may indeed have believed in such a notion. Even if not, however, I think it is clear that the ancient Jewish conception of the morally defiling force of grave sin has left its mark on the Pauline corpus. The defilement with which Paul remains concerned — and with which he wished his followers to be concerned — was of the moral sort. Paul believed that sexual and, perhaps, idolatrous sins would defile sinners and — in place of the land of Israel and temple in Jerusalem — the new communities constituted by those who believed in Jesus.

escaping from boundaries

Although it is not in the Pauline corpus, we turn finally to chapter 9 of the Epistle to the Hebrews, where the relationship between ritual and moral defilement is addressed quite clearly. Moreover, what we do find in Hebrews 9 highlights something that we do not find in the Pauline corpus. In discussing the efficacy of Jesus's sacrificial death, the author of Hebrews makes a number of intriguing statements concerning ritual impurity. The author in 9:13–14 builds an analogy that is strikingly reminiscent of the view articulated by Philo:

Heb 9

> (13) For if the blood of goats and bulls, with the sprinkling of the ashes of a heifer, sanctifies those who have been defiled so that their flesh is purified, (14) how much more will the blood of Christ, who through the eternal Spirit offered himself without blemish to God, purify our conscience from dead works to worship of the living God!

Just as in Philo, there is an analogical relationship established between ritual and moral impurity, and the analogy is drawn by appeal to body/soul dualism (cf. 9:21–23). But there are a number of important differences between what we see here and what we have seen elsewhere. First, the relative importance of cleansing the soul is clearly articulated. Second, the soul is cleansed of sin not by the sacrifices described in Leviticus 16, but by the sacrificial death of Jesus (cf. 10:4). And third, there is a distinction drawn with regard to time. The importance of ritual impurity law ends with Jesus's death (9:9–11). Despite these differences, it is still important to note that some symbolic or analogical relationship is drawn between ritual and moral impurity. The significance of this fact can be seen by contrast, for this is precisely what we do not find in the Pauline corpus. Jesus, it was argued, prioritized the maintenance of moral purity over ritual purity. But unlike Philo, Jesus did not articulate, as far as we know, any symbolic analogy between ritual and moral defilement. Yet just by prioritizing one over the other, Jesus posited some relationship between the two and therefore did not "compartmentalize" the two, as did the later tannaim. Paul, however, articulates no relationship at all between ritual and moral impurity. Perhaps like the good Pharisee that he claims to have been (Phil. 3:4–6), Paul too had at one time compartmentalized the two issues. And perhaps that is why Paul never refers to ritual defilement, even though he frequently refers to moral defilement.[139]

Is Philo on to something?

— Good Q to probe.

Even with this passage from Hebrews, we have by no means come to the end of the story with regard to conceptions of impurity in early Christianity. Indeed, conceptions of defilement and even biblical rules pertaining to *ritual* impurity continued to have an impact upon early Christians. In certain monastic circles, attention was paid to ritual defilement well beyond the first few centuries of the Common Era,[140] and a number of Christian sources testify to the exclusion of menstruants from sacred spaces.[141] But these phenomena, interesting as they are, bring us well beyond our focus on ritual and moral impurity with regard to the first-century figures of John the Baptist, Jesus, and Paul.

Summary and Conclusion

The distinction between ritual and moral impurity can help elucidate many New Testament writings. The recognition that ancient Jews disagreed on the relationship between ritual and moral impurity is equally helpful to us in trying to understand the baptism of John, and the attitudes of Jesus and Paul toward impurity in particular and law in general.

John's baptism is best seen as an eschatologically oriented ritual of atonement. Its purificatory nature comes not from the fact that John viewed sin as a source of ritual defilement, but from the fact that he came to view baptism as a means of removing moral defilement. What John thought about ritual impurity in general we cannot know for certain, but his use of baptism as a ritual of atonement certainly sets him against the later tannaim, who compartmentalized ritual impurity and sin. John's approach also seems to have been distinct from that of the Qumran sectarians. Although he did not compartmentalize ritual impurity and sin, he did not fully merge the two either, for he apparently did not view sin as a source of ritual defilement.

Jesus's approach to impurity and sin similarly goes in a direction somewhere between the paths taken by the Qumran sectarians and the later tannaim. Jesus too, it appears, did not compartmentalize ritual and moral defilement but at the same time did not fully merge the two conceptions. If we are to accept Mark 7:15 as an authentic Jesus saying — and I can think of no reason not to — then we can assume that Jesus prioritized the maintenance of moral purity over that of ritual purity. This fact in itself indicates that Jesus did not compartmentalize these two issues. If the two issues are to be viewed as separate, then the question of their relative importance is irrelevant. This indeed, I think, is how we are to understand the unstated Pharisaic side to the Jesus–Pharisee debate in Mark 7:1–23. According to the Pharisees, it is not that attention to ritual impurity is more important than attention to sin, it is simply that the issue of the ritually defiling force of unwashed hands has nothing to do with the morally defiling force of grave sin.

Paul takes after both John the Baptist and Jesus. Like John, Paul views baptism as a ritual of atonement that effects purification from moral defilement. Like Jesus, Paul's interest in defilement is focused on moral impurity. Jesus prioritized the maintenance of moral purity over the maintenance of ritual purity. Paul would appear to have taken the next step: In addition to focusing on moral impurity, he does not articulate any interest in issues relating to ritual impurity. So with Paul we see a break with the past, in his rejection of the need to maintain ritual purity, but we still see some degree of continuity in his lasting interest in the notion of moral defilement and the deleterious effect individual sinners can have on the community as a whole. Unlike the later tannaim, John, Jesus, and Paul were not very interested in the dele- *Maybe* terious effect morally defiling sins might have on the land or sanctuary. They were *not* interested, rather, in the effect these sins might have on individual sinners. Whereas the tannaim were not interested in highlighting the morally impure status of individuals, the key figures in early Christianity — like Philo before them — were indeed interested in focusing the notion of moral impurity on individuals. Yet ironically, it is Paul, who rejected ritual purity laws, who maintains a greater attention to the communal nature of the doctrine of moral defilement. This one aspect of Paul's approach to moral impurity is to some extent commensurate with the approach of the later tannaim and, very likely, their Pharisaic predecessors.

With Hebrews 9, we come full circle. We have seen Philo's analogical approach to ritual and moral defilement, Qumran's integration of the two, the "compartmentalization" espoused by the tannaim, Jesus's prioritization of moral purity, and Paul's emphasis on moral purity and rejection of ritual purity. I will next systematically summarize the arguments made throughout this work and then offer some concluding remarks.

Summary and Conclusion

In chapter 1, building on the work of a number of biblical scholars, I argued that there are two distinct conceptions of defilement articulated in the Hebrew Bible. The first, ritual impurity, concerns the impermanent contagion contracted by direct or indirect contact with a number of natural processes, such as birth, death, and sexual relations. The second kind of defilement, moral impurity, concerns the longer-lasting contagion conveyed to persons, the land, and the sanctuary, through the performance of three grave sins: idolatry, incest, and murder. Although the second category is frequently described as metaphorical, I argued that the notion of moral defilement was likely taken just as literally and just as seriously as the notion of ritual impurity. Thus moral impurity should not be dismissed as simply the metaphorical or figurative corollary to ritual defilement. Taken together, these two notions are best understood as two *distinct but analogous perceptions of contagion.*

The distinction between ritual and moral defilement is important — even essential — simply for understanding the biblical text itself, as many biblicists have long noted. But the distinction between ritual and moral impurity is equally important for understanding the literature of ancient Judaism. In order for such a distinction to be understood and utilized, it is important to establish and use a terminology that is both accurate and pliable. Chapter 1 acknowledged that there are imperfections and imprecisions in the terminology adopted here. Yet I hope that the full argument presented in this work argues in favor of the overall accuracy and pliability of the terms *ritual* and *moral* with regard to the two types of impurity in evidence in both the Hebrew Bible and ancient Judaism.

Surveying ancient Jewish literature from the early second temple period, we isolated a number of passages articulating the notion of moral impurity. Many of these passages — from Ezra–Nehemiah, Jubilees, and the Temple Scroll, among other texts — have been misunderstood as articulations of the idea of *ritual* impurity. For the most part, however, the passages analyzed in chapter 2 can be better understood as relatively straightforward articulations of the notion of moral defilement. Thus we saw a great deal of continuity between early biblical texts and later texts from the second temple period. Yet there were some innovations in the early second temple period: some new sources of moral defilement were introduced (e.g., bribery in the Temple Scroll), and some new precautionary measures were suggested (e.g., anti-Gentile polemics in Jubilees). Moreover, we saw some important differences that were manifest in distinct shifts in emphasis: Some texts were more concerned with moral defilement (e.g., Jubilees) and others more concerned with ritual defilement (e.g., the Temple Scroll). These subtle disparities foreshadowed the much greater differences in approach to be articulated in the later second temple period literature.

While many Jews believed that sin was in some way defiling, ancient Jews did not all agree on how the relationship between ritual and moral impurity was to be understood. The second part of this book identified at least four distinct approaches to the question of the relationship between ritual and moral impurity.

Perhaps the clearest answer to this question was articulated by the ancient Jewish philosopher Philo of Alexandria. Philo proposed an analogical, or allegorical, relationship between ritual and moral impurity. While ritual impurity affects the body, moral impurity affects the soul. What is more, ritual impurity and its effect on human bodies served, for Philo, as a systemic reminder of the ways in which moral impurity stains the soul. For Philo, therefore, ritual impurity was the symbolic one of the pair, while moral impurity was by far the more important one. Nonetheless, Philo's dual commitments to allegorical interpretation as well as ritual performance allowed him to maintain his belief in the importance of both types of defilement.

Although the sectarian literature from Qumran never explicitly addresses the relationship between two distinct types of defilement, a number of important sectarian documents present an approach to this issue that remains distinct, at least within the history of ancient Judaism. In the sectarian literature from Qumran, we saw the *Qumran* full identification of ritual and moral impurity: sin was ritually defiling, ritual defilement was sinful, and atonement and purification were likewise closely associated. These views go hand in hand with sectarian notions of separatism. Indeed, the sectarian approach to ritual and moral defilement may well have played a role in the sect's decision to live in relative isolation from the rest of Israel. The sectarians sought to maintain their own ritual purity, viewing outsiders as sinners and believing sinners to be ritually defiling. Thus physical separation from outsiders was something to be desired. The idea of moral impurity in particular may also shed some light on the location of the sectarian settlement: Did they choose to live on the edge of land of Israel because they thought the land of Israel was defiled by sin?

Of course, more than one voice is in evidence in the Qumran literature. It is intriguing that the pre- or protosectarian literature (including the Temple Scroll and 4QMMT) do not yet reflect the idea that ritual and moral impurity were integrated into a single conception of defilement. This observation confirms the emerging scholarly consensus that the Temple Scroll and 4QMMT both stem from a period before the sect fully emerged as a distinct entity. The observation that the sectarian approach to impurity and sin are not yet in evidence in 11QT and 4QMMT also raises the possibility that the integration of ritual and moral impurity played some role in the schism that occurred between the sectarians and the remainder of the ancient Jewish polity. Moreover, we were able to discern that there were two distinct facets of the antitemple polemic articulated in the literature from Qumran: some texts (such as 4QMMT and some portions of 11QT) were concerned that the temple had been *ritually* defiled by improper temple practice. Yet other texts (such as other portions of 11QT and 1QpHab) were concerned that the temple had been *morally* defiled by the sinful behavior of the priesthood. Finally, I suggested that the notion of moral impurity must be kept in mind in discussions of the identity of the sect as well. While there are a number of legal rulings regarding ritual impurity that are common to both the sectarians and the Sadducees, I know of no reason to assume that Sadducees considered sin to be a source of ritual defilement. The issues raised in this book will not by any means solve all of these important questions concerning the Dead Sea sectarians, but it is hoped that the analysis here will shed some new light on our understanding of the history and identity of the Dead Sea sect.

The tannaitic sources present an approach to purity quite different from that articulated at Qumran. To whatever degree possible, the tannaim "compartmentalized" impurity and sin, with the result that ritual and moral impurity became distinct concerns. The tannaitic approach to ritual impurity, therefore, resembles more closely that articulated in the Hebrew Bible: Ritual impurity was conceived as natural, unavoidable, and not sinful. Similarly, the notion of moral impurity remained quite close to what was articulated in the Pentateuch: Moral defilement was produced by a small number of grave sins and resulted in the defilement of the land and the exile of the people (as well as the Divine Presence). The tannaim were indeed familiar with both types of impurity, though they rarely discussed the two in tandem. To the contrary, the discussions of ritual impurity are devoid of reference to moral impurity and vice versa. The tannaim were also remarkably careful and consistent in their use of terminology. Unlike the Dead Sea sectarians, they used the term *niddah* in a very restricted sense and almost always avoided using the term "abomination" (תועבה), unless the term was used in a biblical verse on which they were commenting.

It was also suggested that the conceptual distinction between *halakhah* (law) and *aggadah* (lore) might prove particularly helpful in understanding the tannaitic approach to ritual and moral defilement. While ritual impurity is obviously *halakhic* in nature, the tannaitic conception of moral impurity is *aggadic*. The tannaim are indeed familiar with the notion of the defiling force of sin, but they derive no laws from it — yet a further piece of evidence of the tannaitic compartmentalization of ritual and moral defilement. The importance of the tannaitic compartmentalization of ritual and moral impurity can be seen by contrast with Qumran. The tannaitic approach allows for the articulation of a distinctively nonsectarian ideology of impurity. The tannaim did indeed conceive of sinners as impure in some way, but this conception did not lead them to the idea that sinners must be physically avoided, excluded from the temple or synagogues, or otherwise ostracized in any way.

In the New Testament, a few other ancient Jewish approaches to the question of impurity and sin are in evidence. John the Baptist, it appears, refused to compartmentalize impurity and sin. Although apparently he did not view sin as ritually defiling, he advocated the use of baptism — a ritual more frequently associated in the past with ritual impurity — as an effective means of achieving moral purity. The synoptic Jesus also refused to compartmentalize ritual and moral impurity, and it is likely that Jesus also explicitly prioritized the latter. Paul went even further. While

[handwritten annotations: "why?", "→ Because of Baptism?", "↳ This deserves a paper"]

Paul maintained an interest in the notion of moral defilement, he did not maintain an interest in ritual defilement. There is one way in which the founding figures of Christianity and the later tannaim achieved the same result: Both maintained an interest in moral defilement, without articulating a sectarian ideology of impurity like that espoused by the Qumran sectarians. Yet while the tannaim emphasized the communal significance of the doctrine of moral defilement, the key figures in early Christianity were more concerned with the effects of moral defilement on individual sinners.) *[handwritten: "??? → Xianity was highly communal → see 1 Cor."]*

If there was a "purity society" in ancient Judaism — a community for whom conceptions of defilement played a determinative role in the social hierarchy — it was at Qumran. By almost all accounts, the founders of early Christianity would have opposed such a society. But in order to understand both ancient Judaism and early Christianity properly, we must keep in mind that many groups of ancient Jews would have similarly opposed such a society and found different ways of articulating that concern. Jesus opposed a highly rigid concept of defilement by choosing to emphasize moral purity over ritual purity. The tannaim, and very likely the Pharisees as well, opposed a highly rigid concept of defilement by elaborating ritual purity rules in ways that allowed for high levels of interaction between more pious and less pious Jews, and between Jews and Gentiles. The tannaim also avoided extreme sectarianism by taking the position that ritual and moral impurity were completely separate issues: not to be joined together, not even to be compared. On the one hand, Jesus took a stance that was more "liberal" or lenient than the later tannaim: He downplayed the importance of certain ritual impurity laws. On the other, Jesus took a stance that was decidedly more "conservative": He emphasized the defiling force of certain sins, something the tannaim, and likely the Pharisees before them, were loathe to do.

In the Introduction, I reviewed some attempts to account for the diversity of ancient Judaism that focus on the importance of concerns with ritual impurity. Without denying the importance of ritual impurity to a full understanding of ancient Jewish sectarianism, perhaps the most important ramification of the present study is this: The notion of moral impurity plays an equally important role in the dynamic of ancient Jewish sectarian diversity. *[handwritten: "Most Imp Ramification!!"]*

When characterizing ancient Judaism in all its diversity, we are fortunate to have a good deal of evidence that addresses this diversity: Josephus's catalogues of largely philosophical differences between the Pharisees, Sadducees, and Essenes; the tannaitic lists of legal disputes between Pharisees, Sadducees, and others; the list of temple-related disputes in 4QMMT; and other passages in Philo, the New Testament, and elsewhere, that explicitly ascribe certain opinions to specific groups. But despite the wealth of information that can be gleaned from these texts, scholars cannot assume that all of the important differences were noted or listed in these sources. If the analysis suggested here is at all convincing — even if not in all of its particulars — then an important difference between various groups of ancient Jews has been isolated, one that was not mentioned as such in any of these sources. Perhaps when more such differences can be persuasively identified, scholars will be better able to determine what kinds of information were and were not included in the contemporary accounts and why. Until then, I hope that an additional ramification of this study will be to provide still further motivation to search for and isolate other as yet uncatalogued differences among the diverse groups and individuals in ancient Jewish society. Of course, better understanding of the diversity of ancient Judaism will contribute, in turn, to a better understanding of the early periods of both Christianity and rabbinic Judaism.

A third reflection on the study of ancient Judaism that emerges from this work concerns not ancient Jewish literature strictly speaking, but the Hebrew Bible. We have found throughout this work that understanding the dynamic of defilement in the Hebrew Bible (a process in which we were aided by the work of biblicists) contributes to a better understanding of ancient Judaism. This, of course, stands to reason, since the Hebrew Bible was so important to the various groups of ancient Jews. Yet understanding the dynamic of defilement in the Hebrew Bible helps us appreciate not only what ancient Jews shared, but where they differed as well. Thus we find here confirmation of one of the lasting contributions of Jacob Neusner: the recognition that while Scripture looms large for many groups of ancient Jews — thus providing each of them with a common foundation — Scripture in itself does not determine how it is to be interpreted. The disparate groups of ancient Jews (and early Christians) chose to interpret Scripture in various ways. Tracing such dynamics is not always a simple exercise, but this process might progress further if scholars of the sundry facets of ancient Judaism were to heed the advice of Jacob Milgrom and pay greater attention to the achievements of scholars of the Hebrew Bible.

The Hebrew Bible exists today only because it was so important to the various groups of ancient Jews, who carefully copied and transmitted those documents through many generations. Thus, in a way the Hebrew Bible itself is not only a record of the history and religion of the ancient Israelites who composed much of it, but also an important testimony to the religious concerns of the second-temple–period Jews who cared to preserve and transmit it. We could thus say, in a matter of speaking, that the Hebrew Bible is very much an ancient Jewish text. Those who would describe varied groups of ancient Jews with reference only to a certain set of (or piece of) literature would do well to recognize that much of the theological underpinnings of ancient Jewish literature (and tannaitic literature in particular) is to be found in the Hebrew Bible itself.

One final reflection that emerges from this work concerns the complexity of the concept of defilement. Given that the relationship between impurity and sin is so important for an understanding of ancient Judaism, related questions come to mind. Were there other times in Jewish or Christian history when this question came to the fore? Are there other religious traditions in which similar debates have raged? These questions can likely be answered affirmatively. More than thirty years after the publication of Mary Douglas's *Purity and Danger*, while we are much closer to understanding the functions and meanings of purity systems in various religious traditions, there is much that remains to be understood. I hope the present study has at least contributed to that process by clarifying the dynamic between impurity and sin in an important period of the history of both Judaism and Christianity.

Notes

Preface

1. Translations from the Hebrew Bible are taken from or based upon *Tanakh* (Philadelphia: Jewish Publication Society, 1985), henceforth referred to as NJV. However, where NJV uses "uncleanness" to translate the Hebrew *tameh*, I use "impurity."

2. *Leviticus 1–16. A New Translation with Introduction and Commentary*, vol. 3 of *The Anchor Bible* (New York. Doubleday, 1992), pp. 1004–1009.

Introduction

1. Jacob Neusner, over the years, has devoted dozens of volumes to the subject, including *The Idea of Purity in Ancient Judaism* (Leiden: E. J. Brill, 1973), *A History of the Mishnaic Law of Purities*, 22 vols. (Leiden, E. J. Brill, 1974–1977), esp. vol. 22; and most recently, *Purity in Rabbinic Judaism: A Systemic Account* (Atlanta: Scholars Press, 1994). Other recent books include Hannah K. Harrington, *The Impurity Systems of Qumran and the Rabbis: Biblical Foundations* (Atlanta: Scholars Press, 1993); Howard Eilberg-Schwartz, *The Savage in Judaism* (Bloomington: Indiana University Press, 1990); E P Sanders, *Jewish Law from Jesus to the Mishnah: Five Studies* (London: SCM Press, 1990); L. William Countryman, *Dirt, Greed & Sex* (Philadelphia: Fortress Press, 1988); and Michael Newton, *The Concept of Purity at Qumran and in the Letters of Paul* (Cambridge· Cambridge University Press, 1985). In addition, numerous articles have been published in recent years, especially by Joseph Baumgarten, Shaye Cohen, David Flusser, Jacob Milgrom, and Lawrence H. Schiffman. And of course one would always do well to begin with Mary Douglas, *Purity and Danger: An Analysis of the Concepts of Pollution and Taboo*, 2nd impression with corrections (London: Routledge and Kegan Paul, 1969).

2. *Studies in Sin and Atonement in the Rabbinic Literature of the First Century* (London: Oxford University Press, 1928), pp. 212–269 (Bible) and pp. 270–374 (postbiblical and rabbinic literature).

3. On Jesus, impurity, and sin, see chapter 6 of this book.

4 *Leviticus 1–16* (vol. 3 of *The Anchor Bible*); Jacob Milgrom's contribution to this topic is taken up later.

5 See especially *In the Wilderness· The Doctrine of Defilement in the Book of Numbers* (Sheffield: JSOT Press, 1993).

6. For instance, in Jacob Neusner's *The Idea of Purity*, one can find useful discussions of the views of William Robertson Smith, Yehezkel Kaufmann, Baruch Levine, and Mary Douglas. Neusner's discussions focus both on the nature of impurity (whether it is a demonic or rational force) and on the anthropological functions of such conceptions. In Howard Eilberg-Schwartz's more recent book, *The Savage in Judaism*, one can find useful surveys of the relevant anthropological literature (including Douglas and Victor Turner), as well as discussions of the views of Neusner and Jacob Milgrom E. P. Sanders's "Did the Pharisees Eat Ordinary Food in Purity?" (in *Jewish Law from Jesus to the Mishnah: Five Studies*, pp. 162–166) includes detailed discussions of scholarly views of pharisaic eating practices, paying special attention to Gedalyahu Alon, Ellis Rivkin, and Neusner. Finally, Hannah K. Harrington's *The Impurity Systems of Qumran and the Rabbis* is introduced by a chapter that surveys the views of, among others, Büchler, Alon, Milgrom, Yigael Yadin, Neusner, R. P. Booth, and E. P. Sanders. These discussions are, for the most part, accurate and balanced, and thus there is no need to rehearse their contents here.

7. On Adolph Büchler's life and work, see Isidore Epstein's introduction to Büchler's *Studies in Jewish History* (London: Oxford University Press, 1956).

8. On the historical significance of Büchler's *Studies in Sin and Atonement*, see Frederick C. Grant's prolegomenon to the 1967 reprint by Ktav (Library of Biblical Studies, ed. Harry M. Orlinsky), pp. xvii–xxxix.

9. Büchler wrote his *Studies* just a year after he wrote his essay, "The Levitical Impurity of the Gentile in Palestine Before the Year 70" (*Jewish Quarterly Review* n.s. 17 [1926–1927]: 1–79). I have argued elsewhere that Büchler's treatment of Gentile impurity has not received the attention it deserved. See my "Notions of Gentile Impurity in Ancient Judaism," *AJS Review* 20.2 (1995)· 285–312. In my view, Büchler's *Studies* are even more significant, though they have received even less attention than his article on Gentile impurity.

10. *Studies*, p. ix.

11. *Studies*, p. 224; Hoffmann's work is cited and discussed later.

12. *Studies*, p. 270.

13. *Studies*, p. i.

14. *Studies*, e.g., pp. 214 and 229.

15. *Jews, Judaism and the Classical World: Studies in Jewish History in the Time of the Second Temple and Talmud*, trans. Israel Abrahams (Jerusalem: Magnes Press, 1977), pp. 190–234 (Hebrew original: Tarbiz 9.1 [1937]: 1–10; 179–195). On Alon's life and work, see Shmuel Safrai's preface to *Jews, Judaism, and the Classical World*.

16. "The Bounds," p. 232.

17. See the discussion of Alon's work in E. P. Sanders, "Did the Pharisees Eat Ordinary Food in Purity?"

18. Roger P Booth, *Jesus and the Laws of Purity* (Sheffield. JSOT Press, 1986), pp. 152–153; Harrington, *The Impurity Systems*, pp. 4–5, Yigael Yadin, *The Temple Scroll*. 3 vols (Jerusalem. Israel Exploration Society, 1983), vol. I, p. 277.

19. Jacob Milgrom, "Scriptural Foundations and Deviations in the Laws of Purity of the *Temple Scroll*," in *Archaeology and History in the Dead Sea Scrolls*, ed. Lawrence H. Schiffman (Sheffield: JSOT Press, 1990), pp. 83–99.

20. "On the Halakhot of the Early Sages," *Jews, Judaism and the Classical World*, pp. 138–145. Alon in this essay deals with the tradition (reflected in M. Eduyot 5:6 and elsewhere) that sinners under the ban were excluded from the temple. Alon cites the Targum to 2 Samuel 5:8, to the effect that sinners were prevented from entering the temple. Alon does not cite M. Bekh. 7:7, which explicitly permits the murderer to enter the temple, nor for that matter does Alon refer to the biblical traditions (e.g., Exod 21:14) that operate under the assumption that murderers will seek sanctuary at the horns of the altar. Again, Büchler understood the issue bet-

ter: "Not even the gravest crime, like that of murder, would prevent the sinner from approaching the altar and seizing its horns, and he did not defile thereby the sanctuary and its altar" (*Studies*, p. 235). Curiously, I could not find anywhere in Alon's oeuvre his interpretation of biblical traditions like Leviticus 18:24–30, which were so central to Büchler's argument.

21. *Jews, Judaism and the Classical World*, pp. 146–189 (Hebrew original: *Tarbiz* 8 [1937]: 137–161)

22. These and other relevant essays, including Douglas's brief 1968 encyclopedia article "Pollution," can be found in *Implicit Meanings: Essays in Anthropology* (London: Routledge and Kegan Paul, 1975). *Natural Symbols* first appeared in 1970 (London: Routledge and Kegan Paul), was revised in 1973, and has recently been reprinted with a new introduction (London: Routledge, 1996). Douglas's "Critique and Commentary" to Neusner's *The Idea of Purity* will be discussed later along with Neusner's work.

23. For an overall evaluation of this stage in Mary Douglas's work, see the excellent summary and evaluation by Sheldon R. Isenberg and Dennis E Owen, "Bodies, Natural and Contrived. The Work of Mary Douglas," *Religious Studies Review* 3 1 (1977): 1–17 For a treatment of her early work in historical perspective, see William G. Doty, *Mythography· The Study of Myths and Rituals* (Tuscaloosa. University of Alabama Press, 1986), esp. pp. 97–98 and 115–121, and Eilberg-Schwartz, *The Savage in Judaism*, pp. 75–84. On Mary Douglas's life and work, see Richard Fardon, *Mary Douglas: An Intellectual Biography* (London: Routledge, 1999). On *Purity and Danger*, see pp 75–101 My treatment of Mary Douglas's works was written before this biography was published, but I find that my summaries and analyses cohere largely with Fardon's.

24 One error made in *Purity and Danger* is the assumption that Israelites considered all that exudes from the body to be ritually defiling (see p. 121). In reality, as we will see, the biblical purity system problematizes only certain bodily substances. Milgrom (*Leviticus 1–16*, p. 720–721), lists seven errors in Douglas's early work

25. See especially the first two chapters of *Purity and Danger*.

26. *Purity and Danger*, pp. 29–40, esp. pp. 35 and 40.

27. *Purity and Danger*, pp. 29–40, esp. pp. 37–40. Douglas develops her take on anomalies throughout *Purity and Danger*, and then she rethinks her views in "Deciphering a Meal" and "Self-Evidence," in *Implicit Meanings*, pp. 249–318.

28. See *Purity and Danger*, pp. 7–28 for Douglas's assessment of the work of Henry Burnet Tyler, William Robertson Smith, James Frazer, and Emile Durkheim.

29. In this respect, Douglas's work can be profitably compared with that of Claude Lévi-Strauss; see, for example, Lévi-Strauss, *Totemism*, trans Rodney Needham (Boston: Beacon Press, 1963) But Douglas goes only halfway down the road taken by Lévi-Strauss. Douglas has no patience for Lévi-Strauss's search for simple universal structures, insisting instead that we stand to learn much more by recognizing the degree to which ritual and mythic structures cohere with specific cultural ones. See "The Meaning of Myth," in *Implicit Meanings*, pp. 153–172, and *Natural Symbols*, pp. 70–71. On Douglas and Lévi-Strauss, see Isenberg and Owen, "Bodies, Natural and Contrived," p. 4

30. See, for example Milgrom, *Leviticus 1–16*, p. 729. Milgrom builds his argument on Anna S Meigs, "A Papuan Perspective on Pollution," *Man* 13 (1978): 304–318. Surely ancient Israelites did not view all misplaced objects as sources of defilement. But Douglas's opposition has pushed her definition too far. Her definition, I believe, was never meant to be reversible. not all matter out of place is to be understood as defiling! Douglas's point, as I understand it, is simply that impure things fall outside the category patterns of the system in question.

31. *Purity and Danger*, pp. 114–128; "Self-Evidence," in *Implicit Meanings*, pp. 276–318, and *Natural Symbols*, pp. 69–87

32. *Purity and Danger*, pp 41–57.

33. For critiques of Douglas's specific interpretations of biblical material, see Eilberg-Schwartz, *The Savage in Judaism*, pp. 177–179, 189–190, and 218–219; and Milgrom, *Leviticus 1–16*, esp. pp. 704–742. See also Isenberg and Owen, "Bodies, Natural and Contrived," pp. 2–5.

34. See, for example, Jonathan Z. Smith, *To Take Place: Toward Theory in Ritual* (Chicago· University of Chicago Press, 1987), p. 108.

35 In subordinating function to symbol in this discussion, I follow Douglas's own advice. see *Natural Symbols*, p. 37.

36. Douglas, *Purity and Danger*, pp. 3–4 and 112–113; cf. her "Critique and Commentary" in Neusner, *The Idea*, esp. p. 141, quoted below in this chapter.

37. Generally, see *Purity and Danger*, pp 129–158; quote from p. 142

38. *Purity and Danger*, p. 113.

39. *Purity and Danger*, p. 129.

40. See Isenberg and Owen, "Bodies, Natural and Contrived," pp. 10–15.

41. *The Idea*, p. x. Despite the fact that Büchler's *Studies* are cited in Neusner's bibliography, the work is never referred to within the body of Neusner's text, and Büchler's argument is never presented, let alone refuted in any way.

42. *The Idea*, p. x

43. *The Idea*, p. 108. Neusner's detailed analysis of the defiling force of sin in biblical literature can be found on pages 11–15 of *The Idea*. There, too, Neusner assumes that all juxtapositions of sin and defilement are of a metaphorical nature.

44. *The Idea*, p. 54.

45 *The Idea*, p. 117 Neusner needlessly refers to this view as "extreme" (see the discussion in the *Negaim* section of chapter 4 of this book). And here too Neusner fails to recognize that the tannaim, in this respect, are building on a scriptural base: Miriam was afflicted with "leprosy" when she spoke against Moses's Cushite wife (Num. 12). On Neusner's failure to account for the scriptural origin of later ideas, see Milgrom, *Leviticus 1–16*, pp. 1004–1009

46. The issue of defining metaphor is problematic; it will be taken up later when we turn to the biblical passages themselves (see especially chapter 1, under "Moral Impurity as a Metaphor?").

47. "Critique and Commentary," appendix to Neusner, *The Idea*, pp. 137–142; quote from p. 140 Neusner subsequently accepted this point. See Neusner's *History of Mishnaic Law of Purities*, vol. V, p. 253.

48. *The Idea*, p. 141

49. The second chapter of *The Impurity Systems* analyzes the categories of impurity at Qumran: corpses, leprosy, etc. Sin is not one of the subtopics of the chapter. Harrington does address here the connection between leprosy and sin (pp. 81–83), but the issue of the defiling force of sin at Qumran is not otherwise directly addressed.

50. *Jewish Law from Jesus to the Mishnah. Five Studies*, pp. 131–254, esp. pp. 134–151.

51. *Jewish Law*, pp. 133, 137.

52. Sanders cites Büchler's *Studies* and even compliments them (*Jewish Law*, p. 348, n. 3; he refers to the work as "masterful"). But Sanders believes he can discuss the concept of impurity, and not just its "ritual" type, without addressing the question of sin. Thus it appears as if Büchler's *Studies* did not make a great impact on Sanders This fact can more clearly be seen when, in discussing ritual defilement in the Bible, Sanders notes without qualification that "adultery, child sacrifice, homosexuality, and bestiality make one impure" (*Jewish Law*, p 139; Sanders cites Lev. 18·19–24). Yet elsewhere Sanders has stated categorically that impurity and sin are not to be confused; see his *Jesus and Judaism* (Philadelphia: Fortress Press, 1985), pp. 182–187.

53. Recent studies that overlook or underestimate the importance of the defiling force

of sin include Roger P. Booth's *Jesus and the Laws of Purity*, Michael Newton's *The Concept of Purity at Qumran and in the Letters of Paul*, and L. William Countryman's *Dirt Greed, and Sex*. Booth makes an attempt at describing what he calls "ethical defilement" (pp. 210–215), yet he does not define the term or explain what he means by ethical defilement; see the review of Booth and Newton by P. Sacchi in *Journal for the Study of Judaism* 18.1 (1987): 94–98. Michael Newton's work is at once clearer and less accurate than Booth's work. As is suggested by the singularity of Newton's title — *The Concept of Purity* — Newton nowhere recognizes the distinctive nature of sin's defiling force. This despite the fact that Newton cites Büchler's *Studies* on p. 124, n. 70. Newton was criticized on this very point by L William Countryman in the latter's *Dirt, Greed, and Sex* (p. 98, n. 2). Indeed, Countryman begins his book with the recognition of two distinct purity codes in the Bible, one focused on ritual impurity and the other on sin (pp. 20–44). Unfortunately, however, Countryman does not carry through with the implications of this observation: His treatment of subsequent developments does not trace the history of the defiling force of sin.

54. Neyrey's article appeared in *Semeia* 35 (1986): 91–128; cf. also Neyrey, "The Symbolic Universe of Luke–Acts: 'They Turn the World Upside Down,'" in *The Social World of Luke–Acts*, ed. Jerome H. Neyrey (Peabody, Mass.: Hendrickson, 1991), pp. 271–304 Malina's article constitutes chapter 6 of his *The New Testament World. Insights from Cultural Anthropology*, rev ed. (Louisville: Westminster/John Knox Press, 1993), pp 149–183. Rhoads's article constitutes chapter 6 of *Mark and Method· New Approaches in Biblical Studies*, ed. Janice Capel Anderson and Stephen D Moore (Minneapolis: Fortress Press, 1992), pp. 135–161. I thank Carol B. Selkin for bringing this book to my attention.

55. Neyrey, "The Idea of Purity," pp. 98, 101; Rhoads, "Social Criticism," p. 149; and in a rather idiosyncratic way, Malina, *The New Testament World*, pp. 154–157.

56. See discussion of Borg's work in chapter 6 of this book.

57. For a recent survey of scholarly approaches to ritual impurity, see Philip Peter Jenson, *Graded Holiness: A Key to the Priestly Conception of the World* (Sheffield· JSOT Press, 1992), pp. 56–88.

58. *Das Buch Leviticus*, 2 vols. (Berlin: M. Poppelauer, 1905–1906), see esp. vol. 1, pp. 303–304. A Hebrew translation of Hoffmann's commentary has been produced (2 vols., [Jerusalem. Mossad HaRav Kook, 1953]), but all references here are to the German original; the Hebrew terms quoted above are used by Hoffmann in the German edition. On Hoffmann's life and work generally, see Louis Ginzberg, *Students, Scholars, and Saints* (Philadelphia: Jewish Publication Society, 1928), pp. 252–262.

59. Regarding Hoffmann's terminology, see, for example, "bodily impurity" in B. Yoma 80b, and Rashi ad loc.; and "defilement of the soul" in Ibn Ezra on Leviticus 18:24. Regarding Hoffmann's conceptual distinction, various medieval Jewish commentators were acutely aware of the distinctive use of impurity terminology in certain passages of Leviticus. See, for example, the comments of Ibn Ezra and Ramban (Nachmanides) on Leviticus 18:24–30. Both articulate a literal interpretation of the passage, without confusing the defilement caused by sexual sin with the ritual impurities described in Leviticus 11–15.

60. *Leviticus*, vol 1, p. 315

61 *Leviticus*, vol. 1, p 303; vol 2, p 22.

62 *Leviticus*, vol. 1, p. 303; vol 2, p. 59. In Hoffmann's scheme, the prohibitions against eating impure food fall under this second category. But the defilement that originates in contact with carrion (נבלה) and reptilian carcasses (שרץ) falls under the rubric of what Hoffmann calls bodily impurity, which is roughly equal to our ritual impurity. On the dietary restrictions and their relation to purity law, see "The Dietary Laws" section of chapter 1

63. *Leviticus*, vol. 1, p. 315; Leviticus 16:16.

64. *Leviticus*, vol. 2, p. 22.

65. *Leviticus*, vol. 1, p. 303; Hoffmann translates נפש as "Seele." Hoffmann does not go into any detail here about ancient Israel's conception of the soul. The question, though important, is not directly relevant to the topic at hand.

66. *Leviticus*, vol. 2, p. 22; cf. vol. 1, p. 340.

67. Commenting on Leviticus 18:20· "damit is nicht wie 15:18 die Unreinheit gemeint, die durch Baden beseitigt werden kann, sondern die Befleckung von Körper und Seele." *Leviticus*, vol. 2, p. 22

68. *Leviticus*, vol. 2, p. 59: "denn ihr würdet euch durch solches Treiben nur verunreinigen, und zwar nicht blos symbolish, sondern concret. . . . Ihr würdet dadurch eure Person, Körper und Seele, von Gott ab- und dem Wahne und der Unsittlichkeit zuwenden."

69. *Leviticus*, vol. 1, p. 340; vol. 2, p. 59

70. Milgrom, "Israel's Sanctuary: 'The Priestly Picture of Dorian Gray,'" *Revue Biblique* 83 (1976): 390–399.

71. Milgrom, "Sin-Offering or Purification-Offering?" *Vetus Testamentum* 21 (1971): 237–239; cf. Milgrom, *Leviticus 1–16*, pp. 253–254. A brief treatment can be found in Milgrom, *The JPS Torah Commentary: Numbers* (Philadelphia: The Jewish Publication Society, 1990), pp. 444–447; the fullest development of these ideas to date is *Leviticus 1–16*, pp. 253–292.

72. "Israel's Sanctuary," p. 392 (= *Leviticus 1–16*, p. 257).

73. "Israel's Sanctuary," p. 392 (= *Leviticus 1–16*, p. 256).

74. "Israel's Sanctuary," p. 398 (= *Leviticus 1–16*, p. 260).

75. "Israel's Sanctuary," p. 393 (= *Leviticus 1–16*, p 257)

76. "Israel's Sanctuary," p. 393 (= *Leviticus 1–16*, p. 257). Note too the useful illustration in "Israel's Sanctuary," p. 394 (= *Leviticus 1–16*, p. 258).

77. John G. Gammie, for instance, rejects Milgrom's suggested translation, holding that some *chattat* sacrifices serve other purposes. Gammie also feels that the sacrifices in question purged people as well as places See his *Holiness in Israel* (Minneapolis: Fortress Press, 1989), pp. 38–41; here Gammie is following Baruch A Levine, *In the Presence of the Lord* (Leiden: E. J. Brill, 1974), pp. 101–104. For more on Milgrom's interpretation, see Jenson, *Graded Holiness*, pp. 155–160 and the literature cited there.

78. Milgrom recognizes this in his comments on Leviticus 18:24–30 in the Harper Collins Study Bible, cf. Milgrom, *Numbers*, p. 302, n. 5; *Leviticus 1–16*, p. 1055. Presumably, Milgrom will devote more attention to this issue in the second volume of his Anchor Bible Commentary on Leviticus.

79. Tikva Frymer-Kensky, "Pollution, Purification, and Purgation in Biblical Israel," in *The Word of the Lord Shall Go Forth: Essays in Honor of David Noel Freedman in Celebration of his Sixtieth Birthday*, ed Carol L. Meyers and M. O'Connor (Winona Lake. Eisenbrauns, 1983), pp. 399–414.

80. Frymer-Kensky's article is not even cited in the extensive bibliography in Milgrom's *Leviticus 1–16* I learned of this article from an anonymous outside reviewer for the *AJS Review*, who cited her work in a reader's report on my "Notions of Gentile Impurity." Building on Büchler's *Studies*, I had already developed the distinction I will draw between ritual and moral impurity. Thus Frymer-Kensky's work was for me more of a confirmation than a revelation. It appears, in turn, that Frymer-Kensky developed her ideas independently of Büchler and Hoffmann, neither of whom are cited in her bibliography

81. "Pollution," p. 399.

82 "Pollution," p. 405; cf. Leviticus 7 20–21; 22:3–9.

83. For more on the restrictions necessary to avert danger, see David P. Wright, *The Disposal of Impurity: Elimination Rites in the Bible and in Hittite and Mesopotamian Literature* (Atlanta· Scholars Press, 1987), pp. 163–228; see especially p. 227: "If communicably impure persons and objects were allowed full access to the community, other persons and

objects would become contaminated. This would in turn threaten cultic matters. With severe impurities running loose, the average impurity of the community would increase, causing a greater chance of defiling sancta."

84. "Pollution," pp. 403–404.

85. "Pollution," p. 408.

86. For one, Frymer-Kensky does not explicitly state how the bulk of the dietary restrictions fit into her schema. Also Frymer-Kensky's speculative analogy between exile and the flood (pp. 409–412) is not entirely convincing.

87. "Pollution," p. 408.

88. David P. Wright, "The Spectrum of Priestly Impurity," in *Priesthood and Cult in Ancient Israel*, ed. Gary A. Anderson and Saul M Olyan (Sheffield: JSOT Press, 1991), pp. 150–181; cf Wright, "Unclean and Clean (OT)," in *The Anchor Bible Dictionary*, ed. David Noel Freedman (New York: Doubleday, 1992), vol. VI, pp. 729–741.

89. "Unclean and Clean," pp. 729–730.

90. "The Spectrum," p 158.

91. Wright correctly recognizes that the dietary prohibitions pose particular problems for any schematization of purity laws ("The Spectrum," pp. 165–169). For more on how the dietary restrictions relate to the other purity laws, see "The Dietary Laws" in chapter 1 of this book.

92. Now Wright does, to be sure, distinguish between intentional and unintentional violations of prohibited impurity ("Unclean and Clean," pp 737–738; "The Spectrum," pp. 158–159) Thus the unintentional violation of, for example, a Nazirite vow, would not be treated in the same way, or have the same result, as an intentional act of pollution. Yet even with this distinction, it is best not to juxtapose the defilements connected to murder, idolatry, and sexual sins with the prohibitions related to contagious impurities. To be fair, Wright does recognize that there is overlap between the categories ("Unclean and Clean," p. 738).

93. See "Unclean and Clean," pp. 731–732; cf. "The Spectrum," p. 157, and *The Disposal of Impurity*, pp. 115–128

94. See "The Spectrum," p. 157.

95. *Jewish Law*, p. 151.

96. These studies include "Atonement in Leviticus," *Jewish Studies Quarterly* 1.2 (1993/19994). 109–130; "A Bird, a Mouse, a Frog, and Some Fish· A New Reading of Leviticus 11," in *Literary Imagination, Ancient and Modern: Essays in Honor of David Grene*, ed. Todd Breyfogle (Chicago: University of Chicago Press, 1999), pp. 110–126; "The Forbidden Animals in Leviticus," *Journal for the Study of the Old Testament* 59 (1993): 3–23; "The Glorious Book of Numbers," *Jewish Studies Quarterly* 1 3 (1993/1994): 193–216; "Holy Joy: Rereading Leviticus: The Anthropologist and the Believer," *Conservative Judaism* 46.3 (1994): 3–14; "Poetic Structure in Leviticus," in *Pomegranates and Golden Bells: Studies in Biblical, Jewish and Near Eastern Ritual, Law, and Literature in Honor of Jacob Milgrom*, ed. David P. Wright, David Noel Freedman, and Avi Hurvitz (Winona Lake, Ind.: Eisenbrauns, 1995), pp. 239–256; "Sacred Contagion," in *Reading Leviticus: A Conversation with Mary Douglas*, ed. John F. A. Sawyer (Sheffield: Sheffield Academic Press, 1996), pp. 86–106; and "The Stranger in the Bible," *Archives Européennes de Sociologie* 35.1 (1994). 283–298. I thank Mary Douglas for kindly sending me drafts and offprints of many of these articles

97. The volume on Numbers is entitled *In the Wilderness* (cited above), and the volume on Leviticus is entitled *Leviticus as Literature* (Oxford: Oxford University Press, 1999) Mary Douglas's book on Leviticus reached me only after this introduction was complete. I hope to evaluate her newest contribution to this field in another context.

98 It is her significant rethinking of what we call here "ritual impurity" that is commensurate with the analysis in chapter 1. Douglas is less interested in the distinctive nature of

the defiling force of grave sin. See, for example, "The Forbidden Animals," p. 7; and "Sacred Contagion," p. 90.

99. "Atonement in Leviticus," pp. 112–113.

100. Cf. "The Forbidden Animals," pp 5–8, *In the Wilderness*, pp. 150–159; "Poetic Structure," pp. 239–240; "Sacred Contagion," pp. 95–96; and *Leviticus as Literature*, p. viii

101. See "The Forbidden Animals," and "Holy Joy." Cf. *Leviticus as Literature*, pp. 134–175.

102. "The Stranger."

103. For a remarkable statement on the interrelatedness of her work from 1963 to 1985, see *How Institutions Think* (Syracuse: Syracuse University Press, 1985), pp. ix–x. See also her introduction to the 1996 edition of *Natural Symbols*.

104. See, for example, "Atonement in Leviticus," p. 110.

105. Her interest in structures is in evidence throughout, but see particularly "The Glorious Book" and "Poetic Structure." For familiar statements on body symbolism in her new work, see "Atonement in Leviticus," pp. 120–128, and "Holy Joy," pp. 11–12.

106. Compare the introductions and conclusions of "The Forbidden Animals" and "Holy Joy" with the introduction to *Purity and Danger* and the first chapter of *Natural Symbols*.

107. "Holy Joy," p. 10

108. This is especially true with regard to the New Testament scholarship discussed in chapter 6.

109 (Austin: University of Texas Press, 1989). See also Mary Boyce, *A History of Zoroastrianism* (Leiden· E. J. Brill, 1975), vol. 1, pp. 294–324.

110. *History of Religions* 30.1 (1990): 1–24. I thank Barbara R. von Schlegell for bringing this article to my attention.

111. Choksy's description of impurity in Zoroastrianism is in some ways akin to what we will see at Qumran, in chapter 3 of this work.

112. In this respect, Reinhart's description of impurity in Islam is not unlike the way ritual impurity in the Hebrew Bible will be described in chapter 2.

113. Louis Dumont, *Homo Hierarchicus: The Caste System and Its Implications*, trans. Mark Sainsbury et al., Complete Rev. English ed. (Chicago: University of Chicago Press, 1980), esp. pp. 33–64.

114. See Robert Parker, *Miasma: Pollution and Purification in Early Greek Religion* (Oxford: Clarendon Press, 1983); and Walter Burkert, *Greek Religion*, trans. John Raffan (Cambridge Mass.: Harvard University Press, 1983), esp. pp. 75–84.

115. Reinhart, "Impurity/No Danger," pp. 8–9.

116. Shiites consider non-Muslims to be ritually defiling, Sunnis do not. See Ignaz Goldziher, *Introduction to Islamic Theology and Law*, trans. Andras and Ruth Hamori (Princeton: Princeton University Press, 1981), pp. 213–217.

117. I do not mean to deny the value of the comparative enterprise by any means. Influenced by the challenges raised by Jonathan Z. Smith, I believe that the more helpful type of comparison is that which takes account of the fact that each of the traditions being compared is in some stage of an ongoing process of historical evolution. See "In Comparison a Magic Dwells," in *Imagining Religion: From Babylon to Jonestown* (Chicago: University of Chicago Press, 1982), pp. 19–35; and *Drudgery Divine On the Comparison of Christianities and the Religions of Late Antiquity* (Chicago: University of Chicago Press, 1990). A recent gallant attempt at a broad treatment of conceptions of pollution can be found in James J. Preston, "Purification," in *The Encyclopedia of Religion*, ed. Mircea Eliade (New York: Macmillan, 1987), vol. 12, pp. 91–100. A quite different comparative treatment of the concepts of defilement and purification can be found in *The Encyclopedia of Religion and Ethics*, ed. James

Hastings (New York: Scribners, 1919), vol. 10, pp 455–505 There, under the same heading, "Purification," one can find literally an "A to Z" collection of articles, by as many different authors, on purity in various religious traditions. Dated the articles may be, but I believe that the broad spectrum covered by these articles can be of greater use than some of the generalizations to be found elsewhere. Further, on comparison and purity in ancient Judaism, see Jacob Neusner, *A History of the Mishnaic Law of Purities* (Leiden· E. J. Brill, 1974–1977), vol. XXII, pp. 10–23

1. Ritual and Moral Impurity in the Hebrew Bible

1. Generally (and briefly), on biblical source criticism see John Barton, "Source Criticism (OT)," in *The Anchor Bible Dictionary*, vol VI, pp 162–165; and Joseph Blenkinsopp, *The Pentateuch· an Introduction to the First Five Books of the Bible* (New York: Doubleday, 1992), esp. ch 1, "Two Centuries of Pentateuchal Scholarship," pp 1–30.

2. On P and H, see Milgrom, "Priestly ('P') Source," in *The Anchor Bible Dictionary*, vol. V, pp 454–461; Israel Knohl, *The Sanctuary of Silence: The Priestly Torah and the Holiness School* (Minneapolis: Fortress Press, 1995), and with regard to purity in particular see Robert A. Kugler, "Holiness, Purity, the Body, and Society: The Evidence for Theological Conflict in Leviticus," *JSOT* 76 (1997): 3–27.

3. For one attempt to isolate priestly traditions in the entire Pentateuch and designate them as either P or H, see Knohl, *Sanctuary of Silence*, pp. 59–110; see esp. the chart on pp. 104–106.

4. See Milgrom, *Leviticus 1–16*, pp. 3–35 (on the date of P) and pp. 35–42 (on the distinction between P and H); and Knohl, *Sanctuary of Silence*, esp. pp. 1–45 (on the priority of P over H) and pp 199–224 (on the dates of P and H). These scholars continue in the tradition of Yehezkel Kaufmann, who articulated a critique of Wellhausen's postexilic date for P in his *Toledot ha-Emunah ha-Yisraelit*, 8 vols. (Tel Aviv: Dvir, 1937–1958); see esp. vol. 1 Many of the arguments are reproduced (without notation) in Kaufmann, *The Religion of Israel: From Its Beginnings to the Babylonian Exile.* trans. Moshe Greenberg (Chicago: University of Chicago Press, 1960), esp. pp. 153–211.

5. See Wright, "The Spectrum," p. 151–152, n 3 and the literature cited there

6. Neusner, *The Idea*, pp 1–2; Sanders, *Jewish Law*, p. 137.

7. One of the more eloquent spokespersons against such views is Mary Douglas. See the introduction to *Purity and Danger*, pp. 1–6; "The Forbidden Animals," pp 20–23; and "Holy Joy," pp. 13–14.

8. Note Wright's suggestion that the term "cultic" be used to refer to those impurities that come about as by-products of certain sacrificial procedures. See his "Unclean and Clean," p. 732.

9. See Wright, "The Spectrum," pp. 152–153, n. 3. See the section on David P Wright in the introduction to this book for a discussion of Wright's terminology.

10. Wright, "Unclean and Clean," p. 732.

11 See Milgrom, *Leviticus 1–16*, esp pp. 42–63; the rule that carrion is defiling is echoed in H (Lev. 17·15)

12 On the particulars of biblical purity law, see Frymer-Kensky, "Pollution"; Wright, "The Spectrum"; Sanders, *Jewish Law*, pp. 131–254; and Hoffmann, *Leviticus*, vol 1, pp 303–308

13. Frymer-Kensky, "Pollution," p. 403; Wright, "The Spectrum," p. 157. The same claim may well hold true for ritual impurity in Islam as well; see Reinhart, "Impurity/No Danger," p 19

14. And the Holiness Code prohibits having sexual relations with a menstruant (Lev.

18:19; 20:18), an act which in the priestly tradition is viewed as a severe source of defilement (Lev. 15:24).

15. Frymer-Kensky, "Pollution," p. 403; Sanders, *Jewish Law*, pp. 140–142; Wright, "The Spectrum," p. 157.

16. Sanders, *Jewish Law*, pp. 141–142; Wright, "The Spectrum," p. 158.

17 Choksy, *Purity and Pollution in Zoroastrianism*, pp. 108–110.

18 Cf. Ezek. 44:23, and discussion in Milgrom, *Leviticus 1–16*, pp. 615–617.

19. Frymer-Kensky, "Pollution," pp. 403–404; Douglas, "Sacred Contagion," pp. 95–99; cf Wright, *The Disposal of Impurity*, pp. 84–85.

20. The guilt-offering brought by the leper serves to address not any moral sin, but rather the possibility that the afflicted person accidentally defiled holy things while impure (Milgrom, *Leviticus 1–16*, pp. 822, 857). Milgrom, nonetheless, brings the narrative and legal material together in his argument that the disease is in fact brought about by sin (*Leviticus 1–16*, pp. 820–823).

21. On *karet* see Frymer-Kensky, "Pollution," pp. 404–405; and Milgrom, *Leviticus 1–16*, pp. 457–460.

22. For more precise data on the duration and severity of ritual impurities, see Frymer-Kensky, "Pollution," pp. 399–403; Sanders, *Jewish Law*, pp. 134–151; and Wright, *The Disposal of Impurity*, pp. 163–228.

23. Miriam's affliction was brief (Num. 12:14), as was, presumably, Moses's (Exod. 4:6–7); Naaman's affliction was lengthier, but he was cured (2 Kings 5). The exception is Uzziah, whose affliction lasted until his death (2 Chron 26:21)

24. Generally, cf. Büchler, *Studies*, pp. 212–269, and Frymer-Kensky, "Pollution," pp. 404–409.

25. Other biblical traditions also consider such acts to be defiling; see below. Generally, Büchler, *Studies*, pp 212–26; cf Baruch A. Levine, *The JPS Torah Commentary: Leviticus* (Philadelphia: Jewish Publication Society, 1989), pp. 243–248.

26. These acts are often referred to as abominations (תועבות), especially in the Holiness Code (e.g., Lev. 18), Jeremiah (e.g., ch 44), the deuteronomic history (e.g., 2 Kings 21), and Ezekiel (chs 8–11, 18, etc.). Importantly, the term תועבה is not used with regard to the sources of ritual impurity.

27. Thus while ritual impurity is generally not a punishable offense, moral impurity — or, better, the actions that produce it — is. According to Leviticus 20:1–3, for example, the Israelite (or resident alien) who commits idolatrous sins is to suffer death. On the relationship between these defilements and the punishment of extirpation (כרת), see Frymer-Kensky, "Pollution," pp. 404–405; cf. Wright, "The Spectrum," p. 162

28. Frymer-Kensky, "Pollution," p 404

29. Frymer-Kensky, "Pollution," pp. 406–407.

30. On Ezekiel 36:25, see later in this section. Also see Leviticus 16:30, which sees the purgation of sin on the Day of Atonement as a purification of the people According to Milgrom, 16.29–34a are to be assigned to H (*Leviticus 1–16*, pp. 37 and 1056).

31. Some other sins, as well as sinfulness in general, are also referred to on occasion as תועבות: cross-dressing, Deuteronomy 22.5; deceit, Deuteronomy 25:16; arrogance, Proverbs 16:5; sinfulness in general throughout Proverbs. And Deuteronomy 14:3 refers to unclean food as an abomination (on the dietary prohibitions as distinct from the other ritual impurities, see "The Dietary Laws" in this chapter). Still, the terms "abomination" (תועבה) and "pollute" (חנף) are not used with regard to the sources of ritual defilement The uses of the term נדה will be discussed in chapter 2. Generally, on impurity terminology in the Hebrew Bible, the Dead Sea Scrolls, and the New Testament, see Wilfried Paschen, *Rein und Unrein: Untersuchung zur biblischen Wortgeschichte* (Munich· Kösel-verlag, 1970), on תועבה see, pp 28–30 and 67–68

32. Büchler, *Studies*, pp. 214–215.

33. Now it is true that one of the sins listed in this chapter — sexual union with a menstruant (Lev. 18:19) — is also considered to be a ritually defiling act (Lev. 15:24; cf. Milgrom, *Leviticus 1–16*, pp. 940–941). But of course, *all* sexual acts — proper or sinful — are ritually defiling to some degree (Lev. 15:18; cf. Milgrom, *Leviticus 1–16*, pp. 930–934). Thus the point of Leviticus 18 24 can hardly be to indicate that these sins result in ritual defilement.

34. Büchler, *Studies*, pp. 216–217.

35. 1 Kings 14:24; Ezek. 33:26; cf. Amos 2:7 (sexual immorality as a profanation of God's name) Hosea 5:3 and 6:10 also juxtapose adultery and defilement. I believe that the defilement spoken of here should be understood as moral impurity, but it remains unclear to me whether the prophet here is speaking literally of Israel's adulterous sins, or figuratively of Israel's idolatrous sins.

36. Cf. Milgrom, *Numbers*, pp. 37; 302, n. 35; 350–354.

37. Baruch Levine, *Numbers 1–20, The Anchor Bible*, Vol 4 (New York: Doubleday, 1993), p. 207.

38. Cf. Milgrom, *Numbers*, p. 37.

39. Other examples of the same usage can be found in Genesis 34 5, Deuteronomy 24:4; see below in this section for more details.

40. See especially Psalm 106, quoted below. See also Deuteronomy 18:9–12; 2 Kings 16:3; Jeremiah 7.9–15, 16:18; Ezekiel 20.30–31, 22:4, 36:18, 37:23

41. Jeremiah 7.30; 32:34; Ezekiel 5:11, 8:10; cf. 2 Chronicles 29:5, 16.

42. Büchler, *Studies*, pp. 212–214; cf. Wright, *The Disposal of Impurity*, pp. 283–285. It is true that tannaitic texts consider idols to be defiling (see chapter 4 of this book). Yet, importantly, rabbinic sources recognize the fact that the ritual impurity of idols is a rabbinic innovation, and not an idea clearly articulated in Scripture. See M. Shabbat 9:1; B. Shabbat 83b, Maimonides, *Commentary on the Mishnah*, Introduction to Tractate Kelim (Qafiḥ, ed vol. 3, part 2, p. 14).

43 Büchler, *Studies*, pp 218–219.

44. Ezekiel 9:7, 9; 22:1–4; 33:25; cf. Deuteronomy 21:23 (the defilement of the land by the impaled capital offender); 1 Chronicles 22:8 (David cannot build the sanctuary because he has shed too much blood).

45. Büchler, *Studies*, p 235.

46. There is in this respect some similarity to the ancient Greek belief in the pollution (*miasma*) caused by blood-guilt. See Parker, *Miasma*, pp 104–143, esp. pp. 120–125.

47. Büchler, *Studies*, pp 221–226.

48. Cf. Ezekiel 20:7 (idolatry).

49. Hosea 6:10, and see Frymer-Kensky, "Pollution," p. 410.

50 Cf. Ezekiel 18:6, 11, 15.

51. On this difficult passage, see Moshe Weinfeld, *Deuteronomy and the Deuteronomic School* (Oxford: Clarendon Press, 1972), pp. 269–270, and Jeffrey H. Tigay, *The JPS Torah Commentary: Deuteronomy* (Philadelphia: The Jewish Publication Society, 1996), pp. 220–222.

52. Cf the note to Deuteronomy 24:4 in NJV, which suggests that the root אמט in this context is to be understood as connoting disqualification. Levine, in *Numbers 1–20*, notes that the guilty adulteress would be "permanently disgraced and declassed, to be sure" (p. 201, cf. p 205).

53. "The Spectrum," p. 162

54. See also 1 Kings 1:50–53 and 2:28–30; cf. Büchler, *Studies*, p. 235.

55 See discussion in the Introduction, section on Milgrom.

56. Büchler, *Studies*, pp. 216–218; Frymer-Kensky, "Pollution," pp. 406–409

57. E.g., Ezekiel 36; cf. Isaiah 24. See discussion in Frymer-Kensky, "Pollution," pp. 408–412; cf. the brief statement in Milgrom, *Numbers*, p. 302, n. 5.

58. *Contra* Alon, "The Levitical Uncleanness of Gentiles," pp. 180–186; on the tannaitic attitude toward foreign lands, see the Excursus on Gentiles and Gentile Lands, following chapter 5 of this book.

59. M. Ohal. 2:3.

60. Buchler, *Studies*, pp. 217–218.

61. Cf. Levine, *Leviticus*, p. 244.

62. B. Shabbat 14b; Y. Shabbat I 3d.

63. Milgrom, *Leviticus 1–16*, pp. 1009–1083

64. While the sancta are purged "of the impurity and transgression of the Israelites, whatever their sins" (Lev 16:16), the Israelites themselves are purged "of the iniquities and transgressions of the Israelites, whatever their sins" — not of their impurity It is possible, but not certain, that "impurity" in Leviticus 16:16 refers to the purification of the sanctuary from the moral defilement of grave sinners. Regardless, the service for the Day of Atonement still does not provide any means for individuals to atone for moral impurity they themselves may have contracted from the commission of grave sin.

65. On the simile comparing Israel's sin to the impurity of a menstruous woman, see the section on "Metaphor" in this chapter

66. Cf. 2 Chronicles 34.3–8, which describes the process by which, ostensibly, the Israelites purified the land of Judah from idolatrous sins during the time of Josiah.

67. Milgrom, *Leviticus 1–16*, pp. 656–659.

68. Hoffmann, *Leviticus*, vol 1, pp. 303–304, 340.

69. Note the Hebrew phrase used in these passages: ‏ולא־תשקצו את־נפשותיכם‎.

70. "The Spectrum," pp. 165–169; "Unclean and Clean," pp. 730–731.

71 E.g., Douglas, *Purity and Danger*, pp 41–57; and more recently, Douglas, "The Forbidden Animals." See also Eilberg-Schwartz, *The Savage in Judaism*, pp. 217–219; Walter Houston, *Purity and Monotheism: Clean and Unclean Animals in Biblical Law* (Sheffield: JSOT Press, 1993), and Milgrom, *Leviticus 1–16*, pp. 704–742.

72. Ringgren distinguished between cultic and "figurative" usages of purity language ("‏טהר‎," in *TDOT*, vol. V, pp. 291–295) In another treatment, Ringgren and G. André distinguished between ritual uncleanness and "metaphorical" usages of purity language ("‏טמא‎," in *TDOT*, vol. V, pp 331–340). In both treatments, Leviticus 18 and similar traditions are considered to belong to the second category. Baruch Levine views Leviticus 18 as an illustration of a "figurative" sort of impurity. See his *Leviticus*, p. 134; cf. *Numbers 1–20*, p. 207, where he refers to a process of "modulation," whereby the terminology of ritual impurity is applied in a new context. Baruch Schwartz speaks of the transformation of ritual defilement into a symbolic, metaphysical concept in "Selected Chapters of the Holiness Code: A Literary Study of Leviticus 17–19," Dissertation (Hebrew), Hebrew University, 1988, p. xii.

73. Milgrom, *Leviticus 1–16*, p. 37; Wright, "The Spectrum," p. 163 Wright also quotes Buchler to a similar effect on p. 150. Buchler does indeed recognize and discuss the figurative use of purity language in moral contexts (*Studies*, pp. 230–237), but he does not include all references to moral impurity in this category. For Buchler, there is nothing figurative about the defilement of the land by the three cardinal sins (*Studies*, pp. 221–230). Indeed, Buchler explicitly contrasts moral impurity with metaphorical use of impurity language (e.g., *Studies*, p. 289, n. 3).

74. It would bring us too far afield to speculate on why these traditions have been assumed to be metaphorical. David Weiss Halivni suggested to me that there may be some connection between the metaphorization of moral impurity and the tendency in western thought to view sin in general in an abstract, figurative manner.

75. Generally, see the helpful collection of essays in Sheldon Sacks, ed., *On Metaphor* (Chicago· University of Chicago Press, 1978). Among the essays in this volume is Donald Davidson's "What Metaphors Mean," which challenges the traditional distinction between what is metaphorical and what is literal. The challenge has been effectively answered by Eva Feder Kittay in her *Metaphor: Its Cognitive Force and Linguistic Structure* (Oxford: Clarendon Press, 1987). Kittay convincingly resurrects the traditional distinction between metaphorical and literal utterances by making use of semantic field theory. The term "figurative" is both more general and less troublesome, at least as far as contemporary philosophy is concerned. Yet common usage, including the scholarship quoted above, makes no meaningful distinction between these terms. Indeed, in *The New Shorter Oxford English Dictionary* (2 vols. [Oxford: Clarendon Press, 1993]), the definitions of these terms overlap: The term "metaphorical" is employed in the definition of "figurative," and vice versa. As far as the NSOED is concerned — and from here on, as far as we are concerned as well — these two terms are essentially synonymous.

76. The philosophical/linguistic debate on metaphor is only beginning to have an impact on biblical studies. See, for instance, Eilberg-Schwartz, *The Savage in Judaism*, pp. 115–140.

77. On the level of common usage, this definition finds support in NSOED. On a more philosophical and linguistic level, this definition finds support in Kittay, *Metaphor*. Kittay uses semantic field theory to define both "literal" and "metaphor" and to support the traditional distinction between them. A thumbnail summary of her thesis follows: Literal language operates within a single semantic field, while in metaphor, at least two semantic fields are operative simultaneously. It is the incongruity between the two (or more) semantic fields that signals to the audience that the utterance in question is metaphorical.

78. Ringgren and André, "אמט," *TDOT*, vol V, pp 337–338, Milgrom, *Leviticus 1–16*, p. 37; Neusner, *The Idea*, p. 15.

79 The clearest statements to this effect are Zechariah 2·16 and Psalms 78·54–55.

80. Generally, see Kaufmann, *Toledot ha-Emunah*, vol 3, pp. 618–619; vol. 5, pp. 455–457; and Weinfeld, *Deuteronomy and the Deuteronomic School*, pp. 228–229.

81. E.g., Joshua 22:19 and 2 Kings 5:15, cf. 1 Samuel 26.19.

82. E.g., Leviticus 25:23 and Deuteronomy 11:12; cf. Samuel E. Loewenstamm, "Nahalat Hashem," in *Studies in Bible* (= *Scripta Hierosolymitana*, vol. 31), ed. Sarah Japhet (Jerusalem: Magnes, 1986), pp. 155–192.

83. E.g., Leviticus 18:26 and Numbers 35:15; this view is especially indicative of the Holiness Code. Generally see Weinfeld, *Deuteronomy and the Deuteronomic School*, pp. 230–232, and Knohl, *Sanctuary of Silence*, pp. 195–196.

84. See the section on David Hoffmann in the Introduction.

85. "The Spectrum," pp. 162–163, cf "Unclean and Clean," p. 743.

86. In fact, all three of the morally defiling sins involve, in most cases, direct contact with the land. Murder, of course, is conceived as blood spilled *upon the land* (Gen 4:10). Idolatry takes place on altars, which are on the land, and forms of chthonic worship involve the pouring of libations into the ground. Sexual sins, also, are not so removed from the land· ancient Israelites slept (literally and figuratively) on the ground.

87. Levine, *Leviticus*, p. 134; Schwartz, "Selected Chapters," p. xii; and Wright, "The Spectrum," p. 163.

88. Cf. Frymer-Kensky, "Pollution," p. 410.

89. Cf. Genesis 35:2, Jeremiah 33:8; Proverbs 20:9; Job 4:17; cf. Ezekiel 36:17, discussed in the section on "Moral Impurity." See Levine, *Numbers 1–20*, p. 208, and more generally, Buchler, *Studies*, pp. 229–245

90 Isaiah 30:22, Ezekiel 36:17; Lamentations 1:8, 17.

91. 2 Chronicles 29.5; Wright, *The Disposal of Impurity*, pp. 283–287.

92. "Critique and Commentary," in Neusner, *The Idea*, p. 138.

93. "The Spectrum," p. 165, pp. 170–173.

94. "The Spectrum," p. 170.

95. *Aristeas* §§ 128–171; Philo, *Special Laws* I· 256–261. We will examine these texts in the Introduction to Part II.

96. "The Spectrum," p. 164; cf., in this respect, Eilberg-Schwartz, *The Savage in Judaism*, pp. 191–192.

97. Wright ("The Spectrum," p. 174) grants this point too.

98. "The Spectrum," pp. 162–164.

99. Hoffmann, *Leviticus*, vol. 1, pp. 314–322. Interestingly, this is one aspect of Hoffmann's argument that Büchler does not care to take up. I think the reason is the fact that Büchler sets out to emphasize the difference between the two types of defilement.

100. Hoffmann, *Leviticus*, vol 1, p. 340; vol. 2, p. 59.

101. Indeed, Wright tellingly links his argument on the symbolic interrelatedness of the impurity systems to Clifford Geertz's definition of religion ("The Spectrum," pp. 175–177).

102. Douglas, "Sacred Contagion," p. 106; cf. Reinhart, "Impurity/No Danger," p. 4.

103. On this point, see chapter 4, section on *Niddah*, which treats menstrual impurity in tannaitic sources.

104. Cf. Ilana Be'er, "Blood Discharge: On Female Im/Purity in the Priestly Code and in Biblical Literature," in *A Feminist Companion to Exodus to Deuteronomy*, ed Athalya Brenner (Sheffield: Sheffield Academic Press, 1994), pp. 152–164. (Thanks are due to Ross Kraemer for this reference.) Be'er correctly calls for a contextual treatment (p. 152). Her analysis of the impurity regulations, however, leans too much toward the view of impurity as sinful (p 161). This leads her to overemphasize the difference between the priestly view of menstruation, which she incorrectly views as negative, and the view of biblical narratives, which she correctly views as more neutral. When the menstrual taboo is viewed as but one aspect of a general perspective that genital flows are ritually defiling, a more balanced picture emerges. This point is emphasized by, among others Eilberg-Schwartz, *The Savage in Judaism*, pp. 179–182, and Carol Meyers, *Discovering Eve: Ancient Israelite Women in Context* (New York: Oxford University Press, 1988), pp. 36–37 Generally, see Milgrom, *Leviticus 1–16*, pp. 763–768 and 948–953.

105. Eilberg-Schwartz, *The Savage in Judaism*, p. 182. Compare Tikva Frymer-Kensky's claim that the religion of the Hebrew Bible is "gender-blind," and it asserts the "essential sameness of the sexes." See Frymer-Kensky, *In the Wake*, esp. ch. 11, "Gender and Its Image" (pp. 118–143), and p. 189 on ritual impurity in particular.

106. See the charts in Frymer-Kensky, "Pollution," p. 402, and Milgrom, *Leviticus 1–16*, pp. 986–987.

107. Be'er, "Blood Discharge," p. 158; Milgrom, *Leviticus 1–16*, p 953.

108. *Contra*, e.g , Judith Romney Wegner, "Leviticus," in *The Women's Bible Commentary*, ed. Carol A. Newsom and Sharon H Ringer (Louisville: Westminster/John Knox Press, 1992), pp. 36–44 More in line with the view taken here is Mayer I. Gruber, "Women in the Cult According to the Priestly Code," in *Judaic Perspectives on Ancient Israel*, ed. Jacob Neusner, Baruch A. Levine, and Ernest S. Frerichs (Philadelphia: Fortress Press, 1987), pp. 35–48; see esp. pp. 39–40.

109. "Atonement in Leviticus," pp 112–114, and "Sacred Contagion," pp. 95–96.

110. For discussion of this discrepancy, see Be'er, "Blood Discharge," pp. 160–161; Frymer-Kensky, "Pollution," pp. 400–401; and Milgrom, *Leviticus 1–16*, pp. 750–751.

111. See Jubilees 3:8–14, and the discussions in Milgrom, *Leviticus 1–16*, pp. 750–751, and Joseph M. Baumgarten, "Purification after Childbirth and the Sacred Garden in 4Q265 and

Jubilees," in *New Qumran Texts and Studies: Proceedings of the First Meeting of the International Organization for Qumran Studies, Paris 1992*, ed. George J. Brooke and Florentino García Martínez (Leiden: E J. Brill, 1994), pp. 3–10.

112   This is true in the biblical system, as we will soon see, and it is undoubtedly true in the rabbinic system (see M. Yad. 4:6, and discussion in the first section of chapter 4).

113   Milgrom, *Leviticus 1–16*, pp. 750–751; and Gruber, "Women in the Cult," p. 43, n. 13 I mention this not to claim that the birth of a female resulted in greater defilement than the birth of a male because women were better than men in the ancient Israelite perspective. I simply want to underscore the complexity of the problem and the need to recognize that many issues other than gender determine the sources and severities of ritual defilements in ancient Israel.

114.   Possibly the circumcision of the boy child on the eighth day plays a role here (this possibility is mentioned, but not endorsed, by both Be'er, "Blood Discharge," p. 161, and Frymer-Kensky, "Pollution," pp. 400–401). The best explanation I have heard for the prolonged defilement of the mother after the birth of a daughter is that it is tied to the fact that the female infant too will in time menstruate and give birth herself, while the male infant will not (Bamberger, "Leviticus," p. 826). Also, vaginal bleeding is known to occur to some infant girls, and it is possible that a concern with defilement from such discharge is what lies behind Leviticus 12:5. See Jonathan Magonet, "'But if it is a Girl she is Unclean for Twice Seven Days. . .' The Riddle of Leviticus 12.5," in Sawyer, ed., *Reading Leviticus*, pp 144–152.

115.   This exclusion, however, was not complete. See Gruber, "Women in the Cult"

116.   On the sexual laws of the Hebrew Bible, see Frymer-Kensky, *In the Wake*, esp. ch. 17, "Sex in the Bible," pp. 187–198; cf. Frymer-Kensky's related article, "Law and Philosophy: The Case of Sex in the Bible," *Semeia* 45 (1989): 89–102.

117   Frymer-Kensky, *In the Wake*, p 196.

118.   Frymer-Kensky, *In the Wake*, p. 191.

119.   Ross Shepard Kraemer, *Her Share of the Blessings. Women's Religions among Pagans, Jews, and Christians in the Greco-Roman World* (New York: Oxford University Press, 1992), p. 103.

120   Frymer-Kensky, *In the Wake*, p. 192–194.

121.   On the doctrine of communal responsibility as articulated in priestly writings, see Milgrom, *Leviticus 1–16*, pp. 258–261.

2. Moral Impurity in the Second Temple Period

1.   The date of Nehemiah's first term in office is widely recognized as being 445 BCE. Ezra's arrival in Judah is commonly dated to 458 BCE, although some (such as Bright) argue for a later date. On the dates of Ezra, Nehemiah, and their service in Judah, see Joseph Blenkinsopp, *Ezra–Nehemiah: A Commentary* (Philadelphia. Westminster Press, 1988), pp. 139–144; John Bright, *A History of Israel*, 3rd ed. (Philadelphia: Westminster Press, 1981), pp. 391–402, and Morton Smith, *Palestinian Parties and Politics that Shaped the Old Testament* (New York: Columbia University Press, 1971), pp. 90–92. On the date of the books of Ezra and Nehemiah, see Jacob M Myers, *Ezra & Nehemiah*, Vol. 14, *The Anchor Bible* (New York Doubleday, 1965), pp lxviii–lxx (Myers dates the books to c. 400 BCE)

2   Ezra 9:1–10:44; Nehemiah 9.1–4, 10:28–31, 13:1–3, and 13:23–30; cf. 1 Esdras 8:68–9:36.

3.   Consider, for example, the assessment of Morton Smith purity law "was also the basis of the attack on mixed marriages, for ritual purification is a legal privilege. A Gentile cannot be purified. Accordingly, Ezra attacked mixed marriages as communicating to the married the impurity of the Gentiles, and divorce was recommended as 'the immersion pool for

Israel' [sic.]" (*Palestinian Parties*, p. 137). See, too, the comments of David J. A. Clines in *The Harper Collins Study Bible* (on Ezra 10:3): "apparently the law is here being applied to the case of the (ritual) 'uncleanness' of foreign birth."

4. Klawans, "Notions of Gentile Impurity in Ancient Judaism."

5. Büchler, *Studies*, p. 215. For a more precise analysis of the various traditions alluded to in this passage, see Blenkinsopp, *Ezra–Nehemiah*, pp. 184–185, and Myers, *Ezra & Nehemiah*, pp. 78–79 Yehezkel Kaufmann, too, identifies the allusions correctly, though he is not precise enough in identifying the nature of the defilement in question; Kaufmann, *Toledot ha-Emunah*, vol 8, pp. 292–293

6. On the different usages of נדה in P and H, see Milgrom, *Leviticus 1–16*, p. 38.

7. Cf. 2 Chronicles, 29:5, where נדה is used to refer to an idol. Yet as was argued in chapter 1, idols are not viewed as a source of ritual defilement in the Hebrew Bible The analogy between an idol and a menstruant introduced in 2 Chronicles 29:5 proves important in subsequent rabbinic literature; cf. B. Shabbat 82a–83b.

8. On the meaning and etymology of the term נדה see Milgrom, *Leviticus 1–16*, pp 744–745, and Paschen, *Rein und Unrein*, pp. 27–28.

9 Deut. 7:1–4, 23:2–9; for an assessment of the various biblical traditions and their implications, see Shaye J. D. Cohen, "From the Bible to the Talmud: The Prohibition of Intermarriage," *Hebrew Annual Review* 7 (1983): 23–39.

10. On this and other ideological differences between Ezra and the Holiness Code, see Mary Douglas, "The Stranger in the Bible."

11. In a similar way, the prohibition of intermarriage that is articulated in Nehemiah also builds on a deuteronomic tradition (Neh 13:1–3; Deut. 23:2–9).

12. E.g., Judges 3:5–6; 1 Kings 16:31.

13. The deuteronomic history does not by any means emphasize this point at every opportunity. many intermarriages are noted without being criticized (e g., Gideon's Shechemite concubine, Jud. 8:30–31). Moreover, Deuteronomy permits marrying captives (21:10–14). See Shaye J. D. Cohen, "Solomon and the Daughter of Pharaoh: Intermarriage, Conversion, and the Impurity of Women," *Journal of the Ancient Near East Society* 14 and 15 (1985): 23–38, esp. pp 24–25.

14. *Contra* Kaufmann (*Toledot ha-Emunah*, vol. 8, pp. 289–291), who unconvincingly claims that idolatry was not the concern and that nonsinful women were banished because of their Gentile background and their sexually sinful behavior Kaufmann *may* be right — we will never know for sure whether or not the women were idolatrous — but the point is that the wives' Gentile origins caused them to be perceived by Ezra and his supporters as leading Israelites down the road to idolatry (Neh. 13:26).

15 This could be the case because the institution of conversion did not yet exist (so Kaufmann, *Toledot ha-Emunah*, vol. 8, pp. 294–297). Alternatively, it could be that the idea of conversion did exist but that Ezra and Nehemiah were nonetheless ideologically opposed to the idea of integrating foreigners into the community. A favorable attitude toward conversion is articulated in second temple period texts such as Isaiah 56:3–7 and the book of Ruth. On the history of conversion, see Shaye J. D. Cohen, "Conversion to Judaism in Historical Perspective: From Biblical Israel to Postbiblical Judaism," *Conservative Judaism* 36.4 (1983): 31–45.

16. Blenkinsopp, *Ezra–Nehemiah*, pp 176–177; Myers, *Ezra & Nehemiah*, pp 77–78.

17. Smith's translation of מקוה לישראל (Ezra 10:2) as "the immersion pool for Israel" is suspect (*Palestinian Parties*, p. 137) Here NJV and NRSV read "hope for Israel"; cf. Jeremiah 14:8, 17.13, and 1 Chronicles 29:15. In biblical Hebrew, מקוה means "pool" only when it appears in conjunction with מים, cf. Genesis 1:10, Exodus 7:19, and Leviticus 11:36. It is only later, in the period of the tannaim, that the term מקוה standing alone means "pool." And incidentally, tan-

naitic sources (e.g., M. Yoma 8.9) do make the wordplay that Smith here inaccurately attributes to Ezra.

18. Cf. Christine Hayes, "Intermarriage and Impurity in Ancient Jewish Sources," *Harvard Theological Review* 92.1 (1999): 3–36. Focusing more closely on the question of intermarriage, and providing fuller bibliography on that subject, Hayes independently considers some of the same issues and texts, and reaches conclusions that are commensurate with but not identical to those reached here. On Ezra–Nehemiah in particular, see pp. 6–14.

19. Generally, see Eileen M. Schuller, *Non-Canonical Psalms from Qumran: A Pseudepigraphic Collection* (Atlanta: Scholars Press, 1986). The translation here is based on Schuller, *Non-Canonical Psalms*, p. 203.

20. Schuller, *Non-Canonical Psalms*, pp. 204–210.

21. *Non-Canonical Psalms*, pp. 21–60.

22. For more on the date of Jubilees, see James C. VanderKam, *The Book of Jubilees*, 2 vols. (Louvain: Peeters, 1989), pp. v–vi; O. S. Wintermute, "Jubilees: A New Translation and Introduction," in James Charlesworth, ed., *The Old Testament Pseudepigrapha: Vol. 2* (Garden City, N.Y.: Doubleday, 1983), pp. 43–44; cf. Emil Schurer, *The History of the Jewish People in the Age of Jesus Christ*, rev. and ed. Geza Vermes et al., 4 vols. (Edinburgh: T. & T. Clark, 1973–1987), vol. III, pt. 1, pp 311–312, Michael Stone, ed., *Jewish Writings of the Second Temple Period. Apocrypha, Pseudepigrapha, Qumran Sectarian Writings, Philo, Josephus*. Section Two, vol. II, *Compendium Rerum Iudaicarum ad Novum Testamentum* (Assen: Van Gorcum, 1984), pp. 101–103.

23. On Jubilees's provenance, see Schürer and Vermes, *The History of the Jewish People*, vol. III, pt. 1, pp 313–314; Stone, *Jewish Writings*, p. 103, Regardless of where Jubilees originated, it was clearly quite significant to the sectarians at Qumran, for some fifteen or sixteen copies have so far turned up among the Dead Sea Scrolls. On Jubilees at Qumran, see James C. VanderKam, *The Dead Sea Scrolls Today* (Grand Rapids, Mich.: William B. Eerdmans, 1995), pp. 39–40.

24. This is assuming, of course, that we should not consider Ezra and Nehemiah to be sectarian works; but cf. Smith, *Palestinian Parties*, p. 132

25. Translation here and below from VanderKam, *The Book of Jubilees*. Unfortunately, the Qumran manuscripts of Jubilees overlap only intermittently with the passages that are of concern to us here. See the edition of 4Q216–228 prepared by James VanderKam and Jozef Milik in Harold Attridge et al., *Qumran Cave 4, VIII: Parabiblical Texts, Part 1, Discoveries in the Judaean Desert*, vol. XIII (Oxford: Clarendon Press, 1994), pp. 1–185.

26. See also 1:9, 12.2, 20:7, and 21:15, which all suggest that idolatry is defiling.

27. In 7:33 and 21:19, murder defiles the land. In 16.5 the sin of Sodom and Gomorrah defiles the inhabitants and the land (that their sins were sexual in nature can be seen in 20:6) The defiling force of sexual sins is also clearly expressed in 4.22, 7:21–22, 20:3–5, 30.3, 33:7, and 33:18–20.

28. Further passages generally juxtaposing sin with defilement include 7:20, 9:15, 21:21, 22:14, 23:14, 23:17, and 41:25. On innocence as purity, see 1:21, 22:14, and 50.5. Buchler identified a number of these passages in *Studies*, pp. 279–282

29. On the influence of Holiness Code traditions on Jubilees, see Betsy Halpern-Amaru, *Rewriting the Bible: Land and Covenant in Post-Biblical Jewish Literature* (Valley Forge, Penn.: Trinity Press International, 1994), pp. 28 and 44–45

30. In the few cases in which the 4Q texts provide Hebrew originals for the passages of interest to us, we do find uses of moral impurity terminology, such as "abomination" (תועבה) and "perversion" (תבל). See 4Q 219 II.24, 28 = Jubilees 21.21, 23 (VanderKam, *DJD XIII*, p. 47) and 4Q 221 frg. 1, line 5 = Jubilees 21:23 (*DJD XIII*, p. 66).

31. On Jubilees and the land of Israel, see Halpern-Amaru, *Rewriting the Bible*, pp. 25–54.

32. E.g., 7:33, 16:5, 21:19, 23:18–21, and 30:15.

33. Cf. 21:21, 23:18–21.

34. Again, regarding intermarriage and impurity in Jubilees, see Hayes, "Intermarriage and Impurity," esp. pp. 15–25. Hayes counters Cana Werman, "Jubilees 30: Building a Paradigm for the Ban on Intermarriage," *Harvard Theological Review* 90:1 (1997): 1–22.

35. E.g., Bruce J. Malina, *The New Testament World: Insights from Cultural Anthropology*, rev. ed. (Louisville· Westminster/John Knox Press, 1993), p. 160; Jacob Milgrom, "The Concept of Impurity in *Jubilees* and the *Temple Scroll*," *Revue de Qumran* 16.2 (1993): 277–284; see also Klawans, "Notions of Gentile Impurity," p. 286, and the literature cited there in n. 3.

36. Jubilees allows for the ownership of Gentile slaves (15:12–13, 24), a practice that would not be condoned if Gentile persons were considered an inherent source of ritual defilement. Presumably, the behavior of slaves can be controlled. And Joseph, who is praised for his refusal to fornicate with Potiphar's wife, is apparently left unaffected by the physical contact that occurred when she embraced him (39:9).

37. The concern with eating with Gentiles (22:16) is echoed in other texts of the period as well; cf. Daniel 1:8; Judith 12:1–2; Tobit 1:10–12; Joseph and Asenath 7:1, 8:5; Additions to Esther 14:17; and 3 Maccabees 3:4. The concern with "intereating" results generally from concern with impure foods, but idolatry is also noted as a concern (Joseph and Asenath 8:5; Additions to Esther 14:17; and *Aristeas* 139, 142, 145).

38. For the text of the Temple Scroll, see Yigael Yadin, *The Temple Scroll*, 3 vols. (Jerusalem: Israel Exploration Society, 1983); and also Elisha Qimron, *The Temple Scroll: A Critical Edition with Extensive Reconstructions* (Beer Sheva: Ben Gurion University of the Negev Press; Jerusalem: Israel Exploration Society, 1996).

39. Yadin, *The Temple Scroll*, vol. I, pp. 386–390. The early date is suggested by Hartmut Stegemann, "The Literary Composition of the Temple Scroll and its Status at Qumran," in *Temple Scroll Studies*, ed. G. J. Brooke (Sheffield. JSOT Press, 1989), pp. 123–148. For a discussion of the various views, see Schürer and Vermes, *The History of the Jewish People*, vol. III, pt. 1, pp. 414–417, and Michael Owen Wise, *A Critical Study of the Temple Scroll from Qumran Cave 11* (Chicago: The Oriental Institute, 1990), pp. 26–31.

40. Andrew M. Wilson and Lawrence Wills, "Literary Sources for the Temple Scroll," *Harvard Theological Review* 75(1982): 275–288. See discussion in Wise, *A Critical Study of the Temple Scroll*, pp. 21–22. Among others, Wilson and Wills have convinced Stegemann and Milgrom. See Stegemann, "The Literary Composition," and Milgrom, "The Concept of Impurity," esp. p. 284. Even Yadin entertained the idea that the scroll used earlier sources; cf. Yadin, *The Temple Scroll*, vol. I, p. 390.

41. See discussion in Wise, *A Critical Study of the Temple Scroll*, pp. 23–26

42. Yadin, *The Temple Scroll*, vol. I, pp. 390–397. But see Schürer and Vermes, *The History of the Jewish People*, vol. III, pt. 1, pp. 412–415; Stegemann, "The Literary Composition," pp. 126–131; and Dwight D. Swanson, *The Temple Scroll and the Bible. The Methodology of 11QT* (Leiden: E. J Brill, 1995), pp. 239–241; Vermes, Stegemann, and Swanson all argue (against Yadin) that 11QT had a pre-Qumranic origin.

43. Scholars such as Levine and Schiffman have pointed out a number of philological and lexical differences between 11QT and the sectarian literature from Qumran. See discussion in Wise, *A Critical Study of the Temple Scroll*, pp. 24–25, and the literature cited there Schiffman also argues that the legal approaches of the sectarian literature and 11QT are fundamentally different: "Whereas the other texts from Qumran see the extra-biblical material as derived from inspired exegesis, the author of the *Temple Scroll* sees it as inherent in the biblical text." See Schiffman's *Sectarian Law in the Dead Sea Scrolls: Courts, Testimony and the Penal Code*, vol. 33, *Brown Judaic Studies* (Atlanta: Scholars Press, 1983), pp. 13–17; quote from p. 17

44. Stegemann, "The Literary Composition," pp. 127–128.

45. Schiffman, *Sectarian Law in the Dead Sea Scrolls*, pp. 13–14.

46. Stegemann, "The Literary Composition," p. 124.

47. These columns may well comprise more than one redactional unit. Commonly, XLV to XLVII are considered to belong to the part of the document that deals with the temple, while it is columns XLVIII to LI that are commonly referred to the purity law section of the document (e.g., Stegemann, "The Literary Composition," pp. 133–138; Swanson, *The Temple Scroll and the Bible*, p. 175). And it is indeed possible that these two sections stem from distinct sources (so Wilson and Wills, "Literary Sources"). The fact remains, however, that ritual impurity is the main topic of 11QT, from columns XLV to LI. See Phillip Callaway, "Source Criticism of the Temple Scroll: The Purity Laws," *Revue de Qumran* 12.2 (1986): 213–222.

48. See especially Yadin, *The Temple Scroll*, vol. I, pp. 277–343. Other important studies include Florentino García Martínez, "The Problem of Purity: the Qumran Solution," in García Martínez and Julio Trebolle Barrera, *The People of the Dead Sea Scrolls: Their Writings, Beliefs and Practices*, trans. Wilfred G. E. Watson (Leiden: E. J. Brill, 1995), pp. 139–157, cf. esp. pp. 141–147; Jacob Milgrom, "The Concept of Impurity" and "The Scriptural Foundations and Deviations in the Laws of Purity of the *Temple Scroll*," in Lawrence H. Schiffman, ed., *Archaeology and History in the Dead Sea Scrolls*, pp. 83–99; Lawrence H. Schiffman, "The Impurity of the Dead in the *Temple Scroll*," *Archaeology and History in the Dead Sea Scrolls*, pp. 135–156; Swanson, *The Temple Scroll and the Bible*, pp. 175–214. Passages from 11QT are also dealt with throughout Harrington, *The Impurity Systems*.

49. In this respect, the Temple Scroll resembles Ezekiel 40–48. Indeed, it appears that the book of Ezekiel in general, and chapters 40–48 in particular, were particularly influential at Qumran. See Cothenet, "Influence d'Ézékiel sur la spritualité de Qumran," *Revue de Qumran* 13 (1988): 431–439, and (on Ezek. 40–48 in particular) García Martínez, "L'interprétation de la Torah d'Ézékiel dans les mss. de Qumran," *Revue de Qumran* 13 (1988): 441–452.

50. On the expansive impurity legislation of Ezekiel 40–48, see Moshe Greenberg, "The Design and Themes of Ezekiel's Program of Restoration," *Interpretation* 38 (1984): 181–208; and Jon D. Levenson, *Theology of the Program of Restoration of Ezekiel 40–48* (Missoula, Mont.: Scholars Press, 1976).

51. 11QT XXXIX:7–9 See Lawrence H. Schiffman, "Exclusion from the Sanctuary and the City of the Sanctuary in the Temple Scroll," *Hebrew Annual Review* 9 (1985): 301–320.

52. In XLV:12–14, blind people are banned from the city of the sanctuary, lest they defile (ולא יטמאו) the city in which God dwells. The ruling finds biblical precedent both in the exclusion of priests with various defects (Lev. 21:16–24) and in the Davidic ban of the blind and lame from entering the sanctuary (2 Sam. 5:8). Yet what is unprecedented is the view expressed here that the blind have the power to defile. Had Leviticus considered the blind impure, blind priests would not have been permitted to eat of the holy food (Lev. 21.22). Generally, see Yadin, *The Temple Scroll*, vol. I, pp. 289–291; vol. II, p. 193. Milgrom ("The Concept of Impurity," p. 279) says that 11QT has here "jumbled the categories" (of pollution and profanation).

53. Yadin, *The Temple Scroll*, vol. I, pp. 288–289; vol. II, p. 193; cf. CD XII·1–2.

54. Cf. García Martínez, "The Problem of Purity," pp. 141–147; see also discussion of 4QMMT in chapter 3 of this book, section on "Impurity and Sin in 4Q."

55. Generally, on the ancient Jewish debate regarding the so-called *tebul yom*, see Lawrence H. Schiffman, "Pharisaic and Sadducean Halakhah in Light of the Dead Sea Scrolls· The Case of Ṭevul Yom," *Dead Sea Discoveries* 1.3 (1994): 285–299. See also discussion of 4QMMT in chapter 3, section on "Impurity and Sin in 4Q." The scroll's emphatic repetition of this ruling may well serve a polemic purpose; other groups of ancient Jews (including the Pharisees) apparently considered people who had immersed but had not waited for sunset to be ritually pure, at least in some circumstances.

56. Milgrom, *Leviticus 1–16*, pp 968–976. There are other new stringencies as well, such as the demand that the various types of defiled people expelled from the city be separated from each other, even in their ostracization (XLVI:16–18).

57. E.g , exclusions of the blind in 1QM VII:4–5 and 1QSa II:4–11; temple city in CD XII:1–2; first day ablutions in 1QM XIV:2–3; see discussions by García Martínez, Milgrom, Schiffman, and Yadin cited in the four preceding footnotes

58. Trans. Yadin, *The Temple Scroll*, vol. II, pp. 227–228.

59. *The Temple Scroll*, ad loc., and see fuller discussion in vol. I, pp. 383–385.

60. See also 1 Kings 1·50–53 and 2:28–30; cf. Büchler, *Studies*, p. 235.

61. Cf. Milgrom, "The Concept of Impurity," pp 280–281.

62. *The Temple Scroll*, vol. I, pp 74–77.

63. "The Qumran Cult: Its Exegetical Principles," in *Temple Scroll Studies*, pp. 165–180, esp. p. 171.

64. *The Temple Scroll and the Bible*, pp 190, 196–197, 228–229. The thrust of Swanson's valid critique of Milgrom is that the term "homogenization" is imprecise. Swanson's more cumbersome description allows one to see that while the secondary text has an interpretive effect on the base text, there is no evidence of the reciprocity implied by the term "homogenization." In Swanson's words, "there is no implication that the secondary or supplementary texts are affected by the base" (p. 228).

65. Sifra Kedoshim, Perek 4·1 (ed. Weiss, pp. 88d–89a).

66. The Sifra to Leviticus 19:35 and the Sifré to Deuteronomy 25:16 are substantially similar. See Sifra Kedoshim Parashah 8:5 (on Lev. 19:35) (ed. Weiss, p. 91a); Sifre Deuteronomy § 295 (on Deut. 25:16) (ed. Finkelstein, p. 314); cf. Sifre Deuteronomy § 148 (on Deut. 17:2) (ed. Finkelstein, p. 203), and Mekhilta de-Rabbi Ishmael Parashat Yitro 9 (ed. Horovitz, p. 238) These traditions are discussed in chapter 5 of this book.

67. Milgrom, "The Qumran Cult," p. 171.

68. See Yadin, *The Temple Scroll*, vol. II, pp. 208–209. The brief prohibition against defiling the land is, in the manuscript, separated from its immediate context by a *vacat* on either side. The physical separation of the phrase from its immediate context raises the question of whether the prohibition stands on its own or is more directly connected to the content of column XLVIII.

69. This interpretation makes the most sense if we ignore the *vacats* and assume that the phrase is to be interpreted in context. A scriptural precedent for the idea that land can be defiled by unburied corpses is to be found in Ezekiel 39:12–16, which stipulates that the Israelites will spend seven months burying the dead soldiers of Gog, in order to purify the land.

70. This interpretation makes most sense assuming that the phrase is meant to stand on its own. The justification for this interpretation is the fact that 11QT LVIII:11–12 is essentially a restatement of Numbers 35:34, which is concerned with the defiling force of bloodshed, as Yadin correctly noted ad loc.

71. The Temple Scroll's detailed treatments of the evils of idolatry and sexual transgression, even when employing the term תועבה, and while referring to the expulsion of the Canaanites, do not mention the notion that the performance of these deeds defiles sinners, the land, or the sanctuary. For example, 11QT LX:16–21, which rapidly reiterates the prohibitions of child sacrifice, divination, necromancy and the like, alludes to various Holiness Code traditions (e g., Lev. 19:31 and 20:1–3) and speaks of the exile of the land's previous inhabitants. But even so, the idea of moral defilement is not articulated in this passage. Compare LXII:5–16, which speaks of the abominations of the Canaanites without articulating the notion of moral impurity. It is unfortunate that our copy of the scroll breaks off where it does, for LXVI:12–17 reiterates some of the incest laws delineated in Leviticus 18 and 20, and yet, at least in the extant portions, the idea of moral defilement is not explicitly articulated in this passage either.

72 Generally, on the relationship between Jubilees and the Temple Scroll, see VanderKam, "The Temple Scroll and the Book of Jubilees," in *Temple Scroll Studies*, pp. 211–236.

73. Jubilees, in its paraphrase of the narratives in Genesis, finds many opportunities to elaborate on its conception of moral defilement. The Temple Scroll, to the contrary, more often than not actually misses opportunities to elaborate on the defiling force of sin.

74 Schürer and Vermes, *The History of the Jewish People*, vol. III, pt. 1, pp. 395–396; James H. Charlesworth, ed , *Damascus Document, War Scroll, and Related Documents*, vol. 2, *The Dead Sea Scrolls: Hebrew, Aramaic, and Greek Texts with English Translations* (Tübingen: J. C. B. Mohr [Paul Siebeck]; Louisville: Westminster John Knox Press, 1995), pp. 6–7 For a review of scholarship on CD from Schechter until 1983, see Philip R. Davies, *The Damascus Covenant· An Interpretation of the 'Damascus Document'* (Sheffield: JSOT Press, 1982), pp. 1–47. Büchler was among those scholars who rejected Schechter's claims, maintaining that the "Zadokite Fragments" were medieval and not ancient in origin (see Buchler, "Schechter's 'Jewish Sectaries,'" *Jewish Quarterly Review* n.s. 3 [1912–1913]: 429–485). Thus we should not be surprised that CD is not discussed in Büchler's *Studies*

75. Eight manuscripts have been identified among the Cave 4 documents, and one each from Caves 5 and 6. For now, see Charlesworth, *The Dead Sea Scrolls*, vol. 2, pp. 59–63, and Joseph M. Baumgarten, *Qumran Cave 4, XIII· The Damascus Document (4Q266–273)*, *Discoveries in the Judaean Desert*, vol XVIII (Oxford: Clarendon Press, 1996), esp. pp. 1–22. The 4Q fragments do not contain significant parallels to the passage discussed below. The connection between CD and Qumran was actually noticed shortly before the discovery of the first Qumran MS of the work. See H. H. Rowley, *The Zadokite Fragments and the Dead Sea Scrolls* (London: Oxford, 1952), pp. 31–40.

76. Generally, see Schürer and Vermes, *The History of the Jewish People*, vol. III, pt. 1, pp. 389–395; Charlesworth, *The Dead Sea Scrolls*, vol. 2, pp. 6–7.

77. Davies, for instance, argues that CD stems from the pre-Qumranic phases of the sect's history. See *The Damascus Covenant*, pp. 56–104. Jerome Murphy O'Connor, on the other hand, argues that the document served a missionary purpose, propagating a toned-down version of the sect's teachings. See his "An Essene Missionary Document? CD II, 14–VI, 1," *Revue Biblique* 77 (1970): 201–229. The most common explanation is that CD was intended for those group members who did not dwell at Qumran, cf. Charlesworth, *The Dead Sea Scrolls*, vol. 2, p. 6; VanderKam, *The Dead Sea Scrolls Today*, p. 57.

78. Although I am not convinced by Davies's reconstruction of the text-history of CD, I have been convinced by his work that the document has both a complex history and a composite nature

79. Translation of CD (slightly adapted) from Charlesworth, *The Dead Sea Scrolls*, vol. 2.

80. Solomon Schechter, *Fragments of a Zadokite Work*, vol. 1, *Documents of Jewish Sectaries* (Cambridge: Cambridge University Press, 1910), p. XXXVI, ¶ VII, n. 22: "some words must be missing." Chaim Rabin, *The Zadokite Documents* (Oxford: Clarendon Press, 1958), p. 15, n.2 to line 19, also speaks of a lacuna. Cf Charlesworth, *The Dead Sea Scrolls*, vol. 2, p. 19.

81. See Geza Vermes, "Sectarian Matrimonial Halakha in the Damascus Rule," *Journal of Jewish Studies* 25 (1974): 197–202, and the literature cited there for a survey of the views expressed from 1910 to 1974. Subsequent important treatments include Joseph A. Fitzmyer, "Divorce among First-Century Palestinian Jews," *Eretz-Israel* 14 (1978): 103*–110*, and Joseph M. Baumgarten, "The Qumran–Essene Restraints on Marriage," in Schiffman, ed., *Archaeology and History in the Dead Sea Scrolls*, pp 13–24.

82 At the crux of the debate is the meaning of בחייהם: Whose lives are meant? If it is the lives of the men, then presumably even a second marriage following the first wife's death

would be prohibited. So J. Murphy O'Connor, "An Essene Missionary Document? CD II, 14–VI, 1," *Revue Biblique* 77 (1970): 201–229, esp. p. 200. O'Connor's view is endorsed by Davies, *The Damascus Covenant*, p. 116. But this view is now generally considered unlikely, in light of 11QT LVII:17–19, which states that the king must remain with his wife "all the days of her life," but that if she dies, he may take another (Yadin, *The Temple Scroll*, vol. I, pp. 353–357; vol. II, p. 258; and Fitzmyer, "Divorce," p 108*). If the term בחייהם is meaningless or extraneous, then only polygamy would be prohibited. This is Vermes's view as expressed in "Sectarian Matrimonial Halakha." As Fitzmyer correctly notes, we ought not ignore the significance of בחייהם, despite the difficulties. Fitzmyer errs, however, in not properly distinguishing between a prohibition of divorce and a prohibition of remarriage after divorce. But if the lives of the women are meant—which is possible, despite the masculine suffix (see Fitzmyer, "Divorce," p 109*, n. 29, and the literature cited there)—then remarriage after divorce would be forbidden, but not remarriage after the first wife's death. This was Schechter's view (*Fragments of a Zadokite Work*, p. XVII, cf. p. XXXVI, ¶ VII, n. 3), and it remains the dominant position. Cf. Baumgarten, "The Qumran–Essene Restraints on Marriage," pp. 14–15. Schechter's view is accepted here as well.

83. *The Damascus Covenant*, p. 108.

84. "The Ideology of the Temple in the Damascus Document," *Journal of Jewish Studies* 33(1982): 287–301; quote from page 289; cf. *Behind the Essenes: History and Ideology in the Dead Sea Scrolls* (Atlanta: Scholars Press, 1987), p. 73.

85. *An Unknown Jewish Sect* (New York: Jewish Theological Seminary, 1976), p. 157.

86. *An Unknown Jewish Sect*, p. 158.

87. *An Unknown Jewish Sect*, p. 158, esp. n. 22; Ginzberg was followed in this respect by, among others, Rabin, Vermes, and Fitzmyer. See Rabin, *Zadokite Documents*, p. 17, n. 2 to line 20, and p. 19, n. 2 to line 8; Vermes, "Sectarian Matrimonial Halakha," p. 197; and Fitzmyer, "Divorce," p 107*

88. J. Murphy O'Connor, "A Literary Analysis of Damascus Document VI, 2–VIII, 3," *Revue Biblique* 78 (1971): 210–232, esp. pp. 212–214, 217.

89. It is not clear whether the flux in question is menstrual or nonmenstrual; Leviticus 15 uses the same term (זבה) in both cases. And while CD V:7 does not use the more specific term for menstruation (נדה), the phrase "who sees her blood of flowing" (הרואה את דם זובה) does parallel standard tannaitic terminology for menstruation (e.g., M. Nid. 1:4; cf. Schechter, *Fragments of a Zadokite Work*, p. XXXVI, ¶ VII, n. 15). As far as the biblical tradition is concerned, it is only cohabitation with a menstruant that is explicitly considered to be morally defiling (Lev. 18:19). But it is only a short step from the prohibition in Leviticus 18:19 to the idea that cohabitation with a woman with a nonmenstrual flow of blood would likewise be morally defiling (Rabin, *Zadokite Documents*, p. 19, n. 2 to line 7). Regardless, it is clear that the prohibition in question falls well within the conceptual realm of the sins viewed as morally defiling in the Holiness Code.

90. A number of ancient and medieval Jewish sects espoused such a reading of Leviticus 18. See Schechter, *Fragments of a Zadokite Work*, p. XXXVII, ¶ VII, n. 21; Ginzberg, *An Unknown Jewish Sect*, pp. 23–24.

91. Biblical law and narrative throughout assume that polygamy (for men) is permitted. And Deuteronomy 24:1–4 prohibits a man from remarrying a woman he has divorced, if she has in the interim been remarried to any other man. Deuteronomy 24:1–4 assumes therefore (a) that divorce is permitted and (b) that a woman is permitted to remarry after a divorce. Presumably, this law also assumes that a man can remarry after divorce, provided again that he does not remarry his first wife if she has in the interim been married to any other man.

92 Generally, on the books contained in 1 Enoch, see Schurer and Vermes, *The History of the Jewish People*, vol III, pt. 1, pp. 250–268; cf. E. Isaac, "1 (Ethiopic Apocalypse of) Enoch,"

in Charlesworth, ed., *The Old Testament Pseudepigrapha: Volume 1*, pp. 55–89; and M. A. Knibb, "1 Enoch," in H. F. D Sparks, ed., *The Apocryphal Old Testament* (Oxford: Clarendon Press, 1984). The "Book of Watchers" is generally considered to be one of the oldest of the Enoch books, dating from the late third or early second century BCE (Schürer and Vermes, *The History of the Jewish People*, vol. III, pt. 1, p. 256) For the Qumran fragments, see J. T. Milik, *The Books of Enoch: Aramaic Fragments of Qumran Cave 4* (Oxford: Clarendon Press, 1976).

93. Büchler identified a number of these passages in *Studies*, pp. 278–279. We can only assume, of course, that the extant Greek and Ethiopic manuscripts faithfully reflect the original Aramaic on this point. The author used the Greek text found in M Black, *Apocalypsis Henochi Graece* (Leiden: E. J Brill, 1970), pp 1–44. Unfortunately, the Aramaic fragments published by Milik do not preserve the original Aramaic of the verses in question.

94 Generally, on the Testaments of the Twelve Patriarchs, see Schürer and Vermes, *The History of the Jewish People*, vol. III, pt. 2, pp. 767–781; cf. Marius de Jonge "The Testaments of the Twelve Patriarchs," in Sparks, ed., *The Apocryphal Old Testament*, and Howard C. Kee, "Testaments of the Twelve Patriarchs," in Charlesworth, ed., *The Old Testament Pseudepigrapha: Volume 1*, pp 775–828.

95. Marius de Jonge has been the strongest proponent of the Testaments' Christian origin. See discussion in Schürer and Vermes, *The History of the Jewish People*, vol. III, pt. 2, pp. 770–772.

96. For a list of the Hebrew and Aramaic documents related to the Testaments, see Schürer and Vermes, *The History of the Jewish People*, vol. III, pt. 2, p. 776–777. On the Genizah manuscripts, see R. H. Charles, *The Greek Versions of the Testaments of the Twelve Patriarchs* (Oxford: Clarendon Press, 1908), pp. 245–256; cf. Michael E Stone and Jonas C. Greenfield, "Remarks on the Aramaic Testament of Levi," *Revue Biblique*, 86 (1979): 214–230

97. See J. T. Milik, *The Books of Enoch*, p. 23 n. 1.

98. "Enoch, Aramaic Levi, and Sectarian Origins," *Journal for the Study of Judaism* 19 (1988): 159–170; see esp. pp. 159–160, n. 2. The author consulted M. de Jonge, *The Testaments of the Twelve Patriarchs: A Critical Edition of the Greek Text* (Leiden: E. J. Brill, 1978).

99 T. Rub. 1:6, 4:8, 6:1; T. Sim. 2.13, 5:3–5, T. Jud. 14:3–5; T Iss. 4:4, T Ash. 4.3–5, 7.1–2, T. Jos. 4:6; T. Ben. 6:7, 8:2–3. The passages from T Levi will be noted below. Büchler identified a number of these passages in *Studies*, pp 283–285.

100. Translation by Marius de Jonge, in Sparks, ed., *The Apocryphal Old Testament*.

101. Indeed, in his commentary on the Damascus Document, Schechter pointed to this passage in addition to Jubilees 30:15 (quoted in the section on Jubilees in this chapter) as parallels to CD IV:18 (*Fragments of a Zadokite Work*, p. XXXVI, ¶ VI, n. 20).

102. Cf. T. Asher 7:1–2, quoted below

103 Jonas C. Greenfield, "The Words of Levi Son of Jacob in Damascus Document IV, 15–19," *Revue de Qumran* 13 (1988): 319–322.

104. E.g., see lines 9 and 15–16 of MS Bodleian b (in Charles, *The Greek Versions*, p. 247) and line 14 of the Athos MS, published in Michael E Stone and Jonas C. Greenfield, "The Prayer of Levi," *Journal of Biblical Literature* 112 (1993): 247–266.

105. Generally, on the Psalms of Solomon see Schürer and Vermes, *The History of the Jewish People*, vol. III, pt. 1, pp 192–197, Cf. M. Whittaker, "Psalms of Solomon," in Sparks, ed., *The Apocryphal Old Testament*, pp. 683–732; and R. B. Wright, "Psalms of Solomon," in Charlesworth, ed., *The Old Testament Pseudepigrapha: Volume 2*, pp. 639–670. A Greek text of the Psalms of Solomon can handily be found in Rahlfs's manual edition of the Septuagint.

106. See 1:8, 2:3, 2:10–13, 8:8–13, 8:22, 9:6, 17:22. Büchler discusses some of these passages in *Studies*, pp. 274–277.

107. Cf. Büchler, *Studies*, p. 274; he suggests a connection between the Psalms of

Solomon 2.9 (which refers to the earth abhorring the sinners) and Leviticus 18:28 (which refers to the land spewing out the Canaanites).

108. Other references to sanctuary defilement in particular include 2.3 and 8:8–13, 22. It is unfortunate that we do not have the original Hebrew of this composition, for without it one cannot understand fully 8:8–13. It is possible that the concern there is the ritual defilement of the sanctuary by sinners who enter it, but it is also possible, considering the fact that the passage begins by discussing incestuous sins, that moral impurity is the concern.

Part II: Introduction

1. One who would ought simply to peruse the second chapter of Neusner's *The Idea of Purity in Ancient Judaism*, where many passages of ancient Jewish literature dealing with ritual defilement are identified and analyzed.

2. Generally, on Philo, see Schurer and Vermes, *The History of the Jewish People*, vol. III, pt. 2, pp. 809–889; and P. Borgen "Philo of Alexandria," in Stone, *Jewish Writings*, pp. 233–282 On impurity in Philo see Neusner, *The Idea, pp.* 45–51; and É. Cothenet, "Pureté et impureté: Nouveau Testament," *Dictionnaire de la Bible· Supplement* 9 (1979): 508–554, esp. p. 529. A thorough treatment of conceptions of purity in Philo's thought remains a desideratum. In addition to the above works, I also consulted the indices in the Loeb and Cohn-Wendland editions of Philo's works, as well as the useful anthology compiled by David Winston, *Philo of Alexandria: The Contemplative Life, the Giants, and Selections, The Classics of Western Spirituality* (Ramsey, N.J.: Paulist Press, 1981).

3. Translation adapted from F. H. Colson, *Philo*, vol. VII [LCL] (Cambridge: Harvard University Press, 1934), pp. 249–251.

4. Cf. 1·269–270; see also *The Unchangeableness of God*, 131–137, where Philo does essentially the same thing, specifically with regard to "leprous" impurity. Compare also Hebrews 9:11–28, discussed in chapter 6 of this book.

5. Cf., e.g., Plato, *Phaedo* 65d–69d. See Robert Parker, *Miasma*, pp. 281–283.

6. *Unchangeableness of God* 135; *Migration of Abraham* 67; *Who Is the Heir* 184–185, 239–240, 276; *On Flight and Finding* 80; *The Decalogue* 10; *Questions and Answers on Exodus* 2:51.

7. Cf. Samuel Belkin, *Philo and the Oral Law: The Philonic Interpretation of Biblical Law in Relation to the Palestinian Halakah* (Cambridge, Mass.: Harvard University Press, 1940), p. 156; Belkin briefly notes that when Philo speaks of sinners as impure or defiled, he does not use the terms "in the sense of levitical impurity, for which certain ablutions and other acts of purification are prescribed. He uses them in the same moral sense as when the prophets speak of defiling the land by murder and idolatry."

8. Philo is aware of the notion that sin defiles land; see, for example, *On Rewards and Punishments* 68.

9. *Contra* Wright, "The Spectrum," pp. 172, 180–181; see discussion in chapter 1 of this book, section on "A Single Symbolic System?"

10. *On the Change of Names* 240; *Special Laws* 1:269; 3:209

11. *Who Is the Heir* 276.

12. *On the Migration of Abraham* 93.

13 Cf. Daniel Boyarin, *Carnal Israel: Reading Sex in Talmudic Culture* (Berkeley: University of California Press, 1993), esp. pp. 8–9, 37–42, 230–235. Discussing gender issues, Boyarin notes repeatedly that Philo's allegorical approach to Scripture allows the philosopher to prioritize matters of the spirit over matters of the flesh, all the while without rejecting entirely the importance of the latter.

14. *Special Laws* 1:117–119; Philo refers matter-of-factly to the ritual defilement contracted from human corpses in *Life of Moses* 2:228–231.

15. E.g., leprosy (*Special Laws* 1:118) and corpse impurity (*Special Laws* 3:205–208).

16. *The Worse Attacks the Better* 20.

17. E.g., *Unchangeableness of God* 8; *On Flight and Finding* 79–80; *Special Laws* 3: 88–92.

18. *On the Creation* 16; *On Dreams* 1:186–188.

19. *Contra* Neusner, *The Idea*, p. 46, where he uses the phrase "second-level metaphor" to describe Philo's approach to impurity. And cf. *Special Laws* 3:209.

20. Translation from R. J. H. Shutt, "Letter of Aristeas· A New Translation and Introduction," in Charlesworth, *The Old Testament Pseudepigrapha*, vol. 2, pp 7–34 Generally on *Aristeas*, see Schürer and Vermes, *The History of the Jewish People*, vol. III, pt. 1, pp. 679–684; and Moses Hadas, *Aristeas to Philocrates* (New York: Harper & Brothers, 1951).

3. Impurity and Sin in the Literature of Qumran

1 The enigmatic place that the Damascus Document (CD) holds in the Qumran Corpus has been noted already (see "The Damascus Document," chapter 2). To reiterate briefly· Following Davies and others, CD is viewed here as a composite. Thus while parts of the document may well be protosectarian or quasi-sectarian, others are truly sectarian Because of this state of affairs, CD will not be discussed in this chapter in great detail. However, aspects of it that appear to jibe with what we find in sectarian texts will be noted.

2. Generally, on the question of the Dead Sea sect as Essene, see VanderKam, *The Dead Sea Scrolls Today*, pp. 71–98.

3. See, for example, Cothenet, "Pureté et impureté," pp. 511–518; Eilberg-Schwartz, *The Savage in Judaism*, p. 211; David Flusser, "The Dead Sea Sect and Pre-Pauline Christianity," in *Aspects of the Dead Sea Scrolls*, ed. Chaim Rabin and Yigael Yadin (Jerusalem: Magnes Press, 1958), pp. 215–266; Flusser, "The Baptism of John and the Dead Sea Sect" (Hebrew), in *Jewish Sources in Early Christianity* (Tel Aviv: Sifriat Poalim, 1979), pp. 81–112; F. García Martínez, "Les limites de la communauté· pureté et impureté à Qumrân et dans le Nouveau Testament," in *Text and Testimony: Essays on New Testament and Apocryphal Literature in Honour of A F J. Klijn*, ed. T Baardia et al (Kampen: J H Kok, 1988), pp. 111–122; García Martínez, "The Problem of Purity," pp. 139–157; Paul Garnet, *Salvation and Atonement in the Qumran Scrolls* (Tübingen: J. C. B. Mohr [Paul Siebeck], 1977), pp. 58–59; Hans Hübner, "Unclean and Clean (NT)," in *The Anchor Bible Dictionary*, ed. David Noel Freedman (New York: Doubleday, 1992), vol. VI, pp. 741–745; Neusner, *The Idea*, pp. 50–55; Helmer Ringgren, *The Faith of Qumran: Theology of the Dead Sea Scrolls* (Philadelphia: Fortress Press, 1963), pp. 120–126; and B. Sharvit, "Impurity and Purity According to the Qumran Sect" (Hebrew), *Bet Mikra* 26 (1980–1981): 18–27. The most detailed analyses are those of Flusser, García Martínez, Newton, and Sharvit.

4. According to VanderKam, fifteen or sixteen copies of Jubilees have been discovered, and at least seven of the Enoch manuscripts preserve parts of the Book of Watchers; see *The Dead Sea Scrolls Today*, pp. 37–40.

5. See VanderKam, *The Dead Sea Scrolls Today*, pp. 55–56.

6. See Stone, "Enoch, Aramaic Levi and Sectarian Origins," esp pp. 159–161; cf. most recently Gabriele Boccaccini, *Beyond the Essene Hypothesis: The Parting of the Ways between Qumran and Enochic Judaism* (Grand Rapids, Mich. William B. Eerdmans, 1998).

7 Generally, on the Habakkuk Pesher, see William H. Brownlee, *The Midrash Pesher of Habakkuk* (Missoula, Mont.: Scholars Press, 1979); and Maurya P. Horgan, *Pesharim: Qumran Interpretations of Biblical Books* (Washington, D.C.: The Catholic Biblical Association of America, 1979); cf. Schürer and Vermes, *The History of the Jewish People*, vol. III, pt. 1, pp. 433–437. The manuscript dates from the late first century BCE, and since it is generally ac-

cepted that the "Kittim" discussed in the Pesher (e.g., IV:5) are the Romans, most believe that the text was composed after 63 BCE.

8. Translation of 1QpHab from Horgan, *Pesharim*, p. 20; cf. Brownlee, *The Midrash Pesher*, p. 196.

9. For a quick summary of the possibilities, and references to the relevant literature supporting each suggestion, see A. S. van der Woude, "Wicked Priest or Wicked Priests? Reflections on the Identification of the Wicked Priest in the Habakkuk Commentary," *Journal of Jewish Studies* 33.1–2 (1982): 349–359. See also the discussion in Horgan, *Pesharim*, pp. 6–8.

10. The "Groningen Hypothesis" involves the combined insights of two Dutch scholars, F. García Martínez and A. S. van der Woude. See F. García Martínez, "Qumran Origins and Early History: A Groningen Hypothesis," *Folia Orientalia* 25 (1988) 113–136; and F. García Martínez and A S. van der Woude, "A 'Groningen' Hypothesis of Qumran Origins," *Revue de Qumran* 14 (1990)· 521–541.

11. The idea that 1QpHab deals with a series of high priests constitutes van der Woude's contribution to the Groningen hypothesis; cf. his "Wicked Priest." For a critical review of the theory, see Timothy H. Lim, "The Wicked Priests of the Groningen Hypothesis," *Journal of Biblical Literature* 112.3 (1993): 415–425.

12. See, e.g., VIII:3–12; IX:3–7; X:1, 10.

13 Similar phrasing can be seen in, e.g., CD III:17; 1QS IV:10; 1QM XIII:4–5; 1QH IX (I):22.

14. In a sense the issue in both of these passages is a grammatical one: What is the force of the *vav* (-ו) that connects the verbs in these passages? But because there are so many possible meanings that can be conveyed by the *vav* consecutive, grammatical rules alone cannot dictate how to interpret these passages. For a list of the possible connotations of the *vav* consecutive in biblical texts, see Kautzsch-Cowley, *Gesenius' Hebrew Grammar* (Oxford: Clarendon Press, 1910) §§ 111 and 112.

15 Brownlee, *The Midrash Pesher*, p. 142. The idea that arrogance is an abomination and therefore a source of moral impurity can be seen in tannaitic sources as well; cf. e.g., Mekhilta Yitro Parashah 9 (Horovitz/Rabin ed., p. 238); the rabbinic traditions to this effect will be analyzed in chapter 5.

16. Philo also associates greed and defilement in his discussion of the Therapeutae (*On the Contemplative Life* 66), and we will see in chapter 6 a number of New Testament references to the idea of greed as morally defiling (e.g., Mark 7:22 and Gal. 5.20).

17. Brownlee is one of the few Dead Sea Scroll scholars who has recognized the influence of these passages at Qumran; cf. *The Midrash Pesher*, p. 206.

18. Brownlee, *The Midrash Pesher*, p. 206.

19. Generally, see Elisha Qimron and John Strugnell, *Qumran Cave 4, V* (Miqṣat Ma'aseh ha-Torah), vol. X, *Discoveries in the Judaean Desert* (Oxford: Clarendon Press, 1994). See also John Kampen and Moshe J. Bernstein, eds. *Reading 4QMMT: New Perspectives on Qumran Law and History* (Atlanta: Scholars Press, 1996).

20. See Qimron and Strugnell, *DJD* X, pp. 109–121.

21. For Qimron's arguments in support of the mid-second century BCE date of 4QMMT, see Qimron and Strugnell, *DJD* X, pp. 109–121.

22 We follow, here and later, Qimron's composite text and translation, and we use the system of reference employed in that volume (a letter from A to C denoting the section of the text, followed by line numbers which refer to the layout of the reconstructed text). On the phrase פרשנו מרוב העם and its significance, see Qimron and Strugnell, *DJD* X, pp. 111, 134

23. Qimron and Strugnell, *DJD* X, p. 116.

24. The text is composed in the first person plural (e.g., B 1; C 7) and it appears to have had a communal authorship; cf. Qimron and Strugnell, *DJD* X, p. 114.

25. Qimron and Strugnell, *DJD X*, p. 121.

26. On the significance of 4QMMT for the history of Jewish law, see Lawrence H. Schiffman, "Pharisaic and Sadducean Halakhah in Light of the Dead Sea Scrolls: The Case of Tevul Yom," *Dead Sea Discoveries* 1.3 (1994): 285–299. See also Y. Sussman, "The History of the Halakha and the Dead Sea Scrolls," (= Appendix 1 in Qimron and Strugnell, *DJD X*). Fuller citation is provided in the original Hebrew version of this article, published in *Tarbiz* 59 (1990): 11–76.

27. Cf. García Martínez, "The Problem of Purity," p. 148. Despite the agreements between 4QMMT and 11QT to be noted later, I still hesitate to identify the two to the same extent that García Martínez does. Because of the composite nature of 11QT as well as the fact that 4QMMT refers to the foundation of the sect while 11QT does not, I feel it is best to view 11QT as coming from an even earlier stage in the sect's (pre-)history than does 4QMMT.

28. Indeed, 4QMMT B 1–3 seems to state explicitly that many of the concerns to be raised in the letter relate to ritual purity And although we do not have the complete document, it is true that ritual impurity is the subject of many of the *halakhot* contained in the extant fragments For a convenient summary of the *halakhot* in 4QMMT, see Qimron and Strugnell, *DJD X*, p. 147.

29. For a survey of some of the significant parallels, see Schiffman, "*Miqṣat Ma'eh ha-Torah* and the *Temple Scroll*," *Revue de Qumran* 14 (1990): 435–457.

30. Cf. B 71–72, which states that the "leper" must not eat sacred food until the sunset following the eighth day of the purification process. The idea that ritual impurity lasts until the sundown following purification is stated in 11QT XLV:9–10 and XLIX:19–21. Generally, see Schiffman, "*Miqṣat Ma'aseh ha-Torah* and the *Temple Scroll*," pp. 438–442, and "Pharisaic and Sadducean Halakhah." Cf. Qimron and Strugnell, *DJD X*, pp. 152–154 and 166–170.

31. On this and other such parallels, see Joseph M. Baumgarten, "The Pharisaic–Sadducean Controversies about Purity and the Qumran Texts," *Journal of Jewish Studies* 31 (1980): 157–170.

32. 4QMMT B 49–54. It is not clear in this case if blind people are considered inherently ritually impure. Possibly the concern is the fact that since they cannot see, they may be likely to defile things accidentally. See Qimron and Strugnell, *DJD X*, pp. 160–161. For discussion of the 11QT passage (XLV:12–14), see Yadin, *The Temple Scroll*, vol. 1, pp. 289–291, vol. 2, p. 193; cf. Schiffman, "Exclusion from the Sanctuary," pp. 309–311. The approach taken in these documents is also in evidence in other sectarian literature. The Rule of the Congregation (1QSa) excludes many categories of handicapped people from participation in the council of the community (1QSa II:3–11); cf. Schiffman, *The Eschatological Community of the Dead Sea Scrolls* (Atlanta· Scholars Press, 1989), pp. 37–52; esp. pp. 43–49. The War Scroll (1QM) also excludes the blind and lame from participating in the eschatological battle (1QM VII: 4–5); cf. Yigael Yadin, *The Scroll of the War of the Sons of Light against the Sons of Darkness*, trans. Chaim Rabin (Oxford: Clarendon Press, 1962), pp 70–73. There is no such exclusion in rabbinic literature (Schiffman, "Exclusion from the Sanctuary," pp. 310–311). Nor is there any such exclusion in the Pentateuch (see Lev. 21:16–24). See discussion of 11QT in "The Temple Scroll" section of chapter 2, and cf. Klawans, "Notions of Gentile Impurity," p. 292. See also, Aharon Shemesh, "'The Holy Angels Are in Their Council': The Exclusion of Deformed Persons from Holy Places in Qumranic and Rabbinic Literature," *Dead Sea Discoveries* 4. 2 (1997): 179–206 I thank Joan E. Taylor for bringing this article to my attention.

33. Many of the important *halakhot* articulated in one of these documents are not paralleled in the other. While both are concerned with the *ṭebul yom*, for instance, only 4QMMT is concerned with the purity of liquid streams (4QMMT B 55–58, Qimron and Strugnell, *DJD X*, pp. 161–162). And despite the fact that 11QT devotes a number of columns to delineating

the laws of exclusion from the city of the sanctuary, 4QMMT bans dogs, while 11QT does not. Differences between 11QT and 4QMMT can be seen even at points of comparison. In the passages discussed in note 32, 4QMMT excludes both the blind and the deaf, while 11QT excludes only the blind; Qimron and Strugnell, *DJD X*, p. 160.

34. García Martínez, "The Problem of Purity," p. 148.

35. Qimron and Strugnell, *DJD X*, pp. 132–134 (on 4QMMT), and Harrington, *The Impurity Systems*, pp. 51–67; Harrington states that the "stringent interpretation of Scripture" is characteristic of the sectarian approach to purity (p. 67). But see Yaakov Elman, "Some Remarks on 4QMMT and the Rabbinic Tradition, Or, When Is a Parallel Not a Parallel?" in Kampen and Bernstein, eds., *Reading 4QMMT*, pp. 99–128, esp pp. 100–105. Elman identifies instances in which, *contra* Harrington, it is the tannaim who advocate a more stringent approach.

36. The classic study identifying ways in which Qumran's ritual purity law resembles that of the Sadducees is Joseph M. Baumgarten, "Pharisaic–Sadducean Controversies." It is Schiffman who has, in numerous articles, taken the argument one step further, advocating the Sadducean identity of the Qumran sect. See, e.g., his " *Miqṣat Ma'aseh ha-Torah* and the *Temple Scroll*," and "Pharisaic and Sadducean Halakhah," and cf. Sussman's appendix to Qimron and Strugnell, *DJD X*. For a recent treatment of this question, see Baumgarten, "Sadducean Elements in Qumran Law," in *The Community of the Renewed Covenant: The Notre Dame Symposium on the Dead Sea Scrolls*, ed Eugene Ulrich and James VanderKam (Notre Dame: University of Indiana Press, 1994), pp. 27–36.

37. García Martínez, "Les limites," pp. 114–116; Yadin, *The Temple Scroll*, vol. I, pp. 277–307; cf. Harrington, *The Impurity Systems*, pp 51–67, where she sees the "effort to extend the holiness of the Temple to the whole Temple City" as one of the distinctive characteristics of the sectarian approach to purity (p. 67).

38. 4QMMT B 27–33, 58–62; cf. Qimron and Strugnell, *DJD X*, pp. 143–145.

39. Schiffman, "Exclusion from the Sanctuary," pp. 315–316.

40. Qimron and Strugnell, *DJD X*, pp. 46–47, 148.

41. Qimron and Strugnell, *DJD X*, pp. 46–47, 149–150.

42. Qimron and Strugnell, *DJD X*, pp. 145–47. See also Shemesh, "'The Holy Angels Are in Their Council'," esp. p. 187.

43. *Jewish War* v:198–204; *Antiquities* xv:319; cf. the discussion of Gentiles in "Sinful Outsiders as Ritually Defiling" in this chapter, and the discussion of M. Kelim 1·8–9 and the exclusion of women from the temple in "The Status of Sinners" in chapter 4.

44. Klawans, "Notions of Gentile Impurity," pp. 291–293, 297–299, 305, and the literature cited there.

45. On sacrifices of Gentiles in rabbinic law, see Israel Knohl, "The Acceptance of Sacrifices from Gentiles," *Tarbiz* 48 (1979): 341–347. On ritual and moral impurity and Gentiles, see Klawans, "Notions of Gentile Impurity"; and Christine E. Hayes, "The Impurity of Gentiles in Biblical Law and Late Antique Judaism" (unpublished MS).

46. Regarding Gentile ritual impurity and intermarriage, see also Hayes, "Intermarriage and Impurity," esp. pp. 25–35.

47. On the Damascus Document and its place in the Qumran corpus, see "The Damascus Document" in chapter 2, and footnote 1 of this chapter.

48. Translations of the Rule of the Community from *The Dead Sea Scrolls: Volume 1*, ed. James H. Charlesworth et al (Tübingen· J. C. B Mohr; Louisville: Westminster John Knox Press, 1993). Generally on 1QS see A. R. C. Leaney, *The Rule of Qumran and Its Meaning· Introduction, Translation and Commentary* (Philadelphia. Westminster Press, 1966); and Jacob Licht, *The Rule Scroll. a Scroll from the Wilderness of Judaea* (Jerusalem· Bialik Institute, 1965); cf. Schürer and Vermes, *The History of the Jewish People*, vol. III, pt. 1, pp. 381–386.

49. We follow here Charlesworth's translation of חנפ as "hypocrisy," but it should be noted that in the Hebrew Bible this term generally denotes the pollution caused by grave sin (cf. e.g., Num. 35:33).

50 See chapter 2, section on "The Temple Scroll."

51. For further evidence of the ritually defiling force of sin at Qumran, see the next two sections.

52 See "Moral Impurity" in chapter 1; cf. Paschen, *Rein und Unrein,* pp 28–30 and 67–68

53 References to 1QH throughout this work follow the revised enumeration of the columns devised by E. Puech and adopted by both García Martínez in *The Dead Sea Scrolls* and Vermes in *The Complete Dead Sea Scrolls in English* (New York: Allen Lane, 1997). For each reference, Sukenik's enumeration is noted in parentheses. Translation from García Martínez, *The Dead Sea Scrolls.* Generally, on 1QH, see Schürer and Vermes, *The History of the Jewish People,* vol. III, pt. 1, pp. 452–457; Jacob Licht, *The Thanksgiving Scroll: a Scroll from the Wilderness of Judaea* (Jerusalem: Bialik Institute, 1957), esp. pp 3–52; and Menahem Mansoor, *The Thanksgiving Hymns. Translated and Annotated with an Introduction* (Leiden: E. J. Brill, 1961), esp. pp 52–93.

54. Cf. Paschen, *Rein und Unrein,* pp. 27–28.

55. It was also noted there that the same usage appears in a noncanonical (and nonsectarian) psalm, 4Q 381.

56 Ringgren, *The Faith of Qumran,* p 97

57. This observation has obvious ramifications for the question of the sectarians' attitude toward women. The status of women in relation to purity issues will be dealt with in greater detail in chapter 4. On the sectarians' attitude toward women, see Lawrence H. Schiffman, *Reclaiming the Dead Sea Scrolls: The History of Judaism, the Background of Christianity, the Lost Library of Qumran* (Philadelphia: Jewish Publication Society, 1994), pp. 127–143, and Eileen M. Schuller, "Women in the Dead Sea Scrolls," in *Methods of Investigation of the Dead Sea Scrolls and the Khirbet Qumran Site: Present Realities and Future Prospects,* ed. Michael O Wise et al. (New York: New York Academy of Sciences, 1994), pp. 115–131 On the sectarian attitude toward marriage, see J M. Baumgarten, "The Qumran-Essene Restraints on Marriage"; further literature on marriage and celibacy is cited in the discussion of CD IV:20–V:6 in chapter 2 of this book, section on "The Damascus Document." The main cemetery of Qumran, with well over a thousand graves, apparently contains primarily the remains of men, though graves of some women and children have been uncovered in adjacent burial grounds; cf. Schiffman, *Reclaiming the Dead Sea Scrolls,* pp. 51–53, and VanderKam, *The Dead Sea Scrolls Today,* 14–15.

58. Yadin incorrectly identifies the former (XLV:10) as a reference to "spiritual" impurity; Yadin, *The Temple Scroll,* vol. II, p. 193.

59. Cf Neusner, *The Idea,* p. 54.

60. Cf. Leaney, *The Rule of Qumran,* pp. 139–140; and Newton, *The Concept of Purity,* p. 41

61. V:10: "the people of deceit" כול אנשי העול.

62. II:25 "all who refuse to enter" כול המואס לבוא.

63. Cf. 4QS MS C frg 1, II:6–8; Charlesworth, *Rule of the Community,* pp. 68–69.

64. It was for this very reason that, in my earlier study, "Notions of Gentile Impurity," I noted that "there is little evidence from the Qumran literature itself to support the claim that all Gentiles were considered to be ritually impure" (p. 300, n 75, but cf Klawans, "The Impurity of Immorality," p 9, n. 43)

65. Harrington, *The Impurity Systems,* pp. 104–108, and Christine E. Hayes, "The Impurity of Gentiles in Biblical Law and Late Antique Judaism," esp. pp. 23–28.

66. Harrington, *The Impurity Systems*, p. 104; Hayes ("The Impurity of Gentiles," p. 23), also alludes to Hippolytus's *Philosophoumena* (IX, iv, 21) to a similar effect.

67. Harrington, *The Impurity Systems*, p. 104; Hayes, "The Impurity of Gentiles," pp. 25–28.

68. See Joseph M. Baumgarten, "The Exclusion of 'Netinim' and Proselytes in 4Q Florilegium," *Revue de Qumran* 8.1 (1972): 87–95; idem., "Exclusions from the Temple: Proselytes and Agrippa I," *Journal of Jewish Studies* 33.2 (1982): 215–225; and Schiffman, "Exclusion from the Sanctuary," esp. pp. 303–305. Hayes ("The Impurity of Gentiles," pp. 25–28) also reviews the passages and these scholarly discussions with regard to the question of ritual impurity.

69. On Qumranic and rabbinic exclusions of proselytes, see also Shemesh, "'The Holy Angels Are in Their Council.'"

70. See discussion of 4QMMT in the first section of this chapter, and Klawans, "Notions of Gentile Impurity," pp. 291–293, 279–299, 305; cf. Qimron and Strugnell, *DJD X*, pp. 145–147.

71. "The Impurity of Gentiles," pp. 27–28.

72. Harrington (*The Impurity Systems*, p. 104) in addition points to 1QM IX:8–9 to the effect that the property of Gentiles was considered to be ritually defiling. I noted above that 1QS V:19–20 and CD VI:15 do indeed appear to consider the property of *all* the wicked people to be ritually impure (and this would, presumably, include that of Gentiles as well as that of nonsectarian Jews), but I do not see how 1QM IX:8–9 can be seen as evidence of this view. What the passage does state is that the blood of the corpses of the slain sons of darkness would ritually defile the priests of the sons of light, were the priests to come into contact with those corpses. This does, by the way, suggest that the corpses of Gentiles defile, since the sons of darkness in this case are the warriors of Gentile nations (1QM I:1–2; II:9–14).

73. Harrington, *The Impurity Systems*, p. 104; cf. Hayes, "The Impurity of Gentiles," p. 24, n. 41, where she correctly dismisses this kind of evidence.

74. E.g., Wolf Leslau, *Falasha Anthology: Translated from Ethiopic Sources* (New Haven: Yale University Press, 1951), p. xxxviii; cf. Alon, "The Levitical Uncleanness of Gentiles," p. 168.

75. I rely heavily here upon Steven Kaplan, *The Beta Israel (Falasha) in Ethiopia: From Earliest Times to the Twentieth Century* (New York: New York University Press, 1992).

76. Kaplan, *The Beta Israel*, p. 132; p. 196, n. 32; cf. Michael Corinaldi, "Purity and Conversion Norms among the Falashas," in *Between Africa and Zion: Proceedings of the First International Congress of the Society for the Study of Ethiopian Jewry*, ed. Steven Kaplan, Tuder Parfitt, and Emanuela Trevisan Semi (Jerusalem: Ben-Zvi Institute, 1995), pp. 113–124, esp. p. 114. I thank Charlie Kalech for bringing this article to my attention.

77. In addition to Kaplan, *The Beta Israel*, see idem., "'Falasha' Religion: Ancient Judaism or Evolving Ethiopian Tradition? A Review Article," *Jewish Quarterly Review* 79.1 (1988): 49–65, esp. pp. 53–55.

78. Kaplan, "'Falasha' Religion," p. 55.

79. Text and translation following Horgan, *Pesharim*, p. 164.

80. See 1QS III 24–26; IV:15; IV:23; IX:12; 1QH VII:16–23 (XV:13–20); IX (I):7–14; XII (IV):38; and 1QM XIII:9–12. Generally, see Ringgren, *The Faith of Qumran*, pp. 52–55 (God as creator) and pp. 66–80 (dualism). Cf. Flusser, "The Dead Sea Sect," pp. 217–220.

81. It is now generally accepted that the phrase טהרת רבים refers to the pure-food of the community, with which initiates can come into contact only after a year (1QS VI:16–17). See Licht, *The Rule Scroll*, pp. 147–148, 294–303; Schiffman, *Sectarian Law in the Dead Sea Scrolls*, pp. 161–168; and García Martínez, "The Problem of Purity," pp. 152–154. On the Pharisaic *havurah*, see chapter 4 of this book.

82. Generally, on the penal code, see García Martínez, "The Problem of Purity," pp. 152–157; Licht, *The Rule Scroll*, pp. 153–158; Newton, *The Concept of Purity*, pp. 40–49; and Schiffman, *Sectarian Law in the Dead Sea Scrolls*, pp. 155–190.

83. For a convenient chart allowing comparison of all the punishment clauses, see Schiffman, *Sectarian Law in the Dead Sea Scrolls*, p. 160.

84. *Sectarian Law in the Dead Sea Scrolls*, pp. 159–161

85. Licht, *The Rule Scroll*, pp. 153–158; and Newton, *The Concept of Purity*, pp. 40–49.

86. Schiffman, *Sectarian Law in the Dead Sea Scrolls*, p. 158, García Martínez, "The Problem of Purity," p. 152.

87. 11QT LI.11–15; 1QpHab XII:6–9; in this book see chapter 2, "The Temple Scroll" section, and chapter 3, "Sin and Sanctuary in the Habakkuk Pesher." For further discussion of the exegetical background of the sectarian approach to ritual and moral impurity, see the last section of this chapter.

88. Deuteronomy 25:16 and Proverbs 16·5

89. *Sectarian Law in the Dead Sea Scrolls*, p. 161.

90. Schiffman, *Sectarian Law in the Dead Sea Scrolls*, pp. 155–159.

91. Leaney, *The Rule of Qumran*, p. 199.

92. Licht, *The Rule Scroll*, pp 153–155; and Newton, *The Concept of Purity*, pp. 41–42.

93. Though this is not directly related to the topic at hand, it ought to be noted, as Prof. Halivni has pointed out to me, that CD here surprisingly contradicts the simple meaning of the Pentateuch, which clearly denies validity to the testimony of a single witness (Deut. 17.6, 19:15; cf Sifre Deut § 189 [ed Finkelstein, pp. 228–229]).

94. E.g., 1QH VIII:20 (XVI:12); XI (III):21; XIV (VI):8; XV (VII):30; XIX (XI):10, 30–31; cf. IX (I):32 and XII (IV):37, as restored; cf. 1QS IV:21–22, XI:14–15, and 4Q 504 frgs. 1–2, VI:1–2; cf. also the nonsectarian Psalm 155:13 (11QPs^a XXIV:12). Incidentally, this usage is characteristically absent from both 11QT and 4QMMT.

95. Indeed, a great deal of the material in 1QH is scripturally based; cf Schürer and Vermes, *The History of the Jewish People*, vol. III, pt. 1, p. 452, and the literature cited there.

96. Psalm 51 is the only instance of the usage in Psalms.

97. E.g., Garnet, *Salvation and Atonement*, p. 58, n. 3; Neusner, *The Idea*, p. 55; Newton, *The Concept of Purity*, pp. 47–49; Ringgren, *The Faith of Qumran*, p. 123, Sharvit, "Impurity and Purity," pp 21–22.

98. Flusser, "The Baptism of John," pp. 84–89; cf. Flusser, "The Dead Sea Sect," pp. 243–244.

99. E.g., Leaney, *The Rule of Qumran*, pp. 137–139; Sharvit, "Impurity and Purity," p 21; cf. Licht, *The Rule Scroll*, p. 76, where he similarly summarizes the matter (presumably, Licht was familiar with Flusser's earlier, less detailed, treatment).

100. Newton, *The Concept of Purity*, pp. 45–46; cf. Ringgren, *The Faith of Qumran*, p. 125.

101. Published by M. Baillet in *Qumran Grotte 4, III* (4Q482–4Q520). Vol. VII, *Discoveries in the Judaean Desert* (Oxford: Clarendon, 1982), pp. 262 ff; cf. Joseph M. Baumgarten, "The Purification Rituals in DJD 7," in *The Dead Sea Scrolls: Forty Years of Research*, ed. Devorah Dimant and Uriel Rappaport (Leiden: E. J. Brill, 1992), pp. 199–209.

102. Text follows the editio princeps, M. Baillet, *DJD VII*, p. 265. Translation from García Martínez, *The Dead Sea Scrolls*, p. 441.

103. Baumgarten, "The Purification Rituals," p. 200.

104. Frgs. 1–6, col. XII; see Baillet, *DJD VII*, pp. 272–274; note the references to "the third day" (line 1; cf. Num. 19:12) and "holy ash" (line 3; cf. Num. 19:10).

105. The editor, M. Baillet, believed this fragment contained the blessing that was to be recited upon purification from sexual impurity — note the phrase ערות נדה (*DJD VII*, p. 263).

That is certainly possible, but considering the wide use of the phrase in the sectarian literature (see "Sin as Defilement" above), one cannot be certain.

106. Compare J. Baumgarten's assessment ("The Purification Rituals," p. 201):

> What may be safely said is that the authors of this liturgy viewed purification from any defilement as a gift of divine grace and a restoration of one's spiritual and social integrity. There was apparently no sharp dichotomy at Qumran between the ablution of neophytes and the bathing to remove ritual uncleanliness.

107. Joseph Baumgarten, "The Laws about Fluxes in 4QTohoraᵃ," in *Time to Prepare the Way in the Wilderness*, ed. Devorah Dimont and Lawrence H Schiffman (Leiden: E. J. Brill, 1995), pp. 1–8; and Jacob Milgrom, "4QTohoraᵃ: An unpublished Qumran Text on Purities," also in *Time to Prepare the Way*, pp. 59–68. See also other 4Q texts quoted in Baumgarten, "Zab Impurity in Qumran and Rabbinic Law," *Journal of Jewish Studies* 45.2 (1994): 273–277.

108. Translation (slightly adapted) from Baumgarten, "The Laws about Fluxes," p. 3.

109 Baumgarten, "The Laws about Fluxes," p. 3; cf Baumgarten, "Zab Impurity," pp. 275–7; Baumgarten in, "Zab Impurity," pp. 274–277, points to another fragmentary document, 4Q 272 (Dᵍ), which implies that zab impurity was believed to result from lascivious thoughts

110 Milgrom, "4QTohoraᵃ," pp. 60–61.

111. On impurity in Zoroastrianism, see Choksy, *Purity and Pollution in Zoroastrianism.* I cannot address here the issue of possible Zoroastrian influence on Qumran; see Shaul Shaked, "Iranian Influence on Judaism: First Century B.C.E to Second Century C.E.," in *The Cambridge History of Judaism, Volume I: Introduction; The Persian Period*, ed. W. D. Davies and Louis Finkelstein (Cambridge: Cambridge University Press, 1984), pp. 308–325.

112 See "The Qumran Cult" and "Scriptural Foundations"; cf discussion in "The Temple Scroll" in chapter 2.

113 On H at Qumran, see Cothenet, "Pureté et impureté," p. 514; On the influence of Ezekiel at Qumran, see Cothenet, "Influence d'Ézékiel," and García Martínez, "L'interprétation de la Torah d'Ézékiel."

114. Cf. 1QS VIII:4: העת בהיות.

115. This instance, however, is a supralineal gloss, and the insertion is not paralleled in 4QS MS E; only parts of the supralineal phrase fit into the appropriate gaps of 4QS MS D; see Charlesworth, *Rule of the Community*, p. 35, n. 205 (1QS); p. 77, n 49 (4QS MS D); p 87, n. 21 (4QS MS E).

116. On the phrase "atone for the land," see Paschen, *Rein und Unrein*, pp. 147–149

117. Indeed, among others, Garnet, Newton, Leaney, and Sanders correctly point to Numbers 35:33–34 in their interpretations of 1QS VIII; cf Garnet, *Salvation and Atonement*, pp. 66–67; Leaney, *The Rule of Qumran*, p. 217; Newton, *The Concept of Purity*, p. 48; E. P. Sanders, *Paul and Palestinian Judaism: A Comparison of Patterns of Religion* (Minneapolis: Fortress Press, 1977), pp. 302–303.

118. Frank Moore Cross, *The Ancient Library of Qumran*, 3rd ed. (Minneapolis· Fortress Press, 1995), pp. 71–73, n. 5

119 I was encouraged in my thinking along these lines by A. I. Baumgarten (personal communication, April 13, 1996)

4. Ritual Impurity and Sin in Tannaitic Literature

1 The terms "tannaim" and "tannaitic" are used to distinguish these earlier sages and sources from the later "amoraim," and their "amoraic" sources. The amoraim were the talmudic sages who flourished in both the land of Israel and Babylonia from the third to the fifth

centuries CE. The terms "rabbis" and "rabbinic" are used here as more general terms, including tannaitic as well as amoraic and even later figures and sources.

2. Neither of these two questions is frequently asked in scholarship on rabbinic Judaism. Büchler addresses the second question — concerning *moral* impurity — in his *Studies in Sin and Atonement*, but he does not directly address the first question: the nature of the relationship between *ritual* impurity and sin. One recent treatment of the seccond question can be found in E. P. Sanders, *Jesus and Judaism* (Philadelphia: Fortress Press, 1985), pp. 182–187. Sanders, however, does not deal with the first question.

3. Generally, on these and other rabbinic texts, see H. L. Strack and G. Stemberger, *Introduction to the Talmud and Midrash*, trans. and ed Markus Bockmuehl, 2nd printing (Minneapolis: Fortress Press, 1996), on the Mishnah, Tosefta, and Talmudim, cf. Shmuel Safrai, ed., *The Literature of the Sages, First Part: Oral Tora, Halakha, Mishna, Tosefta, Talmud, External Tractates* (Assen/Maastricht. Van Gorcum, 1987). On the differences between tannaitic and amoraic sources, see Safrai, *The Literature of the Sages*, pp. 82–88. On tannaitic sources in particular, see also Sanders, *Paul and Palestinian Judaism: A Comparison of Patterns of Religion* (Minneapolis: Fortress Press, 1977), pp. 59–84. The Mishnah and Tosefta will be cited by tractate, chapter, and pericope. The Talmudim will be cited by the folio page numbers of the traditional editions. The situation for the *halakhic* midrashim is, unfortunately, less standardized. Citations by portion or chapter will be provided, as well as page numbers to the standard editions: Mekhilta d'Rabbi Ishmael (Horovitz/Rabin); Mekhilta d'RaSHbY (Epstein/Melamed), Sifra (Weiss); Sifre Numbers and Sifre Zutta (Horovitz); Sifre Deuteronomy (Finkelstein); Midrash Tannaim (Hoffmann).

4. These midrashim are also often referred to as *halakhic* (legal) as opposed to *aggadic* (nonlegal, legendary, or theological). Indeed, on the whole, this corpus of midrashim comments on the legal portions of the Pentateuch and focuses on legal matters. And certainly the *aggadic* midrashim, be they homiletic or exegetical, contain significantly less *halakhic* material than the tannaitic midrashim. Yet there is a great deal of *aggadic* material in the tannaitic midrashim. Lauterbach, for instance, estimated that three fifths of the Mekhilta contains *aggadic* material (Lauterbach, *Mekilta*, vol. I, p. xix). It is for this reason, as well as the conviction that these texts do preserve material from the first two centuries of the common era, that these texts are referred to here as "tannaitic" midrashim. On the distinction between *halakhah* and *aggadah*, and between homiletic and exegetical midrashim, see Strack and Stemberger, *Introduction*, pp. 239–240; on the question of what to call these midrashim, see pp 250–251.

5. In addition to these texts for which the manuscript traditions are relatively secure, there are also the following three tannaitic midrashim, which have been reconstructed from fragmentary manuscripts and medieval quotations· the Mekhilta d'Rabbi Shimon bar Yohai (on Exodus), the Sifre Zutta (on Numbers), and the Midrash Tannaim (on Deuteronomy).

6. The first generation of amoraic sages are also quoted in these midrashim.

7. Generally, see Daniel Boyarin, "On the Status of the Tannaitic Midrashim," *Journal of the American Oriental Society* 112.3 (1992)· 455–465.

8. Generally, see Strack and Stemberger, *Introduction*, pp 45–55, cf. Jacob Neusner, *Rabbinic Judaism· Structure and System* (Minneapolis: Fortress Press, 1995), pp. 1–27, Shaye J. D Cohen, "The Modern Study of Ancient Judaism," in *The State of Jewish Studies*, ed. Shaye J. D Cohen and Edward L. Greenstein (Detroit: Wayne State University Press, 1990), pp. 55–73; Peter Schafer, "Research into Rabbinic Literature: An Attempt to Define the Status Quaestionis," *Journal of Jewish Studies* 37.2 (1986): 141–152, Chaim Milikowsky, "The Status Quaestionis of Research in Rabbinic Literature," *Journal of Jewish Studies* 39.2 (1988): 201–211; and Sanders, *Paul and Palestinian Judaism*, pp 59–84

9. See, e.g., *Rabbinic Judaism*, pp. 1–27. For a critique of Neusner's newer method, see Boyarin, "On the Status"; and Shaye J. D. Cohen, "Jacob Neusner, Mishnah, and Counter-

Rabbinics: a Review Essay," *Conservative Judaism* 37.1 (1983): 48–63. See also the more detailed discussion of method in Klawans, "Impurity and Sin in Ancient Judiasm" (dissertation, Columbia University, 1997), pp 184–198.

10. In particular, Neusner's *History of the Mishnaic Law of Purities* can be accurately described as source critical.

11. Regarding the nature of tannaitic sources, refer to the text-critical works of Saul Lieberman: *Tosefeth Rishonim: A Commentary on Manuscripts of the Tosefta and Works of the Rishonim and Midrashim in Manuscripts and Rare Editions*, 4 vols. (Hebrew) (Jerusalem: Bamberger & Wahrmann, 1937–1939); and *Tosefta Ki-Fshuṭah· A Comprehensive Commentary on the Tosefta*, 10 vols. (Hebrew) (New York: Jewish Theological Seminary, 1955–1988). See especially the source-critical works of Jacob Epstein: *Introductions to Tannaitic Literature* (Hebrew) (Jerusalem: Magnes Press; Tel Aviv: Dvir, 1957), and his *Introduction to the Text of the Mishnah* (Hebrew) (Jerusalem: Magnes Press; Tel Aviv: Dvir, 1948). On the composite nature of the Mishnah specifically, see Abraham Goldberg's treatment in Safrai, *The Literature of the Sages*, pp. 211–244. On the tannaitic midrashim, see Finkelstein, "The Sources of the Tannaitic Midrashim," *The Jewish Quarterly Review* 31 (1940–1941): 211–243 (repr. in Finkelstein, *Sifra on Leviticus Volume V* [New York. Jewish Theological Seminary, 1991] pp. 191*–223*).

12. Generally, on the problem of attributions, see Strack and Stemberger, *Introduction*, pp. 59–62; and William Scott Green, "What's in a Name?—The Problematic of Rabbinic 'Biography,'" in *Approaches to Ancient Judaism. Theory and Practice*, ed. William Scott Green (Missoula, Mont.: Scholars Press, 1978), pp. 77–96. Neusner's documentary approach "simply dismisses as not subject to falsification or verification attributions of sayings to named masters" (Neusner, *Rabbinic Judaism*, p. 24). The irony here is that one of the most articulate statements in defense of taking attributions seriously, at least as far as the Mishnah is concerned, is to be found in one of Neusner's own books (*Judaism: The Evidence of the Mishnah* [Chicago: University of Chicago Press, 1981], pp. 17–18). True to the spirit of tannaitic literature, the tannaitic discussion of how to evaluate anonymous and attributed material (M. Edu 1:5–6) is itself an anonymous source, with an attributed dissenting opinion. For a discussion of M. Eduyot 1:5–6 and the issue of attributed minority opinions in Jewish law, see David W. Halivni, *Peshat and Derash: Plain and Applied Meaning in Rabbinic Exegesis* (New York: Oxford University Press, 1991), pp. 163–167. Also regarding attributions, see Halivni, "Reflections on Classical Jewish Hermeneutics," *Proceedings of the American Academy of Jewish Research* 62 (1996): 19–127, esp. pp. 42–46.

13. Generally, see Boyarin, "On the Status," pp. 455–458; Sanders, *Paul and Palestinian Judaism*, pp. 69–75; and Morton Smith, "On the Problem of Method in the Study of Rabbinic Literature," *Journal of Biblical Literature* 92.1 (1973): 112–113. More specifically, see Shamma Friedman, "The Primacy of Tosefta in Mishnah-Tosefta Parallels—*Shabbat* 16, 1" (Hebrew), *Tarbiz* 62 (1993): 313–338. All these *contra* the extreme position advocated in Neusner, *Rabbinic Judaism*, pp. 23–27.

14. See Albert I. Baumgarten, "The Pharisaic *Paradosis*," *Harvard Theological Review* 80.1 (1987): 63–77; Joseph M. Baumgarten, "The Unwritten Law in the Pre-Rabbinic Period," *Journal for the Study of Judaism* 3.1 (1972): 7–29; Safrai, *The Literature of the Sages*, pp. 3–119; cf. Strack and Stemberger, *Introduction*, pp. 31–44.

15. Generally, on the use of *aggadic* sources, see Renée Bloch, "Methodological Note for the Study of Rabbinic Literature," in *Approaches to Ancient Judaism: Theory and Practice*, ed. William Scott Green (Missoula, Mont.: Scholars Press, 1978), pp. 51–75.

16 There is, of course, no Babylonian or Jerusalem Talmud on Mishnah Seder Toharot, with the exception of tractate Niddah, dealing with menstrual impurity (on this topic, see the section on "*Niddah*" in this book). Yet there is a great deal of tannaitic and amoraic material

in both talmudim dealing with issues of ritual impurity. Often these discussions are prompted by the various discussions of ritual impurity that can be found in the tractates of the Mishnah that do have Talmud commentary. For instance, M. Hagigah 2:5–3:8 deals with issues of ritual impurity, and thus B. Hagigah 18b–27a follows suit. To get an idea of how much related extra-mishnaic tannaitic and amoraic material there is, one could glance at the modern talmudic commentary on Mishnah tractates Kelim and Ohalot compiled by Gershon Chanoch Leiner (*Sidrei Toharot*, 2 vols , 2nd ed., ed. Jeruchim Leiner [New York: Noble, 1960]).

17 *Studies*, pp. 270–374.

18 The greatest contributor to our knowledge of tannaitic ritual purity law is Jacob Neusner, whose relevant publications include *The Idea of Purity in Ancient Judaism* (chapter 4 is devoted to aggadic traditions in rabbinic literature), *The History of the Mishnaic Law of Purities* (a 22-volume commentary on Mishnah Seder Toharot and parallel texts), and more recently, *Purity in Rabbinic Judaism*. See also the important discussion in Jacob Neusner and Bruce D. Chilton, "Uncleanness in Formative Judaism: A Moral or an Ontological Category?" in *The Religious Study of Judaism: Description, Analysis, Interpretation: Volume IV Ideas of History, Ethics, Ontology and Religion in Formative Judaism*, ed. Jacob Neusner (Lanham, Md.: University Press of America, 1981), pp. 81–106 Regarding these works, one fundamental criticism needs to be reiterated· Neusner throughout maintains the perspective that references to defilement in this literature are to be understood either as articulations of the notion of ritual impurity, or as metaphors. See, e.g., Neusner, *The Idea*, ch. 4, and more recently Neusner, *Purity in Rabbinic Judaism*, pp. 71–74.

19. See Mishnah Parah 10:1, M. Zabim 4·6, and Albeck's commentary ad loc ; cf. Neusner, *HMLP*, vol. XXII, pp. 63–71; and Harrington, *The Impurity Systems*, pp. 237–239.

20. On the development of the conception of the tent, see Jeffrey L. Rubenstein, "On Some Abstract Concepts in Rabbinic Literature," *Jewish Studies Quarterly* 4.1 (1997): 33–73. Cf. Neusner, *Purity in Rabbinic Judaism*, pp. 88–89.

21. E.g., Neusner, *HMLP*, vol. III, p. 383; vol VIII, p 221; vol. XVI, p. 194; and vol. XVIII, p. 176.

22. E.g., Neusner, *HMLP*, vol. V, p. 230, 251–252; vol. XIII, pp. 250–251; vol X, p. 207; and vol. XIV, pp. 195–197, 202–205.

23. Neusner, *HMLP*, vol. XXII, p. 99 But even here, Neusner recognizes a scriptural foundation, or at least the potential for it.

24. Neusner, *HMLP*, vol. XXII, pp. 186–189, 261, cf. Howard Eilberg-Schwartz, *The Human Will in Judaism: The Mishnah's Philosophy of Intention* (Atlanta: Scholars Press, 1986), esp. pp. 95–143. Eilberg-Schwartz takes a more nuanced view: Even though human intention is a significant theme in Scripture, the Mishnah breaks new ground in ascribing power to human intention with regard to ritual impurity. Eilberg-Schwartz on this point, see Harrington, *The Impurity Systems*, pp. 157–159.

25. Neusner, *HMLP*, vol. XXII, pp. 85–87, 188–189.

26. Milgrom, *Leviticus 1–16*, pp. 485–487; pp. 1005–1006; cf Eilberg-Schwartz, *The Human Will*, pp. 101–108.

27. On the purificatory power of ablutions, see Harrington, *The Impurity Systems*, pp 126–139, where she builds on Milgrom, *Leviticus 1–16*, pp. 957–968. On collected water, see Harrington, *The Impurity Systems*, pp. 133–139.

28. Harrington's more recent work recognizes this fact more clearly See "Interpreting Leviticus in the Second Temple Period Struggling with Ambiguity," in Sawyer, ed., *Reading Leviticus*, pp. 214–229.

29. Mishnah translations here and below are based on Danby, *The Mishnah* (Oxford: Oxford University Press, 1933) The Hebrew text is Albeck's, although the major manuscripts have been consulted, and significant variants will be noted.

30. Birth, circumcision, and burial come up not as topics of their own, but only insofar as they relate to other issues that do receive systematic treatment. For instance, circumcision is dealt with in relation to the possibility of performing the ceremony on the Sabbath (M Shabbat 19:1–6), and burial is dealt with in relation to the conflict between mourning rites and the sanctity of festival days (Moed Katan 3:5–9). The ritual impurity that results from childbirth does come up, of course, in the Sifra dealing with Leviticus 12 (Sifra Parashat Tazria [ed. Weiss, pp. 57c–59d]).

31. Neusner, *HMLP*, vol. XXII, p. 94. But cf. p. 97, where Neusner speaks of "recurrent and natural sources of uncleanness." Cf. Milgrom, *Leviticus 1–16*, p. 1008.

32. Interestingly, while the Yom Kippur service is no less obligatory in tannaitic *halakhah*, that service is less defiling. While Leviticus 16:24 implies that the ritual of sending out the scapegoat renders the priest defiled, M. Yoma 6:6 states that the scapegoat defiles only after it has left Jerusalem.

33. For greater detail on this point, see the introduction to "Sin, Status, and Atonement" in this chapter.

34. Neusner, *Purity in Rabbinic Judaism*, p. 59. Italics in the original.

35 On this passage and its subsequent interpretation, see Milgrom, *Leviticus 1–16*, pp. 307–318.

36. Sifra Dibura de-Hoba, Perek 12, *halakhot* 8–9 (ed Weiss, pp. 23b–c, ed. Finkelstein, p. 176); M. Shebu. 1:4–6.

37. Neusner and Chilton, "Uncleanness in Formative Judaism," pp. 81–85.

38. Klawans, "Notions of Gentile Impurity," pp 302–303 and 308–309.

39. On this point, Milgrom and Neusner in a way concur. See Neusner and Chilton, "Uncleanness in Formative Judaism," pp. 89–95; and Milgrom, *Leviticus 1–16*, pp. 317–318.

40. As has been noted, Büchler does not comment on the question that we are addressing in this chapter: the general relationship between ritual impurity and sin in rabbinic literature. In the chapters of his *Studies* devoted to rabbinic literature, he identifies, dates, and analyzes traditions dealing with the defiling force of sin, that is, moral impurity (*Studies*, ch. 4) and sin and atonement (*Studies*, ch. 5) Yet Büchler does not discuss the tannaitic approach to ritual impurity in any detail. Nor does he offer many specific comments on the relationship between ritual and moral impurity in rabbinic literature. The silence, though, is a pregnant one: The force of his work is to drive a wedge between ritual impurity on the one hand and moral impurity on the other.

41. M. Ter. 8:12 uses the term "defile" in the sense of "rape," which reflects usage in Genesis 34.5; M. Yoma 8:9 uses the term "purify" in the sense of "atone," which reflects the verses quoted in the text (Lev. 16:30, Ezek. 36:25, and Jer. 17:13). These usages will be discussed in the first and last subsections of "Sin, Status, and Atonement" in this chapter.

42. On the biblical, Qumranic, and tannaitic approaches to this form of impurity, see Milgrom, *Leviticus 1–16*, pp. 820–824; and Harrington, *The Impurity Systems*, pp 78–84 (Qumran) and pp. 181–213 (tannaim). On sin and "leprous" impurity in tannaitic sources, see Neusner, *The Idea*, pp. 81–84, *HMLP*, vols VI to VIII (on tractate Negaim), and *Purity in Rabbinic Judaism*, pp 71–74.

43. There is debate among some modern scholars as to whether the tannaim distinguish between "affliction" (נגע) and "leprosy" (צרעת). See Neusner, *HMLP*, vol. VIII, pp. 226–250, where he maintains that there is a distinction between the two. But see Harrington, *The Impurity Systems*, pp. 193–198, where she argues — more persuasively, I think — that the latter term refers to one specific type of affliction while the former refers to defiling afflictions as a whole. Cf. Milgrom, *Leviticus 1–16*, p. 776. This debate is not directly relevant to the question of whether these afflictions come about as a result of sin, and thus the term "defiling afflictions" will be used generally here to refer to any and all of the disorders that bring ritual impurity upon people, clothing, and houses.

44. See, e.g., M. Avot 5:8–9, Avot de-Rabbi Natan A 38 and B 41 (ed. Schechter, pp. 57a–58b), and B. Ber. 5a–b.

45. On sin and punishment in tannaitic Judaism, see Urbach, *The Sages*, pp. 436–444 and 511–513; and Sanders, *Paul and Palestinian Judaism*, pp. 117–147

46. M. Neg 3:1; cf. M. Neg. 12:5 and Sifra Metzorah Parashah 5:10 (ed. Weiss, p 73a).

47 M. Neg. 7·1, M. Nid. 5:3, cf. Lev. R 15:5 (on Lev 13.2) (ed. Margulies, pp. 331–332), which discusses situations where children are born with these afflictions Cf Maimonides, *Mishneh Torah*, Book of Cleanness, The Uncleanness of Leprosy, 9:1· "Anyone can contract uncleanness from leprosy signs, even a day-old child." (trans. Danby, p. 176).

48. M. Neg. 14:9. Although it is embedded within statements attributed to various second-century authorities, the specific tradition in question is anonymous and self-contained and thus could be earlier.

49. Sifre Deut § 274 (ed. Finkelstein, p. 293); the traditions preserved in the Tosefta and the Sifre are also anonymous.

50. T. Negaim 6:7; Sifra Metzorah, Parashah 5:7–9 (ed. Weiss, p. 73a); Sifre Deut. Ki Tetze § 275 (ed. Finkelstein, p. 294), see Lieberman, *Tosefeth Rishonim*, vol. III, p. 193; and Neusner, *Purity in Rabbinic Judaism*, pp. 73–74

51. Neusner has correctly emphasized this point: Neusner, *Purity in Rabbinic Judaism*, pp. 73–74.

52. Interestingly, the above quoted tradition explicitly connects its moral message to an instance of an afflicted house. (This is true of the Sifra as well, as will be seen.) Yet the Tosefta also preserves a tradition to the effect that there is really no such thing as an afflicted house and that Leviticus 14, which deals with afflicted houses, is just there "to teach a (moral) lesson." (T. Neg. 6:1·בית המנוגע לא היה ולא עתיד להיות למה נכתב אלא לומר לך דרוש; cf. B. San. 71a.) If there is no such thing as an afflicted house, then there can be no practical ramifications for T. Negaim 6:7 as it stands either.

53. Consider, for instance, the ways in which priests are depicted in M. Yoma 1:3–6.

54. Compare the amoraic traditions discussed below (e.g., B. Arakhin 16a).

55. Sifra Metzorah, Parashah 5:7–9 (ed. Weiss, p. 73a).

56. Sifre Deut Ki Tetze § 275 (ed. Finkelstein, p. 294).

57. It is not perfectly clear to me in what way these two traditions relate to one another chronologically, though I would tentatively suggest that Sifre § 275 is an abbreviation of the Sifra.

58. Thus Neusner goes too far in drawing a contrast between Scripture and the tannaim in this regard. See Neusner, *The Idea*, pp. 80–81, cf. *HMLP*, vol. VIII, p. 253. There is no "shattered metaphor." In Scripture, ritual defilements can come about as a punishment for sin, and the same holds true in tannaitic literature.

59 Sifre Num. Naso 1 (ed. Horovitz, p. 4). The tradition is discussed by Neusner in *The Idea*, pp. 80–81; *HMLP*, vol VIII, pp. 252–253; and *Purity in Rabbinic Judaism*, p. 72.

60. M. Neg. 12:5; Sifra Metzorah Parashah 5:10 (ed. Weiss, p. 73a).

61. On the distinction between *halakhah* and *aggadah*, see Bloch, "Methodological Note," pp 53–55; Schürer and Vermes, *The History of the Jewish People*, vol. II, pp. 337–355; and Strack and Stemberger, *Introduction*, pp. 16 and 239–240.

62. Generally, on Lev. R., see Strack and Stemberger, *Introduction*, pp.288–291.

63. Margulies ed., pp. 340–348.

64 The ten sins listed in Lev R. 17.3 are idolatry, incest, murder, the desecration of the Name, blasphemy, robbing the public, taking what is not one's own, arrogance, the evil tongue, and the evil eye; ed. Margulies, pp. 374–377. For a discussion of parallels in other midrashic sources, see Margulies's note on p. 374 and cf. Neusner, *The Idea*, pp. 97–102.

65. Lev. R. 18:2–3 (ed. Margulies, pp. 404 and 407). For the most part, the tannaitic

sources limit such discussions to "leprous" impurities, but there are some tannaitic texts that connect *zab* impurity to sin, e.g., Sifre Num Naso 1 (ed. Horovitz, p. 4); cf. Num. R. 7:1.

66. On the other sources, see Margulies's commentary on Lev. R. 17:3 (pp. 374–377).

67. Lev. R. 16·1, end, (ed. Margulies, p. 348); cf. B. Arakhin 15b.

68. E.g., the discussion of arrogance in B. Sot. 5a does not lead into a discussion of defiling afflictions.

69. *Contra* Neusner, *Purity in Rabbinic Judaism*, pp. 73–74.

70. But this fact can be deceptive: there is a large amount of amoraic material in the Jerusalem and Babylonian Talmuds relating to all sorts of impurity, as was noted earlier.

71. Generally, see Shaye J. D. Cohen, "Menstruants and the Sacred in Judaism and Christianity," in *Women's History and Ancient History*, ed. Sarah B. Pomeroy (Chapel Hill and London: University of North Carolina Press, 1991), pp. 273–299. Cohen cites many of the important medieval sources. For a more thorough treatment of the tannaitic material in particular, see Sanders, *Jewish Law*, pp. 155–162. On the Mishnah specifically, see Judith Romney Wegner, *Chattel or Person? The Status of Women in the Mishnah* (New York: Oxford University Press, 1988), pp. 162–65. Generally, on women in rabbinic sources, see Judith Hauptman, *Rereading the Rabbis: A Woman's Voice* (Boulder, Col.: Westview Press, 1998); Kraemer, *Her Share of the Blessings*, pp. 93–105; and Wegner, *Chattel or Person?* On women in ancient Palestine, see Tal Ilan, *Jewish Women in Greco-Roman Palestine* (Peabody, Mass.: Hendrickson, 1996). Generally, on gender in rabbinic Judaism, Boyarin, *Carnal Israel*; on the same theme, one ought also to peruse Neusner, *Androgynous Judaism: Masculine and Feminine in the Dual Torah* (Macon, Ga: Mercer University Press, 1993).

72. E.g., Milgrom, *Leviticus 1–16*, p. 765; Harrington, *The Impurity Systems*, p. 272.

73. The passage, to be sure, speaks in some way of the seclusion of menstruants. But it speaks of the seclusion of corpse-defiled persons in the same way. If the passage is to be understood to state that menstruants were isolated, then it also must be understood to state that those who have contracted corpse impurity were similarly isolated, which is highly unlikely. See Sanders, *Jewish Law*, pp. 157–158.

74. E.g., Milgrom, *Leviticus 1–16*, p. 765.

75. See discussion in chapter 3, section on "Sinful Outsiders."

76. MSS Kaufmann and Parma have the latter reading. See Hauptman, *Rereading the Rabbis*, pp. 170–171, n. 7; and Harrington, *The Impurity Systems*, p. 271.

77. Cohen, "Menstruants and the Sacred," p. 278; Sanders, *Jewish Law*, p. 156; cf Neusner, *Purity in Rabbinic Judaism*, p. 115

78. Hauptman, *Rereading the Rabbis*, pp. 147–148 and 160–162.

79. Cf. Boyarin, *Carnal Israel*, pp. 57–60, 96–97; Boyarin repeatedly cautions against reading later medieval views about women into earlier rabbinic texts.

80. Chapter 1, section on "Gender and Biblical Impurity Systems."

81. Wegner, *Chattel or Person?* p. 163.

82. Paula Fredriksen, "Did Jesus Oppose the Purity Laws?" *Bible Review* 95.2 (1995): 20–25; 42–47; see esp p. 23 (I thank Henriette Klawans for bringing this article to my attention.) The rabbinic attitude toward Gentile menstruants appears to have changed over time; see Büchler, "The Levitical Impurity of the Gentile," pp. 7–15; and Klawans, "Notions of Gentile Impurity," pp. 302–311.

83. Wegner, *Chattel or Person?* p. 163. Cf Boyarin, *Carnal Israel*, pp. 92–93, nn. 25–27.

84. *Contra*, Wegner, *Chattel or Person?* p. 165.

85. Interestingly, while Josephus (e.g., *Jewish War* V:199) explicitly speaks of the exclusion of pure women from the inner courts of the temple, the tannaitic sources, though they speak of a "women's court," do not preserve an explicit ban on the entry of ritually pure women. T. Sukkah 4:1 assumes the separation of men from women in at least one cultic celebration,

but much of tannaitic legislation—for example, the law of the suspected adulteress, to be discussed later—assumes the admission of individual women to the sanctuary. See Tosafot on B. Kiddushin 52b (*ve-ki*), which is cited along with other sources in Cohen, "Menstruants and the Sacred," pp. 282 and 291, n. 31.

86. Sifra Aharei Mot Perek 13:1, 20 (ed. Weiss, pp. 85d and 86c–d), cf M. Ket 3:1; M. Mak. 3:1, and M. Ker. 2:4

87. See B. Shabbat 31b–32a and T. Shabbat 2:10, on which see Lieberman, *Tosefta Ki-Fshuṭah* vol. III, pp. 34–35. See also Abraham Goldberg, *Commentary to the Mishna Shabbat: Critically Edited and Provided with Introduction, Commentary and Notes* (Jerusalem: Jewish Theological Seminary, 1976), pp. 50–54, and Epstein, *Introduction to the Text of the Mishnah*, pp. 121–122. While the mishnaic tradition is anonymous and undisputed, in the toseftan and talmudic parallels the base tradition is subject to discussion by mid- and late second-century tannaim Although they dispute finer points of the tradition, they do not refute the general thrust of the claims made in M. Shabbat 2:6. See also B. Niddah 31b and Avot de-Rabbi Natan A 2 (ed. Schechter, pp. 4b–5a), both discussed in Neusner, *The Idea*, pp 84–88; and Lev. R. 15:5, (ed. Margulies, pp. 331–332), where it is suggested that women who do not adhere to the laws concerning menstruation will give birth to "leprous" children.

88. E.g., Y. Shabbat 2:6 (5b) See discussions in Boyarin, *Carnal Israel*, esp. pp. 90–94; and Kraemer, *Her Share of the Blessings*, pp. 95–103.

89. *Contra* Wegner, *Chattel or Person?* p. 155, who claims that these are positive time-bound commandments, from which women are exempt; but see p. 156 and p. 241, n. 233, which recognize the complexity of the issue of women and obligation. Also *contra* Wegner on this point, see Boyarin, *Carnal Israel*, p. 92, n. 25.

90. Lieberman, *Tosefta Ki-Fshuṭah* vol. III, p. 35; Wegner, *Chattel or Person?* p. 155; cf. B. Shabbat 32a–b.

91. *Chattel or Person?* pp. 163–164; cf. Hauptman, *Rereading the Rabbis*, pp. 150–153.

92. Wegner, *Chattel or Person?* pp. 164–165.

93. Kraemer, *Her Share of the Blessings*, p 103; cf. Y. Ketubot 2:5 (26c), cited by Hauptman, *Rereading the Rabbis*, pp. 247–248.

94. E.g., Sifre Num. § 124 (ed Horovitz, p. 158). Interestingly, the tannaim use the phrase מי נדה primarily when discussing biblical passages using that terminology. Otherwise, they generally refer to the same substance with the phrase מי חטאת; cf., e.g., M. Kel. 1:1 and M. Par. 6:5.

95. See chapter 3, section on "Sin and Defilement."

96. See discussion in Cohen, "Menstruants and the Sacred," pp. 281–287.

97. There is no dearth of scholarship on the Pharisaic *havurah*. A good place as any to start is the classic treatment by Jacob Neusner, "The Fellowship in the Second Jewish Commonwealth," *Harvard Theological Review* 53(1960): 125–142. For a review of contemporary scholarship on the issue, see Sanders, *Jewish Law*, pp. 152–166. Büchler once argued that these rules were late (after 135 CE) and applied only to priests. See *Der galiläische 'Am-ha' Areṣ des zweiten Jahrhunderts* (Vienna: Alfred Hölder, 1906). In regard to these matters, Büchler's view is not accepted here.

98 See also M. Demai 2:2–3; Y. Demai 22d–23a; B. Bekh. 30b–31a; and Avot de-Rabbi Natan A 41 (ed. Schechter, p. 66b). Many of the sources are discussed in Neusner, "The Fellowship," and Chaim Rabin provides a synoptic translation in *Qumran Studies* (Oxford: Oxford University Press, 1957), pp. 1–21. See also Saul Lieberman, "The Discipline in the So-Called Dead Sea Manual of Discipline," *Journal of Biblical Literature* 71 (1952): 199–206; idem., *Tosefta Ki-Fshuṭah*, vol. I, pp. 209–221; and Richard S. Sarason, *A History of the Mishnaic Law of Agriculture, Section Three· A Study of Tractate Demai, Part One: Commentary* (Leiden: E J. Brill, 1979), esp. pp. 69–107.

99. Saldarini, *Pharisees, Scribes and Sadducees*, pp. 216–220; Sanders, *Jesus and Judaism*, pp. 187–188.

100. Such is the thrust of his essay, "Did the Pharisees Eat Ordinary Food in Purity?" in *Jewish Law*, pp. 131–254.

101. Sanders, *Jewish Law*, pp. 149–151.

102. For a more detailed refutation of Sanders's argument, see Harrington, *The Impurity Systems*, pp. 267–281.

103. See, e.g., Schiffman, "Pharisaic and Sadducean Halakhah"; and the discussion in "The Temple Scroll" (chapter 2) and "Impurity and Sin" (chapter 3) of this book.

104. This term refers, apparently, to some intermediate stage in which the initiate is trusted insofar as the purity of hands is concerned. See Lieberman, "The Discipline," pp. 201–202, esp. n. 25; and *Tosefta Ki-Fshutah*, vol. I, pp. 214–215; cf. Rabin, *Qumran Studies*, p. 19.

105. The classic studies comparing the two include Licht, *The Rule Scroll*, pp. 294–303; Lieberman, "The Discipline"; and Rabin, *Qumran Studies*, pp. 1–21.

106. Lieberman, "The Discipline," p. 199. Of course, sinners would not very likely have desired admission.

107. Cf. Cohen, *From the Maccabees*, p. 119, where he contrasts the associates and the Qumran sectarians and suggests that the sectarians were "righteous and therefore pure" while the associates were "pure and therefore righteous."

108. T. Demai 3:4; B. Bekh. 31a.

109. According to Lieberman, the sages' reply (לא באו אלו לכלל) does not mean that they rejected these qualifications outright, but rather that such folk would never be considered for membership at all; see Lieberman, "The Discipline," p. 199, n. 4. R. Yehudah's statement includes one more problematic phrase, which may or may not be an exclusion and which is too problematic to be dealt with here. Albeck's text reads "or minister at a house of study," which does not sound like such an untrustworthy thing to do. Danby translates this phrase as an alternative option for the rejected prospective: "but he should minister at the house of study," which is one possibility. See Rabin, *Qumran Studies*, p. 12, n. 9, where he follows the emendation suggested by Epstein: "or minister in a house where a banquet is held."

110. Rearing small cattle is problematic because they strip the fields; see also Baba Qama 7:7.

111. Rabin, *Qumran Studies*, p. 12, n. 8; cf. M. Bekh. 7:7 and Lev. 21:1.

112. According to a baraitha preserved in B. Sanh 25b. Indeed, all shepherds were considered invalid; cf. Maimonides's commentary to M. Sanh. 3:3 (ed. Qafih, p. 109).

113. For example, by my reckoning (based on Kasovsky's concordance), the term is used in only six distinct pericopae in the entire Sifra.

114. M. Avodah Zarah 1:9 contains a quotation of Deuteronomy 7:26. Cf T. Sot. 6:9 (with quotation of Ezek. 33:26).

115. Sifre Deut. § 99 (ed. Finkelstein, pp. 159–160) comments on Deuteronomy 14:3

116. Cf., e.g., M. Sotah 1:3, "These women are forbidden to eat priestly dues: a woman who says, 'I am impure to you'" (טמאה אני לך). And even though some texts phrase this prohibition in terms of impurity (Sifre Num. Naso 7 [ed. Horovitz, pp 12–13] "she is impure with regard to priestly dues"), the reason for denying these women access to priestly dues is not one of ritual defilement, but one of status. The woman who says to her priestly husband, "I am impure to you" is no longer a valid wife to him and thus can no longer exercise the rights afforded to her by having married a priest.

117. Generally, in tannaitic law, women who were captured were presumed to have been raped, unless the converse could legally be established (cf. M. Ket. 2:9). As we have seen, tragically, too often in our own century this presumption is all too accurate.

118. Generally, on the testimony of women, see Wegner, *Chattel or Person?* pp. 120–123; Wegner discusses M Ket. 2:5–6 on pp. 122–123.

119. The Tosefta parallel (T. Ket. 2·2) includes formulations involving use of the term amf, e g., a witness reports, "she was captured, and she was defiled."

120. See discussion of this passage in chapter 1.

121. Sifre Num. Naso §§ 7–21 (ed. Horovitz, pp. 10–25), and Sifre Zutta on Num 5:11–31 (ed. Horovitz, pp. 232–239). On the ordeal as delineated in the Hebrew Bible, see the literature cited in the discussion in chapter 1. On the ordeal as delineated in the Mishnah, see Wegner, *Chattel or Person?* pp 50–54, 91–93, and Hauptman, *Rereading the Rabbis*, pp. 15–29.

122. The text is obscure: she is brought לשער המזרח שעל פתח שער נקנור.

123. M Mid. 1·4, cf. M. Kel 1:8 and M. Yom. 3:10.

124. See B. Sot. 20b.

125. In M. Ket. 2:5–6, for instance, the woman says to her husband that she is pure. The same is true of M Ter. 8:12, where the Gentiles say to the women that they will rape one or all of them. Many of the usages of the term in M. Sotah, too, involve instances of reported speech (e g., M. Sot. 1:3, 2:5, 3:6, 4.2).

126. See "Moral Impurity" in chapter 1, and the primary and secondary sources cited there; see esp. Büchler, *Studies*, pp. 212–214; and Wright, *The Disposal of Impurity*, pp. 283–285.

127. On idolatry in particular, compare Neusner, *The Idea*, p. 15 (Bible) and pp. 34–38 (ancient Jewish literature) Neusner's treatment is still helpful in that he points to a great number of important texts. As we have said, however, Neusner's analysis falls short by not recognizing the morally defiling force of idolatry in the sources he collects.

128. MS Kaufmann lacks "four cubits."

129. At the conclusion of the discussion of M. Shab 9.1 on B. Shab. 83b, the (late) anonymous redactors of the discussion state quite clearly that the impurity of idols is a rabbinic *halakhah*

130 Cf. Maimonides, *Commentary on the Mishnah*, Introduction to Tractate Kelim (ed. Qafih, vol. III, part 2, p. 14).

131. The principle being discussed is אף על פי שאין ראיה לדבר זכר לדבר. Notably, many of these scriptural "indications" come not from the Pentateuch, but from elsewhere in Scripture See discussion in Goldberg, *Commentary to the Mishna Shabbat*, pp. 175–187; and Sifre Num. § 8 (ed. Horovitz, p. 15 [see esp. Horovitz's note to line 9])

132. See M. Ker. 1:1 and M. Sanh. 7:4.

133 Chapter 3, section on "Sinful Outsiders," and the literature cited there, including Klawans, "Notions of Gentile Impurity," pp. 291–293, 279–299, and 305; and Qimron and Strugnell, *DJD X*, pp. 145–147.

134. Many of the MSS (including Kaufmann and Parma) lack the phrase "and that has killed a person." In this case, however, the printed editions preserve the *lectio difficilior*. See also Tosafot Yom Tob ad loc

135. Cf. T. Yeb. 6:9, Sifre Deut. § 248 (ed. Finkelstein, pp. 276–277).

136. And of course a *mamzer* who is wise takes precedence over an ignorant High Priest (M Hor. 3.8).

137. Generally, see Büchler, *Studies*, pp. 366–374 (on the differences between John the Baptist and the tannaim), and pp 375–456 (on "Atonement of Sin by Sacrifice" and not by ritual purification)

138 For the tannaitic exegesis of Leviticus 16:16, see chapter 5 in this book. On Leviticus 16·30, see M. Yom. 8:9, quoted and discussed later in this section.

139. Cf. Sifra Aharei Mot Perek 8:2 (ed. Weiss, pp. 83a–b). See Epstein, *Introduction to the Text of the Mishnah*, p. 1306; and Judah Goldin, "Reflections on a Mishnah," in *Studies in*

Midrash and Related Literature, ed. Barry L. Eichler and Jeffrey H. Tigay (Philadelphia: Jewish Publication Society, 1988), pp. 141–149.

140. Cf M. Taan. 4:8; M. Mak. 3:16; M. Edu. 8:7.

5. Siluk ha-Shekhinah: *Sin, Defilement, and the Departure of the Divine Presence*

1. See introduction to chapter 4, and Klawans, "The Impurity of Immorality."

2. Many of the relevant sources are of course treated in Büchler, *Studies*, pp. 270–374; see esp. pp. 288–299. See also Schechter, *Aspects*, pp. 205–206 and 222–233.

3. This point was made long ago by Büchler (*Studies*, p. 270), but he did not recognize its significance.

4. Much of what is contained in Perek 13 of our editions of the Sifra is not original to the Sifra and is not "Akiban" in nature. See Weiss's comment on 85d; Epstein, *Intoductions to Tannaitic Literature*, pp. 640–641; and Strack and Stemberger, *Introduction*, pp. 261–263. The passage quoted here, however, is generally considered to be integral to the Sifra itself. On the prohibition against publicly expounding on the incest laws, which may well be related to the lacunae in the Sifra on Leviticus 18 and 20, see M. Hag. 2:1.

5. Sexual sins alone are mentioned in Sifre Deut. § 258 (on Deut. 23:15) (ed. Finkelstein, p. 282); cf. also Sifre Deut. § 226 (on Deut. 22:5, the prohibitions of cross-dressing) (ed. Finkelstein, p. 258). The following sources articulate the morally defiling force of all three major types of transgression: idolatry, incest, and murder: Sifra Aharei Mot, Perek 4:1–2, on Lev. 16:16 (ed. Weiss, p. 81c–d) (quoted in the second section of this chapter; cf. B. Sheb. 7b); Sifre Deut. § 254, on Deut. 23:10 (ed. Finkelstein, p 280); Midrash Tann. Deut., on Deut. 21:23 (ed. Hoffmann, vol. 2, p. 132); Midrash Tann. Deut., on Deut. 24:4 (ed. Hoffmann, vol. 2, p. 156); and B. Shab. 33a. Possibly we ought also to include the baraitha on B. Pes. 57a, discussed in Büchler, *Studies*, pp. 288–292.

6. Cf. Sifra Aharei Mot Parashah 9 (ed. Weiss, p. 85c).

7. In addition to the sources cited in the previous note that mention all three major sins, see Mekhilta De-Rabbi Ishmael Yitro 9, on Exod. 20:18 (ed. Horovitz-Rabin, p. 238); Sifra Kedoshim Perek 7·11, on Lev. 19:31 (ed. Weiss, p. 91a); Sifre Deut. § 51, on Deut. 11:24 (ed. Finkelstein, p. 116); Sifre Deut. § 148, on Deut. 17:2 (ed. Finkelstein, p. 203) See also the sources discussed in Büchler, *Studies*, pp 297–299.

8 *Contra* Büchler, *Studies*, p. 297; Büchler suggests that idolatry was the main concern of the tannaim.

9. In addition to the sources cited above that mention all three major sins, see, Mekhilta De-Rabbi Ishmael Mishpatim 10, on Exod. 21:28 (ed. Horovitz-Rabin, p. 282); Mekhilta De-Rabbi Ishmael Mishpatim 13, on Exod. 22:1 (ed. Horovitz-Rabin, pp. 292–293); Mekhilta De-Rabbi Ishmael Ki Tissa, on Exod. 31·12ff (ed Horovitz-Rabin, p. 340) (attr to R Ishmael); Sifre Num. § 160, on Num. 35:25 (ed. Horovitz, p. 220); Midrash Tann. Deut., on Deut. 21:4 (ed. Hoffmann, vol. 1, p. 125); T. Yoma 1:12, T. Sheb. 1·4, and B. Yoma 85a.

10. Cf. also T. Yoma 1:12 and T. Sheb. 1:4.

11. My translation is based closely on Neusner's. Cf. also B. Yoma 23a–b; Y. Yoma 2:2, 39d, and Sifre Num. § 161 (ed Horovitz, p. 222); cf. Lieberman, *Tosefta Ki-Fshutah*, vol. IV, pp. 735–737.

12. The Bavli reads "may he."

13. If the young priest has not yet died, the knife has not yet been defiled ritually by contact with a corpse.

14. The significant exception is the version preserved in Y. Yoma 2:2, 39d, which lacks the last paragraph as printed above.

15. Neusner, *The Idea*, pp. 76–78. To my knowledge, Neusner does not revisit the analy-

sis of this source in his subsequent writings on impurity in ancient Judaism. See also Büchler, *Studies*, p. 297, n. 1. On textual matters, of course, see Lieberman, *Tosefta Ki-Fshuṭah*, vol. IV, pp. 735–737.

16. Neusner perhaps bases his view on Lieberman's comments (*Tosefta Ki-Fshuṭah*, vol. IV, p. 736)

17. See Lieberman, *Tosefta Ki-Fshuṭah*, vol. IV, pp 735–736.

18. Lieberman, *Tosefta Ki-Fshuṭah*, vol. IV, p. 736.

19. Neusner, *The Idea*, p. 77.

20. B. Yoma 23a–b

21. Again, cf B. Yoma 23a–b.

22. In addition to the sources cited below, see B. San. 7a. Schechter discusses some of these traditions in *Aspects*, pp. 229–230.

23. The passage is quoted in full in chapter 2, third section.

24. Cf. Finkelstein, *Sifre Deuteronomy*, p. 258, n. to line 12. The definition of *gezerah shavah* is subject to debate. See Strack and Stemberger, *Introduction*, pp. 18–19, and Michael Chernick, *Gezerah Shavah: Its Various Forms in Midrashic and Talmudic Sources* (Hebrew) (Lod, Israel: Haberman Institute, 1994)

25. Sifre Deut. § 295, on Deut. 25:16 (ed. Finkelstein, p. 314)

26. In this respect I do not think we can distinguish too strongly between arrogance and deceit. It is for that very reason that I do not count arrogance as a source of moral impurity in its own right, but subsume the discussion of arrogance under the discussion of deceit.

27. 1QpHab VIII:8–13, discussed in chapter 3, section on "Sin and the Sanctuary in the Habakkuk Pesher. For other tannaitic and amoraic traditions related to arrogance, see B. Sotah 4b–5a.

28. See, e.g., 1QS IV:15–26; cf. discussion in chapter 3, section on "Sin and Defilement."

29. Translation based on R. Hammer, *Sifre on Deuteronomy*.

30. Hoffmann, ed., vol. 2, p. 132.

31. Sifre Deut. § 221 (ed. Finkelstein, p. 254), cf. M. Sanh. 6:4 and B. Sanh. 45b.

32. 11QT LXIV·6–13. On this passage and additional parallels in ancient Jewish literature, see Moshe J. Bernstein, "כי קללת אלקים תלוי (Deut. 21:23): A Study in Early Jewish Exegesis," *The Jewish Quarterly Review* 74.1 (1983): 21–45.

33. (Ed Horovitz, pp. 160–161); cf. Sifre Num. § 129, on Num 19:20 (ed. Horovitz, pp. 167–168); cf also Sifre Zutta Num. 19:13 (ed. Horovitz, pp. 308–309), which interprets Numbers 19·13 along similar lines.

34. See Milgrom, *Numbers*, p. 161.

35. (Ed. Finkelstein, pp. 159–160); cf. Midrash Tann. Deut. 14:3 (ed. Hoffmann, vol 1, p. 74).

36. We could point to further examples: see, e.g., B. Pes. 17a and the exegesis there of Hag. 2:13.

37. On the rabbinic conception of the *Shekhinah*, see Arnold M. Goldberg, *Untersuchungen über die Schekhinah in der Frühen Rabbinischen Literatur* (Berlin: Walter de Gruyter, 1969); Moore, *Judaism*, vol. 1, pp. 434–438; Raphael Patai, *The Hebrew Goddess*, 3rd enlarged ed (Detroit. Wayne State University Press, 1990), pp. 96–101; Gershom Scholem, *On the Mystical Shape of the Godhead: Basic Concepts in the Kabbalah* (New York· Schocken, 1991), ch. 4, esp. pp. 147–157; Urbach, *The Sages*, pp. 37–65; and Ellen Umansky, "Shekhinah," in *The Encyclopedia of Religion*, ed. Mircea Eliade (New York: Macmillan, 1987), vol. 13, pp. 236–239. On the theological issues relating to sin and the Divine Presence, see Reuven (Robert Alan) Hammer, "The God of Suffering," *Conservative Judaism* 31 (1976–1977): 34–41. On the ascent and descent of the *Shekhinah*, see, e.g., Avot de-Rabbi Natan A 34 (ed. Schechter, p. 51b); and Genesis Rabbah 19:8.

38. Generally, see Strack and Stemberger, *Introduction*, pp 247–251. The pioneering work on the tannaitic midrashim in this regard was done by D. Z. Hoffmann, whose work on Leviticus proved so helpful.

39. These terms ("Akiban" and "Ishmaelian") will be used here more out of convenience than out of any conviction regarding the origin and development of these texts.

40. Sifra Kedoshim, Perek 4:1, on Lev. 19:15 (ed. Weiss, pp. 88d–89a). Similar traditions appear in the Sifra and Sifre with regard to various sins: Sifra Kedoshim Perek 8:5, on Lev. 19:35 (ed. Weiss, p. 91a) (also deceit); Sifre Deut. § 148, on Deut. 17:2 (ed Finkelstein, p. 203) (idolatry); § 226, on Deut. 22:5 (ed. Finkelstein, p 258) (cross-dressing); § 295, on Deut. 25.16 (ed. Finkelstein, p. 314) (deceit). See also Sifra Kedoshim, Parashah 10:8, on Lev. 20:3 (ed Weiss, p. 91c), which begins the series not with "defiles the land" but with "defiles the sanctuary." This passage will be discussed in greater detail later.

41. Mekhilta De-Rabbi Ishmael Yitro 9, on Exod. 20.18 (ed. Horovitz-Rabin, p. 238) (deceit); Mekhilta De-Rabbi Ishmael Mishpatim 10, on Exod. 21:28 (ed. Horovitz-Rabin, p. 282) (bloodshed); Sifre Num. § 161, on Num. 35:34 (ed. Horovitz, p. 222) (murder); Midrash Tann. Deut., on Deut 21:4 (ed. Hoffmann, vol. 1, p 125) (bloodshed).

42. For a survey of some of these disputes, see Urbach, *The Sages*, pp. 51–52.

43. E.g., Mekhilta de-Rabbi Ishmael Bo (de-Paschah) Parashah 14 (ed. Horovitz-Rabin, pp. 51–52); Sifre Num. § 84 (ed. Horovitz, p. 83). Although these traditions emphasize that God remains with the people even in their sinfulness, they do not strictly speaking conflict with the idea that moral impurity brings about the withdrawal of the Divine Presence

44 Baraitha attributed to R. Yosi, on B Sukkah 5a (top).

45. The same can be said of the Temple Scroll; see 11QT XXIX:3–10.

46. (Ed. Horovitz, p. 4); cf. Sifre Num § 161, on Num. 35:34 (ed. Horovitz, p. 222). Compare the discussion in Neusner, *The Idea*, pp. 80–82

47. See chapter 4, section on *Negaim*.

48. *Contra* Büchler, *Studies*, p. 297, n. 1.

49. Cf. Sifra Metzora Perek 9:7, on Lev. 15:31 (ed. Weiss, p. 79b). Note also the traditions that emphasize the dangers posed by ritual impurity at Sinai: Mekhilta De-Rabbi Ishmael Yitro 3, on Exod 19:13 (ed. Horovitz-Rabin, p. 213); Mekhilta De-RaShBY to Exod. 19:13 (ed. Epstein-Melamed, p 141). These traditions do not imply that ritual impurity in general causes the departure of the Divine Presence, but only that ritual impurity in close proximity to the sacred could pose such a problem. Indeed, the danger in these sources is not that the Divine Presence will depart if the ritually impure come too close. The danger is that those who are impure will be struck by God (cf. Exod. 19:24).

50. See, for example, Sifra Kedoshim, Perek 4:1, on Lev. 19:15 (ed. Weiss, pp. 88d–89a) quoted above in our discussion of deceit. See also Sifra Kedoshim Perek 8:5, on Lev. 19:35 (ed. Weiss, p. 91a) (also deceit); Sifre Deut. § 148, on Deut. 17:2 (ed. Finkelstein, p 203) (idolatry); § 226, on Deut. 22.5 (ed. Finkelstein, p. 258) (cross-dressing); § 295, on Deut. 25.16 (ed. Finkelstein, p. 314) (deceit).

51. See "Moral Impurity" in chapter 1 for a discussion of the morally defiling force of idolatry in biblical literature. A number of nonpentateuchal passages do state that idolatry defiles the land (e.g., Jer 2).

52. See, for example, Mekhilta de-Rabbi Ishmael Yitro 9 (ed. Horovitz-Rabin, p. 238), quoted in the first section of this chapter, and Sifre Deut. § 148, on Deut. 17:2 (ed. Finkelstein, p. 203).

53 If this observation is correct, then we need to reconsider Milgrom's assumption that sin produces an aerial miasma (*Leviticus 1–16*, p. 257).

54. On the rabbinic avoidance of prophetic sources in the determination of *halakhah*, see, e g , B. Hagigah 10b. The Qumran sectarians, by contrast, did derive law from the prophets. See, e.g., 4QMMT C 10, discussed in Qimron and Strugnell, *DJD* X, pp. 132–133; 1QS VIII·15–16, discussed in Schiffman, *Halakhah at Qumran*, p 26.

55. I owe this observation to Prof. David W. Halivni. On the use of the term *Shekhinah* in rabbinic sources, see Urbach, *The Sages*, pp. 41–44

56. Strack and Stemberger, *Introduction*, p. 16.

57. This, too, is indicative of the *aggadic* nature of these traditions. On the stability of *aggadah*, see Bloch, "Methodological Note," p. 54, and Strack and Stemberger, *Introduction*, p. 16

58 Josephus makes no such claim in his earlier writing. On Josephus and the Pharisees, see Neusner, *From Politics to Piety: The Emergence of Pharisaic Judaism* (New York: Ktav, 1979), pp. 45–66.

59 Cf. *Jewish War* II:455, IV:150, 201; VI:300. See discussion in Steve Mason, *Josephus and the New Testament* (Peabody, Mass.: Hendrickson, 1992), pp. 62–63. I thank Paula Fredriksen for bringing Josephus's view on this matter to my attention

60. Milgrom, *Leviticus 1–16*, pp. 258–261

61. One way of understanding the notion of *Siluk ha-Shekhinah* is by comparison with the better-known notion of *Hester Panim* — the hiding of God's face *Siluk ha-Shekhinah* is similar in that it is a punitive act of transcendence, but since it involves not only hiding, but removal, it would appear to be more severe. Yet interestingly, some tannaitic sources juxtapose the two images. See, e.g., Sifre Deut. § 320 (on Deut. 32:20).

62. Heschel, *The Prophets* (New York: Harper & Row, 1962), p. 14

63. E.g., Douglas, "Sacred Contagion," pp. 95–99; and *In the Wilderness*, pp. 152–157.

64. Harrington, *The Impurity Systems*

65 See chapter 4, section on *Avodah Zarah*.

66. Tannaitic sources (baraithot) quoted on B. Shabbat 83a and B. Niddah 34a state unequivocally that ritual Gentile impurity is a tannaitic innovation. Similarly, a baraitha on B. Shabbat 14b similarly states that the ritual impurity of Gentile lands also came about as the result of a tannaitic decree.

67. Fuller development of this argument can be found in Klawans, "The Notions of Gentile Impurity." Despite the relative length of that article, much more remains to be said about the ritual and moral impurity of Gentiles Indeed, it would require a book-length work to deal fully with the issues relating to Gentiles in tannaitic *halakhah*. The present discussion is limited to the concerns of this book I understand that a book-length study of Gentile impurity is currently being prepared by Christine E Hayes

68. Alon, "The Levitical Uncleanness of Gentiles," p 147.

69. See Klawans, "Notions of Gentile Impurity," p. 286, n. 3. Some of these works will be discussed in the introduction to chapter 6.

70 B. Shabbat 14b; Y Shabbat I 3d.

71. Alon, "The Levitical Uncleanness of Gentiles," pp. 180–186; cf. Gerson D Cohen, "Zion in Rabbinic Literature," in *Studies in the Variety of Rabbinic Cultures* (Philadelphia. Jewish Publication Society, 1991), pp. 19–38, esp. p. 25.

72 Cf Büchler, *Studies*, pp. 216–218.

73. Cf B. Shab. 145b–146a; and B. Avodah Zarah 22b. Translation based on Soncino edition.

74. Büchler, *Studies*, pp. 316–317.

75. For a more general discussion of the significance of the tradition attributed to R Yohanan, with regard to gender and Original Sin, see Boyarin, *Carnal Israel*, pp. 80–84.

6. Ritual and Moral Impurity in the New Testament

1. For a survey of New Testament passages relating to impurity, see Cothenet, "Pureté et impureté," pp. 528–554; Friedrich Hauck, "Clean and Unclean in the NT," *TDNT*, vol. III (s.v. "καθαρός"), pp. 423–426; and Hübner, "Unclean and Clean (NT)," pp. 741–745.

2. Neusner's treatment in *The Idea*, pp. 59–64 is disappointing; cf Booth, *Jesus and the Laws of Purity*, p. 15. It is also important to note that Büchler did not subject New Testament sources to any detailed scrutiny in his *Studies*. He did devote effort to New Testament sources elsewhere, and he even composed a study on Mark 7:1–23: "The Law of Purification in Mark 7:1–23," *Expository Times* 21 (1909–1910): 34–40. But in this article, composed some thirty years before the *Studies*, Büchler displays no interest in the defiling force of sin.

3. See "Sinful Outsiders" in chapter 3 and "The Status of Sinners" in chapter 4; and see Klawans, "Notions of Gentile Impurity," pp. 291–293, 279–299, and 305.

4. Qimron and Strugnell, *DJD* X, pp. 145–147.

5. See chapter 4, section on "The Status of Sinners."

6. See, for example, Malina, *The New Testament World*, pp. 159–162; Neyrey, "The Idea of Purity," pp. 95–97; Neyrey, "The Symbolic Universe," p. 282; and Rhoads, "Social Criticism," pp. 146–149 As we will see in the section on "Jesus and the Pharisees," Marcus J. Borg's works fall into the same trap: see Fredriksen, "Did Jesus Oppose?" pp. 23–25; and Borg, *Jesus in Contemporary Scholarship* (Valley Forge, Penn.: Trinity Press International, 1994), pp. 101–112.

7. See, for example, Malina, *The New Testament World*, p. 160, Neyrey, "The Idea of Purity," p. 100; and Rhoads, "Social Criticism," pp. 144–149. Again, Borg's works make the same error: see Fredriksen, "Did Jesus Oppose?" pp. 23–25. See also the discussions in "Sinful Outsiders" in chapter 3, and Excursus 1; and Klawans, "Notions of Gentile Impurity."

8. Neyrey, "The Idea of Purity," p 98.

9 Rhoads, "Social Criticism," p. 147; again, cf. Fredriksen, "Did Jesus Oppose?" pp. 23–25.

10. Douglas, *Purity and Danger*, p. 35.

11. Malina, *The New Testament World*, pp. 153–154; Neyrey, "The Idea of Purity," pp. 92–93; "The Symbolic Universe," pp. 274–275, 281–282; and Rhoads, "Social Criticism," pp. 151–152.

12. Neyrey, "The Idea of Purity," pp. 98, 101; "The Symbolic Universe," pp. 275–276, 282; Rhoads, "Social Criticism," p. 149; and in a rather idiosyncratic way, Malina, *The New Testament World*, pp. 154–157. Borg too makes the same error (*Jesus in Contemporary Scholarship*, p. 109).

13 Cf. Neyrey, "The Idea of Purity," pp. 105 and 107, and Borg, *Jesus in Contemporary Scholarship*, p. 109.

14. This very point was made clearly years ago by Sanders (*Jesus and Judaism*, pp 182–187) and quite recently by Fredriksen ("Did Jesus Oppose?" pp. 23–25).

15. Even those studies that do distinguish between ritual and moral defilements typically do not define moral impurity and do not trace the notion back to its biblical origins. This is true of both Cothenet, "Pureté et impureté," and Hauck's entry in *TDNT*, s.v. "καθαρός."

16. *Conta* Borg, *Jesus in Contemporary Scholarship*, pp. 97–126, and *Jesus, a New Vision: Spirit, Culture, and the Life of Discipleship* (San Francisco Harper & Row, 1987). Both of these works update and adapt Borg's earlier *Conflict, Holiness and Politics in the Teachings of Jesus* (New York: Edwin Mellen, 1984). See also Borg's introduction to the new edition of *Conflict, Holiness, and Politics* (Harrisburg, Penn.: Trinity Press International, 1998), pp. 1–17.

17. A number of other factual errors could be documented. Neyrey, "The Idea of Purity," p. 101; and Rhoads, "Social Criticism," p. 149, both assume that spittle is a source of ritual de-

filement, which is not the case. Spittle can be a means of transferring ritual defilement (Lev. 15.8), but in itself it is not necessarily ritually impure.

18. As one might imagine, there is no dearth of literature on John the Baptist. One could begin with almost any gospel commentary or any one of the many recent books on Jesus, many of which deal with John as well. One particularly thorough recent treatment of John is in John P. Meier, *A Marginal Jew· Rethinking the Historical Jesus, Volume Two: Mentor, Message, and Miracles* (New York: Doubleday, 1994), pp. 19–233. On baptism in particular, see pp. 49–56; for further bibliography, see pp. 63–64. For a discussion of John situated within the history of Christian baptism, one would do well to begin with G. R. Beasley-Murray, *Baptism in the New Testament* (London: Macmillan, 1962). Finally, John's baptism, asceticism, and his desert locale have occasioned many comparisons to Qumran; it has even been argued that John was a member of the sect or came under its influence. See the classic study by William H. Brownlee, "John the Baptist in the New Light of Ancient Scrolls," in *The Scrolls and the New Testament*, ed. Krister Stendahl (New York: Crossroad, 1992), pp 33–53 (orig. pub. in 1957). A recent thorough treatment of a number of these questions can be found in Joan E. Taylor's *The Immerser: John the Baptist within Second Temple Judaism* (Grand Rapids, Mich.· William B. Eerdmans, 1997). On John and the Essenes, see pp. 15–48, which also appeared as, "John and the Essenes," *Journal of Jewish Studies* 47.2 (1996). 256–285. See also Robert L. Webb, *John the Baptizer and Prophet: A Socio-Historical Study* (Sheffield: JSOT Press, 1991).

19. The most important passages on John's life and message are Matthew 3:1–17; Mark 1:2–11; Luke 3:1–22; and John 1:19–34 (Aland Synopsis §§ 13–18). On John's death, see Matthew 14.3–12 and Mark 6:17–29 (Aland Synopsis §§ 17 and 144). According to some, Matthew 3:7–12, 11:2–19, and parallels are to be assigned to the hypothetical source known as Q. On John the Baptist and Q see Meier, *Marginal Jew*, vol. 2, pp 177–181.

20. *Ant.* XVIII: 116–119.

21. Meier, *Marginal Jew*, vol. 2, p. 21.

22. On Josephus's testimony regarding Jesus, see, Meier, *Marginal Jew*, vol. 1, pp. 56–88.

23. On Josephus's testimony regarding John, see Meier, *Marginal Jew*, vol. 2, pp. 56–62.

24. Although the point is disputed, it is widely accepted (and I tend to agree) that John's baptism was, at least ideally, not to be repeated. Yet it is important to point out that the sources do not state in so many words that it was to be performed only once. See Meier, *Marginal Jew*, vol. 2, p. 51, where he defends the scholarly inference that John's baptism was a one-time rite by noting (1) that John's baptism had to be administered (and thus could not be repeated at will but only when one who wished to repeat it could track John down), and (2) that with John's heightened eschatology it is unlikely that he believed there was enough time for his followers to transgress, atone, and repeat the rite, all before the coming of the end-time.

25. For parallels, cf. Aland's Synopsis, § 13. Translations from the New Testament are taken from or based upon the New Revised Standard Version.

26. Cf. Matthew 3:2//Luke 3:3; Matthew 3.6//Mark 1:5; Matthew 3:8//Luke 3:8; Matthew 3:11.

27. *Antiquities* XVIII:117.

28. *Contra* Flusser, "The Dead Sea Sect," pp. 242–246; and "The Baptism of John," pp. 84–89. Flusser's understanding of John's baptism is surprisingly close to that of Josephus. According to Flusser, atonement was to precede baptism, and the purpose of baptism was to remove ritual impurity. Cf. Taylor, *The Immerser*, pp. 88–100 Taylor's view is close to that of Flusser (and Josephus) although Taylor's treatment is more nuanced.

29. So Meier, *Marginal Jew*, vol. 2, p. 55.

30. See discussions of atonement in Sanders, *Paul and Palestinian Judaism*.

31. Again, cf. Meier, *Marginal Jew*, vol. 2, p. 55.

32. See Meier, *Marginal Jew*, vol. 2, pp. 60–61, on Josephus's attempts to cast John in a certain Jewish-Hellenistic mold; cf. Webb, *John the Baptizer*, pp. 34–35.

33. For more on John's baptism as a ritual of atonement see Beasley-Murray, *Baptism*, pp 32–34; and Meier, *Marginal Jew*, vol. 2, pp 53–55

34. Matthew 3:7–10//Luke 3:7–9 (Aland Synopsis § 14), and Matthew 3:11–12//Mark 1:7–8//Luke 3:15–18//John 1.24–8 (Aland Synopsis § 16). On these passages, see Meier, *Marginal Jew*, vol. 2, pp. 27–40; on eschatology in particular, see pp. 28–33.

35. Meier, *Marginal Jew*, vol 2, p. 55.

36. Meier, *Marginal Jew*, vol. 2, p. 20–21 and 60–61.

37 See, e.g., Borg, *Jesus in Contemporary Scholarship*, pp. 69–96, esp. pp. 77–78.

38. For a discussion of John's baptism in the context of Jewish purity rituals, see Taylor, *The Immerser*, pp 49–100.

39. E.g., *Special Laws* I:256–261, discussed along with other passages in the Introduction to Part II of this book.

40. *Contra* Taylor, *The Immerser*, pp. 49–100.

41. Cf. Meier, *Marginal Jew*, vol. 2, p. 51.

42. Cf. Taylor, *The Immerser*, p. 23, and idem., "John the Baptist," p. 258.

43. Again, *contra* Flusser, "The Dead Sea Sect," p. 244, and "The Baptism of John," p. 111.

44. Meier, *Marginal Jew*, vol. 2, pp. 43–46.

45. On the Spirit in the scrolls and the New Testament, see Flusser, "The Dead Sea Sect," pp. 246–252, and "The Baptism of John," pp. 89–93.

46 Taylor, *The Immerser*, pp. 15–24; cf. "John the Baptist," pp. 256–259.

47. Matthew 3:3; Mark 1:3; Luke 3:4; John 1:23, and 1QS VIII:13–16 and IX:19–20

48. Taylor, *The Immerser*, pp. 25–29; cf "John the Baptist," pp. 259–263; quote from. p. 262.

49. Taylor, *The Immerser*, p. 20.

50. Meier, *Marginal Jew*, vol. 2, p. 51; Taylor, *The Immerser*, p. 20.

51 It is also important to recall that according to Hebrew Bible, ritual immersion was not in itself purificatory, for the individual still had to wait until sunset before becoming ritually pure (e.g., Lev. 15:8). The tannaim (and, I presume, the Pharisees before them) believed that one who bathed before sunset (the *tebul yom*) was partially pure and could come into contact with anything but holy things. John's baptism thus has another dissimilarity to Jewish ritual purification: the former is, presumably, fully effective immediately, while the latter requires the setting of the sun before full purification is achieved.

52. The classic source on the rabbinic conversion ceremony is B. Yeb. 47a–b. See Shaye J. D Cohen, "The Rabbinic Conversion Ceremony," *Journal of Jewish Studies* 41 2 (1990): 177–203.

53. The classic study remains H. H. Rowley, "Jewish Proselyte Baptism and the Baptism of John," *Hebrew Union College Annual* 15 (1940): 313–334. See also Beasley-Murray, *Baptism*, pp. 18–31; Meier, *Marginal Jew*, vol. 2, pp. 51–52; and Taylor, *The Immerser*, pp. 20 and 64–69.

54. See Shaye J D Cohen, "Conversion to Judaism in Historical Perspective," pp. 37–39; cf Beasley-Murray, *Baptism*, pp. 19–20; Meier, *Marginal Jew*, vol. 2, p. 52; and Taylor, *The Immerser*, pp. 64–65.

55 The same conclusion is reached by Beasley-Murray, *Baptism*, p. 42; Meier, *Marginal Jew*, vol 2, p. 52; and Taylor, *The Immerser*, p. 69.

56 See "A Single Symbolic System?" in chapter 1, cf. discussion of Ezekiel 36 in chapter 1, section on "Moral Impurity" See also the discussion of these passages in Büchler, *Studies*, pp 245–252; and Beasley-Murray, *Baptism*, pp 8–10. One should note too the discussion of John the Baptist in Büchler, *Studies*, pp. 366–374.

57. Mark 11:32, Meier, *Marginal Jew,* vol. 2, pp 28–29 and 46–49; cf Taylor, *The Immerser,* pp. 223–234.

58. Some of the important recent treatments have already been mentioned, including works by Borg, Meier, and Sanders. Other important voices include John Dominic Crossan, Geza Vermes, and the "Jesus Seminar." See, e.g , Crossan, *The Historical Jesus: The Life of a Mediterranean Jewish Peasant* (New York: Harper Collins, 1991); Vermes, *Jesus the Jew. A Historian's Reading of the Gospels* (Philadelphia, Fortress Press, 1981); and Robert W. Funk, Roy W. Hoover, and the Jesus Seminar, eds. *The Five Gospels: The Search for the Authentic Words of Jesus* (New York: Polebridge Press, 1993). For surveys of works on the historical Jesus, see Borg's *Jesus in Contemporary Scholarship;* Ben Witherington III, *The Jesus Quest. the Third Search for the Jew of Nazareth* (Downers Grove, Ill.· InterVarsity Press, 1995); and the collection of essays on Jesus in *Theology Today* 52 1 (1995), which contains articles by Borg, Fredriksen, and Howard Clark Kee, among others.

59. Sanders, *Jewish Law,* p. 90 For a discussion of Sanders's work, see Witherington, *The Jesus Quest,* pp. 116–136. Sanders, to his credit, is reticent to associate the synoptic Jesus with the historic Jesus (*Jewish Law,* p. 1). It would seem, however, that what would apply to Sanders's synoptic Jesus would apply all the more so to the historic Jesus. If the synoptic Jesus did not reject the law, then the historic Jesus most assuredly did not. After reading the first essay in *Jewish Law* ("The Synoptic Jesus and the Law"), one can only assume that Sanders has satisfied the goal he set in *Jesus and Judaism,* p. 265: "I think that further consideration of the evidence, however, will lead to the conclusion that there was no substantial conflict between Jesus and the Pharisees with regard to Sabbath, food, and purity laws."

60. On food, see Sanders, *Jewish Law,* pp. 23–28; on ritual purity, see pp. 29–42; and cf. pp 90–96

61. *Jesus and Judaism,* pp. 51–58. In particular, Sanders discusses Joseph Klausner, *Jesus of Nazareth: His Life, Times, and Teaching,* trans Herbert Danby (New York: Bloch, 1989), and Vermes, *Jesus the Jew.* One should also note the view of Yehezkel Kaufmann in *Christianity and Judaism: Two Covenants,* trans C. W. Efroymson (Jerusalem: Magnes Press, 1988), esp. pp. 49–71. On the history of Jewish scholarship on Jesus, see Susannah Heschel, *Abraham Geiger and the Jewish Jesus* (Chicago: University of Chicago Press, 1998), esp. pp. 235–239.

62. *Jesus in Contemporary Scholarship,* pp. 111–112; cf. also *Jesus, a New Vision,* pp. 125–171, and *Conflict, Holiness, and Politics.* For a review of Borg's work in general, see Witherington, *The Jesus Quest,* pp. 98–108, 115.

63. One important difference concerns eschatology, which is central to Sanders's Jesus but not Borg's. See the reviews by Witherington cited above.

64 Fredriksen, "Did Jesus Oppose?"

65. E.g , Borg, *Jesus, a New Vision,* pp 86–87, and *Jesus in Contemporary Scholarship,* p. 109.

66. *On the Migration of Abraham* 89.

67. 1 Macc. 1:10–15; 2 Macc. 4.7–22. Generally, see Martin Hengel, *Judaism and Hellenism* (Minneapolis: Fortress Press, 1974), pp. 277–314.

68 On Paul, see the third section of this chapter.

69 On "Judaizing" among early Christians, see Marcel Simon, *Verus Israel: A Study of the Relations between Christians and Jews in the Roman Empire (AD 135–425)* (Oxford: Oxford University Press, 1986), pp. 306–338.

70 Translation here modified after NRSV.

71. For parallels see Aland's Synopsis, § 195, and Kloppenborg's Q-Synopsis, § 34. For an analysis of this saying in light of tannaitic sources, see Neusner, "'First Cleanse the Inside': The 'Halakhic' Background of a Controversy Saying," *New Testament Studies* 22 (1976): 486–495.

72 "For, nothing that enters your mouth will defile you [plur.]. Rather, it is precisely what comes out of your mouth that will defile you" (Gospel of Thomas 14 = MS NHC II, 35:24–25). Translation from Bentley Layton, *The Gnostic Scriptures: A New Translation with Annotations and Introductions* (Garden City, N.Y.: Doubleday & Co., 1987).

73. Pap. Oxyrynchus 840. The Greek text can conveniently be found in the Aland Synopsis, § 150, p. 219. English translations can be found in all the major collections of apocryphal Gospels. The manuscript is generally dated to the fourth century, though the composition itself is generally considered to be earlier. (There is no agreement, though, on how much earlier.) See discussion in Booth, *Jesus and the Laws of Purity*, pp. 211–213. For an interesting but dated discussion of the purity practices discussed in the fragment, see Buchler, "The New 'Fragment of an Uncanonical Gospel,'" *Jewish Quarterly Review* (o.s.) 20 (1908): 330–346.

74. See E. P. Sanders and Margaret Davies, *Studying the Synoptic Gospels* (London: SCM Press; Philadelphia: Trinity Press International, 1989), pp. 51–119. Also see the excellent discussion on method for the study of the synoptic Gospels in Meier, *Marginal Jew*, vol. 1, pp. 1–201, conveniently summarized in vol 2, pp. 4–7.

75. This point is widely granted. See, e.g., Booth, *Jesus and the Laws of Purity*, pp. 46–47; and Cothenet, "Pureté et impureté," pp. 533–534, both of whom quickly review earlier scholarship.

76. See Funk et al., *The Five Gospels*, p. 69, where the saying is printed in pink (for an explanation of their color scheme, see p. 36).

77. For a detailed treatment of the chapter as a whole, see Booth, *Jesus and the Laws of Purity*, pp. 55–114; and Paschen, *Rein und Unrein*, pp 153–194.

78. This is the argument made by Heikki Räisänen in "Jesus and the Food Laws: Reflections on Mark 7:15," *Journal for the Study of the New Testament* 16 (1982): 79–100

79. See Booth, *Jesus and the Laws of Purity*, pp. 49–50, for a review of scholarly opinion. Booth's own view is that the phrase is indeed a secondary gloss

80. "Jesus and the Food Laws," pp. 86–88.

81. Sanders argues along a line similar to that of Räisänen, but Sanders's argument is much more nuanced. He generally denies the authenticity of Mark 7:15, because Jesus could not have rejected the food laws, and because if he had, that fact would have been remembered in early Christian debates about food laws. Such is Sanders's argument in *Jesus and Judaism*, pp. 265–266; *Jewish Law*, pp. 23–28. But Sanders also grants that the saying could be authentic if its original intent had nothing to do with food (*Jewish Law*, p. 28). See also Sanders, *The Historical Figure of Jesus* (London: Penguin, 1993), pp. 218–223.

82. Räisänen is taken to task by Dunn in his "Jesus and Ritual Purity: A Study of the Tradition-History of Mark 7:15," *A cause de l'évengile, Mélanges offerts a Dom Jacques Dupont*, Lectio Divina 123 (Saint-Andre: Editions du Cerf, 1985), pp. 251–276. Reprinted with an "additional note" in Dunn, *Jesus, Paul, and the Law: Studies in Mark and Galatians* (Louisville, Ky.: Westminster/John Knox Press, 1990), pp. 37–60. (Pagination here follows the reprint.) Dunn here carefully scrutinizes the variables that one must take into account when discerning the history of a New Testament text: redactional elements, translation, reformulation, and original context. In my opinion Dunn presents a well-organized, reasoned refutation of Räisänen's argument, arguing convincingly for the authenticity of the content, if not the form, of Mark 7:15.

83. On the issue of hand washing in ancient Jewish practice, and Jesus's attitude toward it, see Booth, *Jesus and the Laws of Purity*, pp. 155–203; for another point of view and references to more recent works, cf. also the treatment by John C. Poirier, "Why Did the Pharisees Wash Their Hands?" *Journal of Jewish Studies* 47.2 (1996): 217–233.

84. Booth, *Jesus and the Laws of Purity*, pp. 62–65.

85. If the synoptic Gospels were playing fast and loose with received traditions and they

wished to have Jesus abrogate the food laws, they would have put this saying in a different context: "Jesus and his disciples were eating a pig," for instance. The synoptics do not go this far. But they do go so far as to put Jesus in debate with contemporary Jews over the necessity of maintaining ritual purity.

86. After all, hand washing was an issue among first-century Jews. It is commonly believed that only *some* Pharisees — those who had joined the *ḥavurah* — would have insisted on hand washing before all meals. See Booth, *Jesus and the Laws of Purity*, pp. 190–203.

87. Dunn, *Jesus, Paul, and the Law*, p 51; cf. Booth, *Jesus and the Laws of Purity*, p. 69; and Sanders, *Jesus and Judaism*, pp. 260–264.

88. Cf. parallels, Matthew 9:13 and Luke 5:32.

89. Interestingly, idolatry is not on the list.

90. See, e.g., 11QT LI:11–15, discussed in "The Temple Scroll" in chapter 2; and Sifra Kedoshim 4:1, discussed in the first section of chapter 5.

91. Sifre Deut. § 254 (on Deut. 23:10), discussed in the first section of chapter 5.

92. See 1QpHab VIII:8–13, discussed in chapter 3, section on "Sin and the Sanctuary in the Habakkuk Pesher."

93. *Contra* Booth, *Jesus and the Laws of Purity*, p. 73; cf. pp. 49–50 and the literature cited there.

94. E.g., Romans 1:29–30, 1 Corinthians 6:9–10; Galatians 5:19–21, and Colossians 3:5. On vice lists in the New Testament and Greco-Roman literature, see Abraham J. Malherbe, *Moral Exhortation, A Greco-Roman Sourcebook* (Philadelphia: Westminster Press, 1986), pp. 138–141.

95. Cf., e.g., Matthew 8:4//Mark 1:44//Luke 5:14 (Aland Synopsis § 42).

96. Daniel Boyarin, throughout his book *Carnal Israel*, traces a similar dynamic regarding attitudes toward gender and the body in Hellenistic Judaism, early Christianity, and rabbinic Judaism. In Boyarin's view, Philo's allegorical and dualistic approach — which prioritizes spirit over flesh, without fully rejecting matters of the flesh — becomes increasingly radicalized by (post-Pauline) early Christians, many of whom eventually come to view bodily and sexual matters even more negatively. The rabbis, in Boyarin's analysis, move in precisely the opposite direction, embracing carnality more readily and rejecting even the dualistic prioritization of the spirit over the body that was characteristic of the Jewish-Hellenistic approach. See esp. pp 1–10, 31–60, 77–106, 230–240; for brief statements, see pp. 56–57, 233–234.

97. See chapter 4, section on "The Pharisaic Ḥavurah."

98. On the authenticity of the Pauline epistles, see Sanders, *Paul and Palestinian Judaism*, pp. 431–433.

99. On Paul and Luke's account of Paul, see Alan F. Segal, *Paul the Convert: The Apostolate and Apostasy of Saul the Pharisee* (New Haven. Yale University Press, 1990), pp. 3–33.

100. Generally, see Heikki Räisänen, *Paul and the Law* (Philadelphia: Fortress Press, 1986), pp. 1–15.

101. On the quest for Paul's Jewish and Hellenistic background, see Peter J. Tomson, *Paul and the Jewish Law· Halakha in the Letters of the Apostle to the Gentiles* (Assen/Maastricht: Van Gorcum, 1990), pp. 31–53. Generally, on Paul's social situation, see Wayne A. Meeks, *The First Urban Christians: The Social World of the Apostle Paul* (New Haven: Yale University Press, 1983). For a study that tries to recognize the different social situations of the communities Paul addresses in his letters, see Francis Watson, *Paul, Judaism and the Gentiles: A Sociological Approach* (Cambridge: Cambridge University Press, 1986).

102. E. P. Sanders's provocative analysis, *Paul and Palestinian Judaism*, published in 1977, was followed by a number of detailed treatments of Paul, many of which endeavored to understand Paul against his Jewish (or Jewish-Hellenistic) background and to identify more precisely Paul's attitude toward Jewish law. Some even speak of a "new perspective" on Paul

and the law. See James D. G. Dunn, *Romans 1–8*, vol. 38a of *Word Biblical Commentary* (Dallas: Word Books, 1988), pp. lxiii–lxxii; and Dunn, "The New Perspective on Paul," *Bulletin of the John Rylands Library* 65 (1983): 95–122, reprinted with an additional note in *Jesus, Paul and the Law*, pp. 183–214.

103. On twentieth-century Pauline scholarship, see Sanders, *Paul and Palestinian Judaism*, pp. 1–12, 33–59, and 434–442. For a more recent survey on writings related to Paul and the law, see Tomson, *Paul and the Jewish Law*, pp. 1–30

104. That Paul's rejection of the law is complete is the thesis of, for example, Räisänen, *Paul and the Law*, pp. 42–93. Another view is that Paul rejected the ritual (or "ceremonial") law but upheld Jewish ethical law; see for example, Segal, *Paul the Convert*, pp. 125–133; Sanders's view is that Paul explicitly rejected only some aspects of the ritual law, although he did not insist on observance as an "entrance requirement." See *Paul, the Law, and the Jewish People* (Philadelphia: Fortress Press, 1983), esp. pp. 94–96.

105. Circumcision: Galatians 5:2, Philippians 3:2; food laws: Galatians 2:11–14, 1 Corinthians 8, 10; Sabbaths and holidays: Galatians 4:8–11. See Sanders, *Paul, the Law, and the Jewish People*, pp. 93–105.

106. See, e.g., Dunn, "The Incident at Antioch (Gal. 2:11–18)," *Journal for the Study of the New Testament* 18 (1983): 3–57; reprinted with an additional note in *Jesus, Paul, and the Law*, pp. 129–182, esp. pp. 142 and 167–168.

107. Generally on the incident at Antioch, see Dunn, *Jesus, Paul, and the Law*, pp. 129–182; and Segal, *Paul the Convert*, pp. 187–223.

108. On the requirements of apostolic decree (Acts 15:20) and the Jewish Noachide laws, see Segal, *Paul the Convert*, pp. 194–201.

109. Dunn, *Jesus, Paul, and the Law*, pp. 142 and 167–168, Segal, *Paul the Convert*, pp. 172 and 194; cf. Stanley K. Stowers, *A Rereading of Romans: Justice, Jews, and Gentiles* (New Haven: Yale University Press, 1994), pp. 95–97

110. See discussions in chapter 3, section on "Sinful Outsiders," Excursus 1; and Klawans, "Notions of Gentile Impurity."

111. For a thorough treatment of the *halakhic* issues that may have had an impact on Jewish–Gentile table fellowship, see Tomson, *Paul and the Jewish Law*, pp. 222–258; on the issue of food offered to idols, see pp. 151–220.

112. The most thorough treatment of impurity in Paul's writings that I know of is Michael Newton's *The Concept of Purity at Qumran and in the Letters of Paul*, which has already been referred to in the discussion of Qumran. There are other treatments of purity in Paul's writings (Neusner, *The Idea*, pp. 59–60; Cothenet, "Pureté et impureté," pp. 546–552; and Hübner, "Unclean and Clean (NT)," p. 743), but Newton's work is by far the most thorough and influential. While Newton is correct in saying that purity remains important to Paul, he is not specific enough. Paul's concerns are not with ritual impurity, but with moral impurity.

113. Generally see Newton, *The Concept of Purity*, pp. 52–114.

114. Generally, on Romans as a whole and on this passage in particular, see Dunn, *Romans 1–8*, esp. pp. 51–76; and Stowers, *Rereading Romans*, pp. 83–125.

115. B. Yeb. 103b. One could also identify Greco-Roman literary parallels; see Stowers, *Rereading Romans*, p. 85.

116. E.g., 2 Corinthians 12:21 and Galatians 5:19; see Hübner, "Unclean and Clean (NT)," p. 743; Newton, *The Concept of Purity*, pp. 86–87, 102–106; Segal, *Paul the Convert*, p. 170; and Tomson, *Paul and the Jewish Law*, pp. 97–103.

117. E.g., Dunn, *Romans 1–8*, pp. 345–347 (on Romans 6:19); cf. p. 62 (on 1:24–25).

118. Generally, on Galatians as a whole, and this passage in particular, see Hans Dieter Betz, *Galatians: A Commentary on Paul's Letter to the Churches in Galatia* (Philadelphia: Fortress Press, 1979), esp. pp. 281–290.

119. 1 Thessalonians 2:3 and 4:7; cf. Ephesians 5:3 and Colossians 3:5.

120. See Betz, *Galatians*, pp. 281–283, and cf. the discussion of Mark 7:20–22 and Matthew 15:19 in the sections on Jesus in this chapter.

121. On 1 Corinthians 5, see Newton, *The Concept of Purity*, pp. 86–97; Segal, *Paul the Convert*, pp 169–170; and Tomson, *Paul and the Jewish Law*, pp. 97–103

122. Cf. Newton, *The Concept of Purity*, pp 90–93

123. See discussion in Tomson, *Paul and the Jewish Law*, pp. 101–102.

124. The exclusion, apparently, applies only to backsliding insiders Social contact, even marriage, with unbelievers was tolerated; see 1 Corinthians 7:12; 10:27.

125. See, for example, these classic treatments: Joseph A. Fitzmyer, "Qumran and the Interpolated Fragment in 2 Cor 6:14–7:1," *Catholic Biblical Quarterly* 23.3 (1961): 271–280; and Joachim Gnilka, "2 Cor. 6.14–7.1 in the Light of the Qumran Texts and the Testaments of the Twelve Patriarchs," in *Paul and Qumran: Studies in New Testament Exegesis*, ed. Jerome Murphy O'Connor (Chicago: Priory Press, 1968), pp 48–68

126. *The Concept of Purity*, pp. 110–114; cf Segal, *Paul the Convert*, pp. 166–169.

127. For a detailed review of the evidence and argument in defense of this last possibility, see Victor Paul Furnish, *II Corinthians: Translated, with Introduction and Commentary*, vol. 32a of *The Anchor Bible* (Garden City, N.Y.: Doubleday & Co , 1984), pp. 359–383; cf. Segal, *Paul the Convert*, p. 167.

128. This point has been made already with regard to John's baptism in the first section of this chapter With regard to Paul's baptism, see Segal, *Paul the Convert*, pp. 137–138.

129 Generally, on baptism in Paul see Beasley-Murray, *Baptism*, pp. 127–216. For a discussion relating to purity in particular see Newton, *The Concept of Purity*, pp. 81–84; and Segal, *Paul the Convert*, pp. 133–138.

130. On this passage in general, see Beasley-Murray, *Baptism*, pp 162–167; Newton, *The Concept of Purity*, pp 82–83, and Segal, *Paul the Convert*, pp 177–178 On the verb "to wash" (ἀπολούω) in particular, see Newton, *The Concept of Purity*, pp. 82–83.

131 Generally, on Paul's eschatology, see Segal, *Paul the Convert*, pp. 158–161. On Paul's eschatology in relation to purity in particular, see Newton, *The Concept of Purity*, pp. 84–86.

132. See also Romans 4:24–25, 5:8; 1 Corinthians 15:3; Galatians 1:4; cf. Ephesians 5:25–26. See discussion on baptism and death in Segal, *Paul the Convert*, pp. 134–137.

133. See Newton, *The Concept of Purity*, pp. 75–77 and 83 On Romans 6, see Beasley-Murray, *Baptism*, pp. 127–146; and Segal, *Paul the Convert*, pp. 133–138. Cf. also Colossians 2:12.

134. See, for instance, the more nuanced discussion in Sanders, *Paul and Palestinian Judaism*, pp. 463–468 For a discussion of various understandings of expiation (ἱλαστήριον) in Romans 3:24, see Dunn, *Romans 1–8*, pp 161–183, esp. pp. 169–171; and Stowers, *Rereading Romans*, esp. pp. 206–213. One point that Stowers raises is that many of the discussions of the expiatory power of Jesus's death operate on misunderstandings of sacrificial atonement in Judaism. Stowers, building on Jacob Milgrom's work discussed in the introduction to this work, reminds us that sacrifices of atonement purified not the sinner, but the sanctuary I thank Paula Fredriksen for bringing Stowers's work to my attention.

135. *The Concept of Purity*, pp. 52–78; esp. pp. 53–60

136. Cf. 1 Corinthians 6:19; 9:13–14; and see Segal, *Paul the Convert*, pp. 168–169.

137. Segal, *Paul the Convert*, pp. 151–158.

138. Cf. the discussion in Newton, *The Concept of Purity*, pp 83–84.

139. Generally, on the dynamic among Philo, Paul, and the rabbis, see Boyarin, *Carnal Israel*, pp. 1–10, 31–60, and 230–240. With greater emphasis on Paul, see also Boyarin, *A Radical Jew· Paul and the Politics of Identity* (Berkeley: University of California Press, 1994).

140. See David Brakke, "The Problematization of Nocturnal Emissions in Early Christian Syria, Egypt, and Gaul," *Journal of Early Christian Studies* 3.4 (1995): 419–460.

141. Cohen, "Menstruants and the Sacred," pp. 287–290.

Bibliography

Aland, Kurt, ed. *Synopsis Quattor Evangeliorum*. 13th ed. Stuttgart: Deutsche Bibelgesellschaft, 1990.

Albeck, Hanoch, ed. *Shishah Sidre Mishnah*. 6 vols. Jerusalem: Mosad Bialik, 1952–1958.

Alon, Gedalyahu "The Bounds of the Laws of Levitical Cleanness." In *Jews, Judaism, and the Classical World*, 190–234. Jerusalem: Magnes Press, 1977.

———. "The Levitical Uncleanness of Gentiles." In *Jews, Judaism, and the Classical World*, 146–189 Jerusalem: Magnes Press, 1977.

Attridge, Harold, et al. *Qumran Cave 4, VIII: Parabiblical Texts, Part 1*. Vol. XIII, *Discoveries in the Judaean Desert*. Oxford. Clarendon Press, 1994.

Baillet, M. *Qumran Grotte 4, III (4Q482–4Q520)* Vol. VII, *Discoveries in the Judaean Desert*. Oxford: Clarendon Press, 1982.

Bamberger, Bernard J. "Leviticus." In *The Torah: A Modern Commentary*, ed. W Gunther Plaut. New York: Union of American Hebrew Congregations, 1981

Baumgarten, Albert I. "The Pharisaic *Paradosis*." *Harvard Theological Review* 80, no. 1 (1987): 63–77.

Baumgarten, Joseph M. "Exclusions from the Temple. Proselytes and Agrippa I." *Journal of Jewish Studies* 33, no. 2 (1982)· 215–225.

———. "The Pharisaic-Sadducean Controversies about Purity and the Qumran Texts." *Journal of Jewish Studies* 31, no. 2 (1980): 157–170.

———. "The Purification Rituals in DJD 7." In *The Dead Sea Scrolls: Forty Years of Research*, ed. Devorah Dimant and Uriel Rappaport, 199–209. Leiden: E. J. Brill, 1992.

———. *Qumran Cave 4, XIII: The Damascus Document (4Q266–273)*. Vol. XVIII, *Discoveries in the Judaean Desert* Oxford· Clarendon Press, 1996.

———. "The Qumran-Essene Restraints on Marriage." In *Archaeology and History in the Dead Sea Scrolls*, ed. Lawrence H. Schiffman, 13–24. Sheffield: JSOT Press, 1990.

———. "Recent Qumran Discoveries and Halakhah in the Hellenistic-Roman Period." In *Jewish Civilization in the Hellenistic-Roman Period*, ed. Shemaryahu Talmon, 147–158. Sheffield: JSOT Press, 1991.

———. "Sadducean Elements in Qumran Law." In *The Community of the Renewed Covenant: The Notre Dame Symposium on the Dead Sea Scrolls*, ed. Eugene Ulrich and James VanderKam, 27–36. Notre Dame, Ind. University of Notre Dame Press, 1994.

———. "Zab Impurity in Qumran and Rabbinic Law." *Journal of Jewish Studies* 45, no 2 (1994): 273–277.

Beasley-Murray, G. R. *Baptism in the New Testament*. London: Macmillan, 1962.

Be'er, Ilana. "Blood Discharge: On Female Im/Purity in the Priestly Code and in Biblical Literature." In *A Feminist Companion to Exodus to Deuteronomy*, ed Athalya Brenner, 152–164. Sheffield: Sheffield Academic Press, 1994.

Betz, Hans Dieter. *Galatians: A Commentary on Paul's Letter to the Churches in Galatia*. Philadelphia. Fortress Press, 1979.

Blenkinsopp, Joseph. *Ezra–Nehemiah: A Commentary*. Philadelphia: Westminster Press, 1988.

Bloch, Renée. "Methodological Note for the Study of Rabbinic Literature." In *Approaches to Ancient Judaism: Theory and Practice*, ed. William Scott Green, 51–75. Missoula, Mont.: Scholars Press, 1978.

Bokser, Baruch M. "Approaching Sacred Space." *Harvard Theological Review* 78, no. 3 (1985): 279–299.

Booth, Roger P. *Jesus and the Laws of Purity: Tradition History and Legal History in Mark 7*. Sheffield: JSOT Press, 1986.

Borg, Marcus J. *Conflict, Holiness, and Politics in the Teachings of Jesus*. Harrisburg, Penn.: Trinity Press International, 1998.

———. *Jesus, a New Vision: Spirit, Culture, and the Life of Discipleship*. San Francisco: Harper & Row, 1987.

———. *Jesus in Contemporary Scholarship*. Valley Forge, Penn.: Trinity Press International, 1994.

Boyarin, Daniel. *Carnal Israel: Reading Sex in Talmudic Culture*. Berkeley: University of California Press, 1993.

———. "On the Status of the Tannaitic Midrashim." *Journal of the American Oriental Society* 112, no. 3 (1992): 455–465.

Brownlee, William H *The Midrash Pesher of Habakkuk*. Missoula, Mont.: Scholars Press, 1979.

Büchler, Adolph. "The Law of Purification in Mark 7:1–23." *Expository Times* 21 (1909–1910): 34–40.

———. "The Levitical Impurity of the Gentile in Palestine Before the Year 70." *Jewish Quarterly Review* n s. 17 (1926–1927): 1–81

———. *Studies in Sin and Atonement in the Rabbinic Literature of the First Century* London: Oxford University Press, 1928.

Cazelles, H. "Pureté et impureté: Ancien Testament." *Dictionnaire de la Bible· Supplement* 9 (1979): 491–508.

Charlesworth, James H., ed. *Damascus Document, War Scroll, and Related Documents* Vol 2, *The Dead Sea Scrolls: Hebrew, Aramaic, and Greek Texts with English Translations*. Tübingen: J. C. B Mohr (Paul Siebeck), 1995.

———, ed. *The Old Testament Pseudepigrapha*. 2 vols. Garden City, N.Y.: Doubleday, 1983

———, ed. *Rule of the Community and Related Documents*. Vol. 1, *The Dead Sea Scrolls. Hebrew, Aramaic, and Greek Texts with English Translations*. Tübingen: J. C. B. Mohr (Paul Siebeck), 1995.

Choksy, Jamsheed K. *Purity and Pollution in Zoroastrianism*. Austin: University of Texas Press, 1989

Cohen, Shaye J. D. "Conversion to Judaism in Historical Perspective." *Conservative Judaism* 36, no. 4 (1983): 31–45.

———. *From the Maccabees to the Mishnah*. Philadelphia: Westminster Press, 1987.

———. "Menstruants and the Sacred in Judaism and Christianity." In *Women's History and*

Ancient History, ed. Sarah B. Pomeroy, 273–299. Chapel Hill: University of North Carolina Press, 1991.

Corinaldi, Michael. "Purity and Conversion Norms among the Falashas." In *Between Africa and Zion: Proceedings of the First International Congress of the Society for the Study of Ethiopian Jewry*, ed. Steven Kaplan, Tuder Parfitt and Emanuela Trevisan Semi, 113–124. Jerusalem· Ben-Zvi Institute, 1995.

Cothenet, É. "Influence d'Ézékiel sur la spritualité de Qumran." *Revue de Qumran* 13 (1988): 431–439.

———. "Pureté et impureté: Nouveau Testament" *Dictionnaire de la Bible: Supplement* 9 (1979): 508–554.

Countryman, L. William. *Dirt, Greed and Sex: Sexual Ethics in the New Testament and Their Implications for Today*. Philadelphia: Fortress Press, 1988.

Danby, Herbert. *The Mishnah: Translated from the Hebrew with Introduction and Brief Explanatory Notes* Oxford: Oxford University Press, 1933.

Davies, Philip R. *The Damascus Covenant: An Interpretation of the "Damascus Document."* Sheffield: JSOT Press, 1982.

Douglas, Mary. "Atonement in Leviticus." *Jewish Studies Quarterly* 1, no. 2 (1993/1994): 109–130.

———. "A Bird, a Mouse, a Frog, and Some Fish· A New Reading of Leviticus 11." In *Literary Imagination, Ancient and Modern: Essays in Honor of David Grene*, ed. Todd Breyfogle, 110–126. Chicago· University of Chicago Press, 1999.

———. "The Forbidden Animals in Leviticus." *Journal for the Study of the Old Testament* 59 (1993). 3–23.

———. "The Glorious Book of Numbers." *Jewish Studies Quarterly* 1, no. 3 (1993/4): 193–216

———. "Holy Joy: Rereading Leviticus: The Anthropologist and the Believer." *Conservative Judaism* 46, no. 3 (1994): 3–14.

———. *Implicit Meanings: Essays in Anthropology*. London: Routledge & Kegan Paul, 1975.

———. *In the Wilderness: The Doctrine of Defilement in the Book of Numbers*. Sheffield: JSOT Press, 1993.

———. *Leviticus as Literature*. Oxford· Oxford University Press, 1999

———. *Natural Symbols: Explorations in Cosmology, with a New Introduction*. London· Routledge, 1996.

———. "Poetic Structure in Leviticus." In *Pomegranates and Golden Bells: Studies in Biblical, Jewish and Near Eastern Ritual, Law, and Literature in Honor of Jacob Milgrom*, ed David P Wright, David Noel Freedman, and Avi Hurvitz, 239–256. Winona Lake, Ind.: Eisenbrauns, 1995.

———. *Purity and Danger: An Analysis of the Concepts of Pollution and Taboo*. 2nd impression with corrections. London: Routledge and Kegan Paul, 1969.

———. "Sacred Contagion." In *Reading Leviticus: A Conversation with Mary Douglas*, ed. John F. A. Sawyer, 86–106 Sheffield: Sheffield Academic Press, 1996.

———. "The Stranger in the Bible." *Archives Européennes de Sociologie* 35, no. 1 (1994): 283–298

Dumont, Louis. *Homo Hierarchicus: The Caste System and Its Implications*, trans. Mark Sainsbury et al. Complete rev English ed. Chicago: University of Chicago Press, 1980.

Dunn, James D. G. *Jesus, Paul, and the Law: Studies in Mark and Galatians*. Louisville: Westminster/John Knox Press, 1990.

———. *Romans 1–8*. Vol. 38a, *Word Biblical Commentary*. Dallas: Word Books, 1988.

Eilberg-Schwartz, Howard. *The Savage in Judaism: An Anthropology of Israelite Religion and Ancient Judaism* Bloomington: Indiana University Press, 1990.

Epstein, Jacob N. *Introduction to the Text of the Mishnah* (Hebrew). 2nd ed. 2 vols. Jerusalem: Magnes Press, 1964.

———. *Introductions to Tannaitic Literature: Mishna, Tosephta, and Halakhic Midrashim* (Hebrew), ed. E. Z. Melamed. Jerusalem: Magnes Press, 1957.

——— and E. Z. Melamed, eds. *Mekhilta D'Rabbi Sim'on b. Jochai.* Jerusalem: American Academy for Jewish Research, 1955.

Fardon, Richard *Mary Douglas: An Intellectual Biography.* London: Routledge, 1999.

Feldman, Emanuel. *Biblical and Post-Biblical Defilement and Mourning: Law as Theology.* New York: Yeshiva University Press, 1977.

Finkelstein, Louis, ed. *Sifra on Leviticus: According to Vatican Manuscript Assemani 66 with Variants from the Other Manuscripts, Genizah Fragments, Early Editions and Quotations by Medieval Authorities and with References to Parallel Passages and Commentaries.* 5 vols. New York. Jewish Theological Seminary, 1983–1991.

———, ed. *Sifre on Deuteronomy.* New York: Jewish Theological Seminary, 1993.

Fitzmyer, Joseph A. "Divorce Among First-Century Palestinian Jews." *Eretz-Israel* 14 (1978): 103*–110*.

Flusser, David. "The Baptism of John and the Dead Sea Sect." In *Jewish Sources in Early Christianity* (Hebrew), 81–112. Tel Aviv. Sifriat Poalim, 1979.

———. "The Dead Sea Sect and Pre-Pauline Christianity." In *Aspects of the Dead Sea Scrolls,* ed. Chaim Rabin and Yigael Yadin, 215–266. Jerusalem: Magnes Press, 1958.

Fredriksen, Paula. "Did Jesus Oppose the Purity Laws?" *Bible Review* 95, no. 2 (1995): 20–25, 42–47.

———. "What You See Is What You Get: Context and Content in Current Research on the Historical Jesus." *Theology Today* 52, no. 1 (1995): 75–97.

Frymer-Kensky, Tikva. *In the Wake of the Goddesses: Women, Culture and the Biblical Transformation of Pagan Myth.* New York: Fawcett Columbine, 1992.

———. "Law and Philosophy: The Case of Sex in the Bible," *Semeia* 45 (1989): 89–102

———. "Pollution, Purification, and Purgation in Biblical Israel." In *The Word of the Lord Shall Go Forth: Essays in Honor of David Noel Freedman in Celebration of His Sixtieth Birthday,* ed. Carol L. Meyers and M. O'Connor, 399–410. Winona Lake, Ind.: Eisenbrauns, 1983.

Funk, Robert W., Roy W. Hoover, and the Jesus Seminar, eds. *The Five Gospels: The Search for the Authentic Words of Jesus.* New York: Polebridge Press (Macmillan), 1993.

Gammie, John G. *Holiness in Israel* Minneapolis. Fortress Press, 1989.

García Martínez, Florentino. *The Dead Sea Scrolls Translated: The Qumran Texts in English,* trans. Wilfred G. E. Watson. Leiden: E. J. Brill, 1994.

———. "Les limites de la communauté: Pureté et impureté à Qumrân et dans le Nouveau Testament." In *Text and Testimony: Essays on New Testament and Apocryphal Literature in Honour of A. F. J. Klijn,* ed. T. Baardia et al., 111–122. Kampen: J. H. Kok, 1988

———. "L'interprétation de la Torah d'Ézékiel dans less mss. de Qumran." *Revue de Qumran* 13 (1988): 441–452.

———. "The Problem of Purity: the Qumran Solution." In Florentino García Martínez and Julio Trebolle Barrera, *The People of the Dead Sea Scrolls: Their Writings, Beliefs and Practices,* trans. Wilfred G E. Watson, 139–157. Leiden: E. J. Brill, 1995.

———, and Eibert J. C. Tigchelaar, eds. *The Dead Sea Scrolls Study Edition.* 2 vols. Leiden: E. J. Brill, 1997–1998

Garnet, Paul. *Salvation and Atonement in the Qumran Scrolls.* Tübingen: J. C B. Mohr (Paul Siebeck), 1977.

Ginzberg, Louis. *An Unknown Jewish Sect.* New York: Jewish Theological Seminary, 1976.

Gruber, Mayer, I. "Women in the Cult According to the Priestly Code." In *Judaic Perspectives on Ancient Israel,* ed. Jacob Neusner, Baruch A. Levine, and Ernest S. Frerichs, 35–48. Philadelphia: Fortress Press, 1987.

Halivni, David Weiss. *Midrash, Mishnah, and Gemara: The Jewish Predilection for Justified Law*. Cambridge, Mass.: Harvard University Press, 1986.

———. *Peshat and Derash: Plain and Applied Meaning in Rabbinic Exegesis*. New York: Oxford University Press, 1991.

Halpern-Amaru, Betsy. *Rewriting the Bible: Land and Covenant in Post-Biblical Jewish Literature*. Valley Forge, Penn.: Trinity Press International, 1994.

Hammer, Reuven. *Sifre. a Tannaitic Commentary on the Book of Deuteronomy*. New Haven: Yale University Press, 1986.

Harrington, Hannah K. *The Impurity Systems of Qumran and the Rabbis: Biblical Foundations*. Atlanta: Scholars Press, 1993.

———. "Interpreting Leviticus in the Second Temple Period. Struggling with Ambiguity." In *Reading Leviticus: A Conversation with Mary Douglas*, ed. John F. A. Sawyer, 214–229 Sheffield. Sheffield Academic Press, 1996.

Hauck, Friedrich, and Rudolf Meyer, "καθαρός." In *Theological Dictionary of the New Testament*, ed. Gerhard Kittel and Gerhard Friedrich, trans. Geoffrey W. Bromiley. 10 vols. Vol. III, 413–431. Grand Rapids, Mich.: William B. Eerdmans, 1964–1976.

Hauptman, Judith. *Rereading the Rabbis: A Woman's Voice*. Boulder, Col.: Westview Press, 1998.

Hayes, Christine E. "The Impurity of Gentiles in Biblical Law and Late Antique Judaism." Unpublished MS. 1995.

———. "Intermarriage and Impurity in Ancient Jewish Sources." *Harvard Theological Review* 92, no. 1 (1999): 3–36.

Hoffmann, David Z. *Das Buch Deuteronomium: Übersetzt und Erklärt*. 2 vols. Berlin: M. Poppelauer, 1913, 1922.

———. *Das Buch Leviticus*. 2 vols. Berlin: M. Poppelauer, 1905–1906.

———, ed. *Midrash Tannaim on Deuteronomy*. 2 vols. Berlin, 1908–1909.

Horgan, Maurya P. *Pesharim· Qumran Interpretations of Biblical Books*. Washington, D.C.: The Catholic Biblical Association of America, 1979.

Horovitz, H. S , ed. *Siphre D'Be Rab, Fasciculus primus: Siphre ad Numeros adjecto Siphre zutta*. Jerusalem: Shalem, 1992.

———, and I. A. Rabin, eds. *Mechilta D'Rabbi Ismael*. Jerusalem: Wahrmann Books, 1970.

Houston, Walter. *Purity and Monotheism: Clean and Unclean Animals in Biblical Law*. Sheffield: JSOT Press, 1993.

Hübner, Hans. "Unclean and Clean (NT)." In *The Anchor Bible Dictionary*, ed. David Noel Freedman. 6 vols. Vol. VI, 741–745. New York: Doubleday, 1992.

Isenberg, Sheldon R., and Dennis E. Owen "Bodies, Natural and Contrived: The Work of Mary Douglas." *Religious Studies Review* 3, no. 1 (1977): 1–17.

Jenson, Philip Peter. *Graded Holiness: A Key to the Priestly Conception of the World*. Sheffield: JSOT Press, 1992.

Kampen, John, and Moshe J. Bernstein, eds. *Reading 4QMMT· New Perspectives on Qumran Law and History*. Atlanta· Scholars Press, 1996.

Kaplan, Steven. *The Beta Israel (Falasha) in Ethiopia: From Earliest Times to the Twentieth Century*. New York: New York University Press, 1992.

———. "'Falasha' Religion Ancient Judaism or Evolving Ethiopian Tradition? A Review Article." *Jewish Quarterly Review* 79, no. 1 (1988): 49–65.

Kaufmann, Yehezkel *Christianity and Judaism· Two Covenants*, trans. C. W. Efroymson. Jerusalem Magnes Press, 1988.

———. *Toledot ha-Emunah ha-Yisraelit* 8 vols. Tel Aviv Dvir, 1937–1958.

Kittay, Eva Feder. *Metaphor. Its Cognitive Force and Linguistic Structure*. Oxford: Clarendon Press, 1987.

Klawans, Jonathan. "Idolatry, Incest, and Impurity: Moral Defilement in Ancient Judaism." *Journal for the Study of Judaism* 29, no. 4 (1998). 391–415.
———. "Impurity and Sin in Ancient Judaism." Dissertation, Columbia University, 1997.
———. "The Impurity of Immorality in Ancient Judaism." *Journal of Jewish Studies* 48, no 1 (1997). 1–16.
———. "Notions of Gentile Impurity in Ancient Judaism." *Association for Jewish Studies Review* 20, no. 2 (1995). 285–312.
Knohl, Israel. *The Sanctuary of Silence: The Priestly Torah and the Holiness School.* Minneapolis. Fortress Press, 1995.
Kraemer, Ross Shepard *Her Share of the Blessings: Women's Religions among Pagans, Jews, and Christians in the Greco-Roman World.* New York· Oxford University Press, 1992.
Lauterbach, Jacob Z., ed *Mekilta de-Rabbi Ishmael: A Critical Edition on the Basis of the Manuscripts and Early Editions with an English Translation, Introduction and Notes.* 3 vols. Philadelphia. The Jewish Publication Society, 1933.
Leaney, A. R. C. *The Rule of Qumran and Its Meaning: Introduction, Translation and Commentary.* Philadelphia: Westminster Press, 1966.
Leiner, Gershon Chanoch *Sidrei Toharot.* 2nd ed. 2 vols New York: Noble, 1960.
Levine, Baruch A. *In the Presence of the Lord* Leiden: E J. Brill, 1974.
———. *The JPS Torah Commentary: Leviticus.* Philadelphia. The Jewish Publication Society, 1989.
——— *Numbers 1–20: A New Translation with Introduction and Commentary.* Vol. 4, *The Anchor Bible.* New York. Doubleday, 1993.
Licht, Jacob. *The Rule Scroll: A Scroll from the Wilderness of Judaea* Jerusalem: Bialik Institute, 1965.
———. *The Thanksgiving Scroll. A Scroll from the Wilderness of Judaea.* Jerusalem: Bialik Institute, 1957.
Lieberman, Saul. "The Discipline in the So-Called Dead Sea Manual of Discipline." *Journal of Biblical Literature* 71 (1952): 199–206.
——— *Tosefeth Rishonim: A Commentary on Manuscripts of the Tosefta and Works of the Rishonim and Midrashim in Manuscripts and Rare Editions* (Hebrew). 4 vols. Jerusalem: Bamberger & Wahrmann, 1937–1939.
———. *Tosefta Ki-Fshutah: A Comprehensive Commentary on the Tosefta* (Hebrew). 10 vols New York: Jewish Theological Seminary, 1955–1988.
Malina, Bruce J. *The New Testament World: Insights from Cultural Anthropology.* Rev. ed. Louisville: Westminster/John Knox Press, 1993
Mansoor, Menahem. *The Thanksgiving Hymns: Translated and Annotated with an Introduction.* Leiden: E. J. Brill, 1961.
Margulies, Mordecai, ed. *Midrash Wayyikra Rabbah· A Critical Edition Based on Manuscripts and Genizah Fragments with Variants and Notes.* 3rd ed. 2 vols. New York: Jewish Theological Seminary, 1993.
Meier, John P. *A Marginal Jew: Rethinking the Historical Jesus, Volume One: The Roots of the Problem and the Person* New York: Doubleday, 1991.
———. *A Marginal Jew· Rethinking the Historical Jesus, Volume Two: Mentor, Message, and Miracles.* New York: Doubleday, 1994
Milgrom, Jacob. "The Concept of Impurity in *Jubilees* and the *Temple Scroll.*" *Revue de Qumran* 16, no. 2 (1993): 277–284.
———. "Israel's Sanctuary: The Priestly 'Picture of Dorian Gray.'" *Revue Biblique* 83, no. 3 (1976): 390–399.
———. *The JPS Torah Commentary. Numbers.* Philadelphia: The Jewish Publication Society, 1990.

———. *Leviticus 1–16. A New Translation with Introduction and Commentary*. Vol 3, *The Anchor Bible* New York. Doubleday, 1992.

———. "The Qumran Cult· Its Exegetical Principles." In *Temple Scroll Studies*, ed. G. J Brooke, 165–180. Sheffield: JSOT Press, 1989.

———. "The Scriptural Foundations and Deviations in the Laws of Purity of the *Temple Scroll*." In *Archaeology and History in the Dead Sea Scrolls*, ed Lawrence H Schiffman, 83–99. Sheffield. JSOT Press, 1990.

Myers, Jacob M. *Ezra & Nehemiah*. Vol. 14, *The Anchor Bible*. New York: Doubleday, 1965

Neusner, Jacob. *Androgynous Judaism: Masculine and Feminine in the Dual Torah*. Macon, Ga.: Mercer University Press, 1993.

———. *HMLP = A History of the Mishnaic Law of Purities*. 22 vols. Leiden: E. J. Brill, 1974–1977.

———. *The Idea of Purity in Ancient Judaism*. Leiden: E. J. Brill, 1973.

———. *Judaism. The Evidence of the Mishnah*. Chicago: University of Chicago Press, 1981

———. *Purity in Rabbinic Judaism, A Systemic Account: The Sources, Media, Effects, and Removal of Uncleanness*. Atlanta. Scholars Press, 1994

———. *Rabbinic Judaism: Structure and System*. Minneapolis: Fortress Press, 1995.

———. *Sifra· An Analytical Translation*. 3 vols. Atlanta: Scholars Press, 1988.

———. *The Tosefta: Translated from the Hebrew* 6 vols New York: Ktav, 1977.

———, and Bruce D. Chilton. "Uncleanness in Formative Judaism: A Moral or an Ontological Category?" In *The Religious Study of Judaism. Description, Analysis, Interpretation, Volume Four Ideas of History, Ethics, Ontology and Religion in Formative Judaism*, ed. Jacob Neusner, 81–106 Lanham, Md.· University Press of America, 1986

Newton, Michael. *The Concept of Purity at Qumran and in the Letters of Paul*. Cambridge: Cambridge University Press, 1985.

Neyrey, Jerome H. "The Idea of Purity in Mark's Gospel." *Semeia* 35 (1986): 91–128.

——— "The Symbolic Universe of Luke-Acts: 'They Turn the World Upside Down.'" In *The Social World of Luke-Acts*, ed. Jerome H. Neyrey, 271–304. Peabody, Mass.: Hendrickson Publishers, 1991.

Parker, Robert. *Miasma· Pollution and Purification in Early Greek Religion* Oxford: Clarendon Press, 1983.

Paschen, Wilfried *Rein und Unrein: Untersuchung zur biblischen Wortgeschichte*. Munich: Kösel-verlag, 1970.

Preston, James J. "Purification." In *The Encyclopedia of Religion*, ed. Mircea Eliade 16 vols. Vol. 12, 91–100. New York. Macmillan, 1987.

Qafih, Joseph, ed. and trans. *Mishnah with Maimonides' Commentary* (Hebrew translation of Arabic original). 3 vols. Jerusalem: Mosad Ha-Rav Kook, 1976–1978.

Qimron, Elisha. *The Temple Scroll. A Critical Edition with Extensive Reconstructions, Judean Desert Studies*. Beer Sheva: Ben Gurion University of the Negev Press, 1996

———, and John Strugnell. *Qumran Cave 4, V (Miqsat Ma'aśeh ha-Torah)*. Vol. X, *Discoveries in the Judaean Desert*. Oxford: Clarendon Press, 1994.

Räisänen, Heikki· "Jesus and the Food Laws: Reflections on Mark 7:15." *Journal for the Study of the New Testament* 16 (1982): 79–100.

———. *Paul and the Law*. Philadelphia: Fortress Press, 1986.

Rabin, Chaim. *Qumran Studies* Oxford: Oxford University Press, 1957.

———. *The Zadokite Documents*. Oxford: Clarendon Press, 1958

Reinhart, A. Kevin. "Impurity/No Danger." *History of Religions* 30, no. 1 (1990): 1–24

Rhoads, David "Social Criticism: Social Boundaries." In *Mark and Method: New Approaches in Biblical Studies*, ed Janice Capel Anderson and Stephen D. Moore, 135–161 Minneapolis· Fortress Press, 1992.

Ringgren, Helmer. *The Faith of Qumran: Theology of the Dead Sea Scrolls.* Philadelphia: Fortress Press, 1963.

———. "טהר." In *Theological Dictionary of the Old Testament,* ed. G. Johannes Botterweck, Helmer Ringgren, and Heinz-Josef Fabry; trans. John T. Willis, Geoffrey W. Bromiley, and David E. Green. 8 vols. to 1996. Vol. V, 288–296. Grand Rapids, Mich.: William B Eerdmans, 1974–1996.

———, and G. André. "טמא." In *Theological Dictionary of the Old Testament,* ed. G. Johannes Botterweck, Helmer Ringgren, and Heinz-Josef Fabry; trans. John T. Willis, Geoffrey W. Bromiley, and David E. Green. 8 vols. to 1996. Vol. V, 330–342. Grand Rapids, Mich.: William B. Eerdmans, 1974–1996.

Safrai, Shmuel, ed. *The Literature of the Sages First Part: Oral Torah, Halakha, Mishna, Tosefta, Talmud, External Tractates,* Section Two, Vol. III, Part 1, *Compendium Rerum Iudaicarum ad Novum Testamentum.* Assen: Van Gorcum, 1987.

Saldarini, Anthony J. *Pharisees, Scribes and Sadducees in Palestinian Society: A Sociological Approach.* Wilmington, Del.: Michael Glazier, 1988.

Sanders, E. P. *Jesus and Judaism.* Philadelphia: Fortress Press, 1985.

———. *Jewish Law from Jesus to the Mishnah: Five Studies.* London: SCM Press, 1990.

———. *Paul and Palestinian Judaism: A Comparison of Patterns of Religion.* Minneapolis: Fortress Press, 1977.

———. *Paul, the Law, and the Jewish People.* Philadelphia: Fortress Press, 1983.

Sawyer, John F A., ed. *Reading Leviticus: A Conversation with Mary Douglas.* Sheffield: Sheffield Academic Press, 1996.

Schechter, Solomon, ed. *Aboth de Rabbi Nathan.* Vienna: Ch. D. Lippe, 1887.

———. *Aspects of Rabbinic Theology: Major Concepts of the Talmud.* New York: Macmillan, 1909.

———. *Fragments of a Zadokite Work.* Vol. 1, *Documents of Jewish Sectaries.* Cambridge: Cambridge University Press, 1910.

Schiffman, Lawrence H. "Exclusion from the Sanctuary and the City of the Sanctuary in the Temple Scroll." *Hebrew Annual Review* 9 (1985): 301–320.

———. *The Halakhah at Qumran.* Leiden: E. J. Brill, 1976.

———. "Miqṣat Ma'aśeh ha-Torah and the Temple Scroll." *Revue de Qumran* 14, no. 2 (1990): 435–457.

———. "Pharisaic and Sadducean Halakhah in Light of the Dead Sea Scrolls: The Case of Tievul Yom." *Dead Sea Discoveries* 1, no. 3 (1994): 285–299.

———. *Reclaiming the Dead Sea Scrolls: The History of Judaism, the Background of Christianity, the Lost Library of Qumran.* Philadelphia. Jewish Publication Society, 1994.

———. *Sectarian Law in the Dead Sea Scrolls: Courts, Testimony and the Penal Code.* Atlanta: Scholars Press, 1983

Schuller, Eileen M. *Non-Canonical Psalms from Qumran: A Pseudepigraphic Collection.* Atlanta: Scholars Press, 1986.

Schürer, Emil, and Geza Vermes et al. *The History of the Jewish People in the Age of Jesus Christ.* 4 vols. Edinburgh: T. & T. Clark, 1973–1987

Segal, Alan F. *Paul the Convert: the Apostolate and Apostasy of Saul the Pharisee.* New Haven: Yale University Press, 1990.

Sharvit, B. "Purity and Impurity According to the Dead Sea Sect" (Hebrew). *Bet Mikra* 26, no. 4 (1980/1): 18–27.

Shemesh, Aharon. "'The Holy Angels Are in Their Council': The Exclusion of Deformed Persons from Holy Places in Qumranic and Rabbinic Literature." *Dead Sea Discoveries* 4, no. 2 (1997). 179–206.

Smith, Morton. "The Dead Sea Sect in Relation to Ancient Judaism." *New Testament Studies* 7, no. 4 (1960–1961)· 347–360.

———. *Palestinian Parties and Politics that Shaped the Old Testament.* New York: Columbia University Press, 1971.

Sparks, H. F. D., ed. *The Apocryphal Old Testament.* Oxford· Clarendon Press, 1984.

Stegemann, Hartmut "The Literary Composition of the Temple Scroll and Its Status at Qumran." In *Temple Scroll Studies*, ed. G. J Brooke, 123–148. Sheffield: JSOT Press, 1989.

Stone, Michael E. "Enoch, Aramaic Levi and Sectarian Origins." *Journal for the Study of Judaism* 19, no 2 (1988): 159–170.

———, ed. *Jewish Writings of the Second Temple Period: Apocrypha, Pseudepigrapha, Qumran Sectarian Writings, Philo, Josephus.* Section Two, Vol. II, *Compendium Rerum Iudaicarum ad Novum Testamentum.* Assen. Van Gorcum, 1984.

Stowers, Stanley K. *A Rereading of Romans: Justice, Jews, and Gentiles.* New Haven: Yale University Press, 1994

Strack, H. L., and Günter Stemberger *Introduction to the Talmud and Midrash*, trans. and ed. Marcus Bockmuehl. 2nd printing. Minneapolis: Fortress Press, 1996.

Swanson, Dwight D. *The Temple Scroll and the Bible: The Methodology of 11QT.* Leiden: E. J. Brill, 1995

Taylor, Joan E *The Immerser: John the Baptist within Second Temple Judaism.* Grand Rapids, Mich.: William B. Eerdmans, 1997.

———. "John the Baptist and the Essenes." *Journal of Jewish Studies* 47, no. 2 (1996): 256–285.

Tomson, Peter J. *Paul and the Jewish Law: Halakha in the Letters of the Apostle to the Gentiles,* Section Three, Vol. I, *Compendium Rerum Iudaicarum ad Novum Testamentum.* Assen/ Maastricht. Van Gorcum, 1990.

Urbach, Ephraim E. *The Sages: Their Concepts and Beliefs*, trans. Israel Abrahams. Cambridge, Mass.· Harvard University Press, 1987.

VanderKam, James C *The Dead Sea Scrolls Today.* Grand Rapids, Mich.: William B. Eerdmans, 1995.

Vermes, Geza. *The Complete Dead Sea Scrolls in English.* New York: Allen Lane, 1997.

———. *Jesus the Jew. A Historian's Reading of the Gospels.* Philadelphia: Fortress Press, 1981.

———. "Sectarian Matrimonial Halakha in the Damascus Rule." *Journal of Jewish Studies* 25, no. 1 (1974): 197–202.

Webb, Robert L. *John the Baptizer and Prophet: A Socio-Historical Study.* Sheffield: JSOT Press, 1991.

Wegner, Judith Romney. *Chattel or Person? The Status of Women in the Mishnah* New York: Oxford University Press, 1988.

———. "Leviticus." In *The Women's Bible Commentary*, ed. Carol A. Newsom and Sharon H. Ringer, 36–44. Louisville: Westminster/John Knox Press, 1992.

Weinfeld, Moshe. *Deuteronomy and the Deuteronomic School.* Oxford: Clarendon Press, 1972.

Weiss, Isaac H., ed. *Sifra D'Be Rab (Torat Kohanim)* Vienna: Jaocob Schlossberg, 1862.

Wenham, Gordon P. *The Book of Leviticus.* Grand Rapids, Mich.· William B Eerdmans, 1979.

Wilson, Andrew M., and Lawrence Wills "Literary Sources of the Temple Scroll." *Harvard Theological Review* 75, no. 3 (1982): 275–288.

Wise, Michael Owen. *A Critical Study of the Temple Scroll from Qumran Cave 11.* Chicago: The Oriental Institute, 1990.

Witherington III, Ben. *The Jesus Quest: the Third Search for the Jew of Nazareth.* Grand Rapids, Ill.: InterVarsity Press, 1995.

Wright, David P *The Disposal of Impurity: Elimination Rites in the Bible and in Hittite and Mesopotamian Literature.* Atlanta· Scholars Press, 1987.

———. "The Spectrum of Priestly Impurity." In *Priesthood and Cult in Ancient Israel*, ed. Gary A. Anderson and Saul M. Olyan, 150–181. Sheffield: JSOT Press, 1991.

——— "Unclean and Clean (OT)." In *The Anchor Bible Dictionary*, ed. David Noel Freedman. 6 vols. Vol. VI, 729–741. New York: Doubleday, 1992.

Yadın, Yigael. *The Scroll of the War of the Sons of Light against the Sons of Darkness*, trans. Chaim Rabin. Oxford: Clarendon Press, 1962

———. *The Temple Scroll.* 3 vols Jerusalem. Israel Exploration Society, 1983.

Index of Citations

227

General Index

abomination *See toevah*

adultery. *See* sexual sins

aggadah, 102, 107, 116, 117, 122, 130–131, 195 n.4, 199 n 61, 207 n.57

Albeck, Hanoch, 197 n 19, 202 n.109

Alon, Gedalyahu, 4–7, 10, 12, 134, 174 n.58, 192 n.74

amoraim, 93, 103, 104, 107–108, 194–195 n.1

ancient Judaism, relation to Israelite religion, vii

anomalies, 8, 10, 165 n.27

Aristeas, 36, 65–66

arrogance, as source of moral impurity, 70, 98–104, 123–124

atonement, 26, 30–31, 35–36, 85–88, 98–104, 109–116, 138–143, 154–155

See also moral impurity, resolution of; ritual impurity, resolution of

Atonement, Day of, 15, 30, 116, 126

attributions (in tannaitic sources), 93, 196 n 12

Baillet, M., 193 nn 101–102 and n 105

Bamberger, Bernard J , 177 n.114

baptism, 116, 138–143, 154–156

See also John the Baptist

Barton, John, 171 n.1

Baumgarten, Albert I., 194 n.119, 196 n 14

Baumgarten, Joseph M , 87, 176 n 111, 183 n 75 and n.81, 184 n.82, 189 n 31, 190 n.36, 191 n.57, 192 n.68, 193 n 101, 194 nn 106–109, 196 n.14

Beasley-Murray, G. R., 209 n.18, 210 n 33 and nn.53–56, 215 nn.129–130 and n 133

Be'er, Ilana, 176 nn.104, 107, and n 110, 177 n.114

Belkin, Samuel, 186 n.7

Bernstein, Moshe J., 205 n.32

Betz, Hans Dieter, 214 n.118, 215 n.120

blasphemy, as source of moral impurity, 83, 124–125, 148–149

Blenkinsopp, Joseph, 171 n 1, 178 n.5 and n.16

Bloch, Renée, 196 n.15, 199 n.61, 207 n.57

Boccaccini, Gabriele, 187 n 6

Booth, Roger P., 208 n.2, 212 nn.73, 75, 77, 79, and nn 83–84, 213 nn.86–87 and n.93

Borg, Marcus J., 12, 144–145, 208 nn.6–7 and nn.12–13, 209 n.16, 210 n.37, 211 n.58

Borgen, P., 186 n.2

Boyarin, Daniel, 186 n.13, 195 n.7 and n.9, 196 n.13, 200 nn.71, 79, and n.83, 201 nn.88–89, 207 n.75, 213 n 96, 215 n.139

Brakke, David, 215 n.140

bribery, as source of moral impurity, 50, 70–71, 83, 123–124

Bright, John, 177 n.1

Brownlee, William H., 187 n.7, 188 n.8, 209 n 18

Buchler, Adolph, 3–7, 10–17, 27, 28, 30, 44, 93, 135, 172 nn.24–25, 173 nn.45, 47, and n.54, 174 n.73, 175 n.89, 176 n.99, 179 n.28, 183 n.74, 185 nn.93, 99, and nn.106–107, 195 n.2, 198 n.40, 200 n 82, 201 n.97, 203 n 126 and n 137, 204 nn.2–3, 5, and nn 7–8, 206 n.48, 207 n.72 and n.74, 208 n.2, 210 n.56, 212 n 73

burial, 16, 17, 24, 51, 96, 124–125, 137, 140, 198 n 30

Burkert, Walter, 170 n.114

Callaway, Phillip, 181 n.47

Charles, R. H , 185 n 96

Charlesworth, James H., 183 nn.74–77 and n.80, 190 n.48, 191 n.49 and n.63, 194 n.115

236

Printed in the United States
203860BV00001B/223-231/A